CURATING

Curating

Journeys through Storyscapes

of the American Past

AMERICA

RICHARD RABINOWITZ

with illustrations by RICHARD T. HOYEN

The University of North Carolina Press

Chapel Hill

© 2016 Richard Rabinowitz
All rights reserved
Set in Miller and Didot
by Tseng Information Systems, Inc.
Manufactured in the United States of America

The University of North Carolina Press has been a
member of the Green Press Initiative since 2003.

Cover image: *Quodlibet #3*. Limewood sculpture by
David Easterly (1944). Private collection.

Unless otherwise noted, all illustrations by Richard T. Hoyen

Library of Congress Cataloging-in-Publication Data
Names: Rabinowitz, Richard.
Title: Curating America : journeys through storyscapes of the American past /
by Richard Rabinowitz ; with illustrations by Richard T. Hoyen.
Description: Chapel Hill : The University of North Carolina Press, [2016] |
Includes bibliographical references and index.
Identifiers: LCCN 2016009980| ISBN 9781469629506 (cloth : alk. paper) |
ISBN 9781469629513 (ebook)
Subjects: LCSH: Public history—United States—History—20th century. | Public
history—United States—History—21st century. | Museums—United States—
History—20th century. | Museums—United States—History—21st century.
Classification: LCC E175.9 .R33 2016 | DDC 069.0973/0904—dc23
LC record available at http://lccn.loc.gov/2016009980

MIX
Paper from
responsible sources
FSC
www.fsc.org   FSC® C013483

For Lynda

For twenty-two years stinks in my nose this store.
I wanted to smell in my lungs some fresh air.

— BERNARD MALAMUD

And where would a girl like that find any kind of life
that asked more of her than just standing up to hardship?

— MARILYNNE ROBINSON

CONTENTS

Introduction 1

PART ONE. BECOMING A PUBLIC HISTORIAN

1 Discovering a Calling 15

2 No Ideas But in Things 27

3 Twentieth-Century Minds Dissecting Nineteenth-Century
   Problems 43

4 Other Hands, Other Minds 60

5 The Elements of Interpretation 68

PART TWO.

FINDING OURSELVES: INTERPRETING PLACE

6 History, Dislocated 89

7 Envisioning Place on Gallery Walls 105

8 Museum Visitors on Center Stage 120

9 Museums without Walls 132

10 Visitors Reinsert Human Presence into the Landscape 146

11 Storyscapes Everywhere 160

PART THREE.

BEHOLDING: INTERPRETING STUFF

12 The Object of the Object 179

13 The Object as Evidence and Experience 199

14 The Invention of the Cluster 214

PART FOUR.

BELONGING: INTERPRETING IDENTITY AND COMMUNITY

15 The Body Politic in the Museum 237

16 History Turns Critical 251

17 Taking the New Social History Public 271

18 The Community as Curator 285

19 Can the History Museum Fix It? 297

Postscript 319

A Reader's Reflections 337

Acknowledgments 361

Index 367

INTRODUCTION

I have wanted to write this book for more than forty-five years, since the night I returned home from my first visit, solo, through the snowy lanes of Old Sturbridge Village (osv)—an outdoor history museum in central Massachusetts—on the last Sunday in January 1967. Since then I have wanted to record a simple and sudden revelation, that the people of the past were living, breathing creatures, as complex, intriguing, and elusive as the people in our own lives.

How foolish of me, of course, to think otherwise. But becoming a professional historian had trained me to seek out more abstract stories. I had learned to speak of "ideological origins," "mimetic strategies," and "nationalist impulses." That frosty day, instead, as I walked about the re-created nineteenth-century rural village and its surrounding landscape, I felt the more concrete urgencies of the past: how to reach a warm room, how to find enough light to read by, and how to dry my shoes.

What happened on that "road-to-Damascus" Sunday has continued to shape my work every day since. A door had opened, and I've never stopped exploring the rooms within. On the day itself, my eyes, my ears, my fingertips, and my (nearly frozen) toes were constantly charged with

Moving an 1832 Baptist church to OSV in 1948 created an instant Village common and years later ensured that the museum would have to interpret the era of rural industrialization in New England.

new sensations. I stepped into the osv meetinghouse, and it suddenly loomed above me, a huge, drafty hulk of wood and glass. Immediately I was greeted by an amiable fellow wearing a woolen cape, scarf, and broad-brimmed hat from another century. He invited me to take refuge in a pew and closed its door behind me. In a few words, he presented a brief introduction to the building's history. Assaulted by the cold, I instantly sensed how useful it would have been to bring along the family mutt, as well as every blanket and piece of woolen clothing the household could muster, to keep the gospel message from freezing in the winter air.

From there I strolled over to the McClellan Law Office, where an older gentleman with a British accent offered a painted side chair, a chance to glance through the statute books of Connecticut, and a leisurely half-hour chat about "riparian rights." First, he role-played lawyer McClellan's case in helping local mill owners recover the cost of repairing damages done by careless farmers on the frozen Quinebaug River nearby. Then he cooked up a good defense for the farmers. We shook hands, and though I'd never imagined myself in need of advice on such matters, I knew I had found the right man.

Next I came to the Fenno House, where a kindly old lady showed me an apple she was implanting with tiny cloves. The fruit took on the appearance of one of those spiked flails that medieval knights swung at each others, but the purpose, I discovered, was much more innocent: to create a scented pomander that would ward off bad odors (and maybe evil spirits) in one's cupboards and clothing chests. We exchanged greetings, and I took my seat in a "stick" chair facing the fire. She invited me to look over a reproduction of an 1820 edition of the *Massachusetts Spy* newspaper sitting on a nearby candlestand. My eyes were better in those days, but I had to strain to read the tiny print in the skimpy light offered by a single candle, the graying afternoon, and the reflections of the firelight.

On and on I went, alternately chilled by the snow underfoot and warmed by the conversation of osv costumed interpreters. I felt like I had the place to myself. At the Freeman Farmhouse kitchen, I was refreshed by newly baked cornbread and repelled by a smelly turnip rescued from the root cellar below. Entering the raw, acrid, and smoky atmosphere of the blacksmith shop, I had a childish delight in tracing the changing colors—red, yellow, white—of the ductile iron on the anvil and the golden sparks that leaped up in rhythm with the hammer's strokes. By contrast, the polite parlor of the Towne House seemed to lock my hands tightly by my side. After a day of swinging my arms, now I felt like the bull in the china shop.

I registered the senses, one by one. Later that night, I began to realize

The Law Office, OSV: On my first visit, the museum made American law, religion, and politics leap off the page and into my physical experience.

A revelation: Cultural moments are composed of furniture, weather, words, light, and human action (Fenno House, OSV, 1967).

what all this might mean for me as a historian. I'd been studying these New Englanders for years and years. Now I could no longer recall what images I had previously had of them or where they lived or what they did for an honest livelihood. Maybe I didn't have any images at all! All this time I'd known them only as disembodied wordsmiths, unlocated, only as instruments for weaving intricate arguments. For all the sermons I had read, I had never before entered a building where one was actually delivered. I knew their grace only in words and never in movement, their strength and skills only in abstract virtue and never in physical action.

In the silence of the osv meetinghouse, I had suddenly discovered an orchestra's worth of sound! Every one of those sermons I'd been studying had been delivered orally, some even theatrically. Now, sitting in the pew, I understood how much energy it took for the parishioners to listen to their reasoning. (It was a whole lot easier, I thought, to read and take notes about these sermons at the comfortable and well-lit tables in Harvard's Widener Library.) And then there were my newly imagined sounds of the congregation—bawling babies and scolding parents, the scratches of a merchant's pencil remembering a debt, the whispering of adolescents,

My imagination filled the empty meetinghouse with the sermons, gestures, murmurs, and even the snores of a Sunday worship service.

and the answering reprimands of the official "tithingman" who kept order in the galleries. Feet stamping for warmth, dogs escaping out the back door, cordwood being fed into the stove, the ticking clock, the resounding bell— my imagined nineteenth-century cacophony transformed the silence I'd experienced hours earlier.

Oh, and those moments in the Fenno House. Thank goodness I'd had a stick (or Windsor) chair to sit in. In my hostess's upholstered wing chair, I'd never have been able to swerve and catch the last rays of daylight. How could anybody read this old newspaper in such gloom? As the shadows lengthened, I had felt my lips moving as I read, and suddenly I gained entry into a new way of understanding how words, the precious words I'd been studying so carefully, were spoken and heard among these Yankees. With only one candle, it was a good bet that only one person was going to be reading. And that reader would share those words aloud with companions gathered around. In five minutes, my body and my mind had linked together the furniture design, the newsprint, the ambient and direct light, how one read, and the family's reconnecting at twilight. Usually we think of these as quite distinct from one another, each the subject of its own historical evolution. As a cluster of artifacts and social patterns in space and time, assembled by my sense-impressions, imagination, and reasoning, they now fit together to form a single, synthesized historical phenomenon.

I didn't write the book for almost another half-century. Instead, on the very next day, I got up early; drove west along the Mass Pike; found my way to Barnes Riznik, the museum's head of interpretation; and persuaded him that he would risk little by hiring me for $1.10 an hour to walk about in a big hat and buttoned-fly trousers and share stories of old-time New England with tourists and schoolchildren. And later that week, I took an elevator journey up to tell Harvard's dean of graduate studies that I wanted to take a leave. "One step away from the Charles," he warned, "and you'll wind up in the Mekong." Undaunted, I traded in my Smith-Corona for a quill pen, a schoolmaster's ferule, and my new role as a costumed interpreter. According to the day of the week, for the next seven months I was a parson, a teacher, a banker, or a lawyer. After my initial stint at OSV in 1967, I returned to Harvard, completed the course work and exams for my Ph.D., and served as a tutor in American history and literature. I then began my professional career by returning as assistant director and then director of Sturbridge's educational program. I tried college teaching for a year after leaving Sturbridge, but I was soon drawn back to museum work. In 1980, along with my neighbor, historian Sam Bass Warner Jr., I cofounded American History Workshop (AHW). Side by side with dozens of historians and curators, museum administrators, designers, filmmakers, institutional planners, and public officials, AHW has since undertaken more than 550 projects in thirty-four states and the District of Columbia. The workshop has created programs about virtually every era in American history, from the prehistoric to the day before yesterday, and every place in the country, from the center of Manhattan to the Mississippi Delta, from Rust Belt cities and the wheat lands of eastern Oregon to the sprawling suburbs of Phoenix. Among our projects have been interpretive master plans for new and innovative institutions such as the Birmingham Civil Rights Institute, the Lower East Side Tenement Museum, and the National Underground Railroad Freedom Center and for many state industrial heritage parks. In 2005–11, AHW produced six blockbuster history exhibitions at the New-York Historical Society, winning accolades for *Slavery in New York*, *New York Divided: Slavery and the Civil War*, and *Revolution! The Atlantic World Reborn*. In its work for the new National Museum of African American History and Culture in 2010–11, AHW "laid the crucial foundation," as Director Lonnie Bunch says, for its interpretive exhibition about the history of slavery.

I've thus been a witness to a remarkable transformation of American public history, to the stories we tell about our people and to the way we tell them. Fundamental to that change has been the inclusion of a much wider cast of characters. It seems scarcely credible today that the Smithsonian's American history museum, when it opened in 1964, should have shown almost no images of African Americans or Indian peoples in its galleries. Not a single working-class home or neighborhood in the United States was then deemed worthy of preservation or interpretation. The enormous architectural legacy of American industrial communities, from Maine through New York's Soho district and west through the Great Lakes states, was in danger of being destroyed by urban renewal programs. At plantation museums in the South, the lives of enslaved people were invisible and the work of the "servants" was reduced to passive constructions: "meals were served" or "cotton was harvested." The immigration stations at Ellis Island and Angel Island were abandoned ruins. Museums of decorative arts often cut off their collections at 1820, deeming unworthy the public's interest in machine-made furniture.

All that has changed. The National Park Service now interprets Ellis Island, Lowell's cotton mills, and the Manzanar camp where Japanese Americans were interned during World War II. The conflict over slavery is interpreted as the central issue in the coming of war at most Civil War battlefield sites. In travel magazines, New York's Tenement Museum, whose building was once home to generations of working-class and immigrant families, vies with the National Air and Space Museum as among the most highly regarded non-art museums in the world. Colonial Williamsburg has had an active program of African American interpretation for over thirty years, sparking personal discomfort among visitors and sometimes public controversy. Sally Hemings's story is told at Monticello. Dozens of American museums now address troubling aspects of American and world history—slavery, the Holocaust, the struggle over civil rights, conflicts between Indians and Whites, immigrant and ethnic histories, the pain of returning veterans, and so on. Local and national controversies about preservation, interpretation, and commemoration periodically land on page 1 these days. Public efforts to interpret our history matter.

I have not tried here to write a comprehensive history of this wide-ranging transformation. That would be nearly impossible. So many of these public history presentations have been ephemeral and local, often mounted and demolished with little public or professional notice. Museum staffs revise and update "permanent" installations all the time. Reviews of these projects, which only began to appear in the 1970s, are still few and far between and seldom attentive to the work of small institutions in remote corners of the nation. The archival records of exhibitions are seldom complete, and catalogs are rare in the history museum world. Websites for past exhibitions usually contain only a paragraph or two and almost never include photographs of the installation or interviews with visitors.

Instead, I have focused here on what I've professionally done and what I've personally witnessed. This is a practitioner's book. I did not start out to become a museum professional but learned to define museums as I was imagining, planning, and executing all these projects. The preponderance of my work has been in history museums and historic sites, not museums of art or natural history, science centers, children's museums, botanical gardens, or zoos—though I've had experience in all of those as well. As a professional staff member and as a freelancer, I did not rush about with long-cherished proposals in my breast pocket, seeking funding. AHW did not choose its projects. The clients chose us. I was never commissioned to go off and write a symphony to my own liking. AHW was always hired to work on some organization's behalf and to accomplish its purposes. Nor did I set out to revolutionize museum interpretation. Being a restless soul, I instead took up opportunities as they arose to think anew about history and teaching and collections and institutional urgencies. I ardently avoided finding a formula that could be applied to all these different projects. History is different in every place, and history museums must reflect that distinctiveness. Only in writing this book did I begin to see precisely how the continuities and transformations in my work, taken all together, ultimately brought me to a radically distinctive vision of public history and history museum practice.

When I began this work in 1967, there was scarcely any scholarly literature and few instructional guides in museum studies, material culture, or public history. One or two graduate programs had begun to attract students interested in museum careers, but even they relied most heavily on hands-on experience rather than readings and classroom work. Since then, there has been a remarkable explosion of writing, teaching, and public commentary about museums. Some of it aims to "theorize" the museum, often using it as evidence of everything that is disappointing in contemporary social and intellectual life. Others take the current museum as a given, recommending the "best practices" to overcome its myriad operational challenges. Though I've enjoyed dipping into this literature, it has had only limited influence upon my work.

My own museum theory (if I have one), like my approach to history and to teaching and learning, has emerged instead from the individual projects I have done, from observations of the work of my peers, and from the general intellectual culture around me. This book records my evolving understanding of the media by which I have practiced public history for almost a half-century. If I had focused on refining my museum theory rather than responding to the demands of each project, I would certainly have aligned my thinking with other museum scholars, or consciously deviated from them. This is not that sort of book. It does not aim to evoke the singular essence of modern-day museums—which, after all, vary from wacky roadside attractions to the monumental galleries of the Smithsonian. Nor is it a one-size-fits-all instruction manual for museum interpretation. In reviewing my past projects in this book, I try to excavate what I learned in the process of work on each one and how it connected to the larger evolution of interpretations of the American past.

Public history is far more than the dissemination of scholarly research to a wider audience. It is itself an alternative method of intellectual discovery. Without making facile analogies between past and present, I believe that public historians have first to respond to the urgent inquiries of contemporary society. In the 2010s, for example, we might ask how we find contexts in American and global history for today's political polarization, for our difficulties in extricating ourselves from war, for our delicate balancing of national security and privacy considerations, for our drift into greater inequality and political disenfranchisement, or for our apparently endless appetite for racial stigmatization and exclusion.

Public history is also, inevitably, a political act. My career has been animated by the radical possibilities unleashed by the 1960s protest movements. On behalf of the entire body politic, I think my role as a public historian is to appropriate things of great value—important documents, beautiful objects, significant places, and crucial ideas—and make them accessible, physically and intellectually, for all of us. In every one of my many projects, I have tried to extract and emphasize the stake in the past that we have in common and how it might contribute to a well-informed conversation about our shared present and future. That Black lives in the past are everyone's concern, for example, is a predicate to the idea that Black lives matter today.

All good historians, in this attentiveness to current issues, are public historians. Beyond that, each of us shapes the history we teach by the media we employ. Writing historical monographs, delivering historical lectures, or creating documentary films and videos are no more fundamental to the historians' practice than leading tours of historic sites, conducting high school history classes, or creating historical exhibitions and on-site media presentations. Each has (1) its own target audience, (2) its own supply of appropriate and useful evidentiary sources, and (3) its own pedagogical methodology. And because of these distinctions, each mode of conveying history will create a (4) historical narrative somewhat different from the others. This book focuses on how one public historian working in the world of history museums and historic sites developed ways of thinking about these four concerns. Not all my colleague historians and curators, by any means, share my assumptions and approaches.

My approach has clearly been shaped by my having started my career as a front-line costumed interpreter in an outdoor history museum. I loved that work. I loved exploring New England history with traveling honeymooners on Monday afternoons, retirees on weekday mornings, and suburban families on weekends, and I have never lost my conviction that the visitor is the heart of the museum enterprise—more than the stuff and more even than the story. I am aware that not all visitors are so positively transformed by their visits to museums and historic sites. I've seen my share of bawling infants, sleepy toddlers, surly teenagers, reluctant spouses, and tourists exhausted by efforts to add one more museum to their life lists. There are plenty of cultural critics—though few working in these institutions—who accuse museums of "dumbing down the history" and who view visitors as submissive consumers of souped-up presentational media and the "hegemony" of elites. But in the thousands of hours I've spent talking to museum visitors, I've scarcely met one person whose experience fit the picture of a mindless tourist. Instead I see visitors as complicated and dynamic minds, eager to learn and even inclined to welcome challenges to their preconceptions.

I have invariably learned a great deal from taking visitors as seriously as I take history, and for good reason. Visitors bring a lot of historical evidence with them. They know about immigration and social mobility, about changes in economic life and the applicability of education and training for jobs, and about how families sustain themselves through periods of economic difficulty. They do not know all the possible scholarly contexts or explanations for those experiences; in some measure it is my job to tell them that they are already able to "speak history." Interpretation is a two-way street, a chance for me to learn as well as to teach or, more accurately, for us to create the sort of collaborative learning I found myself cherishing on that first visit to Old Sturbridge Village. Historic sites share characteristics of the tourist experience, of course, and successful interpretation has to provide visitors with all the right amenities. But none is so important as intellectual respect.

Each of the four parts of this book explores one of the large challenges that led to the invention of a new way of thinking about teaching history in museums and in the outdoor landscape. Part 1 recounts the development of a historiography, a pedagogy, and a community of practice in my work at osv and in the years leading to the establishment of ahw. I started with no clear ideas about what sort of history could be effectively taught in the outdoor history museum, or how or what this would mean to my interests in historical research and the learning process. With a rush, the opportunities of this first job generated a series of rewarding experiments that have fueled decades of reflection and further elaboration. In Part 2, "Finding Ourselves," I trace ahw's effort to recount the histories of a hundred different American places. Slowly, the puzzle revealed itself: How could the museum exhibition and the outdoor installation teach history while providing a way to enhance the visitors' physical and psychological "sense of place" at the same time? In Part 3, "Beholding," I record a decades-long partnership with imaginative and empathetic museum visitors to preserve the excitement of encountering authentic or original collection objects while constructing powerful dramatic narratives out of this "stuff." Part 4, "Belonging," explores the ongoing struggle to use the civically important site of the museum as an arena in which visitors define layers of personal, family, ethnic, and national identities. The postscript asks where these major transformations of the history museum have brought us—as learners and as cultural actors—and how museums continue to navigate the new challenges of technological innovation.

My first artistic love was the theater, and readers will see how much my museum thinking owes to the performing arts. I have long observed how visitors experience the museum in time as well as space, with their companions as well as alone, and through a constant interplay of ideas and sensory impressions. My sort of history museum, then, is a place where visitors actively and dramatically encounter the stories of past lives. Over the years, I've come to call that landscape of engagement a "storyscape." As a storyscape, the museum becomes a process of narrative engagement— a verb, if you will, rather than a noun. Older notions of these institutions as repositories, destinations, monuments, and memorials have given way. Visitors, understood as active meaning-makers, use their visits to confront challenges to (and sometimes to affirm) their sense of time and place, their personal memories of family and community, and their definitions of self and world. In the best of circumstances, they emerge with an energized and widened idea of where they stand in the flow of historical time.

Witnessing thousands and thousands of such visits, such complex performances, has given me a front-row seat on the cognitive process by which visitors apprehend the past. To me—as a teacher, a scholar, a parent, and a grandparent—nothing is more amazing in life than the human mind's appropriation of the world in its all its material, intellectual, and emotional dimensions.

Now it is time to share these observations and reflections with my fellow historians, museum professionals, artists, and others interested in the transformations of American culture since the 1960s. There are many valuable things to be learned from theoretical disquisitions and instruction manuals. I hope that readers will find useful a different sort of account, the record of one man's journey through the social and intellectual storyscape of the last half-century in the United States, a cultural history in the form of a professional memoir.

PART ONE

Becoming a Public Historian

1 ::: DISCOVERING A CALLING

My first stint at Old Sturbridge Village (osv) in 1967 had been a lark. I loved the dressing-up part, pulling on my boots and remembering to remove my anachronistic watch and sunglasses before I took up my post in the law office or the schoolhouse. I occupied my early mornings and late evenings poring over dusty volumes of local history, digging up juicy anecdotes about crazy old Yankees. On my days off, I drove on country roads to remote villages from Maine to Connecticut. My technique was to seek out the oldest meetinghouse in town and measure its distance from rundown farmhouses, abandoned mill buildings, and fine village residences that had been converted into antiques shops. History was everywhere—underfoot, through the windshield and the camera lens, and up and down the rickety stairs of old buildings. On my next workday, I was well primed to deliver this miscellaneous information, my "findings," to any and all who would listen. I didn't yet know the word for it, but I was entering a life in the work of public history.

Much to my surprise, those seven months at Sturbridge reshaped my return to graduate work at Harvard in 1967–68. The university was a mess. Signs of turmoil were everywhere. Massachusetts Avenue in Cambridge was crowded with marches, rallies, and protests against the war in Vietnam and a dozen other injustices. The evening news featured one shock after another, from the Tet offensive to the assassinations of Martin Luther King Jr. and Robert Kennedy to the violence at the Chicago Democratic convention. What a year!

Because of these distractions, the university's authority seemed to melt away. Harvard's graduate program in the history of American civilization allowed students to combine seminars and courses in many departments—history, English, art history, government, philosophy, and so on. Having taken so many of the available upper-level courses and even seminars as an undergraduate, I was trusted to steer my own path. My advisers seemed to prefer exempting me from various requirements to grappling with what I wanted to learn, so I signed up instead for a series of sporadically supervised "reading courses."

If "Am Civ" had any coherence at all for me, it came from the legacy of one of the program's founders, Professor Perry Miller. To Miller and his disciples, who were most of my teachers, history was a journey through  intellectual debating chambers in which fierce political contentions were channeled into debates over the nature of the divine, the complexities of the human mind, the locus of authority, and the fundaments of social order. All the major conflicts in American history found their truer, deeper meaning in the opposing positions taken by theologians, literary men and women, lawyers, politicians, or scientists.

By the winter of 1968 and spring of 1969, the civility of campus life was breaking down completely. Many of my students protested, some occupied university offices, one or two suffered police beatings, and virtually all of them went out on strike. On the other side, my teachers felt besieged, betrayed, and threatened. One reportedly barricaded himself overnight in Widener Library to protect the books from vandals. I just dug more deeply into teaching and learning. After Sturbridge, I was startled to discover how poorly prepared I was to teach in the university. I bore down on observing and recording the moment-to-moment flow of ideas and of teacher and student roles, experimenting with methods of drawing my group of tutees together toward a shared understanding.

Sitting at my library carrel, I began to design a course that would engage the next year's juniors in investigations of critical transformations in several American settings—the New England village on the cusp of industrialization, the antebellum plantation on the eve of civil war, and the urban tenement as it received the massive immigration of the first fifteen years of the twentieth century. An obvious starting point was to plan a field study at OSV, and so on a bright February day in 1969, I took the Mass Pike west to Sturbridge once more. This time, Barnes Riznik listened carefully, made some good suggestions, and then shocked me by offering an alternative: a real professional job, as assistant director for interpretation and education, at $8,000 per annum. "There is," he wrote to me that evening, "a very good history teaching job here as well as an opportunity to become involved in museum education experimentation." At Sturbridge, he assured me, I could help create a community engaged in the sort of pedagogical and historiographical questions I was pondering on my own in Cambridge. I'd passed my Ph.D. orals and started my dissertation with long days of reading at the American Antiquarian Society in Worcester. Newly married and eager to get on with adult life beyond the strife and isolation of the academy, I grasped at the opportunity. Now I was truly a "fast-fish," as Herman Melville called it, hooked on a career in public history.

When I returned to Sturbridge that summer as the youngest member of the professional staff, I felt the weight of new duties and the charge of new ambitions. I was perhaps the first academically trained historian brought to osv without any responsibility for expanding our collection of objects or buildings or even historical themes. I was to be an educator. My role was to communicate new scholarship about New England history in training sessions for the interpreters and the museum educators, many of whom had been my colleagues two years earlier, who met the visiting public. I helped start up and teach a graduate program in history and historical museum work, in collaboration with the University of Connecticut. I initiated a work-study internship program for college students and arranged for osv to serve as a site for alternative service for Vietnam-era conscientious objectors.[1]

osv was thriving in 1969. Since it had opened in 1946, its annual attendance had climbed from 5,000 to over half a million. (Indeed, more than 5,000 people now typically came on single days like Memorial Day or Columbus Day.) As the busiest outdoor museum in the Northeast, it had re-erected more than thirty exhibition buildings on the site near the junction of the main highways to Boston from Hartford and Springfield. On billboards and stationery it proclaimed itself "New England's Center of Living History."[2]

1. Philip F. Gura records a generous remembrance of his experience as an OSV intern in "Industrious, Ingenious Artisans," *Reviews in American History* 39 (December 2011): 587–88.

2. I prefer to call OSV an "outdoor history museum" rather than a "living history museum." The practice of "living history," whereby costumed interpreters either

osv was not a "real" historical place. The museum was about a half-mile from the common and center village of the actual town of Sturbridge. Even as it gradually evolved into a representation of a "typical" inland New England village and surrounding farmland, osv was still fundamentally a collection of collections. The museum had its origins in the object-gathering enthusiasms of two brothers, Albert B. and Joel Cheney Wells, who owned and managed the family business, the American Optical Company in Southbridge, Massachusetts. Cheney Wells assembled a superb array of New England glassware, clocks, furniture, and guns. A. B. Wells preferred hand tools and farm implements, folk art, and the utensils of ordinary life.

The Wells family had rejected a proposal by Perry, Shaw and Hepburn, the Boston architects who had worked at Colonial Williamsburg, to house the collections in a series of stately Georgian brick manor houses. Instead, following the advice of Boston landscape architect Arthur Shurcleff, they re-erected old frame residences, shops, mills, and outbuildings from all over New England and laid them out along unpaved footpaths. As the news spread, many New Englanders, before the era of local historical commissions and preservation groups, were happy to have the museum cart off their oldest houses and outbuildings for re-erection at Sturbridge. Some contained cases and shelves to display formal collections. Period room settings, drawn from the museum's collection of furniture and decorative accessories, occupied the residences.

Gradually, almost inadvertently, the place began to look like the center village of a New England town, especially after the museum acquired a Greek Revival meetinghouse in 1948 and set it down on a knoll overlooking what immediately became known as the "Village common." (Twenty-five years later, geographers determined that residences began to encircle town commons in this part of New England only in the second quarter of the nineteenth century—too late to relocate the four eighteenth-century houses already in place at osv by the 1950s.)

By the time of my second tenure there, the museum had grown to include five residences in all, often with diverse outbuildings, gardens, and yards; a dozen sheds and shops for working craft demonstrators; several buildings housing its prize collections of glass, guns, and clocks; eight more-or-less

---

reenact historical roles or describe historical activities in re-created settings, has always been only one of the interpretive methods at OSV, which also includes conventional museum displays of original objects, multimedia presentations, and regularly scheduled staged theatrical performances.

public structures (two meetinghouses, a bank, a law office, a schoolhouse, a general store, an animal pound, and a tavern, which also housed the museum's painting collection); a covered bridge; three water-powered mills for sawing timber, carding wool, and grinding grain (though the sawmill was inoperative); and the beginnings of a working period farm.

Visitors plunked down their admissions fees, got a map and a hearty welcome, and proceeded to stroll through country lanes and in and out of the exhibition buildings randomly, pausing perhaps for a lunch at the mock tavern or a treat of rock candy at the mock general store. A certain imprecision in historical details prevailed. The common was planted in bluegrass and mowed to an inch of its life before the gates opened. Outside the meetinghouse, visitors lined up to take photos of their children (and sometimes husbands) "locked" in the pillory and stocks, though these shaming punishments had long been exiled from nineteenth-century rural villages. Mythologies persisted. For many visitors, the overall impression was that New England folk lived in self-sufficient, preindustrial communities, isolated in space and frozen in time. Acquiring and equipping each of the museum's crafts shops seemed to feed popular misconceptions of fairy-tale towns where "the butcher, the baker, and the candlestick-maker" bartered goods with one another. The osv map made it appear that every town needed one, and just one, of each specialty to survive.

In *The Story of Old Sturbridge Village*, his 1965 address to a convocation of business leaders, osv president Charles van Ravenswaay attributed much of America's success to the no-nonsense, independent, and enterprising New England spirit represented by the Village. From these modest rural communities, he claimed, the nation had grown into a great power. Growth had meant progress, but there were now dangers. "The population growth, the spread of our cities and of urban blight, the industrialization of our countryside—developments such as these make us realize how completely family and community ties with the past have been destroyed," van Ravenswaay warned. Fortuitously, "places like this Village provide a sense of the continuity of time and man."[3] osv could be an antidote to the ills of modern consumer society. The same interstate highways that carried away Worcester County's steel rods and optical devices on weekdays could bring leisure-time visitors to this restorative pastoral museum on weekends.

At osv the best of the past could be preserved. Here people were still

3. Charles van Ravenswaay, *The Story of Old Sturbridge Village* (New York: The Newcomen Society in North America, 1965), 8.

connected almost as family members. Visitors, van Ravenswaay claimed, "have adopted the Village as a kind of ancestral home where, in contrast to their restless and mobile everyday lives, they can put down personal roots and feel a kinship to the past."[4] Forget, for a moment, that osv sits near the convergence of the three most heavily Roman Catholic states in the nation, or that many of its visitors were the grandchildren of immigrant industrial workers. All these ethnic and class distinctions could be safely erased at osv. The museum could help preserve the nation's moral fiber and political unity as it confronted the challenges of the Cold War.

Van Ravenswaay's Village was an oasis of heritage, a parklike setting in which the ferocity of the American industrial machine could be tamed by showing its descent from small-scale workshops. As magazine feature articles frequently said, osv was "a place that time forgot," a locus of nostalgia for a past that never happened in a place that never was. For the general visitor, the objects produced in Village workshops and displayed on Village shelves were simply "quaint," a code word for their passage from utilitarian to decorative value. The labor of the past had been transformed into the stuff of hobby craft.

One could easily lump osv with the other heritage sites savaged for their artificiality, ethnocentrism, and commercialism by geographer David Lowenthal in 1966. The past in America, Lowenthal wrote, "is fenced off in a preserve called History. It may be touched, handled, tasted, even participated in, as at Williamsburg; it is not part of everyday life." But osv had already undertaken a more serious commitment to historical scholarship. Its mission, board chairman Philip Morgan wrote in 1965, was "to preserve and present the story of New England farm and village life as it existed in the period before major industrial growth began (about 1840) and to do this as completely, and in as many different dimensions, as is possible in the 20th century."[5] Behind the scenes, osv's curators and researchers were producing first-rate investigations of New England's architectural, artisanal, and mechanical practice, usually in preparation for the acquisition, reconstruction, and furnishing of new buildings, such as a blacksmith shop, a pottery, an exhibition of glassmaking, or a water-powered carding mill. For the collectors and fanciers of pre- and proto-industrially made products, osv

4. Ibid.

5. David Lowenthal, "The American Way of History," *Columbia University Forum* 9, no. 3 (Summer 1966): 27–32, quotation at 27; Philip Morgan, introduction to van Ravenswaay, *Story*, 6.

could be an extraordinarily rewarding resource. On quiet days I could see them engaging our crafts demonstrators for hours, talking over auger bits and the chemical content of glazes.

But until the mid-1960s, this sort of research seldom challenged the heritage mythos of "Ye Olde Golden Age of Homespun." osv's Research Department then began to churn out more highly contextualized histories, usually linking what was happening in rural New England to wider contexts. In succession, the department turned out studies of the professionalization of rural medicine, of mechanical innovation in the countryside, of advances in progressive agriculture, of the expansion of overland commercial traffic, and most significant, of the emergence of industrially produced textiles, using waterpower, in mill villages planted along New England's numerous river valleys. One by one, the old shibboleths—self-sufficiency, isolation, the prevalence of cashless "exchanges" of goods and labor among neighbors—dissolved as the historians fleshed out the picture of a rapidly changing rural landscape in the quarter-century after 1815. Drawing on notions of modernization and the "take-off" period developed by analysts of the Third World during the 1960s, the osv researchers began to represent rural New England as a cauldron of dynamic economic development.

Gradually, the museum landscape began to register this research. In the late 1960s, led by Darwin Kelsey and John Mott, the museum vigorously initiated a full-scale working historical farm, representing the seasonal cycle of work, complete with the historically correct varieties of crops, swine, sheep, cattle, and poultry. The common was replanted in timothy and clover, the power mowers returned to the garage, and osv's flock of sheep there chewed away, to the amusement of visitors. Heaps and piles of fenceposts and broken barrel staves cluttered formerly well-ordered farmyards. The place began to smell like a real farm, and so did some of the interpreters. And even more ambitiously, osv acquired land and laid out plans for a "second village," a small-scale manufacturing community with a working cotton mill, workers' and mill agent's cottages, and a company store, adjacent to its original property.

My new job was to bridge the worlds of van Ravenswaay's "heritage" and the new, more disruptive history of the osv Research Department. I had to channel the enthusiasm of my visitors for a personal and collective attachment to a world they felt was lost to them into an inquiry as to the process by which that loss occurred. If done poorly, such an inquiry would insult visitors' affections for that way of life or trivialize the history by viewing our historical characters as simpletons frozen in time.

Return the tractors to the garage, plant new "old grasses," and let the flock take over the mowing (OSV, 1972).

It helped, no doubt, that I was the child of a woman who had spent her childhood in a Polish shtetl, in a time and place that was similarly being transformed, and who had matured in 1930s and 1940s New York. Her memory was an encyclopedia of ambivalence about modernization. From firsthand experience she knew why "sliced bread" (industrially packaged and free from the sawdust that old-time local bakers liked to add) was so great, and why the filth of a cold-water tenement was so much worse than the desperately scrubbed floors of a rural cottage. She prepared me for an ironic perspective on historical transformations. On one of her visits, we went to see the film version of *Fiddler on the Roof.* Coming out of the theater, she smiled and said, "Such a great family success story! From a dirty stinking village in Poland to a dirty stinking village in Massachusetts—in only one generation!"

During the two years I'd been back in Cambridge, I had lived with earth-shattering news almost every day. Politics was on everyone's lips. The sexual revolution was in full swing. Bold new historical scholarship carried women's history "up from the pedestal" and traced Black life from "before the Mayflower." Our graduate study of American history was all about change. This made the stillness of the New England rural past increasingly implausible to me. If only we looked more carefully, wouldn't we discover turmoil and conflict in the nineteenth-century countryside? Beyond its museum collections, beyond the small-bore scholarship underlying its fastidious reconstructions of nineteenth-century physicality, osv needed to become more serious about the history it was communicating.

osv was not alone in questioning its pedagogy. "Does the Museum of History Teach History?" asked James J. Heslin, director of the New-York Historical Society, at a 1965 Smithsonian symposium. Simply mounting portraits of the founders, he conceded, "cannot adequately communicate the history of . . . the American Revolution." Old-line historical agencies like Heslin's seemed to have lost their way. They had entrusted their longtime efforts in research and publication to universities but were now poorly equipped to develop education and exhibition programs for an audience "in which visual and aural impact may be dominant in the spread of knowledge."[6]

osv had all the visual and aural resources it needed, but to what end? What history would we teach? We surely needed to say something more definitive about the meaning of this era in American history. At Plimoth Plantation, which tried to reconstruct the life of the Pilgrim community and its Wampanoag neighbors in 1627, or at Colonial Williamsburg, which represented the momentous events leading to American independence, visitors could attach the museum to familiar narratives in history textbooks. Not so at osv. Our pastoral setting, just an hour beyond the suburbs of Boston, Hartford, Providence, and Springfield, seemed to evoke a "timeless way of living" that I knew was never humanly possible.

The role of the public historian, I decided, was to pierce through the platitudinous pieties of our audience, as gently as possible, and to invite visitors into an exciting exploration of the largely untold story of New England's unsteady stumbling into the nineteenth century. Delivering academic lectures on "the countryside in the age of capitalist transformation" was a nonstarter. Somehow we had to make the palpability of the outdoor museum vibrate with the tremors of historical change. We knew that our visitors were living through a tumultuous time—could they see antebellum New England that way, and thereby gain some perspective on the transformations in their own lives?

Part of the problem, I decided, was the fragmentary quality of the mu-

6. Heslin's paper appeared in *Museums and Education*, ed. Eric Larrabee (Washington, D.C.: Smithsonian Institution Press, 1968), 153–65, quotations at 159, 163.

seum visit. Visitors experienced OSV one building at a time. Nothing linked the visit together. Each building, like the paintings on an art museum's wall or the books in the vitrines of a library show, was interpreted independently. No orientation program framed the Village's intellectual agenda, no wrap-up gallery aimed to summarize the big ideas. Nowhere was the character or significance of this era of New England history spelled out. On my darkest days, I feared that visitors were simply rolling through our buildings and our pathways like marbles on a descending track, with nothing sticking to them. Would they remember that Eli Terry's wooden clock wheels initiated a manufacturing system of interchangeable parts and made timekeeping almost universal? Would they recall that the center hallway replaced the old central chimney in eighteenth-century houses, a reflection of a broader interest in bilateral symmetry? Could they see a relationship between the striped woolen cloth woven at the Mashapaug House and the printed cotton curtains in the Salem Towne House? Was there a larger narrative into which they could fold these interesting bits of miscellany?

Trained in the university and not in the museum, I intuited that the connective tissue that would link these bits of information were historical themes. Generalizations from one building to another and one activity to the next, one example and a matching counterexample—that's what OSV needed. And an umbrella theme, a master narrative, something that would tie together all the dimensions of rural life. I finally had my chance when, early in my tenure at OSV, Riznik assigned me the chore of rewriting the Village's mission statement. I took direct aim at the vague sentimentality of President van Ravenswaay's 1965 evocation of a blissful past and began my statement boldly: "The early nineteenth century was a time of change in the everyday lives of New Englanders." I filled pages of legal pad with notes about how each interpretive station in the museum could contribute to an overview of the historical change that came to this generation of rural people—in their use of technology, their response to new economic opportunities and challenges, their view of society as improvable, their invention of new institutions to bring about these improvements, their adaptation of new design forms and styles in consumer goods, their new views of marriage and child nurture, their new emphasis upon private spirituality, and so on. I imagined a new OSV map, to be distributed at the entrance, which would immediately announce that visitors were entering "A World of Change."

It was a lovely May afternoon, and I put down my pen and headed out for a stroll to where our "Vermont" covered bridge crossed the Quinebaug

OSV's romantic and bucolic corner: Could this convincingly interpret an era of tumultuous change?

River, a favorite spot for contemplation. I saw sauntering vacationers, older couples seeking a break, and frolicking youngsters searching for frogs. "A time of change," huh? Not so likely. In the real old-time communities that looked like OSV, men and women worried about the weather, about the market, about the well-being of family members, about dying before they experienced saving grace, and about a thousand other things. And if these visitors were asked in 1971, they would probably express similar worries. But not here, in the bucolic rural museum landscape, and not now. Strolling outdoors on that gentle May day contradicted my lectures about the dynamic nineteenth century. A sensible peace was truer than a reputed revolution.

In time, I would come to distrust these high-flown themes, or at least the capacity of the museum to engender them in the minds of visitors. It took a long time to shuck my academic inclination toward systematic explanation. I still had no other method to compose the bits and pieces of unrelated experience and to foster coherence in the stories we told.

OSV was teaching me these things about myself, lessons deeper than any I had found in classrooms or textbooks. Up to then I'd been a student plunging or stumbling forward, trusting that there was a path. I was surprised to discover that at twenty-five I already came well stocked with strong opinions, instincts, and intuitions about things I'd never encountered before. Every day I awakened to learn that I was building up an approach, or laying a groundwork, for a distinctive way of living and working.

> And now, with gleams of half-extinguish'd thought,
> With many recognitions dim and faint,
> And somewhat of a sad perplexity,
> The picture of the mind revives again:
> While here I stand, not only with the sense
> Of present pleasure, but with pleasing thoughts
> That in this moment there is life and food
> For future years.
> —William Wordsworth

2 ::: NO IDEAS BUT IN THINGS

The "time of change" episode taught me that I wasn't going to get far delivering long-winded speeches about historical issues to visitors eager to spend weekend and holiday afternoons at Old Sturbridge Village (OSV) with their friends and families. Over the decades, this lesson has extended to many other aspects of museum teaching, whether it was long graphic panels that looked like "books on the wall" or audiovisual programs that kept visitors pinned down in theater seats when they wanted to be out looking at the real stuff. I had been ready to say that our problem was content, that our interpreters needed better information. I was wrong. Instead, the big question was (and is), how do we move the minds, as well as the feet and the eyes, of visitors?

Superimposing content would not have helped. I would have to start by asking, what is the actual interaction between interpreters (the costumed hosts, hostesses, and crafts demonstrators) and visitors, or between our educators and the children coming in school groups? How can that interaction be strengthened to engage visitors more effectively? So I set out to observe.

In the residences, members of the Hosts and Hostesses Department—most of whom were women—would welcome visitors, explain what sort of family would have lived here, how the house was divided, and perhaps how family work roles were assigned. As the eyes of visitors fixed on particular objects, the interpreter would provide a bit of identification—without too many obscure terms, one hoped—and await a follow-up question or comment. At the public buildings, second-person interpretation, usually by men, was more common: "You would have come to a meetinghouse like this for two long services on the Sabbath, bringing your lunch with you so that it could be warmed and served at a neighboring home in the intervening hour." At the crafts shops, interpretation was yet more distinctive. Here the demonstrator could speak in the first person: "I'm trying to repair this chain for a farmer's plow, so the first thing I have to do is . . . ." At that point, it was up to the visitor to intervene with a question, and here the well-trained interpreter would know how to manage a brief and informative conversation, shifting from the present to the past, from the first to the third person, from the physical to the contextual, and back again.

Workers in the School Services Department greeted visiting school groups with a brief orientation talk. ("Old Sturbridge Village shows what it was like to live in the old days.") Teachers and adult chaperones were then given a list of buildings they were to visit, one after the other. The list ensured that children would be evenly distributed throughout the museum during the two- or three-hour visit day. In the course of their visit, the children would also customarily gather for a brief spell of hands-on learning, at which osv educators would initiate them into the mysteries of dipping candles, grinding corn, or spinning and carding wool.

Under these circumstances, there was little opportunity for our team to engage visitors in a more critical exploration of rural life. Despite all our excellent scholarship behind the scenes, osv's public presentation still consisted of a flood of minutiae. Whether our visitors were ten years old or eighty, they were eventually worn down. There was no framework, or "scaffolding," as we learned to call it, in which to put these disparate factoids into order. We offered few chances to reinforce bits of learning.

Of course, in slow seasons some interpreters and educators could discourse at length on historical subjects. One was the estimable Patrick Meade, who had held forth so brilliantly at the McClellan Law Office on my first visit to osv. But given the brevity of the museum visit, we could never hope to offer the thorough exploration possible in the classroom, in the lecture hall, or between the covers of a book. On the other hand, as I told myself each day, the public historian in the outdoor museum had tools at hand to teach history that were unavailable to classroom teachers, lecturers, or the authors of historical texts. I eventually realized, too, that the documentary filmmaker, the public artist, the poet, the tour guide, or the community griot each approached the challenge of engaging the public with the past in distinctive ways. It was foolish to judge any of them by criteria derived from the work of another.

What indeed were the special qualities of history museum learning? Could I find a way to use these special tools to create memorable encounters with past generations? To puzzle this out, I went back again and again to my personal experience on that frosty January day in 1967. Over time, I distilled that epiphanic experience into three discoveries. The first revelation was the importance of tactility, the touchability of the past, which would engage all of one's senses and skills in addressing the reality of past lives. The second was the witnessing of my own learning, recognizing how senses, words, concepts, and emotions intermingle with one another in the rush of consciousness, or what philosophers call epistemology. And the third was the pleasure I experienced in joining a collaborative investigation—researcher and interpreter, curator and visitor. Here was a world we could explore together. In this study, I would have lots of company.

Tactility, epistemology, and collaboration: from their confluence came a passion for historical imaginings that has never left me.

THE TOUCHABLE PAST

At professional gatherings, museum workers sometimes remark on the experience of passing through their galleries at night, when footsteps resound on marble floors and the dim light of security lamps barely catches the glint of a bronze sculpture. Even the most sober professional can understand the appeal of "The Night at the Museum" movies, when the precious objects come alive. But osv was never like that. Even before opening hours, the place was already alive—with weather, with light and shadow, and with birdsong and animal calls. As the costumed interpreters took their places, there was always something new to notice: how different people looked as they crossed the Village common in their winter capes, how much time it took for the cabinetmaker to turn a chair leg on his lathe, how a dry April affected the gardens, and how the ice melted in the morning sun. Being outdoors in the historical environment constantly generated new angles of vision, new phenomena to see, and new life-patterns to explain. Opening myself to the sensuality of the past, I kept discovering how time and space, light and color, and stillness and sound *mattered*. For Thoreau, the philosopher Stanley Cavell observes, "The return of a word requires the recovery of its object for us. . . . To discover what is being said to us, as to discover what we are saying, is to discover the precise location from which it is said; to understand why it is said from just there, and at that time" (*The Senses of Walden* [New York: Viking, 1974], 63).

The touchable past, by its nature, abolished an arbitrary boundary between the historical and the contemporary. In my university classes, everything we knew about the past, including its persistence into the present, had to be attributed anew at every moment. A source was called for, and usually those sources resided, still somewhat raw, in the archives, or in the cooked concoctions of well-reputed scholars. But the outdoor museum hinted at a different truth, that our forebears and we share a complex commonality of sensorimotor engagement with the universe around us. In this way, accessing the touchable past vastly widened and deepened what I could consider historical phenomena—words spoken as well as written; stuff made, used, discarded, or preserved; the ambience of human life; and its diurnal, seasonal, and annual rhythms.

Tactility thus brought me closer to the quotidian past. It legitimated a past as complex as the present. Past lives, I learned, were always marked by both routine and out-of-the-ordinary behaviors. Men and women acted purposefully and they reacted instinctively. Some of what they did was characteristic, "just like them," but occasionally it was "out of character." Much of their lives was trivial, like ours, but some of it was long planned and life defining. Every one of these actions involved the natural and physical environment. Each changed the surrounding world and was changed by it. Follow a farmer's movements through his day, and one could hardly finish enumerating the repertoire of ordinary and extraordinary things he accomplished. And thus tactility, perhaps paradoxically, brought me closer to a connectedness of action and setting, a shared dependence of all of creation, that I can only call spiritual. Walking through the rural landscape every day, watching how the sky and the ground ceaselessly altered their color and texture and how many of life's rhythms found their pulse in the natural world, showed me what theologian Jonathan Edwards had meant by a "sensible" knowledge.

At osv the noticeable became investigable. My customary technique was to capture a scene in my mind and then reconstruct the sequence of actions that I assumed preceded and followed it. By the way it was built, for example, a fence told you what was intended to be on one side and what on the other, and who and what would be permitted to pass, and how easily. A highly valued vegetable garden, for example, was surrounded by tightly fitted walls of sawn boards notched and nailed together, a comparatively hefty expenditure of capital and labor. By contrast, a farmer edged a hillside pasture with a "worm" or "Virginia" fence, split logs laid loosely in a zigzag pattern. In just a few minutes, a farmhand could disassemble such a fence to allow cattle or sheep to move from one pasture to another.

I explored everything at osv in this way. I felt that I was discovering the basic data-point, as we would now call it, of historical study. It wasn't the individual document or even a single object but, rather, a human action  (mental, physical, emotional, or social) embedded in its environment and engaged with a cluster of objects over the course of a few moments. From these fine-grained, moment-to-moment particulars, many meanings could be deduced. I hypothesized that everything had a history, a social world, an economy, and an aesthetic. History was all around me, in the window lintels and soapstone sinks, in faux-marble decorations, and in the pastoral images painted on mantel clocks. Such tactility was quite different, as later chapters of this book will show, from the study of "art history," "decorative arts," "material culture," "the material turn," or other academic taxonomies that sharpen and focus boundaries for scholarship. These disciplines usually focus on objects surgically removed for investigation from their immediate personal, social, and economic contexts. Usually, scholars view objects as the concrete realization of an originating idea in the creator—the quilt maker or the poet. I have instead wanted to use my "dramatistic imagination" to enmesh tactility in the long flow of human action. Each object is inescapably tied to a history of human fingerprints and eye scans, physical and cultural, over the course of its life, as it engaged a series of people—makers, sellers, owners, users, repairers, and disposers.

This embrace of materiality did not diminish the importance of ideas. As a parent, I observed how most human beings move in the second year of life from physical expressions—moving a block from one pile to another, or pointing to a dog on the street—to verbalizations. Immediately they are caught up in making categorical distinctions—the color of the block, or the size of the dog. But these words are soon almost invariably combined into increasingly complex metaphors and narratives derived from action in the material world—"see, this block is a train crashing into the (toy) dog." By extension, but through the same cognitive processes, complex historical ideas like the "flowering of Jacksonian democracy" or the "expanding web of capital markets" could be located at osv, but our challenge was to see how they were constructed out of these patterns of practice on a more minute level. Can we learn who built the garden fence or whose idea it was for the farmer's girls to weave Panama hats to earn cash for the family? These were the intermediary questions that led from the investigable scene to richer historical abstractions.

All this seems obvious now, a matter of common sense. But the idea that historical study would address these matters was new to me and still remains fresh and provocative to this day. The commonplace world is for most scholars a largely unexplored domain of inquiry. Historians, for the most part, gain access to the past by examining the traces surviving in archives, libraries, and museum storage shelves. Among my generation of graduate students, many exploited previously ignored sources, such as the unpublished records of municipal officials stashed away in courthouse basements, and employed new quantitative methods to render portraits of the everyday lives of ordinary people, especially in New England communities. Vital records, census returns, court documents, and the like became the building blocks for a "new social history." Chroniclers of New England's past had conventionally relied on the diaries and letters of highly literate citizens or on their outpouring of theological, political, and literary writing to tell the great stories of regional history (like witchcraft in Salem, the American Revolution, the antislavery crusade, or the Civil War). In the 1960s, a new generation of social historians in New England—John Demos, Philip Greven, Kenneth Lockridge, and Michael Zuckerman, among others—were tackling a different and more puzzling transformation: How did the late medieval world of Puritan authority, dominated by an elite of the wealthy and well educated, evolve into the atomistic, politically competitive, and market-oriented structure of modern American capitalism? This change was not like substituting one kind of fence for another. No one human being could see such historical changes happen or record them. They could only be deduced later by making statistical comparisons between levels of activity across generations.

A recent reviewer of these works surmises that their goal was to create a "history of the daily rhythms of ordinary people."[1] But there was a gulf between my experience at osv and what these historians meant by

1. Nicole Eustace, "When Fish Walk on Land: Social History in a Postmodern World," *Journal of Social History* 37 (Autumn 2003), quotation at 79.

"daily rhythms." I did not discover the tangible past in documents, in wills and court cases. Instead, I interpreted a world of activity as a response to the persistent realities of the landscape. Just as I had eagerly stretched my frozen feet toward the Fenno House parlor hearth in 1967 to thaw out, now I discovered that osv was probably most valuable as a useful compendium of physical and cultural problems and problem-resolving alternatives.

A HISTORIAN OF ACTIONS

Tactility reminded me that all facts are deeds. (In French, of course, the word for facts and deeds, *faits*, remains the same.) Everything I saw around me triggered a search for human actions. When I thought back on my first experience in the Fenno House, I now noted that it was dense with actions that might reward attention and analysis:

- actions of the historical actors: granting the property to the original owners; supplying building materials and making the furnishings; building the house and sheds; writing, editing, and printing the newspaper; and so on;
- actions of the museum's curators: acquiring the house, researching its architecture and furnishings, arranging the space to represent the spatial configuration while providing for other museum purposes (e.g., interpretation, conservation), and so on;
- actions of the scholars consulted (in person and in print): defining typical architectural and furnishing plans for such a historic dwelling, shaping and carrying out a distinctive preservation philosophy, ca. 1950, and so on;
- actions of my osv hostess: welcoming me, explaining how and why she was making a pomander, interpreting the diverse uses of this room, commenting on how the winter altered a woman's work, feeding firewood into the fireplace, and so on;
- actions of mine: visiting the museum, sitting down, stretching out my feet for warmth, picking up and scanning the newspaper, discovering that I had to squint, moving my chair to catch the available light, and so on.

In retrospect, what had originally seemed like a simple act of entering an eighteenth-century house came to seem like my stumbling into a busy movie set, with dozens of people milling about and noisily making contributions to the complexity of the scene.

Years later, even when interpreting world-shaking events like the fed-

The Fenno House, like every human habitation, is a decade-by-decade layering of actions.

eral constitutional convention or the Haitian Revolution, I viewed every document as an invitation to witness the multiple dimensions of actions like these. Take, for example, a famous 1801 letter from Napoleon to Toussaint L'Ouverture. When I held it in the archives in Paris, it felt as eventful as a multipart television minidrama. I was no longer interpreting a piece of paper, but a collision of two powerful men. The scrawl of his huge B for Bonaparte at the bottom of the blue page was only the climax of one scene, marked by his deceitful, threatening words. Later, as I prepared to write my interpretive text, I pondered the first consul at his desk in the Tuileries and then Toussaint's receiving this letter at the house of a sugar plantation near Le Cap. I imagined the meetings of Napoleon's generals as they evolved a strategy to reconquer Saint-Domingue and reinstitute slavery secretly, and I reconstructed Toussaint's calculation: Is this meeting with the French officers a chance to consolidate his regime or, as it turned out, his submission to a death sentence in a prison near the French Alps? And I mused over the two-century-long pilgrimage of this document, surviving the emperor's fall and its preservation in the military archives at the Palais de Vincennes, now located at the end of Paris's number 1 Métro line, to be read by historians and history buffs like me. Its passage to New York for the exhibition was, after all, its third transatlantic voyage. Typing out my draft text on a Brooklyn computer tied me into this dramatic flow of history.

At OSV, I learned that every past action could be seen as durational, situated, and purposeful. Every phrase in a history book invites speculation: How did it happen? What did it look and sound like? How was it produced by the activity of real people? Fortuitously, just at this moment, I stumbled across a perfect manual for these interpretive ruminations, Kenneth Burke's *A Grammar of Motives*. Burke, a fine poet and an even more brilliant literary critic who lived from 1897 to 1993, taught me to construe every sentence as a "symbolic action," composed of these five elements: agent, act, agency, scene, and purpose. Burke's "dramatism," as he called his approach, encouraged me to flesh out every fact and every deed I encountered.

When I thought of William Lloyd Garrison's *Liberator*, for example, I now began to imagine how this abolitionist newspaper arrived at a village postmaster's, where he would keep it, and how he would inform the subscriber to come and retrieve it. I debated whether the postmaster and his cronies might scoff or smile at the paper's appearance. I wondered about whether the local meetinghouse would have welcomed the radical Abby Kelley Foster or permitted any woman to speak from the pulpit. I questioned how sentiments for and against abolitionism would have affected attitudes toward the two or three Black families in the town. I pictured a bystander peeking in the windows of one of the houses on the common to discover an evening prayer meeting of the local ladies. Abolitionism was no longer just a set of entries in a bibliography, as it had been for me in the university library, but an idea that may have been carried like a parcel of explosives through the town.

Burke thus gave me a way to talk about the grammar and the rhetoric of the outdoor history museum. Our Old Sturbridge Village was to be a well-researched if still imaginary reconstruction of the center village and outlying farms, lanes, and mills, of a "typical" New England rural town between 1790 and 1840. Such a place, in Burkean terms, was a useful setting or "scene" for the actions of the historical characters ("agents") who were documented in the Village library's collection of historical sources—primary and secondary sources, documents and images, and manuscripts and printed books and periodicals.

This habit of dramatization transformed the way I read historical documents, slowing me down, drawing my attention to different details. In the Village library, for example, I once came across the diary of a fifty-five-year-old farmer, Horace Clark, of Granby, Connecticut. When Clark notes in May 1837 that he had shattered his old iron-shod moldboard plow, I recognized his dilemma. The plow, it appears, had been made by the inmates of the state prison at Newgate many years before. It was an old companion. "I have followed that plow more miles than any one man did or ever will any plow whatever, in my *opinion*," he writes. In my mind's eye, I can see him standing in a barn like the one at the Village's Freeman Farm, hands on hips, pondering his choices. Months before he had carried the broken implement down to H. Fuller's blacksmith shop in Granby, probably not unlike the Moses Wilder smithy at o s v, where the pieces were welded together on the anvil. But today, he notes, it is "Completely worn out." Now his only choice is to travel to Hartford and purchase an up-to-date cast-iron replacement. And there he is, in my imagination, two weeks later, in a four-wheel wagon, maybe his own or maybe hired from a neighbor, setting out for the twenty-mile-long trip to the city, a good five or six hours each way. And there, in the back of the ironmonger's shop in Hartford, he hears of the advantages of a newly patented three-part cast-iron plow. If one part breaks, the dealer tells him, he won't have to replace the whole plow. Standing in that yard with the bargain struck, he probably passes the time exchanging ideas about the weather, the market, local politics (Clark has served in the state assembly three times), the prospects for the new Van Buren administration, or even, more ominously, the growing panic in Connecticut financial markets following the collapse of cotton prices.

Most of the foregoing is entirely my inference from the fewer than thirty words that Clark devotes to his plow problem in his diary. There is conjecture here, but I prefer to think of it as an invitation to further research. That is what every historian does. OSV encouraged me to situate the story in a time,

place, and material circumstance that I would not otherwise have known or cared about. As I sat back and considered the different elements involved in Horace Clark's little drama, they seemed to compose a pattern of physical, mental, social, cultural, and economic phenomena, akin to what I had experienced in the Fenno House parlor by straining to read the *Massachusetts Spy* on my maiden visit to OSV. This pattern was an integral unit of rural life, tying together consciousness and action and constituting the way of everyday life. I wanted to go further, to explore the consequences of Horace Clark's action, and even to place it in a historical framework. My goal, I wrote to my colleagues in 1973, was to create a complete "experiential history."

I was assisted in this enterprise by reading the work of British anthropologist Mary Douglas (1921–2007). Douglas's first major work, *Purity and Danger: An Analysis of Concepts of Pollution and Taboo* (1966), provided an exciting link between the ordinary, often implicit or tacit, mental constructions of everyday life and a wide variety of social practices. For example, she argued that in abandoning Friday abstinence from meat as a crucial religious observance, the Second Vatican Council had undermined attachment to the faith among British Catholics (she had been born as one). The practice had sustained the faith, not the other way around.

With Douglas's help, I could lift my exploration of Horace Clark to an even more ambitious level of historical narrative. Contrast the "rules and meanings," as Douglas would call it, of the two Horace Clarks. One is a local Granby farmer dependent on a local blacksmith. The other is a Hartford

County farmer increasingly enmeshed in a wider network of progressive farm agents, manufacturers, and traders. In crossing from one to the other, he has done more than buy a new tool. In Burke's terms, he will never have the tools or the skill (agency) to repair the new plow himself, nor will his old blacksmith down the road. What, then, about his "purpose," in Burke's terms? What was Horace Clark up to? Did he think he was participating in a technical transformation of New England farming or joining the march toward a modern economy? We cannot know for sure, but the hypothesis is worth investigating—and there are hundreds of other farm diaries in which to look for evidence.

In this way, Douglas's work encouraged me to probe the key distinctions that helped organize the world of rural New England. On one side, for example, I could identity the few—adult males and a few widows—who were "independent," possessed of a sufficient "competence" to carry on their lives without subordination to others' wills, though they were bound to "honor" the aged and the well born and the educated. On the other side, there was everyone else—women, children, the poor, most Blacks and Indians, hired laborers, and those who had been publicly shamed for some transgression. They were all "dependents," unworthy of being trusted to make decisions rationally and thereby ineligible for town office. Other distinctions flowed from that, like the one between male and female work roles;[2] or between the Sabbath (when heads of households felt obligated to appear in public with all their dependents in tow) and weekdays (when household members might appear on their own in social and commercial settings); or between harvest season (when almost everything was a life-and-death matter) and dead winter (when all sorts of heedless mayhem might be permitted).

Douglas solved some of the problems left by Burke's "dramatistic"

2. A fine illustration of this structuralist methodology appears in my former colleague Jack Larkin's *The Reshaping of Everyday Life, 1790–1840* (New York: Harper & Row, 1988), 17:

Men occupied the realm of major physical force. Most edge tools—plows, axes, saws, scythes—and other heavy implements and vehicles were marked off as their territory. Cooking pots, crockery, washtubs and baskets, butter churns, spinning wheels, needles and thread were counted as distinctively female. Men and boys usually handled the raw materials of farm production and undertook the first steps in processing them—after which they handed them over to women and girls to finish. Finally, and probably most important, American families worked as patriarchal units, governed by their male heads. Men's work, and men's decisions about work, were primary.

method. "Agent" and "scene" were not absolutely distinctive entities but were mutually constructed. Built into every agent was a set of available scenes—a person could not act without them. Even better, by prompting us to locate the rules and meanings of this rural society, Douglas allowed me to tie together artifacts, cognitive processes, and behavioral norms. She provided a scheme to contrast the front and back doors of houses, the differences between redware pottery and porcelain china, and the distinctions between the tools used by a carpenter and those of a cooper: Each of these had a different design quality, a different pattern of use, a different etiquette and terminology, and so on. Each side of the opposition suggested a distinct worldview. And for every opposition, of course, there was also an intermediate sphere, the liminal zone, where things were not all one or the other. In *Purity and Danger*, Douglas suggests how threatening this might be, how dawn and dusk were dangerous times, and how ambiguous kinds of food sources might be nonkosher. New Englanders, the archives tell us, hastened to clear up these confusions. In the municipal world, they organized periodic "perambulations of the bounds" to secure the lines between one town and another, and they voted each year to ensure that unattached persons— impoverished people or vagrants—would either be "warned out of town" or "sold" to local households to be sustained at public expense.

UNDERSTANDING EXPERIENCE

Moral philosophy was a standard course in every nineteenth-century American college, but none of them posed as many challenges in defining what was *appropriate* and *correct* as a rural cooper's shop in the same era. Watching the osv cooper employ his "jointer," the large plane he uses to shave the staves so that they belly out, nest alongside one another perfectly, and in addition taper to fit exactly within the bottom or top "head," presented me with an astonishing range of the most exquisite challenges. Making staved containers—butter churns and firkins, buckets, wet and dry barrels of a half-dozen different sizes, washtubs, bellied-out casks, and gigantic hogsheads—entailed dozens of choices, careful observations about the nature of materials, and skills in handling a wide variety of tools. And then, of course, the cooper needed competence in managing his business, trading for his supplies and materials, supervising apprentices, and teaching the craft. In her book *Natural Symbols: Explorations in Cosmology* (New York: Pantheon, 1970), Douglas concludes, "Cosmologies are the categories in use" (144). My country cooper, viewed as a farmyard cosmologist, seemed to

The nineteenth-century cooper had a jointer in his hands and plenty on his mind.

contain within himself greater intricacy than all the disputants in New England's celebrated religious controversies.

In August 1972, I framed the problem this way:

What was the experience of New Englanders living in rural communities in the fifty years after the establishment of the federal government? How did the lives of these families intersect with the processes of social change transforming the landscape and the mindscape of the region? The museum serves as a stimulus to these questions in all their myriad details. The meetinghouse poses questions of political and religious organization, the carding mill of the impact of new technologies, the parlors of changes in the lives of women, the farm fields of the economic decisions to be made by each household, the shops of changing tastes and commercial development. But these questions are given a certain twist toward the local, the ordinary, the representative by the need to interpret Old Sturbridge Village as a sample of the civilization of four or five million people in the early nineteenth century. Our questions are not about religious and political organization in itself, but about the way a parishioner or a citizen perceived or acted within that organization, the way a choice was made between one kind of chair and another, the alternatives available to a younger son on a central Massachusetts farm in the 1820s.

Much of our work at osv, as this passage indicates, was predicated on locating "the ordinary, the representative" so that we could "interpret Old Sturbridge Village as a sample" of New England life. Of course, the paradoxes stared us in the face. Horace Clark dotted his diary with literally "remarkable" moments, such as a −7°F day in January or the first appearance of a "humblebee" in May. But these striking events were anything but randomly chosen or extraneous to a Connecticut farmer; the arrival of frosts and bees were essential markers of the farmer's year. They fleshed out a regimen of rules and meanings that underlay the practice of typical agricultural life in this place and time.

Consequently, when my evenings turned to writing a Ph.D. dissertation, those daytime museum explorations of the experiential realities of rural life were translated into an alternative history of the well-trod subject of New England religion from 1780 to 1860. Reading hundreds of diaries, conversion narratives, and revival accounts; deducing the experiential ground in hundreds of sermons; and dramatizing the situations posed in dozens of theological treatises, I tried to trace the evolution of the personal experience of grace and spiritual practice. My thesis was that a whole generation of religious New Englanders, whatever their theology or church politics, moved in the same direction in their pattern of spiritual practice, their commonplace understanding of how people engage the divine.

Douglas thus helped me locate the evolving "geography of grace," the step-by-step morphology of salvation, the internal drama of the mind undergoing this transformation, and the social processes that accompanied and sustained these personal changes in the early American republic. Theologians had, of course, interpreted all these experiences, but I found better evidence for the pattern in personal narratives by ordinary folk. The conventional theological distinctions, like the battles between liberal Unitarians and evangelical Trinitarians, dissolved in these readings. I discovered that contemporaries in the 1810s or the 1840s shared a road map of their experiences, no matter what church they attended or which prayer book they used. Praxis was more determinative than theology. For the purpose of clarity, I gathered all my cases into three ideal types—doctrinalist, moralist, and devotionalist spirituality—and I titled the dissertation, correspondingly, "Soul, Character, and Personality" to represent the way the self was experienced in each of these three forms. Finally, I concluded by positing that what was happening in the religious sphere of meaning-making could be witnessed as well in the evolution of teaching and learning, of fictional invention, and of other ways of representing the life of the mind.

The thesis brought to religious life the same sort of attention to moment-to-moment consciousness and action that I had learned at osv to apply to the mechanics of making fenceposts. In focusing on the phenomenology of religious life, dissecting and dramatizing the materiality of the metaphors that ordinary folk use to describe themselves, I was "doing" intellectual history as my Harvard professors had taught me, but in a way that might better link to social and economic life. I found that changes in these patterns of ordinary life were indices of major social transformations, just as Perry Miller could find revolutions in thought by the changing metaphors used by Puritan preachers.

As much as my colleagues in the new social history, I wanted to widen the focus of scholarship to address people usually excluded from the stories of American political and intellectual development. It was easier to demonstrate that enslaved and free Black Americans, immigrants and their children, working-class folk and farm families, transients, the homeless, and disabled people lived in the same physical universe, often toiled with the same tools, and experienced the same rhythms of sun and storm as their more fortunate and privileged neighbors. But I also wanted to test the notion that they, too, had stakes in the political struggle, ideas worth explicating, and complex social and psychological interactions.

When I put it that way, I remind myself that coming to osv—though I'd never been there before—was a turn toward home. I'd also been a child among men and women of considerable skill who seldom received public or scholarly attention. As a youngster I'd spent hours trailing my mother through her daily tasks—there was no preschool in those days. When I watched her sifting flour, starching shirt collars, koshering meat, or pushing chunks of meat and onions through a grinder, I was being initiated into a craftsperson's world. Intuiting the routines of days, weeks, seasons, and generations involved her in complex understandings of the world. Right ways of doing things involved lots of knowledge, and lots of flexibility.

When people asked if my mother was orthodox or observant, I would say that this exercise of *balabatishe* (careful homemaking) skill was actually the core of her religion. Her "theology" was vague and inconsistent, but her Jewish patterns of action were precise and complex. It took more than a Harvard degree to understand how my mother made apple pie (or the way Horace Clark replaced his plow).

"No ideas but in things," William Carlos Williams wrote in 1926, in the first version of his epic poem, *Paterson*. The genius of a museum is its capacity to treat the object directly, to make it present in the eyes and minds of many visitors at a single moment and allow each of them to use a lifetime of recognitions, reasonings, and imaginations to absorb its presence into their lives. They, in turn, become part of the object's character and history. We are connected to all of creation.

3 ::: TWENTIETH-CENTURY MINDS DISSECTING NINETEENTH-CENTURY PROBLEMS

From my very first trip to Old Sturbridge Village (osv), the place provided an exhilarating opportunity for learning. No wonder. I'd been in school forever—reading, taking notes, writing, listening, talking, being tested, and reading some more. Life had devolved into a competition between my right index finger turning the page and my left thumb holding down those already read. By contrast, my first Fenno House parlor visit sparked new ways of learning— by stretching out my legs to thaw out, squinting at an old newspaper, shifting my chair, adjusting my body, voicing the words, as well as decoding the paper's unfamiliar content and layout (with advertisements occupying much of the front page)—each of which communicated something new about the preindustrial world. I didn't have to worry about what some teacher expected me to notice. This was just for me. The faster I learned, the more broadly I smiled. My fingers danced happily on the steering wheel all the way home.

When I returned to osv, first as an interpreter and then as a professional, I realized, of course, it couldn't be just for me. How was I going to get my visitors to tap their fingertips and toes? Could I use the Fenno visit as a model for successful museum interpretation? Here's what I remembered: First, I had been warmly welcomed by the hostess ("please have a seat and thaw out a bit on this frigid day," or words to that effect). Second, I was provided with bits of identification and orientation (she told me I was in "the parlor of a house built in Canton, Massachusetts, in the 1720s"). Third, she provided some information new to me ("the parlor in legend was reserved for receiving company, but it might also serve as a place for the family to have tea or an evening meal"). Fourth, I then had room to toss in my own two cents, asking whether the paper was Federalist or Democratic-Republican and whether it was usual for people to read aloud in those days before whale oil lamps shed better light. The fifth stage came in our mutually wrapping up the conversation. Sixth, and last, we bid each other farewell. The kindly lady suggested that, given my interest in politics, I would find a visit to the law office valuable.

I had already been interested in epistemology, the study of how the mind learns. In an undergraduate literature course, I'd written a paper on William Wordsworth's long poem "The Prelude: The Growth of the Poet's Mind," where he celebrates the assimilating power of a child's mind. From that moment, almost everything I've ever studied and taught stemmed from this fascination with the epistemological moment. By the end of my junior year, I'd carved out a path for myself as an aspiring historian of the way the mind works. Through my senior thesis on Melville, and in virtually all my graduate courses, I continued to dissect representations of interiority in literature, theology, philosophy of mind, and the emerging science of psychology.

THE VISITOR'S WAY OF LEARNING

It wasn't surprising that I used my first OSV visit as the basis for developing a morphology of the museum learning encounter. I became familiar with this sequence: welcome, orientation, information, interaction, culmination, farewell. This six-step process proved a valuable tool for assessing how a visitor might successfully learn in the museum space, and it has since been valuable in training interpreters to be aware of the stages of the visitors' experience. Critical to the success of this sequence was its duration. It seemed to take at least four or five minutes for a visitor to engage, interact, and register a productive encounter. Visitors who had briefer, hit-and-run contacts with interpreters got much less from the experience. Success also seemed to come from making the meeting a true dialogue, with responsibility for agenda-setting shifting back and forth between the museum worker and the visitor.

Assembling the components of a good learning encounter was challenging. First came the "hook," something that would intrigue visitors strongly enough for them to stop. I used my college interns as an experimental team. We discovered that visitors would nod to an idle costumed interpreter they passed on the road, but they would not stop. But when we gave the interpreter a prop—a pitchfork, a newspaper, a basket of fruit, virtually anything—he or she became magnetic. The threshold into a dialogue was thus the merest suggestion of an action that could be described:

- "I'm going up to the farm to join in the haying—it's a good way to pick up some six shillings for a day's work."
- "I've just been reading this piece in the paper about the Barbary pirates—do you think it's right to pay ransom to those thieves so we can get our sailors back?"
- "Old Widow Marcy's doing poorly now and I thought my fruit could cheer her up until her son comes back from taking his heifer to be sold in Brighton."

Openings like these encouraged visitors to participate, to ask questions, or to comment on historical differences. Skillful interpreters could also engage children in the activity of the interpretive station, as in the following questions addressed to younger visitors:

- "Could you please lend me a hand and carry one or two of these pieces of wood to the schoolhouse stove so we'll be able to warm up our lunch later on?"
- "Help me out; we've got a problem with woodchucks in the garden, eating up the vegetables. What are we going to do?"

The best interactivity, of course, drew from both the sensorimotor domain and the visitors' ability to "think historically" or role-play a member of the rural community in the nineteenth century.

Finally, the interpretive encounter needed a reinforcing culmination and farewell, which rewarded the attention of visitors and recognized their empathic imagination and skills in role-playing. The farewell also usefully directed visitors to another station in the Village, to another historic site, or perhaps to a book available in the Village bookstore.

At osv, any given museum visit was composed of as many as twenty to thirty of these encounters. Museums, after all, engage attention only intermittently. Groups of visitors seemed to move through the landscape—indoors or out—in an accordion-like fashion, walking at different paces,

"You look like interesting folks to talk history with!"

spreading out until they were attracted to a particular interpretive station, and then reconnecting with other members of their group. As they arrived at a station, I noticed, visitors generally arranged themselves in a 120-degree arc, with everyone's attention fixed on the "object," which could be a costumed interpreter's talk or a craftsman's demonstration, about eight to twelve feet away. (The widespread use of cameras, of course, influences where the visitor stands.) I began to call this spatial configuration of subject (visitors) and object (interpreters and stuff) "the museum frame." There was a ritualistic quality to the encounter. Arriving visitors leaned forward, straining to catch up with the flow of the presentation. Some held back, waiting for the interpreter to "start again," as if there were a fixed-length script. (There usually wasn't.) Others pushed in, inserting themselves into the conversation. Parents divided their attention between absorbing the content and ensuring that their children were well behaved and "learning properly." The most skilled interpreters "reframed" every few minutes, intuitively welcoming the latest arrivals. I observed that the heart of a presentation, the magical "aha!" moment, often came around the three-minute mark, and then it was skillfully delineated for emphasis by a counterex-

The "museum frame" holds visitors, interpreters, and tools in a shared exploration.

ample or a piece of comic relief. After about four or five minutes, the interpreter offered a culminating remark, summarizing the importance of what he or she had said. At that point, most visitors began to drift away, leaving behind the most engaged to ask their own idiosyncratic questions, to show off their knowledge, or (on occasion) to challenge the interpreter.

In the course of those few moments, many visitors (especially under less crowded conditions) arrived at a comfortable position vis-à-vis the material they were encountering. Within the museum frame, they had situated themselves in a present moment engaging a single moment in the past. The museum had thus physicalized the meeting of people at distinct points in the flow of time. When this happened, visitors could cross this divide in a number of ways: by imagining themselves in the same past moment and situation, by measuring the contrast between then and now, or by puzzling out how the historian makes sense of the difference between the two. In such a "museum episode," as we can call it, the best interpretation tied the key ideas to the sense-experience and was also responsive enough to different kinds of visitor interests and learning styles. This experiential unity was far different from the conventional drone of a "this-is-a . . . and that-is-a . . ." museum tour.

A similar rhythm of engagement and detachment, as I've often observed, prevails in indoor museum installations, including galleries of art and science as well as history. Museum people should acknowledge that visitors pay attention episodically, and they should tailor their presentations of ideas, objects, and demonstrated processes with this in mind. By contrast, films shown in a darkened theater allow little opportunity for viewers to break the flow of their attention and to turn away. Their focus, pulled along by the mechanical pace and lifelike representation of the flow of time in cinema, is more continuous. Live theater stands midway between the museum and film. According to theater scholar Bruce McConachie, breaks in the action (sometimes interrupted by audience applause or other reactions), a dimly lit ambience, and intermission periods permit companions to sense the doubleness of the actors as modern-day people like themselves and also as characters in a story.

The special gift of museums to learning is a kinesthetic engagement, the body's repeatedly approaching and retreating from the museum frame. Somehow I had to learn to use this rhythm productively. In the best of circumstances, as the visitors got closer to the object, their eyes, ears, hands, and legs began unconsciously to mimic the action and the scene in front of them. They shuddered a bit at the clang of the hammer of the anvil, and their eyes followed the quick shot of the shuttle across the loom. Such immersion blocked out the rest of the environment—other visitors, the weather, the time of day. Then, when they disengaged, their bodies could move into another relationship with time and space, reconnecting themselves to the museum map. At this moment, if all went well, the interpreter could offer an overview that contextualized the immersion moments that preceded it.

Immersion and overview, I realized, were the poles of museum learning. Immersion allowed for personal involvement, emotional attachment, and a lengthening of sensory attentiveness. Overview allowed visitors to put the moment into the context of prior knowledge and integrated it into a larger historical context. Experientially, the overview also reminded visitors that they belong to a group proceeding on today's schedule. Both immersion and overview posed risks. Too much immersion, and the visitor would lose touch with the larger storyline. Too much overview, say in hearing the interpreter go on too long about big historical ideas, and the visitor would lose interest in the human drama. A sequence and a balance were necessary.[1]

osv was great at immersion but not so good at overview. As I discovered

---

1. Jay Appleton, in his analysis of environmental perception, refers to this as "prospect and refuge" theory; see *The Experience of Landscape*, rev. ed. (Chichester, U.K.: Wiley, 1996).

in my attempt to rewrite the Village's mission statement, it was impossible to subsume the whole visit as an encounter with a theme like "A Time of Change." The place to start, it turned out, was the museum education program (as it almost always is in museums, since the educators are the most likely to think through the arc of the visit experience from pre-visit information to follow-up exercises in the classroom). Throughout the school year, as many as 400 children came to osv almost every day. They were divided into groups of ten or so, and we had around forty groups daily to test out different ways of navigating the museum's geographical and cognitive map.

What good fortune it was, then, that just when I had felt stymied by the mission statement fiasco, in late May 1971, I got the chance to take over the directorship of osv's education program. We'd already lost one director the year before, and eager to avoid another arduous search process, Barnes Riznik gave me the job—to which I brought almost total inexperience with elementary and secondary education and, indeed, with managing staff altogether. But now I would have a laboratory in which to experiment with understanding the museum as a place for teaching and learning history. It was a lot easier, after all, to shape the program of a school group than it was to herd dozens of adult and family visitors moving at their own pace through the outdoor museum.

Given Riznik's desperation to fill the job, I could lay down some conditions. We would change the name from School Services to the Museum Education Department. I could hire two assistants. We would be free to develop a totally new approach to educating visiting schoolchildren in the Village, and that approach would inform the design of the new learning center that was just beginning its planning process. Surprisingly, at age twenty-five, I was in charge of something big: a working group of about thirty paid docents, three professionals, and three secretaries. More than 70,000 schoolchildren a year would visit.

On my first morning, I got to the library early, found an 1809 cookbook, and xeroxed a dozen copies of a recipe for rice cakes. At 10:00 A.M., I greeted a busload of ten-year-old visitors from Springfield, New Jersey, a bit groggy from their long ride that morning. I took my ten kids aside and gave each a copy of the recipe. One child was appointed recipe reader, another map tracker, a third chief strategist, a fourth scribe, two or three others basket-carriers, and so on. The recipe reader started out, "Take a pound of rice . . . ." The strategist said, "OK, where do we get rice?" A small boy guessed, "the farm?" The mapper pointed the way, and off we went.

At the Freeman Farm, our group met the fellow impersonating old Pliny

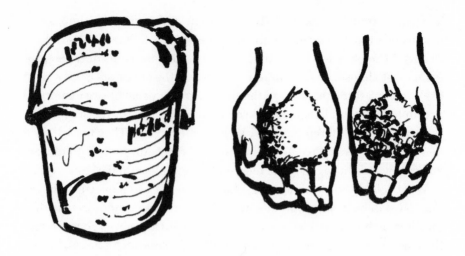

Freeman that day. "You want what?" he asked. A chorus rang out, "a pound of rice!" "Well, where do you think you are? South Carolina?" Puzzled looks. "This is Massachusetts. We haven't any rice here!" he gesticulated emphatically. "What are we going to do?" asked the new Museum Ed director helpfully. "What *do* you have?" piped up the ten-year-old strategist, God bless the child. "Well, I could get you some corn, and you can make cornbread," suggested the smiling farmer. "Oh, and how do we know how to do that?" the littlest boy asked.

Thus began our great adventure. We pestered the farm wife for advice again and again, pondered what a "cup of water" meant in the day before Pyrex measuring vessels, helped churn some butter to make up for the amount we were "borrowing," wondered how much we would need to feed a dozen explorers direct from the twentieth century, and on and on, until we chewed and swallowed every bit of our project. For me, it was the perfect way to teach and learn, an open-ended process and a clear goal, a measure of uncertainty and a collaboration toward a successful conclusion.

Without patter about the name of this artifact or that one, and without nine-syllable phrases like "preindustrial society," the day instead energized the native skills of these children. Some were physically adroit, some were good calculators, some were fascinated by the process, and others were driven by the goal. The chaperone and I coaxed and coached, but it was the children's project to make that cornbread and gobble it down as though it were chocolate truffle cake. Shoes filthy from mud, shoulders weary from carrying buckets of water, and the crumbs of cornbread left on the corners

of a kid's mouth would, I hope, be surer signs of their learning than lists of words and concepts.

Could this become a model for our museum education program? In 1970–71 and for years before, elementary and middle school groups coming to osv had been given a list of buildings they were to visit, one after the other. The list ensured that children would be evenly distributed throughout the museum during the visit day. If a group visited the Quaker meetinghouse, it would skip the Village meetinghouse; those going to the bank would bypass the law office. Watching the potter do his magic on the wheel meant you had to forgo the equally impressive show at the blacksmith's anvil. This made no pedagogical sense at all. Whatever story about the diversity of religions in New England might be told at one meetinghouse surely needed the other. Whatever awareness kids got of the process of making the wheel turn in the dark and dank Hervey Brooks pottery would benefit from the hammer drop in the hot and acrid Moses Wilder smithy.

In the course of their visit, the children would also customarily gather for a brief hands-on learning spell. They lined up to dip a row of candlewicks into a tub of hot bayberry wax sitting on an electric hot plate, one dip per child. Leaving aside the anachronisms of the heat source and the bayberry (in the Village period, candles were made from tallow, or pig fat), what could a child learn from a single dipping? "Did I do it long enough?" "When is it done?" "What happens if I drop the stick into the goop?" No time for questions, no room for answers. And, of course, the children never got a chance to read by candlelight in a darkened parlor, as I had years before.

Applying the "rice cakes" model meant developing a series of thematic tours—on work, family life, and community. An introductory briefing would set up the problem for the "field study." (We banned the trivializing term "field trip.") Students would be given role cards, based on our team's demographic studies of the historical town of Sturbridge. Thus, a ten-year-old child, carrying a label on her coat that read "Jemima Dunton, age 35, wife of blacksmith Zenas Dunton and mother of five," was invited to interact knowledgeably with the issues as her group made its way through the Village. The museum educator used each stop along the tour to encourage students to question, to elaborate, to illustrate, and to question again. In the midst of the tour, a visit to a learning "studio" gave students hands-on experiences with handling farm tools, cooking a meal, spinning and weaving cloth, or printing a broadside. At the end of the day, they joined in summarizing their impressions: How would we deal with a crisis in family life?

How do we organize a task that requires more labor than we have in our own family to get the crops in? What should the town do about building a high school (who would benefit?), locating a tannery (did neighbors have a right to ban that awful smell?), or connecting the old meetinghouse road to the nearest turnpike (would that get our goods to market more efficiently?)?

Unlike my earlier effort to promote "a time of change" as the master theme for all of osv's interpretive efforts, these thematic tours in Museum Ed provided a stronger thread on which to string a sequence of experiences in the Village. We framed the whole visit as a single investigation—with a beginning, middle, and end—rather than a meaningless sequence of stops along the path. We would introduce ideas, exemplify them, reinforce them, challenge them, refine them, wrap them up, and say farewell. The thematic tour turned the group visit into a process, an arc of linked encounters from pre-visit classroom materials to the follow-up exercises back in school, which often had kids compare the social and physical world represented at osv with the one they saw every day in their home towns.

EXPERIENTIAL LEARNING

We were in love with process. Just as we paid close attention to every step in the cooper's craftsmanship, so we watched intently as ten-year-old visitors learned to compare nineteenth-century barrels with modern-day trunks or cardboard containers. Moment by moment, we mapped the learning through a child's facial expressions — curiosity, wonder, befuddlement, resolution, doubt, satisfaction. A visit to osv, we all knew, was not an end in itself. At best, we were proposing a method. We hoped it would catch fire and stimulate parents, teachers, and children to mix the same rich ingredients in teaching history at home or school: immersing themselves in a historic site, observing unfamiliar processes close up, reading and savoring bits of historical documents, trying out the challenge of making something with their hands, enjoying the process, and sharing discoveries with their companions.

One key difference from classroom learning, or from watching television or playing board games, was the enormous variety of learning materials and methods available to us as educators in the outdoor museum. First, our students were immersed in a different world, from which electricity and automobiles had been banished. The students trod on stony roads and woodland paths, crossed a covered bridge, and peered over the rails at the river below. They watched and listened as craftspeople made familiar objects — rolling pins, horseshoes, soup bowls — from stacks and heaps of shapeless stuff. They examined historic artifacts and read aloud from period documents, taking note of how differently people in the past made things and talked about the work they did. Students took on the roles of nineteenth-century farmers and villagers, debating the way they wanted their futures to go. They wrote nature poems, set them in type on an old press, and brought them home to proud moms and dads.

This diversity of learning activities, of course, elicited a remarkable array of native skills. Kids unfamiliar with the name of every artifact in a room constantly surprised us by their quick ability to intuit how something could be used. Teachers told us that boys who usually clung to the back walls of their classrooms, silently and sullenly, came forward and wanted to demonstrate how to make that thing work. One African American boy, advertised by his teacher as a potential troublemaker, turned out to have learned in a summertime visit with his South Carolina grandmother exactly how to make use of every part of the pig osv slaughtered every autumn—its bristles for brushes, the fat for all kinds of soap and candles, the bladder for a drum head, and glycerin for a thousand and one household remedies. His classmates were agape.

We thought anything could be taught this way, and teachers from all grades, of all subjects, and of all sorts of children brought their classes to us. We enthusiastically read Ivan Illich's *Deschooling Society* (1971) and dreamed that teaching like ours could invigorate, enrich, or (as the most radical of us thought) replace the dreary bureaucratized world of our industrial-era education system. To those who haughtily dismissed museums as improbable agents of educational revolution, we pulled out our copies of John Dewey's *School and Society* ([1899; rpt. Chicago: University of Chicago Press, 1956], 89–90). "Take the textile room as an illustration of such a synthesis," Dewey advised those eager to uncork the energies of curious children.

> I am talking about a future school, the one we hope, some time, to have. The basal fact in that room is that it is a workshop, doing actual things in sewing, spinning, and weaving. The children come into immediate connection with the materials, with various fabrics of silk, cotton, linen and wool. Information at once appears in connection with these materials; their origin, history, their adaptation to particular uses, and the machines of various kinds by which the raw materials are utilized.

Hands-on learning about textiles, Dewey said, could connect children as well to investigations of art, literature, science, and cultural history.

> In the ideal school there would be something of this sort: first, a complete industrial museum, giving samples of materials in various stages of manufacture, and the implements, from the simplest to the most complex, used in dealing with them; then a collection of photographs and pictures illustrating the landscapes and the scenes from which the materials come, their native homes, and their places of manufacture. Such a collection would be a vivid and continual lesson in the synthesis of art, science, and industry.

Dewey never specified exactly how teachers and students would move from one element to another in this magical workshop cum industrial museum cum arts studio, and this remained a puzzle for our museum educators at osv. What, in fact, did our children learn through their hands-on investigations? How much about the past could one learn by an abbreviated reenactment of past work processes? Simply lying on one's back with a paintbrush in hand could hardly bring one closer to the art, spirituality, and social context of Michelangelo's work at the Vatican. But the longer that we extended the reenactment and the more we mixed a variety of tasks and end products, the better was the conversation that ensued with students. If a school or college group dressed in period costume, spent the evening preparing and sharing a meal in a museum house, and capped off their day with a simulated nighttime political or religious meeting, the students assuredly began to capture the perspectives of nineteenth-century New Englanders more consistently and coherently.

The secret lay in exploring the value of an imperfect match between past and present. Following in historic footsteps led to a lot of wobbling and missteps. Measuring the wobble was, indeed, a useful research technique. We could never know the past exactly, but we could work at it. To wobble was to become a sympathetic neighbor to the truth. To cook the way old New Englanders did, we would first have to learn this and try that, mostly without much success. To plan a day as one of our historical diarists did, we would have to think of time in a way that reflected the distance between 1840 and 1970. We would have to learn what was behind the way "they" described women or treated children or settled their debts. In each case, the margin of difference generated valuable learning while it conveyed the "historicity" of the phenomena we were encountering. And all the while it was revealing our common humanity, both with the characters of the past and with our fellow seekers today.

After Dewey, the next great giant of cognitive development was the Swiss psychologist Jean Piaget. In a series of epochal works written between the 1920s and the 1960s, Piaget and his coauthor Bärbel Inhelder had linked the child's evolving cognitive, affective, and operational capabilities to his or her biological development. After a hundred generations of educators failed miserably at "hammering something into a child's thick skull," the Piagetians reinterpreted learning as a physiologically necessary and even pleasurable act. In the 1960s, Jerome Bruner, the Harvard psychologist, carried this idea forward. "Bruner's emphasis upon structure and his bold assertion that any topic can be taught to any child at any age have become part of the working assumptions of most curriculum developers," wrote Edwin Fenton, a leader in social studies education (*Teaching the New Social Studies* [New York: Holt, Rinehart and Winston, 1966], 81).

Devoted to a child-centered investigation of education, Bruner drama-tized the step-by-step process of learning as if it were as adventurous as the Apollo space missions. "Discovery," he wrote in *On Knowing: Essays for the Left Hand* ([Cambridge: Harvard University Press, 1962], 82–83), "whether by a schoolboy going on his own or by a scientist cultivating the growing edge of his field, is in its essence a matter of rearranging or transforming evidence in such a way that one is enabled to go beyond the evidence so re-assembled to new insights. It may well be that an additional fact or shred of evidence makes the larger transformation possible. But it is so often not even dependent on new information."

So fertile was the child's Brunerian imagination that it could continue to learn in the absence of new stimuli, simply by reworking fragments of experience already collected. When Bruner came to visit us at osv, he ap-plauded the Museum Education program as a splendid illustration of his pedagogical narrative.

Still, I had my differences. Bruner's work was crucial to the curriculum reform efforts of the 1960s, the most pervasive (and the most often mocked) being "the new math." After children had been forced for centuries to memo-rize multiplication tables and master "long division," Bruner's allies in the American Mathematical Association pressed for a curriculum that would engage children in understanding the commutative, associative, and dis-tributive laws that actually underlay these arithmetical calculations. "Our task as teachers," Bruner said, "is to lead students to develop concepts in order to make sense of the operations they have performed" (*On Knowing*, 102).

This was just what we desperately needed. Our visiting schoolchil-dren had the native skills and the motivation to operate splendidly in the historical museum environment. But were they learning any "history"? osv's teacher training cadre, an adjunct of our band of museum educa-tors, pressed to have school visits fit neatly into the classroom curriculum. Such advocates of the "new social studies" wanted students to move beyond operations (like improvising the making of cornbread) to "master" concepts (like the division of family work roles) and thereby to achieve a grasp of the "structure" of historical study analogous to that championed by the mathe-maticians or the physicists.

Here I parted company. My heart ached to see little kids carrying clip-boards around the Village and filling in the boxes of their "data-retrieval charts." Hands tightly holding pencils would surely never feel the heft of a water bucket or the heat of a Dutch oven. Trouble was, what the Village communicated to visiting children was much richer than the evidence for historical conceptualizing. Maybe someday all those sensory impressions would be captured in propositional form—but not yet! I wanted my students to feel the pulse of a living place, not to stand off to one side as detached observers.

I didn't know about math or physics, but I was beginning to recognize that history was a different kind of creature. I never met a "practicing" historian who pursued the methods set forth by the new social studies. History doesn't seem to be built up out of concepts at all. Instead, what we call historical concepts—for example, the struggle against exploitation, efforts to maintain social order, the conflict of settlers with native populations— are invariably embedded in human situations that change over time. Such stories could be told in a thousand different ways, using a global or a microscopic focus, as tragedies or comedies.

Further, it now dawned on me that one's way of "doing history" depended entirely on what one used as source material for these stories and how one presented them to one's audiences. I was now indelibly a museum historian. I was jealously proud of the immense array of human artifacts and actions I could interpret, of the exciting presentational methods I could use, and of my mission to reach old and young, expert and novice, at the same time.

Perhaps I loved process even more than Bruner. He was, after all, surrounded at lunch in Harvard's William James Hall by men and women reaching conclusions. I preferred to believe that the proper end of learning was the open-ended love of learning. Years later, my friend Nick Westbrook suggested I read David Pye's *The Nature and Art of Workmanship* (1968). Pye distinguished between "the workmanship of risk," dependent upon a moment-to-moment exercise of dexterity and care, and "the workmanship of certainty," which aims to realize a complete preexisting design goal. Every day at osv, children were demonstrating unexpectedly original and dexterous understandings of the past. I didn't know if they were getting the "right" answers, and I didn't care. The more the museum visit was integrated with the classroom curriculum, I feared, the less likely it was to deliver its own special delights.

Museum teaching taught me a lot about nineteenth-century history, even more because I was trying out my ideas with fifth-graders and not fellow graduate students. Ten-year-olds, I discovered, had an enviable habit of viewing the world as desperately in need of assistance. They were great at deducing clues so long as they contributed to the solution of a problem that was truly worrisome. Where older children would know the game was "unreal," and "just a trick to get us to do something we didn't really want to do," ten-year-olds got right into it. The best programs for such kids posed tactical puzzles that engaged their "concrete operational" thought processes, as our readings of Piaget predicted. Visiting students would become so enraptured by the role-playing of a town meeting at osv that they would conclude the day with the urgent question, "Are we really going to build a high school now?"

THE SYNTHESIS OF MUSEUM EDUCATION

The Museum Education program at osv, in sum, addressed the problem of making coherent sense of fragmentary encounters with three methods.

First, there was a focus on *overview themes*. In practice, these became investigations of the anthropology of rural communities.

- FAMILY: How did the different members of a family distribute the work that was needed for subsistence and growth? What activities and rituals of family life bound the members together? How would the family unit respond to crises or to new opportunities? *Compare the families you know in contemporary America.*
- WORK: How were raw materials transformed into food, clothing, shelter, and other goods wanted by the family and community? What skills and tools were required to produce these goods? In what ways did the family and community have access to specialized skills, like medicine, law, and religious instruction? *Compare the work processes you can see in contemporary America.*
- COMMUNITY: How did these New Englanders organize their provision of public goods (schools, roads, poor relief, etc.)? What kinds of social interactions brought people together in early nineteenth-century towns? *Compare the community life in the places you know in contemporary America.*

"A Time of Change" differed from these themes in important ways. Despite its intention to look more critically at the museum's presentations, that theme was merely a verbal overlay on the activities visible in the museum. It was otherwise experientially inaccessible. FAMILY, WORK, and COMMUNITY, by contrast, assumed that students could work with these concepts, even if they could not yet name them. By exploring the division of work rules in practice, the FAMILY program metaphorically represented the interdependence of household members. The WORK program concretely engaged students in the transformation of the raw into the cooked. The

COMMUNITY program asked children to demark the boundaries of public and private spheres. Rather than talking about concepts, these programs invited students to use them.

Second, the Museum Education themes were often given *a narrative twist*—as when the day was devoted to a key question like "should we build a high school here?" Through the entire visit day, museum educators could keep the inquiry proceeding through encounters at different interpretive stations and different kinds of hands-on learning experiences in the Museum Education Center. And they could wrap up the day's work with a culminating exercise, portraying the contrasting characteristics of "then" and "now."

Third, the *diversity of learning modes* itself became a subject for the students' exploration. What could one learn from cooperating to cook a meal at the hearth? What did an examination of a family's succession of census returns tell us? Did a role-playing exercise bring us some new understanding of the roles of different family members, or different people within the community?

It took four years at Museum Education to translate the exhilaration of my personal discoveries into a way of creating exciting experiences for visitors old and young. And it has since taken more than four decades for me to translate what our small band of museum educators learned into joyful ways of teaching history in public settings in every corner of the country. I am still amazed at the magic of the museum moment at its best—when it crystallizes the immediacy of the theater, the meticulous scholarship of the library, the open-ended adventure of the laboratory, and the conviviality of the family table. In my imagination, I have written this chapter a hundred times since 1975, plumbing its deep discoveries again and again. Creating museum education was for me like laying out a fabulous garden, still growing, with many paths, flower beds, ponds, and fountains, all of them providing delights that are refreshed by frequent visits.

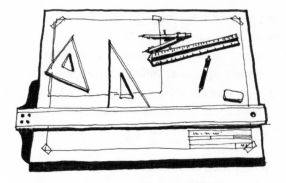

The museum work was a gift. I discovered how history could move from footnotes to fingertips, cropping up wherever I looked around Old Sturbridge Village (osv). I watched in awe the fast-paced drama of minds in motion—my own, my colleagues', and those of the visitors we met. osv channeled my fascination with theatricality and with epistemology into productive work, and it provided me with a foundation for my own career. But perhaps its most lasting bounty was the invitation to start working alongside and to common purpose with men and women of radically different backgrounds, skills, and methods. Over these five decades, collaborative work has been my best teacher and counselor.

Taking a leave from graduate school in 1967 was anything but the loss of a learning community. True, I was no longer seated alongside my mates at library tables or in classrooms. But from that momentous January day, I'd been accompanied for much of the time by museum interpreters. At my side, like the Interpreter in John Bunyan's *Pilgrim's Progress*, they had "show[n] me excellent things, such as would be helpful to me on my journey." Every conversation was a revelation. The lady in the Fenno House parlor, it turned out, was Alice Thompson Taylor. She'd spent a lifetime as a dairy farmer until the death of her husband, and she knew everything about country life in central Massachusetts. Her second husband, Iral D. Taylor, had been an engineer on the Boston and Albany Railroad. He moved into Alice's Greek Revival farmhouse in New Braintree and gladly rented his little house in nearby Warren to me for seventy-five dollars a month. Iral's inexhaustible tales of near-calamities on the B&A came gratis.

The man who portrayed lawyer McClellan on my first visit, it turned out, was the even more exotic Patrick Meade. Born in Ireland, a veteran of the World War I trenches, and then an officer in the imperial police in India, Burma, and Singapore, he'd actually shot (or shot at) tigers, rhinos, and crocodiles. He'd met Mohandas Gandhi, "felt the impelling power of his eyes," and come to distrust him thoroughly. His adventure-drenched memoir, *Born to Trouble* ([New York: G. P. Putnam's Sons, 1939], 215, 366), concludes by wanting "to impress upon the chance reader that although dangers can be met in the jungle and distant parts of the world, so can they be met in the heart of London and New York." Stationed in Washington, D.C., during World War II, Captain Meade was mysteriously involved in providing more war matériel to the British forces than was publicly acknowledged in the Lend-Lease agreement. Now, in wintry New England, he was the embodiment of Anglo-American order and tradition, my own personal Churchill. He cherished rural New England as the perfect tempering of British courtesy and American democracy.

There were many others. Henry Joy, himself the son of a man born during the "Village period" (1790 to 1840), had been an apple farmer in Woodstock, Connecticut, for forty years. Mimicking his Yankee accent has been a constant mainstay of my joke-telling to this day. I once asked Henry how he might account for the sharp decline in "prenuptial conceptions" (the proportion of first births occurring within seven months of a marriage) between 1790 and 1840. Immediately he replied, "Well, Rich-ard, the roads got a whole lot bett-ah. They could send the young men home at night!"

What pleased me most about my comrades in costume was their shared curiosity about the past. Most of them were retired, and they knew the mystery of time's passing, the disappearance of evidence, the irretrievability of absolute certainty. The talented craftsmen of osv—as their leader, Ralph Hodgkinson, told me—could only struggle to recover a mastery of skills that once were almost universal. In the university, the range of skills was comparatively so limited and the sources worth plumbing so narrow. Further, in the modern university, everyone—students as well as faculty—is at work on independent projects. By contrast, osv resembled an odd sort of crash program, where researchers, curators, educators, and interpreters were all looking at the same objects and focusing on the same historical phenomena, the civilization of rural New England as it existed a century and a half ago, though from many different angles of vision.

I had the chance as education director to broaden the museum's teaching staff. We brought together people with a wider range of talents and backgrounds—in scholarship, in classroom teaching, in theater, and in crafts work. Some started as interns at osv; others, as costumed interpreters. We tried hard to integrate these newcomers with the workers I had inherited, most of whom were local women working part time after their children had started school. Several of these veterans took on enhanced responsibilities as master teachers, training other escorts in the increasingly complex program of thematic tours and active-learning studios.

The core of this new program of escorted "field studies" was installed piece by piece over the course of several years to replace the teacher- and chaperone-led visits. As classroom teachers, including history professors from many colleges in the region, heard about the new museum education program, we invited them to collaborate with us on experimental projects. Over the next four years, these experiments expanded our sense of osv's capacity to teach almost any subject. Jack Larkin turned the Village into a physics laboratory for high school and college students, exploring the mechanics of plows and flails, of buildings and waterwheels. Nancy Grey Osterud taught sixth-grade teachers and their students to trace family histories with census data and historical maps. Virginia Westbrook and Pam Kramer fashioned opportunities for students to view the provision of food and clothing in families as a transaction with the natural world, with social and economic systems, with the wisdom and foolishness of folklore, and best of all, with the students' own cognitive, affective, and operational skills. One nearby middle school brought its students to us once a week throughout the school year.

All these experiments were reported with great candor in our in-house collective journal, waggishly called *The Pedagogue's Panoplist: An Irregular Review of Heuristic Happenings at the Horace Mann Space Center, Museum Education Department, Old Sturbridge Village*. In thirteen installments and comprising over 300 pages, it portrays an emergent "community of practice" committed to a constantly innovating program of museum teaching and learning. We expected everyone in museum education to do some original library research, to lead tours, and to share in regular evaluations of our program. Those who worked "full time" were encouraged to spend a day a week outside the museum, taking courses, working in the schools, or pursuing research projects. Museum Education, we often said, belonged to all of us. We encouraged each person to lay out specific goals for each day's work and to report (in a shared notebook and bulletin board) what he or she had learned from the experience. It was vital to overcome the reluctance of group escorts to have other staff members follow their tours. Over time, the conversation in the staff lounge slowly evolved toward an ongoing, lively, and critical dialogue about museum learning.

Rather than press each Museum Ed worker to teach according to what we could describe today as "best practices," which would systematize but inevitably flatten the richness of our program, I wanted to encourage a wide range of experiments. Improvisations by one person were prized for what they could tell all of us about the exciting challenges we faced. In the process, I became fascinated with observing how different minds approached the task of leading a group of students through a series of museum episodes. This proved, over the long years ahead, valuable in learning how to construct and lead teams for museum planning and exhibition development projects.

The most fascinating "different minds" were the architects brought on board to design the new Museum Education Center. I loved watching their distinctive styles of spatial thinking and visual presentation. Allen Moore was a born hands-on teacher, and he imagined a series of studios—for trying out spinning and weaving textiles, hearthside cooking, printing, and threshing grain—that would spread over the open plan of the entire ground floor. He recognized that arriving schoolkids needed to work off steam after their long bus rides, so he placed the drop-off and ticketing hut on the far side of a meadow and connected it to the center by a wooden bridge about 100 feet long and two running children wide. That brought students into the building on the second level, and a ramp allowed them to walk entirely around the outer walls and look down at the studios, as if, we said, "you stood at the top of a stairs on Christmas morning and could see everything in the world that you'd want to play with." Then John Rogers, his more mathematically minded partner, twisted the two levels at a 45-degree angle to create small tuck-in spaces for quieter group work in pods and corners throughout the structure.

Our admittedly utopian effort to construct a "learning organization," enthusiastically sharing the responsibility of innovation, posed obvious problems for an institution like osv, which was based on conventional hierarchies and established methodologies. For years, the old School Services program had processed thousands of visiting students through its "canonical operating procedures" without inquiring too much as to what was being

A hands-on learning center, to be filled with children's voices and handcraft for decades to come (drawing by Serge Bicking, ca. 1971; reproduced courtesy Old Sturbridge Village).

learned or how it might be improved. In any case, it was simply unfeasible to offer specially designed programs—especially tied to classroom curricula—to each of the 2,000 to 3,000 teachers we were welcoming every year.

Dubious about remaining in the role of managing such a huge program, I proposed that osv create a center for teaching and learning, which would be attached to but independent of the regular museum education program, and which would develop "field studies" in and beyond the Village with innovative high school and college teachers. I was able to garner some funding commitments to get it started. But in an era of diminished revenues, brought on by the decline in automobile tourism after the oil embargo of 1973, the magical era of expansion was over at osv. There was little patience in the administration for our experimentation.

I had learned so much in those seven years. To use Thoreau's favorite locution, "I had found myself . . ." in many fascinating learning situations: deciphering old manuscripts, encountering groups of fifth-graders, explaining religious change to seventy-year-old interpreters, writing job descriptions for new positions, directing plays, and decoding the blueprints for the most wonderful educational building in the world. Every historian creates his or her own historiography, and I had found mine at osv—a distinctive focus and range of interests, a method of research and teaching, a productive set of circumstances. It was time to move along.

TOWARD AMERICAN HISTORY WORKSHOP

I took the time after leaving OSV to complete my dissertation and to look around for ways to apply what I'd learned there to a wider sphere—to the history of other times, to the deployment of other teaching methods, and to a vastly different range of publics. Living in Boston at the end of the 1970s, I reconnected with a number of old college friends who were launching their careers in law, design, advertising, government, and public relations. Since they had money and I didn't, I lured them into long lunches, plying them with questions about their current projects: How would they design a children's hospital? How would they sell a tasteless breakfast cereal? How would they win legislative approval for a park system? I inveigled my way into brainstorming sessions in their offices and studios, where everything was at once unfamiliar and fascinating. My notebook filled with diagrams tracking the contest of ideas in play. I developed my skill at decoding every team meeting as an interplay of conventional wisdom, innovative challenges, empirical data, and assertions of authority—all beneath the press of "getting the work done."

Collaboration, I learned, was not just working together on the same job or working alongside one another on distinct tasks, but the fruitful interaction of different physical skills and mental styles. I relied on my experience as a historian of psychology to help me dissect the thinking and anticipate points of convergence among members of the team. I read widely in the works of Peter Drucker, Rosabeth Moss Kantor, Peter Berger, and other students of occupational sociology and psychology. I began to see the drama of every project as the back-and-forth of different minds—as if they were characters in a play being written as we went along. Some colleagues effortlessly spun out alternative approaches; others preferred to synthesize. Some loved process; others were obsessively goal oriented. I discovered a comfort in stepping back to stage the action so that each character would express himself or herself productively.

Through one of my old graduate school friends I found work ghostwriting speeches for the chairman of the National Endowment for the Humanities (NEH), Joseph Duffey. Whenever he had to announce a grant to create a Hittite dictionary or to produce a PBS version of *The Scarlet Letter*, or when he had to introduce Nobelist Isaac Bashevis Singer at a gala dinner, I would turn out 500 clever words. These comments often incorporated bio-graphical events that might connect Duffey to these subjects. "Richard," he once said, "what an exciting life you've given me! I'm not sure if any of this actually happened." On other occasions, we collaborated on longer speeches framing the value of the humanities to an American culture that seemed to be splitting into a specialists' academic ghetto, on one hand, and the rapidly expanding culture of pop music and Disneyland, on the other.

A side benefit of the NEH connection was the chance to attend the meet-ings of the Public Programs Division, reviewing the recommendations made by expert panels for the funding of exhibition and public television projects. Without a role to play, my perch allowed me to see connections and to diagnose persistent problems. The NEH guidelines, for example, in-sisted that the themes of the humanities—history, literature, geography, and the like—be front and center in the implemented projects. As I delved more deeply into the proposals, knowing what I now knew about how insti-tutions worked, I saw how difficult this actually was. Convening a kick-off meeting with eminent scholars was no guarantee that the project's long evolution would sustain the conceptual richness the scholars put forth. Consulting historians often told me that they had no notion how the pro-gram, once it was ready, related to their advice. Much of the NEH funding, in fact, was going to the work of the "nonhumanists" on the team—the de-signers, the exhibition fabricators, and community educators. The quality of the humanities thinking, I believed, depended entirely on the strength of the project director's knowledge and self-assurance.

As these quarterly reviews continued, I was drawn into a number of in-terpretive exhibition projects in the Boston area. I worked with my archi-tect friend Allen Moore, along with designers and filmmakers, on a visi-tors' center for Ocean Spray in Plymouth. The job gave me a chance to do oral history up and down Cape Cod with cranberry growers. Wily old Elna-than Eldridge told me how he'd started picking berries out in Orleans a half-century before: "The fuuhst thing you do," he advised in his non-rhotic local dialect, "is to pop the bucket a few times haahd against yer knee. That way, it don't take quite s'many cranberries to make up a quaaht." Outside the center, adjoining the landscaping of active cranberry bogs, we created a giant walk-through cartoon version of a bog. Inside we commissioned a perfect scale model of a grower's entire operation in full harvest mode. *The Cranberry and Its People* featured ethnographic portraits of the communi-ties in Massachusetts, New Jersey, Wisconsin, and Washington where cranberries were being grown. A video of Cape Verdean growers in southeastern Massachusetts was the product of my first shot at writing a media piece.

I was less happy with other jobs. I soon realized that it was hard to make a living on three days of historical research for a museum project at $100 a day. It generally took me a day to make a proposal, another day to deliver the final product, and an indefinite amount of unpaid time answering questions from the designers who were using my research to mount the show. Furthermore, I knew from experience that the real joy, and the real creative challenge, was in integrating the content and the design. Not only was no one paying me for that; I wasn't even getting into the ring.

Over a series of lunches with my neighbor, the great urban historian and public citizen Sam Bass Warner, we began to cook up a scheme. Let's put the historian at the creative core of interpretive projects like those that NEH was funding. We could hire and direct the other talents, shape the design,  press for effective outreach and education, help raise the necessary funds, and even serve as the interim museum leadership until a professional crew could be recruited. As a "producer," with an organization and an office, we would get to divvy up the pie, build a workforce, welcome young historians into the practice, and explore and expound the professional practice of interpretive design. This led to the creation of the American History Workshop in the summer of 1980. I realized that President Jimmy Carter wasn't long for his job and hence that Joe Duffey would not last long in his. The workshop would be my refuge, my base camp. I didn't realize that it would also be my professional life, from that day to this, 550-plus projects later.

5 ::: THE ELEMENTS
OF INTERPRETATION

After departing from Old Sturbridge Village (osv), I recognized that I would never be an "institution guy." I was
temperamentally more suited to the world of clearly defined projects—"Get in, get done, get paid, and get out." I
would sacrifice the pride one gets in nurturing the development of an organization over time in favor of the energy
and creativity I might bring to institutions at a turning-
point moment. "Projects" are wonderful inventions that
allow human imagination to fill an assumedly empty
future. True, there are dangers to project thinking. To
project, to throw an idea forward from conception to im-
plementation, was a radically new idea in nineteenth- and
early twentieth-century America. A project's success can
be achieved only by some risky assumptions—that there is
a clean slate at the starting gate, that the final product can
really be accurately anticipated in a preliminary plan, that
the surrounding landscape can be safely ignored, and that
the sponsors and stakeholders will remain stable and constant as the work proceeds.[1]

1. The use of the word "project" to signify any collective enterprise, rather than the plan for such an effort, dates from the

I had learned a lot of caution by watching meetings in design offices, law firms, and ad agencies. I fascinated myself by discovering the amazingly distinctive ways that creative thinking happened. But nothing had really prepared me to organize large project teams efficiently, to calculate and control budgets over a long project's life, or to manage the ups and downs of a client's expectations. Mastering those challenges, and learning to use the word "we" for the often diverse approaches of the American History Workshop (AHW) team, would keep the company's doors open.

SELLING INTERPRETATION

But first I needed to define what AHW was selling. At its simplest dictionary-definition level, interpretation is *translation*, making difficult words and concepts accessible to a listener, a viewer, a reader, or a visitor. Beyond that, interpretation can include *explanation*, locating a context for the thing somewhere more familiar to the audience. Finally, interpretation can suggest the *recasting* of the thing in a new form: an interpretive dance turns a source idea, a characterization, or an object, into a physical performance of movement in time. Musicians interpret the silent, written score with sound-making instruments.

What does interpretation mean in the world of public history? Of course, research is a necessary part. Incorporating the freshest and most relevant scholarship to tell a timely, significant, and accessible story right is crucial to us as historians. So, too, is our application of the highest standards to assemble the documents and objects to be shown and explored. But supplying program content has not been the end of our work. As educators, we know that the pedagogical approach we take and the media we employ to communicate are equally critical; too frequently, this has been where the richness of the material often is sacrificed. Diverse audiences, we knew, would present their own challenges in receiving and responding to the programs we devise. And, finally, we assume that every project needed to strengthen its ties to stakeholders, to the funding sources, to the wider community, and to the institution's professional peers.

Interpretation, then, is the whole action of the sponsoring institution in relation to its various and distinct publics. It incorporates the skills of the scholar, of the designer, of the educator, of the expert in collections and/or sites, and of the institutional and project administrator. And it makes room

---

middle of the twentieth century. School projects were a Progressive-era innovation. The first so-called housing projects came in the 1930s.

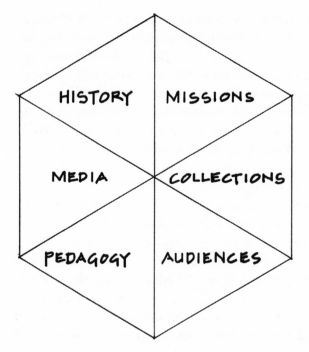

for the active engagement of its audience. Often, when we began a project with meetings of our client's staff, we heard each specialist stake claims to the priority of his or her disciplines. "Without objects there is no museum." "We must get the history right this time." "We have to involve the community productively." "Whatever we do, we've got to preserve the collection." "If our audience is families, then we have to rethink our designs to make it work for them."

All of them, I would explain, are correct. Interpretation is inherently a complex and collaborative work of art. Over time, we came to represent the task in what we called the "interpretive hexagon." The interpretive historian/designer needed to integrate six distinct elements—history, missions, collections, audiences, pedagogy, and media—in forming a successful program.

THE HISTORY WE ELUCIDATE

The historical content has not only been primary in our approach, but historical concepts and narratives helped us shape the other five sides of the hexagon. Design, program, and everything else stemmed from our understanding of the history. When a request for proposals from a city planning agency came in the door or when a museum director called for advice on reconfiguring the focus of her galleries, our first response has been to cast possible storylines. Even before it was possible to consult a reigning expert or convene a panel of scholarly advisers, I wanted to focus the client on the exhibition narrative. My technique, I now see in retrospect, has been to select a few details about a town or a historic site, deduce how they fit into "a system of life," and then posit how that system connected to larger social and regional narratives.

Here's an example, based on our work for the Albany Urban Cultural Park project in 1985–87:

Albany, New York, began as a Dutch trading post, a crossroads—a product of its location near the juncture of two river systems. As in Virginia and New Hampshire, New York's capital moved in the immediate post-revolutionary years to the head of navigation of the state's most important river. Ultimately Albany evolved into a canal and railroad hub. But every crossroads town, with all its demographic diversity, soon becomes a "home town," an industrial center serving its transportation, financial, and governmental sectors. And the conflict among these roles has shaped the social geography of the place thenceforward.

This bit of storyline, overlaid with generalizations about urban systems, then could lead to the scaffolding of an experiential plan.

Visitors will trace the development of the "crossroads" by encountering three mini-galleries, each interactively representing an era of trade, demography, and the relationship of locals and travelers. The fourth gallery, representing the Empire State Plaza of contemporary Albany, shows how the modern city drew its distinctive character from these relationships.

Paralleling these two narratives—the city's story and the visitors' pathway—immediately laid a solid foundation for the overall interpretive plan. All this was casual, off-the-cuff thinking; but it was a start, and it was always better to create a "straw man" for others to criticize than to leave the slate blank. In those early years, AHW's work leaped daily from the Piscataqua to Puget Sound, from jewelry-making factories in Attleboro, Massachusetts, to Dyess Air Force Base in Abilene, Texas. When the job was actually ours, then we could gather the experts and create a research agenda on which to base our plan for public presentations.

But even then, public history called forth its own special challenges. I recall bringing a group together in 1981 to shape a plan for the Fall River

Heritage State Park in southeastern Massachusetts. The scholars unanimously recommended that we conclude our history exhibition with the city's municipal bankruptcy and default in 1930. Here was a great story: the rise and fall of the nation's greatest center of cotton print production, a magnet to immigrants, capitalists, and inventors alike, the key supplier of textiles to New York City's garment industry!

Well, all that was possible for scholars, but not for public storytellers. How could we ignore the last half-century of the place and exclude from our narrative the experience of the 90,000 people who still lived in Fall River in 1980? Didn't the town's response to the collapse of the textiles industry warrant attention from historians? Didn't the settlement of the largest groups of Portuguese and Cape Verdean immigrants in the United States merit as much investigation as we might devote to the Irish and French Canadians who came in the nineteenth century? In other words, our public history project needed to represent the contemporary community as much as its antecedents.

I came to expect two sorts of resistance. To our community meetings came self-taught men and women, sometimes carrying odd objects or wearing strange costumes and always professing to have information that "you professionals" never heard of. Sometimes these "organic historians," as my friend Fath Davis Ruffins calls them, would reveal a vein of ongoing, living folk cultures that had escaped the official chroniclers. In most places, we also met their opposites, the antiquarians who fought to prioritize stories of the founding of places, of pioneers and settlers, and who distrusted anything to do with living, breathing human beings. They knew the genealogy of every parcel of land, every railroad station and general store, and everything that ever happened on the courthouse lawn. Members of both groups professed to have attics full of historical documents that survived nowhere else, and they invariably claimed to be working on long-awaited histories. I spent many hours knocking on those locked attic doors. Occasionally, I got inside and indeed found a real nugget of historical gold.

Over time, as I will explain, this initial focus on the historical content began to loosen its hold on my development of public history programs. Soliciting advice from a wide-ranging team of historians and submitting exhibition plans to panels of academic reviewers seemed to lead, inevitably, to increasingly complicated narratives. Stick an additional paragraph on the end of a text label or insert an extra minute in the middle of an audio-visual presentation, aiming to forestall criticism from one quarter or another, and in a trice you discover that your program has lost its audience.

A 150-word-long label may attract half as many readers as one of only 75 words. Thematic content is the finest generator of program ideas, but it works best as the menu upon which the other five corners of the interpretive hexagon feast. History often warrants complication, but art and learning always require clarity and coherence.

I've also become increasingly aware that the form of a historical narrative—constructed around a clear beginning, middle, and end to the story—can be too definitive. Public pedagogues often insist upon one "big idea," a single "take-away." But a productive engagement with the history does not end, in my view, with visitors reaching the conclusion I have sketched out in advance. Public history is a public dialogue. It is unsealed, open-ended, eddying out forever in new questions and new understandings. Anticipating and welcoming the audience's response is an ethical requisite.

STAKEHOLDER INTERESTS

If it has been relatively easy to find solid footing in preliminarily locating the historical content, the same was not true of the competing purposes of the project's stakeholders. In a project like that in Fall River, the goals of stakeholders, laudable and otherwise, diverged widely. The interest of the Massachusetts state government was largely focused on the economic benefits of the park, its contribution to the revitalization of the waterfront and the nearby downtown that had been damaged by decades of disinvestment. Entrepreneurs emphasized economic development through tourism. The local establishment pressed the case for preservation, education, intergroup harmony, and the documentation of the historical resources. Local political leaders had their own ambitions for the project: jobs and contracts for cronies or just good newspaper publicity or, more simply, a chance to celebrate their grandparents' achievements (a Hall of Fame of Great French Canadians?). On the other hand, those who taught the children of newer immigrants, the core of the city's school population and the most likely weekday visitors to the new park, wanted a history that would inspire their students. All these goals had to be taken into account in organizing the interpretive program.

Over time, I honed my technique. I was at heart a historian, and what I knew best was how to enlist each stakeholder as a fellow investigator of the local history. It was a very bad tactic to bring the representatives of all the interest groups together in the same room, particularly at the start of a project. As I made the rounds to staff and community offices or among museum trustees, I instead tried out fitting the proposed project inside each person's cherished way of telling the history. One on one, I discovered what was really at stake, and by listening to each in turn and considering how the project could be sharpened to accommodate each person's storyline, I could forge a pathway wide enough for all. Coalition building meant shaping the program until all the key voices could sing the chorus in unison, even if their own verses were quite distinct. Only gradually would we bring the group together to share their hard-won enthusiasms for the result.

I have to report that over the years I encountered little overt political influence in the interpretive development process. All museum professionals and many history educators bear the scars of the "culture wars" of the 1980s and 1990s, when right-wing critics attacked the Smithsonian museums and national curriculum-reform efforts. (In Chapter 16 I discuss the debacle of the Enola Gay exhibition controversy in some detail.) My colleagues in Australian museums, almost all of which are heavily dependent on federal and state government funding, have been more relentlessly battered by political partisans on the right—even to the extent of having to rip out and replace core history exhibitions. In the United States, outside the Smithsonian complex, such interference has been rare. The National Park Service's Civil War battlefield parks and monuments have been constantly assailed by neo-Confederate groups angered by efforts to emphasize slavery as a cause of the war, but the revisionist program has mostly proceeded smoothly. Private philanthropy in most established cultural institutions has, in my experience at least, been a protective shield against overt politicization. Even museums that sit on public land are managed by private, nonprofit organizations led by boards of trustees, and trustees have usually been reluctant to impose or even suggest a political cast to a museum's historical interpretation. Exhibitions and museum programs may frequently incur criticism on political grounds, from both right and left and especially from those who have felt excluded from the dominant narrative, but the responsibility for shaping interpretation has fallen in almost all cases to a professional staff committed to inclusiveness.

COLLECTIONS

Beyond a narrative that is compelling, fresh, and relevant to contemporary concerns, the museum historian needs to render a story that can be explored visually, spatially, and kinesthetically. If the historical account can be best accommodated in print and within book covers, it doesn't need our intervention. As my chapters in Part 3 note, many scholars consider collections essential to qualification as museums, despite the fact that many children's museums, science centers, and art-presenting institutions do not own or display any original objects. Clearly, "original" or "authentic" sites, artifacts, or documents play an important role in validating the authority of museums. This legitimacy, however, does not come from the collections or from the museum's sponsors. It is accorded the museum by the public, and therein the tale grows more complicated.

As I will show, much of AHW's interpretive work has been devoted to telling stories of people and events that have been traditionally ignored by established museums. The absence of collections and the silence of the archive about the enslaved, the impoverished, and the oppressed have been more significant facts than what can be gleaned from the few pieces that exist in collections. Take the Lower East Side Tenement Museum (LESTM) as a case in point. I had been working with Ruth Abram, the founding director, and others for several years on the idea of representing immigrant working-class life in New York's Lower East Side, the iconic gateway to America for five or six generations of people from Europe, Asia, Africa, and Latin America. In 1987, Anita Jacobson, deputy director of LESTM, discovered the availability of a building at 97 Orchard Street in Manhattan for display as a "typical" six-story dwelling that housed two dozen households of working-class immigrants. (Around 1900, as many as 70 percent of New Yorkers lived in such places.) Above the first-floor shops, the old apartments had been relegated to use as dusty storage space; penciled notes on the walls indicated someone's long-forgotten inventory of suits, pants, and jackets.

Once the building was identified, it was "authenticated" by the experts. Andrew Dolkart, then a consultant and now head of the preservation studies program at Columbia University, studied the building and attested to its historical integrity as an 1863–64 structure with some evidences of later accommodations to New York's housing laws. One day the building was derelict. On the next, the very same building, still in ruins, was being turned into a museum exhibit, and in a few years it had become a city, state, and national historical landmark. The outdoor latrines have been excavated, the layers of paint and wallpaper stripped, and the plumbing appliances detailed and dated. But since then the tenement has been furnished with the well-documented stories, not the long-discarded objects, of its residents. Almost everything that visitors now see has been acquired and arranged by a stylist, Pamela Keech, rather than by a curator, as if for a commercial photo shoot. But for visitors it rings all the more true. Few seem to notice, none object, but almost everyone is powerfully affected by LESTM's accounts of the dislocations of immigration and poverty. Visitors have, if you will, "authenticized" the tenement at 97 Orchard. The building is real enough, the inhabitants' names are specific enough, and the chosen situations are compelling enough to overcome the question I constantly confronted as a host at osv years ago: Is that real? Attributing authenticity to an object or a place is a complex action. One recovers authenticity by emotionally identifying oneself with the prior, perhaps original, state of the object, rejecting its subsequent layers of history as spoliation. So an old-timer's authenticity is very different from the arriviste's. The historian and archaeologist George McDaniel tells the story of bringing one of its old occupants to a newly installed reconstruction of a sharecropper's cottage at the Smithsonian. "It looks real good," he told George, "but I can't figure out what that plastic thing [the barrier to visitor entry] is doing there."

AUDIENCES

And the audience? Almost every ahw client has hoped that our innovative installations would attract more visitors.[2] Most market studies and a great deal of the audience research in museum and tourism sites focuses on the demography, seasonality, and other social and behavioral dimensions of the visiting public ("Please tell us your zip code"). The predictive power of "comparables" from other sites in the same or other regions was and is often unreliable. Macroeconomic changes, changes in leisure-time tastes, and many other cultural factors constantly churn up patterns of visitation. I began working at osv in the year of Expo 67, which drew large numbers of automobile-driving vacationers up through New England to Montreal. For six years after, attendance at osv grew by roughly 13 percent a year, fueling dreams of expanding into a second museum village devoted to the story of early industrialization in the region. It was not to be. The 1973 oil embargo,

---

2. A quirky exception was the Buten Museum of Wedgwood in Merion, Pennsylvania, with a collection of 8,000 pieces of Wedgwood ceramics that spanned the history of the British company since the mid-eighteenth century. The museum was then still housed in the founder's family mansion, alongside the living quarters of his surviving doyenne. David Buten, the director, devised a scheme to have Wedgwood produce a commemorative plate each year for museum members. He told me that upwards of 25,000 signed up and, of course, renewed their membership annually so that their collections would not suffer an embarrassing lacuna. Only 2,000 people visited the actual museum each year. What a brilliant business plan, keeping the money flowing in and capping the expenses for floor wax and toilet paper! The collection has since been acquired by the Birmingham Museum of Art in Alabama.

A little scary but a lot of fun to role-play Supreme Court justices at the Constitution Works program, New York City, 1989 to the present.

economic stagnation, and then the declining relative costs of air traffic and the global opening of tourist destinations for middle-class Americans have apparently permanently undercut the appeal of outdoor museums like OSV, which were reached in the family car on a vacation to heritage sites. Other, more complex causes may have compounded these trends. *Star Wars* and films like it ushered in a culture in which children's imaginations focused on what was once called outer space. It has been many years since most American children fantasized about hanging out with Johnny Tremain, Davy Crockett, and Laura Ingalls Wilder. Walt Disney World took away one chunk of our audience; Machu Picchu, another.

More important to me than the raw numbers or the sociographic composition of the audience has been the challenge of converting all-too-passive museumgoers into active partners in historical meaning-making. In more recent versions of the interpretive hexagon, we have used the word "re-

sponders" as a substitute for "audiences," thereby emphasizing the importance of designing programs that will provoke active participation. Over
the years, AHW has experimented with many ways to generate this dialogue, using a wide variety of pedagogical tools: role-playing, audiovisual
and computer-interactive media, visitor talkback stations, and even (in the
case of our *Constitution Works* program at New York's Federal Hall) a set of
full-blown, month-long, role-playing curricula for middle and high school
students.

But everything depends on smoothly inserting the museum visit experience into the course of a potential visitor's day. Recognizing that the best
visit begins hours or days before one enters the gallery, we try to learn more
about what will fit most comfortably into the flow of the visiting group's
leisure-time calendar. Our research shows that visitors come with expectations, prior interests, and current needs that must be acknowledged and
respected. This leads us to think of the museum as a process rather than a
place, as an experience in time as well as space. The action of the museum,
we have learned, occurs not in the gallery at all but inside the minds of our
visitors. And our highest ambition is to realize that the best visit ends long
after the visitors' cars and buses have left the parking lot.

PEDAGOGY

After leaving OSV, I fully expected that I would continue to find new opportunities to experiment with new forms of experiential education in the museum. I now report unhappily that nothing since then has matched the exhilarating, rapid-paced learning about learning that our little band achieved
in creating OSV's Museum Education Department in the early 1970s. Gallery exhibitions, of course, can seldom accommodate the kind of hands-
on learning we offered in the outdoor museum. As we have seen, Dewey's
remarkable vision of the ideal classroom/workshop/"complete industrial
museum" fit, of course, within a school building. In this magical realm,
he imagines a collection of threads and fabrics; agricultural equipment;
spindles, spinning wheels, and looms; an encyclopedic collection of textiles from around the world; a library with cloth-making myths and ethnographic information and illustrations; a music library; and so on. Calling
upon all the senses and many skills, Dewey's textile room was the model
for OSV's Museum Education Building, but it's a far cry from even the best-
equipped history museum education facilities created since.

Educational groups are vital in demonstrating the public value of museums to potential supporters, but outside of children's museums and some

science centers, adapting learning environments and teaching methods to visiting groups of schoolchildren has been rare. In surveying dozens of architectural plans for new and expanded museums, I have frequently encountered the space labeled "CLASSROOM," often in a windowless basement near the bus-unloading dock and floored with tiles, furnished with metal chairs and worktables, and lit by cold fluorescent bulbs. Why would our children, who spend as much time as they do in overly sterile school buildings, want to come to a museum, likely jammed to the gills with fascinating stuff, and be expected to learn in such a room?

We often design exhibition galleries, I confess, to afford a good view to only 4 or 5 (adult) visitors at a time. But for many museums, the docent tour includes as many as 30 to 35 students in one group. (At osv, the limit was 10 or 12.) Typically, I've observed, this means that just 4 or 5 kids can see something, 6 or 7 more may jostle to get a glimpse, and the rest linger, out of view and earshot. Worst of all, the docent—unable to make satisfactory eye contact—lectures his or her way through the show, neglecting altogether the visual, tactile, manipulative, and aural richness of the design.

Where museums have done much better work, in my view, is in linking the visit to the school's curricula and thereby bringing much richer visual and sometimes three-dimensional resources into the classroom. In the *Constitution Works* project, described in Part 4, AHW created classroom scenarios that fed directly into a dramatic role-playing experience at Federal Hall in lower Manhattan, but I don't know of many such examples. That curriculum aimed to alter the roles of classroom teacher (into a coach rather than a judge) and students (into a collaborative team in a contest of ideas). Most often, however, museum-generated materials are used in the classroom as any other sources, depending largely on the skill and inclination of the teacher.

Pedagogical concerns, of course, do not relate only to audiences of schoolchildren, and my transition to planning gallery exhibitions and developing new museums pushed me to apply what I had learned at osv to the visit experience for all museumgoers. Here Dewey encouraged me to diversify "the museum object," incorporating original documents but also interpretive texts, hands-on learning devices, scale models, audiovisual and computer-interactive programs, and other treasures of the designer's toolbox. With enough imagination, museum education could, I discovered, mimic the widest range of ways that human beings learn: in schools; in the home and in the street; in libraries, laboratories, and theaters; in the natural landscape; and everywhere else. The key to overcoming the unfamiliarity of the museum space and its objects was to remind visitors, almost by a kind of muscle memory, that they already know how to learn this way—by reading, by examining, by touching, by choosing, by empathizing, and so on. Thinking long and hard about Jerome Bruner during my OSV years inspired my commitment later to a focus on the discovery process in the gallery, wherein visitors would be challenged to synthesize these encounters in making and articulating meaning for themselves. Together these two converge in a constructivist educational theory, based upon the active participation of both the learner's mind and body and the requirement that the learner's conclusions are validated—not by their congruence with an external standard of truth but by whether they "'make sense' within the constructed reality of the learner."[3]

INTERPRETIVE MEDIA

In the first half-dozen years of AHW, I took my compensation, frankly, in learning my craft, slowly and with many missteps. Reconceptualizing stakeholder interests and articulating the character of audiences, collections, and educational approaches fell naturally into my bailiwick. Not so the development of the physical and operational program itself. Taking charge of a whole project meant that AHW had to hire and subcontract out the work of design and media production, price the work of designers and producers, establish performance criteria, and manage several budgets. This was just at the moment that this work was being revolutionized. Up through the 1950s, museum architects and interior designers viewed their work mostly as the creation of containers for art objects, specimens, and exhibition cases. Should there be modernist or classical architectural fittings? Natural light or lighting devices? Terrazzo, wood, or carpeted flooring? An exhibition gallery was usually situated in a purpose-built museum structure whose prominent siting and classical design separated the building from the street by a flight of stairs and then brought visitors through an entry lobby with admissions desks and services (coat check, restrooms, and perhaps an iconic work of art that served as a convenient point for meeting). Even in history museums, galleries were often distinguished by types of collections: guns and farm tools here; quilts, toys, and folk paintings there. A corridor of period rooms, exemplifying successive generations of decorative styles, appeared in both art and history galleries. In the 1930s, the WPA had hired artists to produce historical murals, often in the entry rotunda, as

3. George Hein, *Learning in the Museum* (New York: Routledge, 1998), 34.

well as dioramas of critical moments in national and local history that were fitted neatly into wall cases.

As the historian Gary Kulik explains, modern history museum exhibition begins with Arthur C. Parker's effort, in the second quarter of the twentieth century, at the Rochester (N.Y.) Museum of Arts and Sciences to "revisualize the past for the benefit of the whole community." Parker, an archaeologist and advocate for American Indian causes, laid out the history of Rochester with "portraits, maps, deeds, graphics, objects, period spaces, and several small models."[4] Parker explains in the museum's house organ, "All museum exhibits must be properly interpreted. Interpretation is one of the most important features of exhibition. The visitor not only wants to see an object but wants to know what it means and what value it has to himself and to knowledge in general" (cited in W. Stephen Thomas, "Arthur Caswell Parker: 1881–1955, Anthropologist, Historian and Museum Pioneer," *Rochester History* 17 [July 1955]: 10).

Parker's methodology, expounded in his pathbreaking 1935 *Manual for History Museums*, focused on original objects to tell the city's story. The next great advance, according to Kulik, was *The Farmer's Year*, an exhibition at the Farmers' Museum, sponsored by the New York State Historical Association in Cooperstown. Designed by Per Guldbeck and opened in 1958, the exhibition led visitors through each month of the agricultural cycle, explicating farming practices through superb graphics and displaying tools—outside exhibit cases—so that one could almost feel their heft and imagine the skill they required. As I remember it, the exhibition even included stacks of hay to provide verisimilitude around the objects.

The interpretive toolbox expanded rapidly in the decade that followed. The National Park Service's Mission 66, initiated in 1955, created interpretive centers to welcome and orient visitors to historic (and natural) sites, using an array of models, maps, and reproductions of historic images to illustrate the events that marked the site's importance. In Albany, the New York State Museum's exhibition on the Adirondack region, which I first saw in preparation in 1969, displayed original lake craft, trappers' equipment, mountaineering gear, and habitat settings of native fauna, but also massive faux trees, partially re-created buildings, and a frighteningly realistic soundscape of a thunderstorm heard in the middle of the woods. Out

4. Gary Kulik, "Designing the Past: History-Museum Exhibitions from Peale to the Present," in *History Museums in the United States: A Critical Assessment*, ed. Warren Leon and Roy Rosenzweig (Urbana: University of Illinois Press, 1989), 18.

in British Columbia in 1969–72, the designer Jean Jacques André created a life-sized model of early twentieth-century Victoria, complete with cobblestone streets and its own Chinatown, and surrounded it with astonishingly lifelike reconstructions of a mineshaft, lumber camps, and fisheries (I swear I could smell the fish here!). One could even stride across a large-scale replica of the HMS *Discovery*, the ship under Captain George Vancouver that surveyed and claimed much of the northwest coast for the British.

Rooted in theatrical design, these innovations immersed visitors in hyperrealistic environments, favoring sensory experiences over information.[5] The contrary impulse came from graphic designers, influenced especially by Charles and Ray Eames and their work in trade shows and world's fair installations. Firms like Staples and Charles in Washington, D.C., and Chermayeff and Geismar in New York created dense assemblages of objects, images, and interpretive panels on translucent exhibition walls often made of acrylic or mesh. Exploring a show like *A Nation of Nations*, interpreting the experience of immigration at the National Museum of History and Technology in 1976, felt like walking through a brilliantly laid out magazine, page after page, except that here the sidebars often featured life-sized reproduced objects rather than symbols. Five-foot-high "paper doll" cutouts represented population statistics; dinner plates stood in for types of meals; suitcases symbolized migrants. For many observers, decoding all this information—and perhaps information overload—had become the experience.

The third new bin in the exhibition designer's toolbox was audiovisual media. Orientation films became a regular feature of the entry experience at National Park Service and other visitor centers. The most elaborate and long lasting was *The Story of a Patriot*, an hour-long costume epic introduced at Colonial Williamsburg in 1956. A year later, Acoustiguide launched its first audiotape guide to a historic site, Eleanor Roosevelt's account of life at Hyde Park. Sound installations, in the form of self-guided tours either carried on handheld devices or broadcast in gallery settings triggered by motion sensors, spread quickly over the next decades. Multiple-projector, wide-screen slide or film shows running on computer-driven programs, like *Where's Boston?* (produced for the American Revolution bicentennial in

5. The experience was so immersive that it was impossible to discover how far along one was in the exhibition pathway. When my six-year-old son, accompanying me through the State Museum in Albany, needed to find a restroom, we had to retrace our steps all the way back to the entry, a full five-minute run, only to learn that we had actually been just fifteen feet from the exit.

1975), were hour-long theater pieces presented to a seated audience rather than elements within the galleries themselves. The first IMAX show, the twenty-six-minute-long *To Fly*, opened on the same day, July 4, 1976, as the Smithsonian's Air and Space Museum—without a special fee but separated from the rest of the museum.

Incorporating moving image footage into the gallery was still a technical revolution away. Some history museums put videotape players and monitors, boxy and ugly, right in the middle of the gallery, explicating, say, the technology of a sawmill. A bold step came in 1987, as part of an exhibition at the National Museum of American History titled *A More Perfect Union: Japanese Americans and the U.S. Constitution*. Selma Thomas's five-minute video showed a middle-aged Japanese American man standing in the doorway of a re-created internment camp cabin, where he said he spent his World War II years. Playing on a large monitor mounted sideways (so that the conventionally horizontal aspect ratio could be reversed), the video powerfully registered the succession of emotions of a real person encountering the room and reliving his childhood. The visitors, of course, were also peering into the room from the "fourth wall"—in some measure reenacting the experience of the former internee.

Through these innovations over these years, in sum, the container seemed to vanish. Museums popped up everywhere, in old factory buildings and department stores, on side streets and along otherwise abandoned corners of the old downtown. The exhibition landscape became denser and isolated from its surroundings; the visitor pathway, more highly controlled. In some history museum projects, stage, graphic, and industrial designers exiled the architects from the galleries altogether, relegating the men with the bow ties to the less glamorous tasks of locating galleries, devising schemes for circulation, and designing visitor amenities like admissions areas, rental spaces for community functions, shops, cafés, back-of-house work spaces, loading docks, and parking.

I'd visited these pathbreaking exhibitions as a young museum professional. Now I shared the responsibility to make them happen. I had to learn what actually constituted filmmaking or design development. (We even hired an "imagineer" to give us a behind-the-scenes tour of the mechanics behind the spectacular presentations at Walt Disney World in Orlando.) And though I couldn't tell you the first thing about how a Steenbeck film-editing machine worked, I recognized how critical the judgment of the editor, the cameraperson, the stylist, or any of a dozen other technicians, was to the historical interpretation being produced. Similarly with producing the mechanicals for a graphic panel or finding the basswood for a scale model. I lacked the *Sitzfleisch* to do any of these jobs, but I knew they mattered crucially. Leonard Majzlin and I together crafted the first interpretive piece about the Eldridge Street Synagogue in 1987, but it was Leonard's genius to enlist the stylish Broadway actor Geraldine Fitzgerald and to coach her to bring the centuries-long weight of British theatrical tradition to the voice-over narration that most effectively communicated the significance of this preservation project to both Jewish and non-Jewish supporters.[6]

As I gained these insights, I was better able to understand the value of the media we were choosing. An audiovisual piece, inserted into the course of a narrative exhibition, was not only a way of representing sound, voice, and motion (which are, after all, crucial elements of human experience in the past as well as the present). It also reshaped the visitors' activity. It allowed parents to recapture their straying children and keep them in eyeshot. The media show provided older visitors with a chance to sit down. And by varying the kinetics of the experience, it often relieved visitors of the eyestrain and fatigue of looking at too many paintings, butterflies, or typewriters along the wall.

I have always found this work enormously stimulating: intellectually provocative, emotionally rewarding, and, for many reasons, something of a miracle. I never lost the frisson gained by hanging out backstage during a performance and watching gifted artists strut their stuff. By what miracle did I, with scarcely an ounce of artistic or musical or mechanical talent in my lunchbox, wind up here? Nothing beats the pleasure of watching an idea come back from the artists' studio. On project after project, I've tried so hard to explain the intricacies and subtleties of the historical content and pedagogical strategy to architects, artists, and designers. And then our meeting breaks up, and the waiting starts. A few days or weeks later, I am presented with the result. "This is what your idea did for me, Richard," they—my artist partners—say in ever so many ways. And I look at the drawing or listen to the tape or gaze at the storyboard. And my first reaction is, usually, "Oh, no, this is impossible! Can't you see that this is all wrong?" But I hold my tongue, I bide my time, I recognize the old slogans—"the perfect

6. And then, in the middle of the piece, Leonard inserted a few measures of the great cantor Yossele Rosenblatt intoning the "El male rachamim," the funeral prayer. For observant Jews, this was a signal that the project was infused with reverent Yiddishkeit as well. This is an example of the "wink" that good interpretation makes to inform insiders that their concerns are respected.

is the enemy of the good"—and so on. And then I look and listen more carefully. I embody the work as if my fingers and my voice were one with those of my colleagues, and—still silently—I attempt to explain this, to defend this, to my clients. Concerns about budget, deadlines, and the politics of a project are never completely absent. And, slowly, I begin to recognize my original idea, its swaddling clothes discarded, now outfitted in a new garb, matured and ready to act in the world. I'm an empty nester, with my baby home from college almost totally transformed. As the design comes alive for me, I begin to see its consequences—well, if this is true, then we can do that. The movie has started up again, the soundtrack is in sync, the creative process moves forward. Something unanticipated has come from this miracle of human collaboration, from this creative misreading of my best ideas—and I'm delighted.

COMPLICATING THE HISTORY AND MAKING IT MORE ACCESSIBLE AT THE SAME TIME

As a producer, the public historian complicates the act of producing and presenting coherent historical narratives by adding other concerns: by synthesizing competing institutional and personal purposes, by understanding how the communicative process engages the minds of our audiences, by discerning the messages imparted by the relationship of audiences to the objects we present, and, perhaps most important, by recognizing the shaping power of the media we deploy. All historians, whether they say it out loud or not, do these things. The writer of a research monograph or the lecturer in the first-year survey course also responds to institutional and personal concerns, audience interests, strengths and weaknesses in the evidence, and methods of communicating. I have lived my career inside the intricate relationships of this interpretive hexagon, constantly stimulated and challenged. In the early years of my career, my friends in university history departments would ask, "When are you going to try to get a real job?" I could only laugh, and move on to the next project.

PART TWO
Finding Ourselves:
Interpreting Place

6 ::: HISTORY, DISLOCATED

Since the founding of American History Workshop, more of its projects have focused on histories of place and places than on any other subject. It's small wonder. The vast majority of the 30,000 museums in the United States are history museums, and most are devoted to interpreting state and local history. Historic sites, house museums, markers, and preservation districts are everywhere.

Nearly every place in America advertises its historical significance. Guidebooks from Frommer, Fodor, and a hundred competitors direct tourists to historical attractions. Almost every city, county, and state has a tourism agency, and virtually all their websites link to sites of local and regional historical importance. With all this activity, one might think that anyone can easily discover the unique qualities of a place, how it shapes local life, and how it came to look and feel the way it does. For most of the twentieth century, the past of a community was usually located in a list of "historical features"—public buildings where famous events occurred, sites of battles, or the elaborate homes of noteworthy citizens. Tourist maps dotted the landscape with "historically significant" buildings, implying that the others around them deserve little notice. The

National Geographic Society regularly compiled these places in its editions of *America's Historylands*.

The Freedom Trail links a dozen sites related to Boston's Revolutionary-era history while remaining silent about the financial district towers, presumably of no historical interest, that dwarf them. Alternately, almost all the buildings surrounding Independence Hall in Philadelphia were destroyed in the 1950s to create a mall that would magnify the prominence of what was actually a rather small seat of national government. And then there's Colonial Williamsburg, where most evidence of post-1780 life (except for that necessary to welcome visiting tourists) was studiously expunged in its 1920s restoration.

Nothing better expresses the idea of local history as the enshrinement of historical features than the movement to place historical monuments and markers. American monuments were born in the impulse to commemorate the republic's founders: Robert Mills's column commemorating George Washington in Baltimore (1815–29), and subsequently his Washington Monument on the National Mall (1848–84), and Solomon Willard's Bunker Hill Monument in Charlestown, Massachusetts (1825–42). By the end of the nineteenth century, commemorative statues graced courthouse squares, town commons, and city plazas in every part of the nation, particularly in recognition of the sacrifices made by Civil War soldiers on both sides. Monuments were essential to the turn-of-the-twentieth-century City Beautiful movement, which aimed to overlay the haphazardly evolved and disorderly urban landscape with wide boulevards, ceremonial centers, and impressive public buildings and cultural institutions. The ideology of the movement was clear from the outset. To art critic Evelyn Marie Stuart in 1915, monuments played a major role in civic improvement: "Away from the sordid cares of the work-a-day world, the statue of hero or allegorical group, leads our thoughts to clearer heights, where the mind may walk with the souls of the great, or commune with the spirits of the virtues. This is one of the reasons why monuments exist and persist as they will until the end of time" ("Monuments: Their Place in the Scheme of Civic Improvement," *Fine Arts Journal* 32 [1915]: 91–93).

The City Beautiful movement had little interest in the "workaday world," which of course is usually what makes a city truly distinctive to us: its historical relationship to the local topography, the particular economic niches it occupied over time, and the cultures and customs that persist and shape contemporary life. The effect of all this has often been to ghettoize the Big

The workaday world swirls around and beneath the grandeur of
Daniel Chester French's Dupont Circle, Washington, D.C.

Historical Sites and to view history as a community ornament, safely isolated from present conditions.

On the local and state level, the historical marker served to cordon off
the past from the present. Among the best-documented state programs
has been the one sponsored by the Pennsylvania Historical Commission,
founded in 1913 with the goal of ensuring that all local citizens knew what
had happened nearby and to whom they owed their privileges as Americans. The Keystone Staters aimed for an inclusive enterprise. "No one of
the varied historic elements which entered into the making of Pennsylvania should be either unnoticed or over-emphasized. . . . In its personnel the
Commission represents distinctly the principal separate strains of race and
religion which made up the composite citizenship of the Commonwealth."
To be sure, in the 1910s, the range of significant Pennsylvanians was ethnically rather narrow: "the English Episcopalian, the English and Welsh
Quaker and Baptist, the Scotch-Irish Presbyterian and the Pennsylvania
German church and sect people" (*First Report of the Pennsylvania Historical Commission* [Lancaster, Pa.: New Era Printing Co., 1915], 12). Markers
are wonderful ways of determining who counts most to the powers that
be. At that historical moment, no one from Eastern or Southern Europe,
Africa, Asia, or Latin America, apparently, had yet played a role worth ac-
knowledging—and this at a time, of course, when immigration from those

areas was swelling the state. The 1910 census, for example, reported that the state's population included 200,000 Italian-born Pennsylvanians.

The Pennsylvania marker program devoted itself entirely for many years to commemorating colonial settlements, pioneers, and events of the Revolution and the Civil War era. Typical of those plaques was the one marking an Indian massacre on the frontier:

> On October 25, 1755, John Harris, founder of Harrisburg, and a party of 40 men, who came up the river to investigate the (John) Penns Creek Massacre, were ambushed by a party of Indians near the mouth of this creek, at the head of the isle of Que, about one-third of a mile south of this spot. (*Second Report of the Pennsylvania Historical Commission* [n.p., 1918], 68)

The marker is silent on the context. Who were these forty White men, and who were these Indians? Why the massacre, and why the ambush? Actually, this was no random Indian attack. It was one of the first skirmishes of the war between British Pennsylvanians, on one hand, and the Delaware Indians and their French allies, on the other—which would later erupt into a global war pitting Britain and its German allies against France and Spain, with indigenous and settler populations taking sides on local battlefields. After the Seven Years' War, the site and John Harris were remembered, but the Indians dissolved into oblivion.

After World War II, the state marker program was newly reinvented, and the now-familiar blue signs with gold lettering proliferated on more than 1,350 metal posts around the state. Perhaps as an ironic reflection of the state's slow loss of its productive might, the markers increasingly took note of industrial sites—railroads and canals, glassworks, oil exploration, and the homes of inventors. Now a wider segment of the population was deemed noteworthy, and a marker was placed, for example, at St. Michael's Church in Shenandoah, Pennsylvania, founded in 1884 by Ukrainian immigrants as the first Greek Catholic Rite congregation in the United States. Some Underground Railroad "stations" were also marked. By the 1990s, commission signs announced the site of the Prince Hall Grand Lodge of Masons, an important African American organization, as well as the residences of Paul Robeson in Philadelphia. More recently, the site of gay rights protests has been marked.

Broader in scope as these new markers were, they were still historically evasive. They raised more questions than they answered. How did the Underground Railroad divide Pennsylvanians in the antebellum decades?

What kind of work and domestic life did the Ukrainians in Shenandoah have? Why have Masonic lodges in the United States been segregated since the Revolutionary era? Why did Paul Robeson, one of the greatest talents of the American stage in his time, end his days in this modest West Philadelphia house?[1]

As early as the 1950s, the City Beautiful ideal began to spark resistance in urban centers. In New York, activists and visionaries like Jane Jacobs decried the large-scale projects that threatened to turn the city into an array of dreary single-purpose zones—a new district of glass-curtain skyscrapers along Third Avenue, a new complex of performing-arts facilities lifted above the street at Lincoln Square, gigantic new housing projects with few commercial or cultural amenities along the city's old waterfront and warehouse districts—all tied together by superhighways. What was neat and tidy on the planners' drawing boards felt increasingly deadly in the neighborhoods, and artists took the lead in spilling over the boundaries set for them, colonizing old manufacturing buildings as their homes and studios and using the parks, streets, and subways as their galleries. The official city landmark commission focused on great buildings and then on elegant residential districts.

City and state officials no longer had a monopoly on what was historically significant. And history escaped from its imprisonment in the monumentality and elitism of the City Beautiful. In 1989, a group of writers, artists, and historians enrolled under the banner of REPOhistory (repos-

1. As incomplete and ineffective as the Pennsylvania markers are, they are not politically tendentious like those in southern states that express regret for the "Lost Cause" of the Confederacy or maintain a white supremacist viewpoint. On the site of the horrible massacre in Colfax, Louisiana, for example, where Blacks defending the local courthouse after a bitterly contested state election were overrun and slaughtered by White militias linked to local versions of the Ku Klux Klan, the Louisiana Department of Transportation mounted this marker in 1950: "COLFAX RIOT: On this site occurred the Colfax Riot in which three white men and 150 negroes were slain. This event on April 13, 1873 marked the end of carpetbag misrule in the South." It still stands. Bryan Stevenson of the Equal Justice Initiative has begun a campaign to mark the sites of 4,000 lynchings across the country. Still, I'm not sure that coming across them, one at a time, in small towns and urban centers, does as much as is needed to denote the terrain of terror that plagued Black families, generation after generation, for the first century after emancipation. See Sanford Levinson, *Written in Stone: Public Monuments in Changing Societies* (Durham: Duke University Press, 1998).

sessing history) to "retrieve, relocate and document absent historical narratives at specific sites in New York City, through public installations, performances, educational activities, printed matter and other visual media." What caught the public's attention most was the Lower Manhattan Sign Project, which mounted thirty-nine aluminum historical markers on lampposts. Their narratives stretched back in time from the earliest moments of European colonization (situating themselves as a countercelebration to the official recognition of the Columbus Quincentenary) to episodes of public unrest and civil disorder in every century since. They revealed traces of the slave trade, immigrant settlements, union organizing, and pitched political battles in precincts of the modern city characterized by huge corporate office buildings and judicial courts. They reminded passersby of tragic miscarriages of justice:

"They Died Very Stubbornly" wrote justice Daniel Horsmanden of those executed during the New York Conspiracy or "Great Negro Plot" of 1741,

and they marked tragedies in our own day:

On the fourth day of the month of March in the year nineteen ninety-one, three homeless Americans passed a very cold and bitter night on this spot in lower Manhattan.

An initiative called "Queer Spaces" located a dozen landmarks of gay and lesbian organizing before the Stonewall riots of 1969. REPOhistory reminded New Yorkers that the abortion clinic of Ann Lohman, alias Madame Restell, dubbed by the press "the evilest woman in New York," was shut down by the police in 1878, almost a century before *Roe v. Wade*. The signs went beyond historical marking to provoke questions about justice in the contemporary city: "What is the Effect of Urban Renewal on Crime?" or "Who Owns Your Life?"

As New York recovered from its fiscal crisis in the 1980s, REPOhistory's brilliantly inspiring projects reminded passersby that there was a hidden history of poverty, exploitation, racial discrimination, and violence beneath the new glitziness. Perhaps more than the specific history on any one sign, the project elicited, as the art critic and historian Lucy Lippard noted, "a 'Hey, I never learned that in school' response."[2] And that, in turn, could gen-

2. Cited in Andrew Wasserman, "Contemporary Manhattan Cartographies: Ephemeral Public Projects in New York" (Ph.D. diss., Stony Brook University, 2012), 37.

erate the idea that the contemporary cityscape, despite its surface polish, represented a suppression of a divergent past. The annals of REPOhistory tell of continuing conflicts with the city department of transportation, especially after Rudolph Guiliani's administration succeeded the more sympathetic mayoralty of David Dinkins.

By being explicitly oppositional in form and message in its many successful projects in New York and Atlanta, REPOhistory left a powerful legacy in the public art and public pedagogy movement, but it had little impact on the preservation movement, urban design, or more institutionally based interpretations of place. It has been even more disappointing, then, to see how old-fashioned marker programs have gone on and on. In the mid-1990s, a group called Heritage Trails New York installed over forty new brightly colored panels in downtown New York, often right next to older markers describing the same site. (Lower Manhattan might eventually evolve into a museum of historical markers.) Few tied "what happened here" to aspects of its physical site or its geographical role in the city's evolution. None invited visitors to see themselves as parts of New York City's history. The new

markers were initially linked by dots pasted on the sidewalks, color coded to encourage thematic connections, which of course soon vanished under the heavy foot traffic of these streets. The writing in the new panels was indeed livelier, and certainly the appended historical images were better chosen and reproduced more clearly. The maps did help tourists locate themselves on the gridless streets of lower Manhattan. But the sum total of understanding how this landscape came to be was in no way augmented by these stories of landmark structures and noteworthy events. The markers sat in heavy black frames that bore no relationship to the traditions of street furniture in New York. In my view, the expensive experiment cluttered the streetscape with miscellaneous information that was largely meaningless to native and visitor alike.[3]

3. American History Workshop proposed an alternative and more integrated approach for Heritage Trails New York, including a visitors' center, a children's discovery program, and a series of "adventure tours" through downtown New York (*Downtowners in Every Sense: An Integrated Approach to the Creation of a Vibrant New Cultural Institution*, February 25, 1997, AHW Records, University of Massachusetts, Amherst). Our sample program, "Wheeler-Dealers," describes a competi-

To all of that, the poet Jorge Luis Borges, with remarkable insight, says, "Nadie es le patria."

> No one is the homeland. Not even the rider
> High in the dawn in the empty square,
> Who guides a bronze steed through time
> Nor those others who look out from marble
> Nor those who squandered their martial ash
> Over the plains of America
> Or left a verse or an exploit
> Or the memory of a life fulfilled
> In the careful exercise of their duties.
> No one is the homeland. Nor are the symbols.

"The homeland," Borges concludes, "is a continuous act / As the world is continuous.... It is all of us" ("Ode Written in 1966," trans. W. S. Merwin, in *Jorge Luis Borges: Selected Poems, 1923–1967*, ed. Norman Thomas di Giovanni [New York: Delacorte Press, 1972], 205–7).

The older generation of markers signified the reverence of officialdom. The newer ones convey meager reparations for achievements or injustices unfairly ignored in the past. But both fracture the "continuousness" of our history. Both neglect the ways in which history is "all of us." The tales they tell seem to come out of nowhere. The drama, not to say the blood, of the Indian massacre has gone cold. Why did it occur? And why here? And how has it left its real mark on those who are here now? If they bespeak the people who came before us, they arrived here and departed without notice. As much as anything, such markers denote the irretrievability of the past. They erupt, it seems, out of the placidity of the contemporary countryside or city street. They elevate the absent at the cost of the present. They never tell you where you are, right now, or who is here with you.

The form of the conventional historic markers poses other problems. Sticking up out of nowhere, they don't offer shade, seating, or refreshment; they simply interrupt our journeys along the street or highway with words

---

tive game-tour of lower Manhattan. Each player started with three beaver pelts and at strategic historic locations in the neighborhood could sell his or her property for sugar, slaves, cotton, and coffee; canal, railroad, and steamship shares; and coal, oil, automobile, and biotechnology stocks. Each trade opportunity was also a way of looking at the local architectural elements of succeeding regional, national, and global economies.

and (now sometimes) pictures. They ask us, suddenly, to switch to a different perceptual apparatus, to enter a world of reading and decoding. Even when they describe ancient landscape features—the original shorelines of Boston or Manhattan, or the routes of long-abandoned canals and millraces—they poorly communicate the long-departed sense of being in those places. Even when they mention previous settlements—of native peoples or immigrants from Europe or Asia—they say nothing about how their lives here have affected ours today. It would be helpful at least if the marker told us something about the ground and air we occupy: "This was the tallest structure in the city when it was built." "In the 1850s you would have seen piles of merchandise six times higher than this sign." "The bricks came down the river and were unloaded at the pier just west of here." "Every World War II sailor passed down this street." And so on. Then the marker would operate like a well-informed sidekick and not an old-fashioned busybody droning on about trivia.

Like every other interpretive medium, markers dictate their own kind of history. They work best for what the French call *l'histoire évènementielle*, a chronology constructed around significant events—wars, earthquakes, elections, riots, the first this, or the oldest that—rather than the deeper, more continuous patterns of everyday social, economic, or cultural life. Even after the rise of a more inclusive approach to social history in the 1970s, markers have tended to ignore topography and landscape, the experience of work, the diverse ethnic groups who settled or resided in this place, long-festering social conflicts, and the slow change over time that connects the famous event to our own day. In so doing, markers tend to obscure the lives of most ordinary people, even to erase their presence from history.

So, too, with the history museums of my early professional life. Even though they were ostensibly dedicated to interpreting the history of a distinct geographical area, the core exhibitions in local and state history museums also said little or nothing about the specificities of place. By 1970, virtually every state historical society hosted a variant of the same chronologically arranged history show. In these exhibitions, the geography, topography, and landscape of the state or the city were viewed as a blank backdrop for historical events, as if the state's history was a series of empty boxes along a timeline. History was a sequence of dominant groups, each of which did their own thing, left behind some strange objects, and then vanished forever.

The first gallery, inevitably, focused on local Indian tribes, whose lives "in harmony with nature" were illustrated by a diorama and display case with a dozen dark brown archaeological specimens—pots and fabrics and arrowheads. Succeeding exhibition cases featured a predictable progression of Pioneers (flintlocks and wolf traps); Settlers (axes and aprons); Founding Fathers (inkwells); Farmers and Farm Wives (plows and Dutch ovens); Canal and Railroad Men (maps, schedules, tickets); Inventors (patent models); Civil War Soldiers (uniforms, breech-loading rifles); Captains of Industry (engravings of sprawling factories); Immigrants (colorful folk costumes); Governors or Presidential Candidates (campaign buttons picturing men with beards); and Veterans of the World Wars (posters, packs of Lucky Strikes, ration cards). Oddly enough, this arrangement worked equally well in Maine, in Nebraska, and in Oregon. Though the objects on display were drawn from local examples, the story they told was generic. They communicated the same message: America was anywhere and everywhere a tale of endless economic progress, democracy, and the expansion of science and industry.

The materiality of Old Sturbridge Village sensitized me to the history on every street corner. To acknowledge that is to reclaim the city for its ordinary people. The modern-day landscape is always being packaged for sale. Tourism promoters emphasize its attraction to sports fans and theater buffs. Economic development agencies advertise its livability, business friendliness, and creative resources. Local politicians proclaim its menu of needs, for which they prescribe public remedies. Neighborhood groups often aim to lock in their current image of the area and protect it from intrusion and change. The role of the historian is to interpret all of these in the context of this moment, to see the longer-term continuities of the place, and to represent the city as an ever-changing dynamic layering of life-worlds. In that effort, history makes the city visible to itself and to "all of us" as fellow citizens.[4]

COMING FROM AN UNNOTABLE PLACE

My public history agenda was doubtlessly shaped by the strangeness of coming from an obscure, unnotable corner of one of the most noteworthy

4. Public historian Karilyn Crockett observes that "Boston remains a mystery for many of its own residents, and particularly its young people. . . . A visitor on the typical Boston tourist trek could blanch when they learn that the city is 53 percent non-white. 'What?!' they might exclaim. 'Where?' There are two perplexing issues entangled here: Boston's residents, particularly its nonwhite majority, are not a regular or visible part of the city's public face; and visitors seeking to encounter Boston's real heartbeat, its multiracial resident population, leave town mostly disappointed" ("A City Invisible to Itself," *ArchitectureBoston* 17, no. 1 [Spring 2014]).

cities in the world. Our geographical marginality felt like the physical analogue of my family's position as social and ethnic outsiders in this citadel of American prosperity. And yet, becoming a historian of the United States enabled me to see that even such apparently insignificant places and people are richly revealing. That they too deserve to be dignified by the historian's narrative, and thereby cherished by residents past and present, became the animating motive of my professional career.

I was born and reared in the out-of-the-way New Lots section of the East New York neighborhood in the southeast corner of Brooklyn. For most New Yorkers it is quickly and unnoticeably traversed on the way to and from Kennedy Airport. The only historic marker you will find there announces that the old Dutch Reformed Church on New Lots Avenue was built in 1823-24. (The church was designated a city landmark in 1966 and added to the National Register in 1983 as "an outstanding example of rural church architecture.") By the 1930s, when my family came, the Dutch farmers were long gone. So too were the Yorkers and Yankees and German immigrants who came after, working in the factories, railroad yards, and breweries that had been plunked down on the old farm fields. On a particularly clear day, an attentive child could see the Empire State Building in Manhattan eight miles away as the crow flies—if one could find a crow that would fly over the cityscape. That trip took almost an hour by the IRT Seventh Avenue line, and we rarely went there.

The streets of my immediate neighborhood, bounded by my elementary school's catchment area, were lined with two- and six-family semidetached brick houses. The main drag, New Lots Avenue, was dotted with luncheonettes, small food stores, kosher butchers, and shops selling hardware, toys, and clothing. Of supermarkets we had not yet heard. Boys played stickball and a hundred other games in the streets, only rarely disturbed by a passing automobile, and we built makeshift forts and set fires in the empty lots. Occasionally we crossed Linden Boulevard to roam in "the swamps" that bordered Jamaica Bay, foraging for treasures that might be stashed away in secret places.

Our neighbors were almost all Jews born in Eastern Europe, like my mother, or on Manhattan's Lower East Side, like my father. They'd grown up in the 1920s in Brownsville, the neighborhood just to the west, which had become the largest Jewish community in the world by that time. Our fathers had come out of military service or wartime work during World War II to run small businesses or work in factories, department stores, or government offices around the metropolitan area. A few of the mothers had gone to work after their children had grown, as teachers or school secretaries. Many families had an ancient grandmother living with them, dressed in black, speaking Yiddish (then invariably called "talking Jewish"), and respecting the dictates of Judaism more scrupulously than the rest of us. Lives were closely observed. Family arguments echoed across alleyways and down stairwells, but angry threats at midnight were silently forgotten by morning. It was an orderly place, a safe refuge for a generation that felt it had somehow survived pogroms, immigration, depression, and world war.

There was scant room to improve private lives. No decorative treatment would have altered the row of brick houses, lined in white trim, on Bradford Street—each of them marked in the keystone with the ominous date, "1929." There was no space for a garden. The tiny rooms inside, laid out like a railroad flat, left little space for the expression of personal taste. We did our homework on the dinette table, and our mothers shooed us out to play whenever the weather permitted.

The neighborhood was a world for mothers and children. Our fathers, to a man, worked long hours and far from home. The mothers patronized the shops, kept watch over the children at play, and gathered on the stoops to kibitz, share recipes, and complain of mothers-in-law. These daughters of immigrants banded together and lobbied city and state officials to foster the educational and cultural development of their children. They scrimped and saved to build a community center, the East New York Young Men's and Young Women's Hebrew Association, with a swimming pool, gymnasium, studios, and workshops for art classes. They created a branch library in a storefront in 1949. They pushed and pushed until the city's capital budget included funds for a gleaming two-story modernist building for the library and a new junior high school, in the shape of a piano, named for local hero George Gershwin. The librarians and teachers, of course, were mostly also Jewish women, lucky to have a college education, who thirty years later would have had the opportunity and encouragement to become neurosurgeons and investment bankers. They vented their ambitions on us. Open School nights operated like a giant neighborhood conclave, where parents and teachers conspired to wrest the last drop of childhood laziness out of my classmates.

It was home, but transitory for all that. The neighborhood was defined mostly by what it was not. It was far from the "fancy" Jewish enclaves of Flatbush or Eastern Parkway and a million miles from uptown Manhattan or Westchester. Nor did it denote upward mobility, like the new suburbs out on "the Island." Most important, it was definitely not Brownsville, still

*My block of Bradford Street, in a calm corner of Brooklyn,
with tidy houses and no room for ostentation.*

quite nearby and whose poverty and crime, now associated with growing
populations of Black and Puerto Rican New Yorkers, threatened to spill
over into this refuge. Our East New York was thus a generational way station, not a place of attachment. I never heard anybody say they were proud
of the neighborhood. All of us—the next generation—were told from Day
One that we were on our way up and out. As in Alfred Kazin's day, loyalty
to our community of origin, in other words, would be "measured . . . by our
skill in getting away from it" (*A Walker in the City* [New York: Harcourt
Brace, 1951], 12). By the early 1960s, our parents' generation thought they
had finally left the turmoil of history behind. The threats seemed far off, in
the brinksmanship of Cold War rivals, but the American economy roared
forward. The cars on the block got bigger. The earnings from skilled labor
were being invested in laundromats and delicatessens. Almost all my contemporaries were on the way to college and professional life.

And then, in the blink of a historian's paragraph, it was all gone. As the sociologist Frances Fox Piven notes, "The central part of East New York in Brooklyn, home to 100,000 people in 1965, was largely destroyed in the following decade" (cited in Walter Thabit, *How East New York Became a Ghetto* [New York: New York University Press, 2003], 1). "I could have lived there for the rest of my life," my mother often said, but within two years, from 1966 to 1968, bankers and realtors savagely terrified, blockbusted, and redlined this stable community out of existence. Our tightly knit band of householders on Bradford Street, frightened by the prospect of being "the last on the block to sell," dispersed—as did hundreds of thousands of their fellow lower-middle-class New Yorkers—to high-rise co-ops on the edges of the city, in Coney Island, the Rockaways, or the southeast Bronx. All that they had worked for was gone. The "Y" was sold or given to the city, and Gershwin is now slated for closure as a "failed school."

Of course, that was not the end of the East New York story. As the Dutch had reinvented the landscape of the indigenous Canarsie people, as the industrialists and workers transformed the farmscape, and as my parents' generation converted it into a minisuburb for lower-middle-class commuters, so it has been reconstructed, redesigned, and reinhabited by successive waves of in-migrants. As the British archaeologist Christopher Tilley writes in *The Phenomenology of Landscape: Places, Paths and Monuments*, "The landscape is an anonymously sculptural form already always fashioned by human agency, never completed, and constantly being added to, and the relationship between people and it is a constant dialectic and process of structuration: the landscape is both a medium *for* and outcome *of* action and previous histories of action. Landscapes are experienced in practice, in life activities" ([Oxford, U.K, and Providence, R.I.: Berg, 1994], 23).

For my generation, East New York will probably always be a dream destroyed. Almost all of them have moved on, as expected. Some alumni of the local high school, Thomas Jefferson, conduct reunions in Los Angeles rather than in Brooklyn. But I find it hard to turn away from the area. For many of its current residents, life in East New York is daunting. More than half the population survives below the poverty line, unemployment and foreclosures stalk the neighborhood in the wake of the Great Recession, and the local police precinct regularly records the highest rates of murder and robbery in the city. (According to the New York Police Department, however, the number of murders in the 75th Precinct declined from 122 in 1993 to six in 2014; robberies, from 3,152 to 331.) Still, its website registers positive reviews from the parents of the students at my old elementary school, now 83 percent Black and 15 percent Hispanic. Some of the vacant lots have been turned into community vegetable gardens, and a weekly greenmarket operates in the warmer months. When I bike over to look around, about once a year, I see the mix Tilley is talking about. In some measure the current East New York has been shaped by "previous histories of action," like the expansion of public transit during the 1910s and public housing in the 1950s, and to some extent these have merely been the "medium" for new forms of life, positive and negative, different from mine.

For the social historian, districts like East New York—exemplifying all the stages of the city's economic change and ethnic succession—are much more worthy of study than fancy places like the Upper West Side, despite the greater number of famous people who have lived there. By law, historic preservation designates areas that have had a long-lasting architectural character, which virtually ensures that they have been more immune to urban dislocation than East New York, Astoria, Chinatown, or the South Bronx. Amid the jumble of building types and streetscapes that survive from all that tumult, East New York and its current children still have no acknowledged public history beyond that lonely church on New Lots Avenue. All the other layers of the district's history lay far off, resting in archival collections in downtown Brooklyn, Manhattan, Albany, and Washington, D.C. For East New Yorkers of the twenty-first century, there is no "genealogy of place" whereby they can ponder the lives of those who preceded them.

It is important, therefore, to bring such places to light. For current and former residents, it is a form of respect seldom accorded such people in the news media or other vehicles of cultural expression. But it is equally important for nonresidents. If you live in New York City and do not know places like East New York, then you do not know who nurses your sick parents, delivers your mail, or fills your grocery shelves. Many of the comforts of twenty-first-century urban life are purchased with such ignorance.

Recollections of East New York and what I experienced there, as I have said, created a menu for public interpretations of place. In rereading this vignette, I see the intersection of physical place with modes of residence, work, and community life; of "newsworthy" events with the slow rhythms of everyday life; of continuities and contrasts across ethnic lines; of how each place is defined by its relationships with others in memory and daily life; of the virulence of class and racial stigmas; of my roles as witness, analyst, storyteller, and citizen. I love historic landmarks, but that little Dutch church on New Lots Avenue hardly suffices to inform us about the many strands that form the tapestry of collective memory and public history in East New York.

7 ::: ENVISIONING PLACE
ON GALLERY WALLS

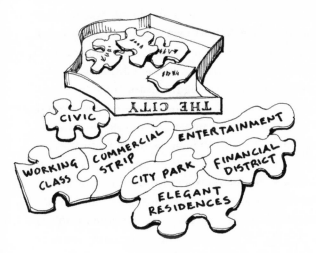

The early years of American History Workshop (AHW) plunged me into a perplexity. I was sure that historic markers could not satisfactorily interpret the layered human history of a place. I was often disappointed at how conventional history museums twisted local stories into a forced march toward America's manifest destiny. I had a credo: History was everywhere and included everyone's story, the present needed elucidation as much as the past, setting history apart from the "workaday" world was foolish, and the official and commercial "branding" of a place obscured much of its real character. And, of course, personal experience is the best teacher, with keen observation of everyday life a close second.

The perplexity was that my chosen specialty was the interpretation of history in public spaces, especially the museum. Of all the possible places to represent the evolving experience of place, the museum gallery seemed among the least likely. This was the Palace of the Immutable, after all, the Sanctuary of the Untouchable. If I wanted to fracture the boundaries that set Historyland off from ordinary city life, could I do this in the museum, the most bounded place of all? In those days, when admission was often free or nominal, visitors were expected to be quiet, unobtrusive, and attentive. Signage was discreet, to the verge of invisibility. The museum shop stocked catalogs, postcards, and a few works of scholarship related to the collections. The café, if there was one, was open from noon to 2:00 P.M. and sold lukewarm coffee and cellophane-wrapped sandwiches with too much mayonnaise. Museums portrayed themselves as a special refuge, cut off from the workaday world. Even more than churches, American museums were sacred spaces.

In contemplating the problem of interpreting the history of place in the gallery museum, two paths lay in front of me. The curatorial path would lead to exhibitions of individual maps and images of a place—paintings, drawings, engravings, photographs—over the course of its history. With images mounted in frames or housed in glass vitrines and annotated with long labels, this approach focuses on the representation of place by artists (and sometimes by scientists or cartographers). Perhaps these may include excerpts from travelers' narratives or other verbal documentation. Implicit in those labels is usually the assumption that "the nineteenth century" viewed the land in this way—as if one individual draftsman could magically channel the whole culture's perceptual framework of the environment at that given moment. And, going a step further, I could lay out a sequence of images to show how the place evolved over time.

Such exhibitions might be aesthetically pleasing—no small matter—but pedagogically I thought this worked for only a small sliver of the visiting public. It depended heavily on the skill and patience of visitors in examining the minute details in period illustrations. They would have to move their eyes (and their attention) from text to image, or from text to map to image and back, again and again. Few people have the commitment to work their way through such material while standing in a museum. Most visitors would, I discovered, be unable to separate the changes in the landscape from the decisions of artists, photographers, or mapmakers to represent the place in a particular manner. This curatorial approach works much better when one can hold a book with the maps, images, and textual commentary close at hand. It's altogether too easy for museum visitors to lose their way in the thicket of details, and many give up in frustration.

The other path was the museum educator's. I could ask a workshop group of visitors to create their own maps, say, of the journey from home to the museum. (Or their own drawings or photos of the buildings seen en route.) Then we could compare their maps or drawings to one or more historical examples. At Old Sturbridge Village (osv) I had discovered that a school group assigned to draw the facade of a building could then better understand its design sources, its construction techniques, and its relationship to the public and private spaces around it. Even one's hastiest sketches are valuable conduits for exploring space, place, and the built environment.

Applying the educator's approach would help visitors learn about the builder's or artist's challenges in representing landscape, or about the way economic or social factors influenced what and how the place is shown. More than through the curatorial route, the workshop participants could competently address issues relating to how things are designed and built today. But the downside was this: The museum educator would not be able to show any more than a one-to-one contrast between the old landscape represented in the historical image and the one audiences produced of the place now.

I chose both paths. It was an important career decision. I would teach history—solid, conceptually rich, archivally informed history. No one would ever be able to criticize my work as stale, ungrounded in scholarship, trivial, or merely of "antiquarian" interest. And, second, I would do so with all the experiential learning tools I could develop. It would be addressed to ten-year-olds as well as to their grandparents, and to both when they visited my museums or sites together. I would apply whatever I could learn about cognitive processing, about performance theory, and about situated learning, all in the cause of helping visitors make their own meanings about the connections of past and present.

Easier said than done. Reconciling and balancing these two commitments has been a knotty professional challenge for me for decades. At osv, I recognized that an alertness to the epiphenomena of everyday life could be linked to a pedagogy asking visitors to reenact the processes of nineteenth-century life for themselves. Since then I've been hard at work hammering out those links between the content of my research methods and my teaching.

That work began in earnest in 1979 and 1980, when I joined teams developing two interpretive exhibitions on the history of place. *The Lay of the Land*, produced by the Rhode Island Historical Society for its new gallery in the Aldrich House in Providence, told the state's history through a sequence of emblematic landscapes. The first planning meeting laid out the chapters of the story: European Visions of the Land and Its People, A Garden of Farms, A Place of Great Trade, Mill Villages in the Valleys, Providence 1900, and Living with Our Landscape. At weekly sessions devoted to each chapter over the next three months, historians and curators brought together maps, charts, plans, engravings, photographs, and dozens of objects that had been used in shaping the landscape, experiencing its character, and recording its features in each of these six generations. Each week the team hewed out a basic theme for each era, chose the best objects, and suggested design directions.[1]

The second of these projects was *Place over Time*, a temporary exhibition for the Boston Landmarks Commission located at Museum Wharf in Boston. *Place over Time* ambitiously explored the development of seven historical areas in Boston's center city. Each "place-unit," as the design team called it, was a setting for constant reinvention, as "'every generation reshapes the city to meet its own needs.'" Some were total transformations, like the replacement of raunchy Scollay Square by the austere new Government Center in the 1960s. Others evolved to accommodate changes in technology and the increasing scale and complexity of urban interaction. As the merchants' counting-houses in State (originally King) Street gave way, for example, to the office towers in Boston's financial district, male clerks were superseded by female secretaries; the ledger books, by typewriters and adding machines; the connections to the sea, by electronic communications; and so on.[2]

The conventional state history museum, as we have seen, surveyed the place's dominant groups, one after another. Historical factoids were everywhere, but they were rarely bound together in actual themes that might characterize the region's continuity over time or its major transformations. *The Lay of the Land*, by contrast, defined Rhode Island's history as a sequen-

1. The Society published a book to accompany the show, Albert T. Klyberg and Nancy Grey Osterud, *The Lay of the Land* (Providence, 1979). The team also included curators Ann LeVeque, Robert Emlen, and Candace Heald, education director Laura Roberts, and designer J. Fred Moore.

2. The project was directed by Pauline Chase Harrell, researched and written by Susan Geib and Margaret Smith, and designed by Emily Hiestand and Fred Golinko, with an introductory film produced by Fred Brink. I consulted on the thematic organization of the show and its diverse interpretive approaches. The seven downtown areas explored were Dock Square (including Quincy Market), Government Center, Downtown Crossing, State Street, Beacon Hill/Boston Common, Copley Square, and Kenmore Square. An additional exhibit unit explored the relationship of central Boston to its nineteen residential neighborhoods, and an Issues Forum presented contending views on urban policy through an audiovisual program. The quotation is from a memo from Emily Hiestand to members of the development team, January 3, 1980, courtesy of Susan Geib, AHW Records, University of Massachusetts, Amherst.

The Lay of the Land *exhibition portrayed Rhode Island as a sequence of landscapes characterized by changing economic uses.*

tial revisualization of its landscape, spurred in each generation by new economic opportunities. The exhibition argued that powerful interests in the colony, state, and nation repeatedly deployed different techniques to exploit the local terrain and generate new ways of seeing and recording the place. The early maps, for example, emphasized the colony's relationship to more powerful neighbors and rivals. Eighteenth-century maps revealed their preoccupations with nautical matters, assiduously documenting the depths of harbor approaches. Maps created around the turn of the nineteenth century showed greater care, by contrast, with the divisions of agricultural land and overland transport networks. The era of early manufacturing came with an upward turn of the head and a discovery of the landscape's verticality, when engineers like Zachariah Allen measured the falls of local rivers to design waterpower systems. Urban development in the century after the Civil War once again brought attention to a top-down view, this time demarking the different economic zones of the city, the variety of ethnic populations,

Place over Time *invited visitors to peer behind the current look of a city they thought they knew (Boston Museum of Transportation, 1980).*

and the trolley and rail networks that connected urban Rhode Islanders to work, community life, and leisure. The last chapters used aerial photography to show suburban sprawl and the rather amazing horizontal spread of airfields and naval facilities in mid-twentieth-century Rhode Island, as well as the reforestation of the inland landscape.

The Lay of the Land started out as a good example of the curatorial path I describe above. But clustering the materials for each era broke the customary mold of library exhibitions, in which individual pieces are arranged in a uniform sequence of cases and panels. Each era was sharply differentiated in design. The interpretive text deftly related issues of land use and genres of representation. The cluster for each era featured objects as well as documents and images: native American digging tools and fishnets, a colonial hay rake and merchant clerk's desk, working drawings and site specifications for the adaptive reuse of abandoned mill buildings, and so on. Most important, when we could not locate adequate original sources—maps of nineteenth-century streetcar routes, the contrasts between city districts, and immigrant communities in turn-of-the-twentieth-century Providence—our team created them ourselves, using archival research and period maps as a base for the graphic design. The exhibition, in other words, was rooted in themes rather than in a checklist of treasures.

Place over Time was equally thematic, but it had few or no original objects. It relied instead on highly inventive caricatures of iconic architectural elements (like the classical columns at Quincy Market, the elaborate doorways of Beacon Hill, or the window treatments of early business offices), scale models, and graphic panels—often shaped to provide references to urban spaces—that superimpose interpretive information on period illustrations. This playful reimagining of the Boston downtown was combined with a rigorous interpretive organization that plotted the sequence of "time-units" (historical eras) against "place-units" (downtown areas). The exhibition began with a film that presented the key themes, narrated by a real Boston cabdriver. His image reappeared as a cartoon figure introducing the subthemes for each zone of the city (and hence of the exhibition).

TYPOLOGIES AND INVENTIONS

Both *The Lay of the Land* and *Place over Time* explored the same overarching theme: the repeated re-visioning and reconstructing of their landscapes by Rhode Islanders or Bostonians. Each exhibition postulated that landscapes were "invented," or "re-invented."[3] These words suggest human contrivance and will and imply something impossible—that men and women deliberately created enormously complex social systems, political orders, and natural settings. And both exhibitions assumed that human beings could again and again impose new ways of organizing space and society onto a blank canvas, a tabula rasa, largely ignoring what had existed before. At one moment, Rhode Island was an early American version of Texas, dense with cattle ranches. A century later it was dotted with miniature Manchesters, rolling out bolts of cotton cloth.

The second shared assumption concerned the organization of the ex-

---

3. The Yale University library catalog lists over 400 books with "Inventing" in the title—*Inventing Virginia, Inventing Wine, Inventing Van Eyck, Inventing Vietnam,* etc. Almost all of them date from 1978 (e.g., Garry Wills's *Inventing America*) or later. "Re-inventing," though rarer, appears in twenty-seven titles, all since 1980. By contrast, the even more common phrase "The Making of" has had a much longer and more consistent usage, with an upsurge around World War I, and clearly stimulated by E. P. Thompson's pathbreaking *The Making of the English Working Class* (1963).

hibition. *To discover a master exhibition theme*, we proposed, *was to develop a typology*. There were six generations of ways to witness and use the Rhode Island landscape and seven distinct zones of human interaction in the downtown Boston streetscape.

In our 1982 plan to commemorate Maine's becoming a state, we described our traveling exhibition, *Doorways to Statehood*, this way: "The exhibit will be constructed as a six-sided, freestanding box, about six feet tall and twelve feet in diameter, made of pine. One of the faces will offer a historical orientation to this period of Maine history. Each of the other five will be faced with a representation of a doorway in a Maine town. Opening that doorway, the visitor will discover how that particular Maine community—and others which share its key historical characteristics—grew to approximate its present form during our period." The five types emblematized Portland as the state's preeminent urban seaport; Bethel and Blue Hill as new farming settlements; Brunswick and Topsham as river towns with dozens of small water-powered mills; Wiscasset as a model of a county seat, focused on a courthouse; and Madawaska as a town settled by the Québecois and laid out by their very distinctive surveying practices.

By using the phrase "others which share its key historical characteristics," we were suggesting that all Maine towns would fall, roughly, into one of these five types. Almost all these early AHW projects were built around such typologies. The influence of my friend Sam Bass Warner is unmistakable. Even as we plotted the creation of AHW over lunch at various Boston cafeterias, I was probing Sam's way of writing urban history. His 1968 book, *The Private City*, posits that Philadelphia's growth took three successive forms: The Eighteenth-Century Town, The Big City, and The Industrial Metropolis. Each is easy to visualize and to grasp. Each becomes the container for lively narratives.

The pedagogical strategies I used in these typology-based shows were similar. Let's give the visitors a set of conceptual tools by which they could connect their own personal experiences (of places in Rhode Island or of types of urban space in Boston) with a set of historical documents. Let that sink in for a moment: "You probably don't realize that your way of moving across this landscape is deeply rooted in this eighteenth-century aspect of the land." Then subsume the two together, the visitor's contemporary experience and the archival document, as evidence of a key historical generalization. In doing so, we were silently conveying the notion that you, the visitor, were as important a figure in the historical evolution of place as anyone.

The whole landscape, not just the parts fenced off as "historical features," was rooted in the past.

The experience in the gallery aimed to fix the typology in the visitors' minds, often with some design element or interactive device that could be memorably associated with one of the types. We theorized that visitors would carry these typologies with them after they left the exhibition gallery. If they could carry around Roger Tory Peterson's *Field Guide to American Birds* as they ventured into the wild, illustrating the differences between nuthatches and warblers, why shouldn't they be able to carry Rabinowitz's guide to city streets, telling how to differentiate an industrial zone from a financial office district, as they ventured downtown? But Peterson came in paperback and was available for constant reference. I depended on visitors' recalling the difference between one ideal type of cityscape and another weeks and months after their museum visits.

That was one problem. Professional historians, if not the visiting public, could detect others. In making classifications of one sort or another, the historian puts himself or herself above the fray of events, watching as one system of landscape or one economic order replaces another. But how and where would we account for the forces that produce these changes? In *The Private City*, Warner had located the responsibility for the constant unwinding of social stability in liberal capitalism, which he called "privatism."

We were so focused on the contrasts among historical eras or landscape types that we glossed over the crucial question of where these typologies came from.[4]

To this we could only reply that the exhibition form presented formidable obstacles to exploring the deeper roots of such distinctions as house forms, furniture types, or village geographies. I wanted the exhibition to represent *action*, but how could I show precisely the actions that led to these variations among types? What do "industrial capitalism" or "the national security state" do, and how can we show that in the gallery without distracting visitors from the immediate concrete story in front of them? When historians—most of whom are academics—suggest that we need to explain the larger social and economic contexts of what we are displaying, they generally fall back on recommending that we insert long-winded text panels full of heavy words like "exploitation," "expropriation," and "hegemony." As teachers we know that these yield more yawns than questions.

A second deficiency of the typological regime was that our categories were completely ad hoc, developed anew for each project. Did every city have exactly these seven zones, every state just this same sequence of economic landscapes? So where did we get these distinctions? We never bothered to ask.

This rather casual attitude fit nicely into a shift in scholarly attitudes toward social science. In academic circles, the 1950s and 1960s had been an era of increasing confidence in the application of positivist methods, including statistical measures, in disciplines like geography, archaeology, and environmental perception. My well-thumbed copy of James H. Johnson's *Urban Geography* textbook (1972) introduced me, for example, to "timeplan analysis," "location theory," and "factorial ecology." The morphology of cities, I discovered, could be directly related to the distribution of demographic and occupational densities. The charts, graphs, and maps in Johnson's book intrigued me.

But in the early 1980s, anthropologists and archaeologists were turning

4. Periodically, over the course of the last few decades, critics of public history programs complain that they obscure power relationships and foster "an incapacitating awe" of a past detached from contemporary social conflicts. The most acute of these observers is Mike Wallace, in *Mickey Mouse History and Other Essays on American Memory* (Philadelphia: University of Pennsylvania Press, 1996). The phrase is from Wallace's essay "Visiting the Past: History Museums in the United States," ibid., 27.

away from such "totalizing frameworks," which had stimulated them to fit their data into generalizations that could be applied across time and across the globe. Instead, they increasingly adopted theories of interpretation derived from philosophy and literary criticism. In these early AHW exhibition projects, we did not think to "interrogate" the grounds for our categorizations, as postmodern theorists would have insisted a few years later. We judged that our categories were useful to visitors, pure and simple. But even if we had dissected the assumptions bound up in our taxonomic schemes, I do not believe that our interpretive approach would have differed.

The job of the museum teacher is to deploy the most valuable instrument in fashioning a successful educational program: the visitors' own background and learning skills. We haven't the time or the authority to do otherwise. To suggest that visitors must first be introduced to the underlying philosophical principles by which we use language to dissect different social and physical phenomena would be disastrous. History museums, for better or worse, accept the world beyond the gallery as it is commonly and concretely described, not as some postmodern conspiracy. And then we seek to enrich and complicate our visitors' ability to make sense of it for themselves. This is one of the profound differences that began to emerge between public and academic historians in the 1980s and 1990s.

THE EXPERIENCE OF GALLERY EXHIBITIONS

Beyond these theoretical objections, the most important deficiency of these gallery exhibitions about places, for all that, was that they had little actual *sense of place* in them. They had tried to explore the histories of landscape within the confines of picture frames, graphic panels, and glass cases. Our pedagogy was more akin to a walk-through illustrated lecture, a book on the wall (though a handsomely designed one, incorporating some three-dimensional artifacts), than it was an evocation of historic places. And if our subject was meant to be the land as it was settled, used, or worked by ordinary people, these elegant displays undermined the vernacular forms and quotidian life-patterns they were supposed to interpret. They could display what things looked like or how they might be designed or what contemporaries did to remember them. But they often reduced the human presence to verbal commentary with a few illustrations. In their stillness, these wall-mounted historical images invited the substitution of words, words, and more words for the tactility and kinetics of life. I missed the intensity that came by immersion in the physical aspects of past worlds and from encountering skilled live interpreters.

In such gallery exhibitions, I relied on a cognitive process that was close to teaching history as I had learned it, in the graduate seminar and through the research article. Such museum learning seemed to use only a tiny fragment of the museumgoer's skill. Successful visitors, we thought, would be able to identify the key points, match evidence to hypothesis, and replicate the argument we were making. At the end of their visit, they would know what we knew—no less and no more. How naive we were! Museums are not schools. Without the social apparatus of formal schooling—without the discipline of enrolling in a course of study and without the incentives of feeling oneself a part of the scholarly guild—we could never make a museum visit achieve what happened in the classroom and research library. Visitors pass no entrance exams and, except for children on school visits, can leave whenever they want. They come to museums to enjoy themselves in the company of friends and family. They trust museums—but learning is just an extra. People like to tell their friends how much they enjoyed museum visits, and some leap to quick judgments about what they did and didn't like. But I've met no visitors who wanted to be tested on their mastery of the intellectual content.

In my early career as a museum historian, my impulse was to develop an interpretive plan thematically, that is, by following the logic of a historical argument. Visitors would be told that they could understand the past if they could notice distinctions among historical phenomena, so the gallery would be divided into treatments of geographical zones, chronological eras, or types of objects. The AHW's 1981 plan for an interpretive exhibition that would introduce nine houses of the Society for the Preservation of New England Antiquities in Maine and New Hampshire envisaged three major themes: Riverways, describing the ecological and economic transformations of the Piscataqua River valley; The Craft of Portsmouth Hands, documenting local artisanship; and The World of Wood, which explored four interrelated domains of silviculture (the Forest, the Ship, the House, and the Fireside). Elegant as this organization would have been, if it had been adopted, it demanded a great deal of visitors to keep all these complex themes straight. These were long answers to questions that the visitors had never quite brought themselves to ask.

Ultimately, we needed to discover and develop another conceptual architecture that would provide an easier framework for the progress of visitors through the gallery, just as the thematic tours did for school groups at OSV. This would allow them to learn as they went, without distracting them entirely from the material in front of their eyes and hands. The layout of the exhibition would have to follow the logic of the visitors' experience, not of the themes—not the logic of complex words, but the bio-logic of visitors' bodies. But how?

THEMATIZING HISTORIC HOUSES

Several other fortunate failures in applying thematic interpretation to historic house museums proved helpful in our understanding of this problem. We were hired in 1981 to plan a bold new interpretation of the James J. Hill House in St. Paul, owned by the Minnesota Historical Society (MHS). Hill, who created the Great Northern Railway and earned the title of "The Empire Builder," was a titanic figure in the history of the upper Midwest. But, after four decades and more as residence and command central of the local archdiocese, his 1891 palatial manor atop Summit Avenue had lost much of its grandeur. A glitzy restoration, even if the original furniture could be reacquired from family members, was beyond MHS resources. We wanted to bring visitors into the presence of the great man himself, rather than refurbish the house with "typical" period furniture and relegate the telling of Hill's story to a dreary panel exhibition.

After consultation with the large and experienced staff of the historical society, we settled on three core themes: (1) the house as a landmark in the career of an extraordinary man; (2) the house as a social system, exploring the code of conduct among family members, guests, and employees in each of its many rooms; and (3) the house as a complex and innovative physical operation—Hill had insisted on his own electric generating and advanced plumbing systems. In our proposal, these would be tied together, thematically and experientially, by a combination of docent-led tours, brief interpretive labels throughout the house, multimedia installations, and (on occasion) live performances by actors in period costumes. We laid out a single integrated interpretive pathway and a dramatic arc to the visit experience. Every space in the house would have to be reconstructed as an episode in an hour-long presentation. Each tour would become more tightly scripted and less variable, with a tighter interweaving of media and the role of MHS guides. But to our clients, this was organizationally too complicated. It seemed easier to retain the conventional room-by-room, object-by-object docent lecture, leaving it up to the guides to judge whether and how to infuse the new thematic material into their presentations. Our plan, apparently, never got beyond its initial presentation.

In a 1982 interpretive plan for the Hermann-Grima House, a house museum in New Orleans, AHW suggested a similar triad of themes: the family history, the house as a site of social interaction, and the architectural and physical character of the building. In St. Paul, our clients had been highly professional historians, curators, and museum administrators, who urged us to articulate more complex themes. In New Orleans, we now had to convince the ladies' committee that the house was at its core a meaningful lens into the history of domestic life, including the troubling aspects of the past, like slavery. The interpretive plan barges straight ahead:

> One point cannot be overemphasized: interpretation is very different from furnishing. If we let the objects "speak for themselves," our tours are likely to consist of name after name of unfamiliar things: "this is a ____, that is a ____." A visitor to such a house, and we have all been there, is left with only a fragmented view of the past. Instead, we have to select among the possible themes those which are most important historically and those we can best illustrate with our collections. The themes come first.

We were wrong. In our zeal to prod the ladies away from a guide's tour spiel full of miscellaneities, we hoped to superimpose larger themes: how the domestic life of an antebellum New Orleans house evidenced all the contradictions of progress and tradition, freedom and enslavement. It didn't work. The executive director who hired us and espoused this approach departed before it could be tried.

THE LIMITS OF THEMATIC INTERPRETATION

No matter how carefully we planned our pedagogy to develop a competent overview of the social science generalizations, visitors shied away from the exercise. Yes, we did say that we were telling stories: "This exhibition tells how Maine's people developed different kinds of communities in the decades before statehood." But these didn't feel to visitors like stories at all. To apply the terms of Kenneth Burke's pentad of elements comprising a dramatic action, the agents were usually collective words for groups of people ("colonial farmers," "Irish immigrants"); the acts were abstract verbs ("develop," "establish"); the agencies were abstract tools ("the traditions they had brought with them"); the scenes were vague ("over the course of the nineteenth century," "the rural countryside"); and the purposes—well, those mostly went unspoken. The scheme was altogether too remote and difficult for visitors to engage with. If one wanted to make the public feel more connected to the places of the past, it was foolish to use a pedagogical technique that intimidated our audience.

Visitors craved a more dramatic form: stories with a beginning, middle, and end, stories with specific characters, indeed with heroes and villains. While advocates of the new social history, including me, cherished the breakthrough that allowed the lives of the previously invisible "little people" in history to take center stage, many visitors were not impressed. Visitors often did not identify themselves with thematic presentations about the everyday lives of ordinary people in the past. After I tried once to make this link explicitly, one visitor told me, "You may think we're ordinary folks, but you don't know us." It was a useful lesson for a historian and a teacher.

8 ::: MUSEUM VISITORS

ON CENTER STAGE

The early years of American History Workshop (AHW) were tough. We paid our bills, barely. We discovered that jobs materialized and disappeared with equal suddenness. Even a project with the greatest ideas, developed with maximum collaboration, could still fall prey to staff changes, the Reagan recession, and the whim of trustees. But I was learning my craft, as well as my business, and even the projects that collapsed taught us valuable lessons about teaching history in public spaces to a sizable and diverse audience.

Gradually I began to see that the relationship of historical theme to visitors' learning could not be reconciled entirely with the toolbox I had inherited from the conventional museum—illustrative images, text panels, and guided tours. Our design colleagues brought us a new generation of interpretive media—stagecraft (lighting, props, mock environments), audiovisual programs, and hands-on interactive devices. More than just presentational tools, they altered the stories that we could tell and the politics of our interpretation.

If we were going to interpret the elegant dining room of the James J. Hill House in St. Paul, for example, it made sense to animate the room by re-creating a dinner party. Since the original table and table settings were gone, we could just as well substitute a video of a simulated event, projected onto a surrogate table (actually a screen) from below, and invite visitors to sit and watch as the splendid meal was served. And while we were at it, we could reconstruct, via the video's sound track, the long-departed conversations between the Hills and their guests—the meatpacking magnate Richard Armour, for one. Gloved hands and serving utensils would be seen, but not the torsos and faces of the characters. And since this was such a winning idea, why not create a parallel show for the servants' dining table in the basement, filled with scuttlebutt about the proceedings upstairs?[1]

Of course, we could fantasize about presenting a full costume drama, à la Masterpiece Theater, but we would never have the money for that, and a projected drama on a screen would undermine this as a site-specific in-

stallation built into the furnish-ings of the room. As a child, I'd listened to radio dramas like *The Lone Ranger* and *The Green Hornet*, and we knew that "the pictures on radio were always better." Our more modest approach, emphasiz-ing the aural world and table ac-couterments of the Hills' dining room, would—with a few introductory remarks from the docent—actually more effectively spark the visitors' imagination. It could be entertaining, to be sure, and much more memorable than the conventional docent's tour of the room's lifeless architecture and furnishings. It also suggested a large number of new research questions—about the cuisine, the decorum of hos-pitality, the interactions of upstairs and downstairs, and the rhythms and substance of conversation.

A few years later, we were invited to plan an interpretive installation for Caramoor, the Westchester estate of Walter and Lucie Bigelow Dodge

1. Twenty-odd years later, the Minnesota History Center, led by exhibition devel-oper Benjamin Filene, added a major element that used many of the same techniques in exploring the diverse immigrant families who had lived in one particular house on the East Side of St. Paul. See Filene, "Make Yourself at Home—Welcoming Voices in *Open House: If These Walls Could Talk*," in *Letting Go? Sharing Historical Authority in a User-Generated World*, ed. Bill Adair et al. (Philadelphia: Pew Center for Arts & Heritage, 2011), 138–55. In 2014, in an exhibition called *Eat Your History: A Shared Table*, the Museum of Sydney (Australia) created a series of videos that showed di-verse historical modes of food preparation and presentation. These videos were much like the ones we imagined in 1981 for the Hill House.

AHW imagined the Caramoor Music Room in Katonah, N.Y., alive with period conversation, music, and a fearful historical moment.

Rosen, which they converted in the late 1920s into an Italian villa filled with choice Renaissance and Asian art objects. The Rosens, we learned, welcomed their friends to summer afternoon concerts in the house's Music Room, with performances given by many recent emigrés from Nazism and fascism. Again, simply annotating the room's furnishings reduced the story to a shell of its historical significance. So AHW designed a sound installation that would allow modern-day visitors to "eavesdrop" on the conversations of such a party on the last Sunday in August 1939. We imagined chatter about the recent opening of the Whitestone Bridge, the failure of the recent Rodgers and Hart musical on Broadway, Joe DiMaggio's brilliant hitting, the silk suits featured in the Paris season, and most ominously, the news of the Hitler-Stalin nonaggression pact just days earlier. And, then, in our plan, someone announced that Hitler was demanding the cession of Danzig from the Poles. Everyone knew war was imminent. The string players took up Schubert's "Death and the Maiden," and our program ended.

What history were we going to tell? I had learned at Old Sturbridge Village (OSV) to interpret a much greater range of historical actions than could be documented in memoirs and statistical charts. Now I began to ask, why

aren't the sounds of the time, the etiquette of interactions, and the ephemera of daily life also not worth researching, interpreting, and presenting in the history museum gallery? Even though they were often dense with objects behind do-not-touch signs, historic sites offered richer opportunities for interpretive installations than gallery shows. As my theater friends knew, the blank slate and the black box allowed for all sorts of illusionary tricks, but there was also magic in site-specific performances. Viewers and visitors brought with them lifetimes of experience in such spaces. They knew that parlors and kitchens spoke in different dialects and that factory lofts and storefronts hosted different kinds of dexterities. They may not have been able to distinguish the Georgian from the Greek Revival style, but they knew "porch-ness" and "classroom-ity." Knowing well how to read the architectural, visual, tactile, graphic, and auditory clues of a space would, we thought, allow visitors to grapple more effectively with the information we presented. Slowly I was discovering how to translate my experiments at osv into a new way of making history come alive inside the museum.

THE MUSEUM VISIT AS A PERFORMANCE

Each project carried us further from dispensing information toward organizing experience. A dozen clients in the 1980s asked us to create a coherent system of interpretation that would link a variety of local sites. Our work in Monterey in 1984–86 is an example. For the capital of the Spanish and Mexican colony of Alta California, where the state's first constitution was written, and a place with very rich historical features but an underfunded state historic park program, we developed a plan for a visitors' center housing a major multimedia orientation program, called *The Rim of Empire*, and we designed outdoor interpretive sites throughout the city. For the newly authenticated homestead of the Revolutionary-era hero Ethan Allen in Burlington, Vermont, AHW designed and implemented a similar program in 1984–89. A barn on the property housed an introductory exhibition, *Ethan Allen: Man and Myth*, interweaving the historical and folkloric figure of the Green Mountain Boy over time. Visitors were then invited to take seats in an adjoining "tavern" room and offered mugs of apple cider. As they sat there, the room darkened, and ambient sounds and then voices emerged. Evoking a wayside inn on a winter's eve, a series of "Tavern Tales" imaginatively brought to mind the era of 1791, the moment of Vermont's

The Ethan Allen Homestead tavern: Take a seat, have a mug of cider, and imagine yourself welcoming Vermont's admission to the Union in 1791.

admission as the fourteenth state in the Union. After the show, the docent explained the history of the site, and visitors could explore the homestead landscape and the preserved house itself.

The South Street Experience, the orientation program at New York's Seaport Museum for which we co-wrote the script in 1982–83, was the longest and most technically elaborate of these programs. Its computerized program coordinated the sequencing of a hundred slide and two film projectors. Fog rolled over the audience during the account of New Amsterdam's origin in the age of exploration, and blasts of smoke accompanied the frightening scenes of devastation in the great fire of 1835. The goal was to stock the minds of visitors so that their subsequent tour of the preserved streets, buildings, and ships would repeatedly call forth images and sounds from the show. As the project evolved, its cost grew along with its ambition, and soon it had become a separately ticketed attraction only tangentially related to the museum's interpretive and educational programs.

THINKING IN TIME

These projects were a watershed. In designing gallery exhibitions and historic house visits, we had been thinking spatially. We had assigned content to the available spaces—introducing the themes, reinforcing and illustrating them, and summing up the key concepts in a concluding space. Typological exhibitions use room divisions as convenient separators of different chapters of the argument. Now, in these multisite projects, spreading over the actual cityscape or museum "campus," visitors would move in and out of the historical program, interrupting their explorations of the themes with episodes of moving from site to site, eating and shopping, kids' play, people-watching, and just hanging out. Given these distractions, keeping visitors focused on the historical argument would be impossible. We needed a new template.

The visitors' time became the organizing frame of the visit. Now we were facilitating a nonlinear series of visitor experiences. We provided a loose-leaf sourcebook for a narrative of events that was being inscribed by visitors, rather than a road map through the historical argument. There might still be conventional gallery exhibitions along the way, with walls of framed documents and cases of labeled objects, but these projects also included audiovisual and interactive programs, with hands-on learning and living history interpreters. The whole district or town or region was being recast as what we began to call a "storyscape." Our template for the historic attraction resembled in some ways what national park planners had created as a basic sequence for visitors. First they would arrive at a visitors' center, where a dramatic multimedia presentation would relate the site, its people, and its significant milestones to larger historical stories that visitors would recognize. Then they would be invited to partake of a menu of time-demarked tours and participatory programs. This would give them access to the core object or site element, the "original" thing that merited historical attention (as, for examples, the Custom House in Monterey, the four-masted *Peking* at South Street, or the actual home of Ethan Allen). And they could conclude their visit with a variety of in-depth learning opportunities or a chance to visit the gift shop and take away books and souvenirs.

THEMES VERSUS EXPERIENCES

I think I lost my faith in centering interpretation around themes when I stood in front of the Old South Meetinghouse on Washington Street in Boston, watching the entry and exit of tourists along the Freedom Trail. AHW had just been hired to work on an interpretive program, in connection with needed architectural repairs. Those poor souls, I thought, schlepping from one landmark of America's struggle for liberty to another, were loaded down with pamphlets and squally children. They surely did not look like the mock Mohawks who assembled here in 1773 to launch their assault on the *Beaver, Dartmouth*, and *Eleanor*, the ships moored in the harbor with their cargoes of East India Company tea. The time was for deeds, not words, I could hear those old revolutionaries say, and that became my slogan for the reinterpretation. Enough of these long panels of historical copy and repro-duced woodcuts.

The National Park Service and the Old South staff, however, had by this time adopted the principle that site interpretation should focus on commu-nicating historical themes. AHW pushed back. We argued that this should be "an exhibit of, not [simply] an exhibit in" the meetinghouse. The AHW report continued:

> Interpretation acts to slow visitors down, focusing their attention, in-tensifying their perceptual grasp of the scene, dramatizing it for them as a human story, and, finally, providing them with a coherent historical, architectural, and cultural context. Generally such an inductive process works better than a more deductive approach, in which the learning ex-perience starts with important-sound phrases ("On this site, the most fundamental event in the long evolution of American liberty . . ."), and then brings visitors down to particulars. In a site interpretation, it pays to start with the things visitors already know, like how to enter and ex-plore the building as a gathering-place. Then and only then do we try to reveal the great meanings inherent within.

The common thread of the building's history was the action of Bostonians in congregating, speaking, listening, and deciding. Built as a house of wor-ship for Congregationalists in 1729, Old South continued to host Sabbath and weekday evening services for almost a century and a half. After its con-gregation moved to the Back Bay in 1872, the building was threatened with demolition. Saving the meetinghouse was among the earliest triumphs of the historic preservation movement in America. As a historic site and as a forum for lively political and religious debate, it has continued to serve the city into our own day. It is now associated with the Boston National Histori-cal Park, though it is still owned and operated by its own board of directors.

AHW's plan focused on the idea and the experience of "meetinghouse." Interviews with visitors revealed that they had little idea of what that word meant and why this was not simply a "church." We would trace the notion,

common in colonial New England, that the town or parish would construct a single building for both religious and governmental purposes, calling it a meetinghouse. In Puritan thought, the "church" was not a building but, rather, the gathering of souls ("saints") who had passed through an experience of redemption through God's grace, evidenced for many in an often-harrowing conviction of their own unworthiness that could be relieved only by a "sensible" infusion of divine favor. By combining the secular and sacred meeting space in one building, and by using taxes to support an "orthodox" (that is, Congregationalist) ministry, colonists demonstrated that spiritual and moral well-being was a responsibility of the whole town. In the eighteenth century, beginning in Boston itself, the municipal functions began to migrate from religious structures to "town houses," and dissenters (such as Quakers, Anglicans, and Baptists) were exempted from such taxes. Still, Old South continued to serve as a convenient site for protest meetings in Revolutionary times, though it was only steps away from the seat of royal authority in the Court House, now called the Old State House.[2] The final disestablishment of the orthodox churches did not occur in Massachusetts, New Hampshire, and Connecticut until 1818–33.

But beyond the ecclesiastical history, chiefly written as a story of negatives (for example, "the Puritans purged their religious services and sites of ornamentation, even of steeples and bells"), I wanted to get at the positive experiential qualities of a setting like Old South. (My first visit to the meetinghouse at osv twenty years earlier proved an inspiration.) How could modern-day visitors grasp the conjoined social and spiritual significance of sitting for hours on the Sabbath in a building flooded with daylight from its remarkably large windows? Without the visual foci of Christian iconography (even the cross), without stained glass, elaborate altars, choir stalls, or baptismal fonts, would the congregants attend the pulpit language more intensively? (Their chosen text was from Romans 10:17: "So then faith cometh by hearing, and hearing by the word of God.") Would

2. The key source, unavailable to me during our work on Old South, is Kevin M. Sweeney, "Meetinghouses, Town Houses, and Churches: Changing Perceptions of Sacred and Secular Space in Southern New England, 1720–1830," *Winterthur Portfolio* 28 (Spring 1993): 59–93. See also Peter Benes, ed., *New England Meeting House and Church: 1630–1850*, Dublin Seminar for New England Folklife, Annual Proceedings, 1979 (Boston: Boston University, 1979).

they hold even more dearly their Bibles? Or would they use the building's excellent sight lines to see who was sitting up front, in the pews assigned to the wealthy, the well-educated, and the well-born? The room's windows thus made the social hierarchy as legible as the gospel message.

Our interpretive plan laid out an experiential pathway for visitors that mimicked the sequence of those attending Sabbath services, political gatherings, or community forums over the centuries. AHW's plan thus split the entire Old South space and the visit experience into three parts and three zones: (1) arrival, welcome, and orientation; (2) the core interpretive experience; and (3) response, wrap-up, and takeaways. The first aimed to integrate the visitor into the centuries-long chain of people who have come to Old South for worship, for political deliberation and action, and as tourists. The second, itself divided into two parts, invited visitors to immerse themselves in each of the architectural settings, social arrangements, and historical significances of the building's major eras. Then they could take seats in the center pews and listen in on audio reconstructions of the debates that resounded in the hall over time. The third zone proposed gathering visitor responses to the great questions posed by Old South's debates through interactive electronic media and summarizing the site's contribution to the city's religious and intellectual life, the Revolution, and the movement for historic presentation.

A wide array of interpretive media would represent this sequence without distracting attention from the centrality of "meetinghouse-ness." Near the entry, visitors could explore a scale model reconstructing the evolution of the architectural design. Further along, they could use headsets to listen in on recorded snippets of sermons, incendiary speeches, and lectures reconstructed from Old South's history. Clues to the experience of congregants were embedded in mock artifacts tactically arranged around the space, re-creations of the contrast between the "box" pews of 1729, expressive of patriarchal sovereignty, and the more egalitarian "slip" pews, benches open at both ends, installed in the 1850s. Mock hourglasses interpreted the duration of religious services. Mock signposts laid out the order of services. And so on.

VISITORS AS CAST MEMBERS IN AN ONGOING HISTORICAL DRAMA

Over the course of the 1980s, exhibition making had been transformed. The differences were often subtle and almost always unstated. But as a cultural activity, the work of curators and designers had been profoundly changed.

Our earnest efforts, assisted by funding from the National Endowment for the Humanities, to transform history museums into miniclassrooms for the new social history had—in my view—failed. We had lost the balance between overview and immersion. Or rather, our interpretive exhibitions in the gallery had failed to deliver the promised mastery of our chosen historical themes for our audience. We knew that we were not pouring knowledge directly into our visitors' heads, as if they could be opened like Terry Gilliam's cartoons on *Monty Python*. We had created learning exercises that were engaging and interactive, and we thought of our visitors as fellow explorers. But the exercise was too cold. Visitors did not share our view of the past as a giant database, and they seemed reluctant to join us in analyzing how all that data could be sliced and diced into typologies or ideal types— the constituent parts of cities, different economic landscapes, diverse ways of organizing family roles, a succession of architectural styles, and so on. Visitors were not chart makers. History was not a clinical investigation.

By the end of the decade, we had moved toward a theatrical analogy, inviting our visitors to see themselves as cast members in an ongoing drama. Whenever they read a historical text, watched a historical documentary, or visited a museum, they themselves were part of the historical narrative. They were not in a de-historicized room, looking at the past through a window. There was no radical break between the place itself (the real "Pittsburgh") when it might have been an "authentic" site of manufacturing or consumption, and when it became a (less-than-authentic) destination for tourists, "a Pittsburgh of the imagination." Tourism was a part of the place's history, and tourists were actors in its life-course just as much as its original settlers or the steelworkers or their unemployed children. A whole shelf of books came off the press during the 1980s portraying the tourist as a new and special breed and tourist destinations as a new type of modern or postmodern place. I was skeptical that one could make these sharp separations. Tourism and pilgrimage are ancient human activities. Pausanius wrote a guidebook to Greece in the second century C.E., and pilgrims to Jerusalem, Mecca, Santiago de Compostela, and Mont St. Michel have been buying souvenirs of their visits for more than a millennium.

But even much more mundane sites have always made accommodations for travelers and provided guideposts that "branded" the place as a valuable destination. The "stranger's path" is a part of every town's geography and economy. Every Polish immigrant who arrived in western Pennsylvania looking for work was, initially, a tourist. She contributed to the site's evolution before she did a stitch of work, just as much as her great-granddaughter does when she visits from Los Angeles. One day I had been a tourist at osv, and the next day I was a museum worker. Had I become a different creature?

Visitors did not need or want to be treated as gawkers. They liked the dignity of connecting their own history, including their visits, to the history of the place. As the title of Peter Laslett's book, *The World We Have Lost* (New York: Scribner, 1965), suggests, the social history scholarship of the 1960s betrayed a tinge of nostalgia. At osv and in my "typological" exhibitions, I had encouraged visitors to contrast that world with "our own." But is the past really lost, or is it still evolving into our present and future? We are not outside the processes of history, peering in. We have a partial view of our situation, of course, but so too did each of our predecessors. No perspective is omniscient. Momentary immersions in the past, which is what museum exhibitions might offer, were efforts to discover, draw out connections, and alter the course of history by our attentiveness to one story and our neglect of another.

Coming back home to New York in 1983 made an enormous difference. For twenty years or so, I had loved Boston and New England as a stage on which to act out all my adolescent dreams—assimilation into a society of bourgeois comfort and intellectual seriousness, of refined tastes and earnest commitment. But something was missing. The region's pitched political battles—between ethnic "Southie" and waspy Weston—seemed very far from my own concerns. The culture was immaculately curated. The music on wgbh and the art at the Boston Museum of Fine Arts were the finest in the world, I knew, and the Boston Athenaeum was (and still is) my vision of paradise. Brooklyn, by contrast, was a mess; but it felt like my mess. Crack vials blossomed outside my brownstone every morning. The drainpipe, my car battery, and even the computer in our basement office had been purloined, probably to pay for somebody's fix. Graffiti were everywhere, the subways were a horror, and almost every streetlamp in Prospect Park was shattered. My son was mugged coming home from school one afternoon, and a little kid no older than twelve tried to jump me as I returned from a Manhattan meeting.

But the streets felt familiar, and the ionized air after a thunderstorm reminded me of how speedily we had been sent to "play outside" as children, just as soon as the rain stopped. I seemed to have returned home endowed with a box of Crayola 64, able now to put all sorts of colors onto my black-and-white memories of Brooklyn in the 1950s. I retraced old passages. Although I was now living on the western edge of Prospect Park, a no-man's-land for Jewish kids in my teens, Brooklyn's old turf boundaries seemed to have been turned upside down and reset to accommodate a flood of immigrants from Asia, the Caribbean, and Africa. I watched as Jack's Bar on the corner of Seventh Avenue and Ninth Street, where a patron had been shot dead in 1947 for predicting the imminent demise of the Dodgers in the World Series, was turned into a semifancy hamburger joint with imported beers. Gentrification was on its way. From my former perch at the top of Beacon Hill in Boston, I had been looking down on a world of transformations. In Brooklyn, pretty much a flat landscape, I was thrown into the middle of all those changes.

And on the radio WNYC was playing a lot of concert music written by people my age or younger. At the end of those crummy subway rides, you would ascend to find new art everywhere—conceptual art, video art, performance art, public art. There was dancing in the streets, crossing disciplines and genres, speaking pidgin, art imported from Texas and Transylvania.

One event sticks out: Matthew Maguire's production in June 1986 of *The Memory Theater of Giulio Camillo* within the cavernous vaults of the Brooklyn Bridge anchorage. That evening, as I scrambled to follow the commedia dell'arte actors and musicians passing through seven different dreamscapes of a fictional seventeenth-century Italian mystic, I saw my work in a new light. Didn't my exhibition visitors also confront triggers to memory and meaning as they passed along the gallery pathways we designed? Forget the classroom. Imagine the museum, imagine the historically self-aware street, as an opportunity to confront the sights, the voices, and the pulsing moments of another time and place. Imagine always being in at least two places at once. Isn't that what diaspora means?

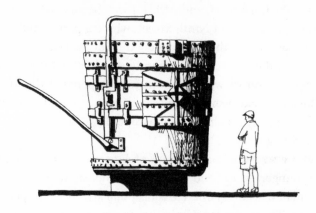

For a century after the American Civil War, U.S. cities grew by developing functionally and demographically distinguishable districts: the civic center, the financial district, downtown shopping streets, an entertainment area, parks or beaches, zones for heavy and light industry, waterfronts or rail yards with warehouses and distribution routes nearby, residential sections distinguished by race, class, and ethnicity, and so on. Every city had more or less the same roster. Each zone had its distinctive architecture, its own decorum, its particular clock and calendar.

In the late 1960s, things began to be jumbled up, and by 2000 every sort of use could be found almost everywhere. Artists began to colonize disused industrial space as production facilities and used the parks and streets as exhibition and performance spaces. Urban Times Squares lost their monopoly on nighttime attractions. Inner-city row-houses, often converted during depression and war years into boarding and rooming houses, were restored to single-family domiciles or condominiums by middle-class families. Developers and local civic associations slapped new names on old neighborhoods, often evoking preindustrial landscapes: Soundview, Boerum Hill, Carroll Gardens.

Some of the energy of that boundary breaking can be found in the spreading appeal of the term "museum without walls." The phrase had its origins in Stuart Gilbert's translation of the title of part 1 of André Malraux's *Psychologie de l'Art*, published in the United States in 1949–50.[1] Malraux's French title was *Le Musée Imaginaire*, and his book investigates the significance of the public's widening access to inexpensive images of famous artworks. For Malraux, it was revolutionary that one could juxtapose color reproductions of photographs of a piece of Chinese jade with a British Victorian portrait in oils. He claimed that art had henceforth lost its parochial boundaries. But so far as I know, Malraux did not use the phrase "musée sans murs" in his own text, and he certainly did not intend for the walls to be taken literally.

Twenty years after the translation's initial publication, the term began to be applied to an ever-widening variety of efforts to package and distribute reproductions of artwork: a film series, packets of slides, videodisks, CD-ROMs, and more recently, smartphone apps. Paradoxical as it seems, in 1976 a Philadelphia group created its own indoor "museum without walls," a giant arcade of 25,000 art images on sixty-four screens. (It failed two years later.)

By 1977, the phrase had jumped the boundary from art to history. Cities, perhaps beginning with Annapolis, Maryland, began to describe their heritage areas as "a museum without walls." Organizations that mounted their programs in the city streets, like Boston's Museum of Afro-American History, called themselves a "museum without walls." By the early 1980s, the term described any site of interest outside the formal, ostensibly confining "walls" of actual institutions like museums and historic houses. In 1981, a *New York Times* travel writer described the ancient Korean capital of Kyongju as a "museum without walls." By mid-decade, nearly any town-beautification scheme earned the sobriquet, even when it didn't draw attention to any specific features of the place. Thirty years later, the National Trust's annual meeting was holding do-it-yourself sessions for local preservationists on transforming their downtowns into "museums without walls." Any program that lent art or artifacts to schools could be called a "museum without walls."

---

1. *The Museum without Walls*, pt. 1 of Malraux's *The Psychology of Art*, 3 vols., trans. Stuart Gilbert (New York: Pantheon, 1949–50). In his subsequent book, *Picasso's Mask* (in French, *La tête obsidienne*), Malraux reports his disappointment at the effort of the Fondation Maeght in Vence, France, in 1973 to concretize this notion of "a museum within the imagination" (Malraux, *Picasso's Mask*, trans. June Guicharnaud with Jacques Guicharnaud [New York: Holt, Rinehart, and Winston, 1976]).

For some museum professionals, of course, the term had negative implications. It suggested that museums were confining places, depriving the public of some form of liberation and personal enlightenment they could instead achieve in the unsanctified outdoor landscape, away from the interference of meddlesome curators, admissions desks, and experts with all their fancy jargon. Tear down the walls! Objets d'art, you have nothing to lose but your wall mounts!

But I preferred to think about the term another way. I had already tested the limits of gallery installations. The notion of a museum without walls opened up the possibility of applying the same concentrated gaze on the "secular" landscape, the world at the edges of our notice, as we have in looking at what is customarily celebrated. Not the statue in the town square but the men and women who lounged at its base during lunchtime. Could we "museumize" or "museumify"—use what term you will to describe our heightened attentiveness—the living cityscape? Could we transform it into a shared storyscape?

A MORE INCLUSIVE HISTORY

Fortuitously, the 1980s also marked a turning point in the culture's view of what was historically worthy. Many old-line historical societies, long neglectful of the industrial and workaday areas of their towns and of the people who lived there, awoke to discover that their constituencies among the local business elite and their spouses had vanished. Newly minted professionals, trained in the new social history, recognized that they needed to attract audiences from among the new arrivals, often ethnically and racially different from the town's founding fathers and mothers. Stories of the original settlers and exhibitions of the oldest, the first, and the loveliest relics in the town's history no longer sparked instant reverence. Teachers and tourism officials urged that programs address issues that are more relevant and employ more modern museum technologies. As government support became more important, programs for schoolchildren, elders, and nontraditional publics celebrated the societies' new relevance.

Public officials in Orlando, Florida, offered space in the now-vacant county courthouse to the county historical society, provided it could contribute to the redevelopment of the downtown. The Ella Sharp Museum in Jackson, Michigan—with a young director and a passionate group of young educators and docents—wanted to connect their art and history exhibition galleries, the historic house museum, and space for community events. In Philadelphia, an umbrella group called Germantown Preserved hoped to connect the interpretive energies of seven or eight splendid historic houses and to find ways to make their high-style architecture and decorative arts collections more accessible and engaging to the racially mixed and economically troubled community around them. American History Workshop (AHW) kept preaching the gospel that downtown revitalization meant encompassing the entire community's history, not merely the disparate landmarks of the old narrative.

Public art projects, akin to the REPOhistory markers but with much bolder intentions to redefine public space, interjected oppositional or whimsical histories into the urban landscape. In 1988, artist Andrew Leicester celebrated Cincinnati's 200th birthday by erecting four flying pigs, reminders of the city's history as a major meatpacking center, as a gateway to the new Bicentennial Commons Park. More discursively, a beautifully crafted sculpture and timeline by artists Sheila Levrant de Bretteville and Betye Saar honors the life of Biddy Mason, the African American woman who fostered the development of a black community in nineteenth-century Los Angeles. A mural and a riverside park in St. Louis celebrates the life of Mary Meachum, a free woman of color who accompanied a daring escape of enslaved people across the Mississippi, and at the same time tarnishes the gilt-edge reputation of local slaveholder Henry Shaw, who established Tower Grove Park and laid the groundwork for the world-renowned Missouri Botanical Garden.[2]

All these projects lowered the threshold once separating the august Museum from the lowly street, precious Culture from commerce and daily life. The museum building or visitors' center became, in the new parlance, a "base camp" from which journeys of exploration (into the untamed city?) could be launched. Sometimes, as in Charleston, South Carolina, the visitors' center orientation program could be combined with convenient parking, jitney connections to the historic downtown, and even arrangements for lodging and entertainment. At the very least, such centers dispensed handy maps and, more recently, apps directing visitors from one significant site to another.

I was seeking a form of landscape interpretation that would integrate

2. Dolores Hayden, *The Power of Place: Urban Landscapes as Public History* (Cambridge: MIT Press, 1995). Andrew Hurley, "Narrating the Urban Waterfront: The Role of Public History in Community Revitalization," *Public Historian* 28, no. 4 (Fall 2006): 19–50, describes the often compromising process of locating the park and winning public approval.

space with event, local circumstance with major historical patterns, the physicality of the environment with the layers of human settlement and cultural reinvention. Amazingly enough, such interpretation became possible in the unlikeliest of American places: the regions left desolate by economic decline in the 1960s and 1970s. The most ambitious programs to embed historical interpretation in the ongoing life of American communities, to take in the stories of historically silenced populations, and to allow for a continuum of narratives throughout a site's history occurred in the deindustrializing cities of America's Rust Belt. Seldom attracting interest from old-line preservationists and scarcely capable of organizing their own revitalization programs, these former industrial cities—from paper mill towns in Maine to grain-processing centers in Iowa—proved to be the canvas for a new kind of landscape interpretation. Without trying to do so, the campaign to preserve elements of the American industrial heritage by state and federal organizations—not academic historians, not architects, not educators, and not publicists—revolutionized the concept of what was "historical."

From the 1930s, the federal government had supported small but critical efforts to survey, document, collect, and publicly interpret the evidences of the nation's architectural and technological history. The National Park Service (NPS) had become the locus of this expertise, housing the Historic American Buildings Survey (established 1933), the National Register of Historic Places (1966), the Historic American Engineering Record (1969), and the Historic American Landscape Survey (2000). The Society for Industrial Archeology (SIA), formed in 1971, spearheaded the historical documentation and analysis of technological artifacts and systems, as well as the buildings, transportation networks, and communities that surrounded them. I recall joining an SIA tour of sites in Massachusetts and Rhode Island in 1972, along with an impressive variety of engineers, curators, architects, and preservation activists, and plenty of old Gasoline Alley tinkerers who loved getting their hands dirty. Curators of the new National Museum of History and Technology at the Smithsonian (opened 1964) played an important role, in keeping with the institution's emphasis on mechanical artifacts. The journal *Technology and Culture* was among the first to commission reviews of exhibitions and public interpretive programs.

As capital flight began to endanger older manufacturing cities and towns in the 1960s and 1970s, and as the errors of massive urban renewal and subsidized suburbanization became clearer, a movement to celebrate, commemorate, and preserve the nation's industrial heritage gathered force. The technology enthusiasts took the lead.

The window of opportunity was closing. Amid the massive movement to the Sunbelt, the allocation of congressional seats to the Northeast was dwindling, but seniority in key appropriations committees still rested with members from Johnstown, Pennsylvania, and Lowell, Massachusetts. (The state of West Virginia, of course, had its own strategy for economic development through federal investment in the person of Senator Robert Byrd.) Within state legislatures, suburban growth left older industrial cities economically weaker but politically still significant. In Massachusetts, New York, Pennsylvania, and Ohio, legislatures authorized state industrial heritage parks—about a dozen in each state—in 1978–82.

A similar process occurred on the national level. Congress steadily expanded the realm of the NPS in these years by designating new parks in Altoona and Johnstown, Pennsylvania; in the Blackstone Valley between Worcester, Massachusetts, and Providence, Rhode Island; and most especially in Lowell, Massachusetts. As with state marker programs, the NPS had concentrated previously on individual and often isolated historical monuments. In the 1980s, it began to think across time and space, designating national heritage areas and corridors. The NPS usually followed and aimed to strengthen local and state commitments to preservation and interpretation of industrial heritage.

On the state level, development of these urban parks was assigned to the state parks departments, which had previously focused only on "natural" areas in coastal, rural, or wilderness regions. They brought many new hands to the public history workbench: state bureaucrats, local officials, development interests, and amateur or "indigenous" historians. In the best of cases, local librarians, curriculum developers, and advocates for newly arrived (and mostly minority) communities were invited to join the deliberations.

For fifteen years or so, AHW worked continually on one or another of these projects. The NPS or the state agencies coordinated the planning, managing a series of staged contracts for conceptualization, design development, construction documents, fabrication, and installation. For the early stages of such projects, AHW hired on as interpretive planning consultants to teams led by architectural and planning firms, and which included marketing and management experts as well. The heritage park invited us to think of the entire industrial city as an entity, even if the interpretive installations were limited to one former mill building or downtown business block. Now we were interpreting the history of Fall River, not only its cotton textile production sites.

The industrial heritage parks pushed AHW further away from defining interpretation as the presentation of complex, verbalized themes. But now we were running into opposition from professional staff converted to the cause of using sites to teach history. It had become standard procedure in the field to begin such projects by convening scholarly panels and creating a list of key concepts. At Lowell, NPS staff and consultants identified five such themes: waterpower, technology, labor, capital, and the industrial city. As they chose sites for interpretive installations and programs—exhibitions, environmental re-creations, tours, school visit programs, and special events—they checked off the core themes each would address. In 1992, NPS historian Marty Blatt described the experience of visitors in the weave room at the Boott mill complex at Lowell:

> Visitors to the Boott pass into the mill yard using the same bridge over the Eastern Canal that mill workers used for over 100 years. Tracing the footsteps of these mill workers, they enter the museum and encounter a partly recreated early-20th-century weave room, with 90 operating power looms. The looms are beltdriven, with their harnesses rocking and their shuttles flying, and some will actually produce cloth. The visit to the weave room provides a frame of reference for subsequent exhibits on the industrialization of America, the textile production process, the work experience, America's fascination with technology, the decline of the mills and a glimpse at Lowell today, and work in the 21st century.[3]

I asked myself, what does it mean to provide a frame of reference? How, actually, does an immersion in the weave room lead to reflections on the economics, technology, and global expansion of textile production? Like Blatt and his colleagues, I had once assumed that illustration was instruction. But all too often, I ultimately found, this cascade of rich ideas—delivered on graphic panels in exhibits or orally by rangers, interpreters, and educators—simply overwhelmed visitors or, worse, distracted them from paying attention to what was unique, absorbing the whole sensory environment of the textile factory as a nexus of production and labor. Site visits, we observed, are hardly the best places to read or listen to verbal accounts of such complex historical phenomena. Would the park interpreter's message about parallels between nineteenth-century New England and twenty-

3. Blatt, "America's Labor History: The Lowell Story," *CRM* 15, no. 5 (1992): 1–5.

first-century Malaysia, for example, help a single mom from Somerville, perhaps a shoe buyer for a Boston retailer, as she tries to explain her Greek great-grandparents' settlement in America to her two kids?

As happened to many progressive teachers, it finally dawned on me that the visit begins and ends in the minds of our visitors and not in our list of curricular objectives. If, then, concepts flow out of the visitors' experiences, different themes should be presented distinctively. Rather than hang up informational signs and pass out brochures at every turn, we should design dramatic experiences to fuse the sensory and the verbal, the kinesthetic encounter and the historical concept, the visitors' pathway and the site's story. This meant reframing the industrial city as a sequence of dramas in which visitors as actors would encounter fragments of the past—streets, buildings, and waterways; technological artifacts and processes; traces of social, cultural, political, and religious life; and most important, stories of the local people—as "props" and "cues" to help visitors script their own understandings of work, family, and community in the past.

ACT 1: THE INDUSTRIAL COMMUNITY

The AHW team rethought our plans and began to construe these industrial communities as three-act plays. Our first act provided an overview. It located the city in its geographical context and described its origins as a community planned and planted by capitalist investors. The second narrative introduced visitors to a close, kinesthetic, highly sensory relationship with the industrial production process and its machinery. The third story addressed the construction and sustaining of a community among industrial workers and their households, often linked by ethnic origins; these involved visitors in explorations of family life, religion, housing, foodways, play, health, civic and social engagement, and other aspects of urban life outside the world of work.

In each of these heritage park projects, we placed Act 1 in the proposed visitors' center, usually located in a redeveloped commercial space in the downtown core. Here we announced that creating an industrial city on this site had been a bold, aggressive action, requiring the engineering of the landscape and of a human workforce, but with social and economic consequences that could hardly been foreseen. We implied that there was nothing "natural" or "necessary" in creating manufacturing towns.

In the early years of such projects, we illustrated this story with enlarged or projected woodcuts of the agricultural landscape that had preceded the heroic exploitation of waterpower "at the falls." Interpretations of the trans-

Orient visitors to the topography of Wheeling, W.Va., through a scale model of the city (Wheeling National Heritage Area interpretive plan, 1995).

formed landscape aimed to restore a sense of verticality to the countryside. Even before the era of Google Maps, modern-day visitors traveling to the park on highways easily lost track of when they were ascending and descending the local hills, crossing small waterways, or rolling through "the flats." Act 1's interpretive exercise tried to re-create the physicality of the route by which historical figures came to the industrial town. We measured the pace of their journey in weeks and days rather than hours and minutes; reminded them of the hazards of travel on road, river, or rail; told stories of seasonal freshets or ice floes at fords along the river; and mentally erased the modern-day signposts to dislocate imaginary travelers. Then we "inserted" the engineering works piece by piece: drainage and grading, metalled and macadam roads, ferries and bridges, standardized rail gauges, stations, marked junctions, steam and gasoline vehicular engines, telegraph, telephone, and standard time zones—that historically converted this particular landscape from an obstacle course into a tool for production. To accomplish this in Wheeling, West Virginia, for example, AHW proposed constructing a large-scale model of the Ohio Valley town, focusing on the convergence of the mighty Ohio and the narrow Wheeling Creek and linking the city to its agricultural and industrial networks.

The second interpretive engagement explored the technology of production. How could we help visitors understand the process of manufacturing in each of these places? Beyond the individual machines and the sequence of operations in the making of textiles, for example, we wanted to communicate the idea that all of this work had been brought together in an integrated system. To many Americans, modern machine production is miraculous. Inexplicably complex processes transform unfamiliar materials into familiar commodities almost instantly. An automobile assembly line can be comprehended. But a textile plant, like an oil refinery or a steel mill, is a mystery.

Museums and science centers are good at explicating machines. They can slow down or speed up processes. They can use graphic diagrams, animated films, and mechanical models to represent the physical process. In the world of history museums, an early standard for such a representation was set by the Merrimack Valley Textile Museum in North Andover (now the American Textile History Museum in Lowell) and its handsome 1965 exhibition *Wool Technology and the Industrial Revolution*.[4] The exhibition graphics allowed visitors to feel the dramatic importance of each advance and to take pleasure in the fine housing of these early machines and in the fabrics they produced.

But the cool, classic modernist aesthetics of the North Andover museum gallery, sited in a tidy suburb, masked any human participation in the manufacturing process. Each machine had been orphaned from its teeming siblings, quieted, pomaded, and lit like a portrait by Yousuf Karsh. The old weaver's bench seemed to invite a viewer into a bodily relationship with the few foot-powered looms on display, as if working the loom was akin to driving an exquisite Lamborghini. This followed a more general trend. Most often, history museums have interpreted technology by preserving and presenting a line of unique surviving examples of mechanical genius. The Smithsonian's Museum of History and Technology arranged its initial exhibition, *Growth of the United States*, in 1967 as a succession of techni-

---

4. Thomas W. Leavitt, "The Merrimack Valley Textile Museum," *Technology and Culture* 8 (April 1967): 204–6. The "handbook" of the exhibition, with photographs of the installation and replicas of the graphics, was published as *Merrimack Valley Textile Museum* (North Andover, Mass.: MVTM, 1965). Malcolm Grear designed both the exhibition and the handbook.

cally sophisticated machines—in agriculture, manufacturing, communications, and other fields.

In Washington, D.C., as in North Andover, this interpretive approach turned the exhibition floor into an extension of the collection storage area and, in the process, erased information about the kinesthetic, sensory, or social experience of the past. Only the objects mattered. They were the stars of the show and cast a long shadow over the anonymous masses of operators. As with other survivors, the museum's machines tell heroic stories, of inventors, mill owners, and even of curators and conservators, but seldom of the multitudes who spent ten- and twelve-hour days making cloth. They win the affection of enthusiasts who can detail every model. Engravings, patent drawings, or models—often elegantly rendered—supplement the machines themselves in museum displays.

For me, nothing in the museum world's representation of textile production had ever equaled the experience of visiting the working woolen mill in Harrisville, New Hampshire, which began in the 1820s and operated until 1970. Shafts of light through huge factory windows swept through oceans of lint thrown upward by the spinning machines. The pounding of the looms hammered our guide's explanations into gibberish. The workers' garb—jeans and sweatshirts cut off at the elbow—felt even trashier when compared with the delicate heather- and burgundy-hued John Meyer of Norwich pullovers they were making that day.

Could we mount museum exhibitions that would allow visitors to explore the phenomenological, moment-to-moment interrelationship of such workers and their tools and settings? Could we use them to create a multisensory, durational immersion that would help visitors see how decisions were made on the shop floor or in the mineshaft, how the workday progressed, and how skill was developed and exercised? In the new industrial heritage parks of the 1980s, social and labor historians wanted to present the human engagement with work in narratives like these. But in most sites, technology won out over representing the conditions of labor. Machine enthusiasts overwhelm labor historians. (And the labor historians often put more emphasis on the social origins, the cultural contexts, and the contests for control of the shop floor and for higher wages and benefits than on the routines, crises, and ordinary strains of the work itself.)

Paradoxically, as the movement to preserve nineteenth- and early twentieth-century industrial architecture (mill buildings, workers' housing, warehouses, lofts, and wharf facilities) succeeded, structures were adapted for residential and commercial uses and lost their stigmatic identification with lower-class life and labor. Seen as embarrassing remnants of failed enterprises and liable to "slum clearance" in the immediate post–World War II years, they now became fashionable. During the long century of industrialization, status-conscious respectability had made worksites and workers' tenements discomforting. Businessmen ventured there for business or to explore the tawdriness of "the wrong side of the tracks." Proper women stayed away, lest they become tainted by being seen there. No one who was anyone would want to live in rooms with exposed brick walls and unsheathed columns, beams, and rafters. But by the 1980s, perfectly respectable middle-class city homes were stripping away plaster from walls and ceilings to reveal raw construction materials beneath. Developers offered newly constructed "loft" buildings on lots from which manufacturing and warehousing had departed long before.

While the middle-class children and grandchildren of mill workers or miners are often proud of their forebears, they seemed to shy away from focusing on the day-to-day labors on the shop floor or in the mineshaft. After all, many report family conversations in which the older generation did everything to dissuade their offspring from following them into these difficult jobs. (In this they resemble the descendants of enslaved and emancipated African Americans, who want little to do with the often degrading details of work in rice or cotton fields.) By contrast, farm museums linger long over the ennobling rhythms of agricultural work and celebrate their virtues.

Over the years some curators and educators fought back by creating exhibition elements that celebrated the dexterity, inventiveness, adaptability, improvisational genius, and even brute strength and endurance of skilled workers. In our program for the Attleboro Area Industrial Museum in 1981–82, we developed four interpretive areas in addition to a live demonstration of jewelry-making craft. They included the Shop Floor, focusing on dexterity; the Bottom Line, addressing management skills; the Drawing Board, exploring engineering and design; and the Store Window, assessing marketing and sales. In other words, the idea of skill could be used, conceptually, to link all the elements of the modern industrial enterprise. In Wheeling, we planned a Bridge-Building park, in which civil engineering concepts and ironworking skills would be interpreted through hands-on playground equipment.

But by and large we have failed to bring the daily experience of industrial work to the fore. The protagonists of the industrial history narrative in American museums remain capitalists such as the Boston Associates, who

organized the mills in Waltham and Lowell, or the inventors who introduced faster and more complex machines. For several years, AHW worked
with local partners to create a Minnesota Labor Interpretive Center, but
funds for its construction were vetoed by Governor Jesse Ventura in 1999.
Failing to reconstruct and represent the experience of industrial labor has
been one of my greatest professional disappointments.

ACT 3: THE ETHNIC COMMUNITY

Finally, the third thematic and experiential focus on our work on industrial
heritage sites addressed the immigrant and ethnic communities formed by
workers and their families. Given the political grounding of these projects,
this was not surprising. The NPS's planners and consulting historians hoped
originally to focus its interpretation at the new park in Lowell, the first explicitly to celebrate industrial labor, on the life and work of "the Lowell
girls." These daughters of New England farmers came there to work in the
1840s, lived in healthful boardinghouses, and cultivated their protofeminist
cultural identities by literary, religious, and political activity. But, as Cathy
Stanton's *The Lowell Experiment: Public History in a Postindustrial City*
(Amherst: University of Massachusetts Press, 2006) shows, the sympathies
of current city leaders lay with their Irish and French Canadian immigrant
forebears rather than these pioneering Yankee lasses, and soon the interpretive priorities shifted to those mid-nineteenth-century working-class
families.

In AHW's industrial heritage projects, in fact, the history of families,
women, children, and the elderly—as well as the parts of the workforce
outside the factory gates themselves—could be elucidated in this third
thematic focus. In exhibitions, tours, and educational programs, we documented the home, the multifamily dwelling, the multihousehold street, the
commercial district, the schools, the religious buildings, and other sites
of social gathering. One of my favorite interpretive proposals, never executed, was Heinrich's Day, in which visitors would be invited to trace an
often forgetful, imaginary fourteen-year-old German American boy as he
made his way around Centre Wheeling, an immigrant neighborhood in the
Ohio River city. Heinrich mistakenly leaves his father's tools at the Centre Market, his schoolbooks at the singing society, his market basket at the
First German Zion Evangelical Church, and the dandelion tea from the
local "Apotheke" at the B&O Railroad Station, where he'd gone to pick up
his aunt arriving from the East. As they visit each of these streetscape elements, visitors would in effect be surveying the geography and lifeways of

Follow Heinrich as he runs errands in Centre Wheeling,
linking a dozen sites into one forgetful teenager's day.

the German immigrant community in Wheeling, but through the eyes of
a young nineteenth-century child rather than a historian. Modeled on my
own childhood navigations in East New York, the plan for Heinrich's Day
tried to turn the exploration of a tightly knit ethnic community into self-
guided experiential learning. Rather than bedeck the city with overly long
and hard-to-read historical markers or graphic panels with obscure images,
we wanted to reanimate the streets with characters, with bodies, with life
situations.

10 ::: VISITORS REINSERT HUMAN PRESENCE INTO THE LANDSCAPE

The Lower East Side Tenement Museum (LESTM) in Manhattan was a landmark in the development of American History Workshop's interpretive approach, refocusing from themes to experiences and deploying the skills that visitors brought with them. I began to work on this project in 1984 when it was still linked to the effort to save the 1887 Eldridge Street Synagogue, the first great house of worship built by Eastern European Jews in New York City. I brought a lot of personal history to the interpretation of the Lower East Side, which had flourished for almost a century and a half as a first stop in America for thousands of immigrants from dozens of countries. I never lost sight of the fact that my father was born in 1914 in a fifth-floor apartment at the tenement at 39 Essex Street, above a pickle store; had read his first books (after showing that his hands had been scrubbed clean) at the public library in Seward Park; started school soon thereafter; and sold Yiddish newspapers on the streets and subways at age eight, before the family moved to Brooklyn. And in 1928, a tenement at 35 Madison Street, a few blocks west, had been my mother's first home in the United States. Whatever nostalgia I might have had for those days was obliterated by her astonishingly detailed and astute memories of being transformed from a twelve-year-old schoolgirl in a Polish shtetl into a sixteen-year-old garment worker helping her family survive the Great Depression in New York. These streets laughed with me, and they cried; but they never left me unmoved.

The LESTM was equally a milestone in the widening focus of American history museums. When I began my public history career in 1967, there were almost no historic house museums in the United States that preserved and presented the life and the belongings of anyone but the rich and famous, except for a few pioneer homesteads. No museum exhibitions told the story of urban working-class people or explored the experience of immigration or enslavement in any detail. On my first visit to the Chicago Historical Society in 1971, I was stunned to discover that the elevated cars, the Cubs and the White Sox, Bronzeville, the stockyards, and anyone of non-Anglo-Saxon extraction were all invisible. (I do recall seeing a painting of John Adams and wondering why it was gracing these walls.) Five years later, Harold Skramstad's staff created *Chicago: Creating New Traditions*, a breakthrough treatment of Chicago's innovative contributions to American culture, urban design, architecture, literature, and social reform. But even this superb show viewed immigrant and working-class life largely through the eyes of urban reformers.

Baltimore's Peale Museum went a bit further in 1981 with a new core exhibition, *Rowhouse: A Baltimore Style of Living*. The show impressively brought attention to the living conditions of "average" Baltimoreans. But it left me a little cold, since it was organized chiefly as an ambitious scholarly and curatorial exploration of five big subjects: (1) architectural history, including rowhouse design, construction, and aesthetics; (2) domestic history, including furnishings, daily activity, and use of space; (3) technological history, including public utility service and production of building components and furnishings; (4) economic history, including commercial activities, local transportation systems, and rowhouse builders; and (5) geography, including the spatial expansion of the city and ethnic and racial differentiation.[1]

Rowhouse celebrated the importance of this kind of housing, but it studiously avoided exploring the daily lives—the work, the families, or the religious, cultural, or ethnic lives—of its residents. The voices of rowhouse dwellers at home or in their communities were totally drowned out by the social historians and curators, who used the exhibition instead to display the research and artifact collections they had gathered. And the words "style of living" in the exhibition title stuck in my craw.

The LESTM was different. Among my earliest undertakings for the museum were a series of "Peddler's Pack" tours of the neighborhood. In various New York libraries, I discovered and copied a batch of manuscript documents, memoirs, and travelers' accounts. (Henry James's visit to "the

---

1. Roger B. White, "Whither the Urban History Exhibit? The Peale Museum's 'Rowhouse,'" *Technology and Culture* 24 (January 1983): 76–90.

Ghetto," recounted in *The American Scene* [1907], was the most perplexing.) I packed them up and led a dozen or so visitors on hour-long excursions. When we stopped at food stores, I asked one person to read a recipe book and decode the necessary ingredients. At a local elementary school, someone else read aloud from a 1920s reader and another recited from a student's report card. On the stoop of one tenement, we read the names of dozens of residents from the building's census return for 1900.

I vividly recall the discovery in 1988 of the tenement at 97 Orchard, unoccupied since the 1930s, above the underwear shop on the ground floor. And I remember climbing the stairs, feeling my way in the dark, pushing aside the smells of vacancy, and entering an apartment on the second floor: broken glass, empty seltzer bottles, an inventory of men's coats and pants penciled on the wall, the horrific twin toilet stalls in the hallway, and a nailed-shut transom over a door between the apartments, evidence that the first fire-safety laws, passed in 1867, could be easily bypassed.

It had been about twenty-five years since Ada Louise Huxtable dealt a first death blow (using Colonial Williamsburg as her target) to scraping away all later additions to a historical structure, but a new orthodoxy had taken hold. Restoring 97 Orchard Street to its condition at the time of its construction in 1863–64 would mean destroying the physical evidence of thousands of its residents in its long history. (And that would mean ignoring the hugely important era of massive immigration to the Lower East Side in the three decades before 1914, which would in turn weaken efforts to gather community support for the museum venture.) Further, the restoration of the Great Hall at Ellis Island had recently been opened to the public and had given a bad name to an overzealous erasure of historical grime. Ruins were suddenly in fashion in the United States, perhaps for the first time. The history of 97 Orchard Street did not, after all, end when Mayor Fiorello LaGuardia required the owner to install toilets within the apartments on the top four floors in the late 1930s and the owner decided it was not worth his expense. The ensuing fifty years also had their stories to tell.

Ruth Abram's background in social work shaped the museum's distinctive goals: "to promote tolerance and historical perspective through the presentation and interpretation of the variety of immigrant experiences on Manhattan's Lower East Side, a gateway to America." In the popular mind, the old Lower East Side had become identified with Jewish immigrants from Eastern Europe, but the diversity of those immigrants was important to Abram's vision. So she initially assigned apartments to each of New York's major ethnic groups: African Americans, Irish, Germans, Eastern European Jews, Italians, Chinese, and so on. And she contracted with teams of scholars to construct composite family biographies for each of these distinct ethnic groups.

After the German and the Irish groups reported, it was plain that historians are not very good dramatists. Both groups, working independently, featured an intermarriage between Protestants and Catholics. In both, an industrial accident in nineteenth-century New York's dangerous trades crippled the paterfamilias: the Irish longshoreman's shoulder was crushed by a falling crate, and the German furniture-maker lost several fingers to a jigsaw. In each case, the family had three children. The older son became a leader in the ethnic community on the Lower East Side, one in Tammany politics and the other in the Turnverein. But the middle child, a daughter in both cases, married outside the ethnic boundaries, and that posed problems. And the third child—yes, you guessed it, a boy—lost himself to drink and gambling and got into trouble with the law.

It looked as though the museum would become an endlessly repetitive soap opera of immigrant tribulations, masking a lot of ethnic stereotyping, when suddenly we were rescued by research in original documents. Serendipitously, genealogist Marsha Saron Dennis discovered Nathalie Gumpertz's 1883 petition to have her husband, Julius, missing for nine years, declared legally dead, so that she could cash in on his East Prussian inheritance. Nathalie, God bless her soul (or *neshumah*), had actually lived at 97 Orchard Street and had solicited help in searching for Julius from people we "knew" from other research (the building's original builder and owner, Lucas Glockner, for one). A furious research process began. Nathalie could indeed be located in two federal censuses, shifting from "keeping house" when the family was intact in 1870 to earning a livelihood for herself and the three surviving daughters as a "seamstress" in 1880. Was Nathalie Catholic, Protestant, or Jewish? Germans in New York's Kleindeutschland were all of these, and even assertive free-thinkers. But soon we discovered that one of the daughters had married a man named Cohen, and another had wed a fellow named Stern. Nathalie herself was buried in a Jewish cemetery in Queens.

From that point the museum's interpretation has focused on the lives of documented historical figures, not fictionalized composites. Their stories are far more unpredictably interesting than those our historians had scripted, underscoring the truth of historian David Thelen's dictum that "each of us is larger than the groups to which we belong." Once the news of the museum got out, Brooklyn resident Josephine Baldizzi arrived to share

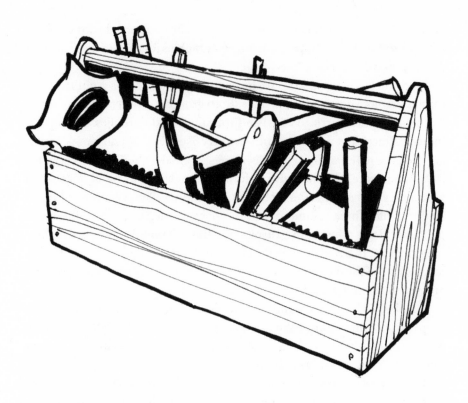

her family's story of living at 97 Orchard Street in the 1920s and 1930s. Mrs. Baldizzi brought her father's toolbox with her as well as richly detailed stories of her Lower East Side childhood during the Depression. With hand, voice, and eye, she helped the museum furnish the apartment adjoining the Gumpertzes'. The oral history, family memory, and material legacies of a twentieth-century family supplanted the work of archaeologists and curators, complementing it in some ways and contradicting it in others.

The apartments at 97 Orchard began to talk to one another. The years 1874 and 1929 had each thrown the lives of newly arrived Americans into severe distress. What provision was there for support from neighbors, local organizations, or the government? How did husbands and fathers confront their failure as providers? How did their wives and daughters go beyond the traditional homemaker's role in order to make ends meet?

As in the best public history projects, the discovery process has never stopped. Did the New York police note that Julius was missing? Did the Gumpertz girls go to school? When Josephine's younger brother Johnny was hit by a car, as she reported, what kind of medical care was available? How did the children in these two families overcome the scourge of infectious disease on the Lower East Side? What did it mean for Nathalie to become a seamstress? Ready-made clothing was just beginning to appear for the men's market but hardly existed for women. So what kinds of skills were called upon in dressmaking in the 1870s? Did she involve her children in the work? New dresses were an extravagance, so it's likely that she had to build a clientele among the wives of doctors, lawyers, and businessmen in the German community. How? What sort of relationship did she have with these women? We know that when Nathalie finally received the roughly $600 Julius had inherited, she moved her family up to the quieter precincts of Yorkville, in the east Eighties of Manhattan. Why did she choose to move? Was she wary of how the Lower East Side was changing now, in light of the huge influx of Russian and Polish Jews to New York that followed pogroms sparked by the assassination of Czar Alexander II in 1881?

This Tenement Museum project was a turning point for me. Its pedagogical purpose was less to teach historical concepts than to generate curiosity, historical empathy, and imagination. The museum introduced visitors, in prescheduled groups, to hour-long tours of the Gumpertz and Baldizzi apartments. We did not start them off with orientation programs narrated by authoritative voices. We did not use graphic panels to chart the rise and fall of immigration or the population of New York City in the years since 97 Orchard had been built in 1863. No maps compared population density or subethnic concentrations on the neighborhood streets. There were just a few contextual comments offered by a guide while the group prepared to enter the startlingly dark hallway of the tenement. The project aims to teach history but without interposing the five-dollar words we often insist upon as necessary preliminaries. In fact, words like "immigration," "urbanization," "ethnicity," "economic change," and "urban renewal" have seldom been used. Visitors, even students and foreigners, have always seemed to come equipped with concepts like these already in mind and ready to be applied to the particular stories they explore in the museum.

The LESTM is an immersive experience, but it is not a Disneyland. For more than twenty years, as the number of apartments and stories at the museum has grown to nearly a dozen, LESTM has embedded its selected social history themes in a series of concrete human situations. The best interpretive tours bring visitors to a moment of high drama, when they have to confront the stark and limited choices available to poor Americans facing hunger, filth, cold, desertion, humiliation, discrimination, and epidemic disease. Empathizing with such historical characters, visitors generally use their native wit to figure out what they might do, and how little they can do, in similar circumstances. As in real life, the stories leave visitors unresolved. Since many, if not most, visitors come as members of family groups, the Tenement Museum's uncertain "situations" become opportunities for members of visiting families to hug one another a little bit more tightly. (This was a brilliant confluence of interpretive and marketing strategies.)

This focus on individual family narratives has also had the unanticipated effect of diminishing the museum's emphasis on tolerance. Intergroup relationships became less important as the distinctive story of each family rose in importance. For one thing, there are no longer "Jews" and "Italians," but a variety of each: Visitors can note generational and subethnic differences (say between Ashkenazim from Poland and Sephardic Jews from Syria, or between Sicilians and Neapolitans). The museum continued to assist newly arrived Americans by sponsoring English and citizenship classes, but the story of immigration has changed dramatically in my lifetime. The city of my childhood, the world of *West Side Story*, was rife with second-generation ethnic rivalries and coalitions. Fewer and fewer New Yorkers were foreign-born.

But after the passage of the Hart-Celler Act of 1965, which opened the United States to many more immigrants from Latin America and Asia, this narrative of ethnic rivalry has made less and less sense. Now that New York City's schoolchildren speak over 150 different mother tongues, and when mosques, temples, and meeting halls spring up to foster dozens of religious traditions, the centrality of the World War I–era story has receded. Gradually, the LESTM has defined the city anew, as an ongoing absorption process for families from everywhere who rely on family and communal resources to find a niche for themselves: small businesses for men having to reinvent themselves in adult life, high schools and colleges for children eager for entry into the high-tech economy, and neighborhood support networks for mothers and elders less able to navigate in the mainstream. Tolerance, "mere" tolerance, now seems a tepid response to the heightened drama of these family transmutations. The museum is now planning an expansion to include the families that lived in a neighboring tenement, 103 Orchard Street, after World War II—immigrants from China and Puerto Rico, as well as a family of Holocaust survivors.

Work on the development of the LESTM climaxed my transition from a historian working with museum collections to a museum dramatist evoking historical experiences for visitors. For a decade or so, I'd been creating exhibitions about places, but I should have recognized more quickly what I'd originally learned at Old Sturbridge Village. Experience precedes and blazes the path for information, not the other way around. You could introduce people to a site with a decade of lectures or drag them along a mile-long series of well-illustrated panels, and the visual, tactile, and above all narrative power of the place would overwhelm all that verbal proliferation in a single moment. Stories "take place," and places whisper stories we will never forget.

SITUATED LEARNING

For many of those who have visited the LESTM in its first quarter-century, the museum has evoked an emotional identification with people in trouble. The circumstances of their difficulties seem so concrete—too many people sharing too few beds; rooms, clothes, and children impossible to keep clean; privacy practically nonexistent. We feel as they must have felt. In their absence, our emotion fills the gap. When their efforts to solve the challenges of daily living in this awful place are exhausted, we rack our brains to find the solutions for them. We, the living, are the renewed human response to their pained situations. In sharing their space, we put place in its place, as the surroundings of dramatic human interactions.

In my earlier projects, when we had been describing the evolution of whole communities—rural New England, modern-day Boston, Rhode Island, industrial Wheeling, and many others—we were usually inviting visitors to take pleasure in the journey toward American modernity. The exhibition passageway somehow became identical with the path of historical progress. Who would want to go to a museum to see misery? It turned out we were wrong. In the course of an hour-long tour, guides and visitors became firm allies of the challenged historical characters portrayed in the apartments at 97 Orchard Street. The museum showed us that plunking visitors down in the midst of others' troubles actually made them trust us all the more, for being honest, for renouncing rosy scenarios when they did not suit the historical facts.

The LESTM thus helped us at the American History Workshop screw up our courage and tackle much more complex human dilemmas in the vast American archive of stories. In project after project since then, we have aimed to engage visitors in situations that forced them to shift perspectives, to weigh alternative explanations, to empathize with strangers, and to see discomforting historical parallels. One of my favorites was the *Salmon Stakes* exhibition at the Seattle Museum of History and Industry in the late 1990s.[2] In the museum's storage rooms, away from the public, we had come across a foreboding gizmo with a cast-iron title plate above it that read "The Iron Chink." Designed to gut and clean salmon for canning, this was a machine you would not want to get too close to. But one could not imagine a better avenue for understanding the Pacific Northwest. Like its mechanically sequenced steel blades, the butchering machine laid bare the muscle, bone, blood, and flesh of the region's economy, ecology, science, technology, and demographics. It was Seattle's secret emblem at the turn of the twentieth century.

Invented by Edward A. Smith in 1903–5, each Iron Chink machine was meant to replace fifty Chinese fish-butchers (and hence its name), at a time when their numbers were fast diminishing as a result of the Chinese Exclusion Act of 1882. The demand for canned salmon surged in these years. Much of it was shipped off to Britain to serve as a major, often the only, source of protein in the diet of miners and mill workers. The state and federal government enthusiastically created hatcheries to restore the stocks of salmon thus depleted in this harvest, ultimately endangering the survival of wild salmon in the region's rivers and bays. Despite the difficulty and danger of the labor, the fisheries and canneries along the coast up to Alaska attracted immigrants from Norway, the Balkans, Italy, Finland, Japan, and the Philippines. Immigrant women from these countries replaced the Chinese at the butchering tables. The fight to unionize workers in these industries was fierce and sometimes bloody. The bosses started as local businessmen; but even by 1900 the packing companies were consolidating, and in the twentieth century they were absorbed into giant food conglomerates like Del Monte Foods and ConAgra.

Smith's Iron Chink was a featured exhibit at Seattle's Alaska-Yukon-Pacific Exposition in 1909, which aimed to promote local businesses, particularly in mining and timber, to celebrate Seattle's role as a nexus of trans-

---

2. *Salmon Stakes* opened at the old Montlake location of the Seattle museum. A version of the show was installed in the new museum building after the move to South Lake Union in 2012 and was adapted as a traveling exhibition as well. Designed especially for schoolchildren and families, this version of *Salmon Stakes* abbreviated the historical context, but it explored the technology and labor issues and included splendid hands-on learning opportunities.

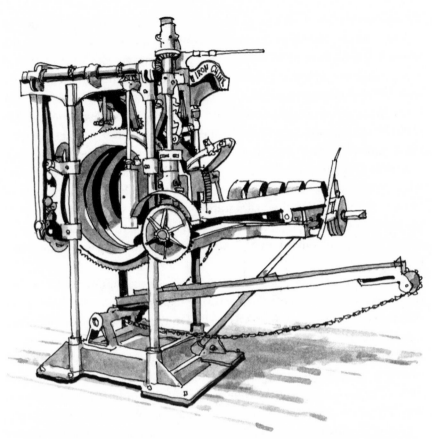

The Iron Chink, an artifact with meaning for the history of technology, ecology, demography, politics, and economics in the Pacific Northwest (Seattle Museum of History and Industry).

pacific trade and to interest American tourists in the region's natural beauty and the burgeoning sport of motorboating. Although casual Asian visitors were apparently excluded from the fair's attractions, Eskimo, Japanese, and Chinese "villages" were erected to provide titillating glimpses into these exotic and "primitive" cultures, complete with actual native peoples whom visitors could gaze at and take snapshots of.

The planners of the *Salmon Stakes* exhibition portrayed Seattle in 1900 as a boomtown exploiting international flows of labor, capital, technology, transportation, and consumption to put the region on the map of statesmen and investors around the world. Beneath the boom, however, there were other ambitions: to install and maintain racial and social hierarchies, to manipulate natural environments in order to maximize the exploitation of local resources, and to deploy new technologies that would standardize production and facilitate global trade. The four corners of the gallery represented the worlds of the butchering-floor, the workers' barracks, the cannery front office, and the hatchery, providing visitors with historical contexts for the dynamic transformations occurring in each area. Within each of these corners, designers planned interactive devices to let visitors listen in on personal narratives of the diverse lot who played the "salmon stakes"—immigrants and their families, capitalists and managers, naturalists and engineers. An interpretive area dedicated to the World's Fair served as a conclusion, suggesting a link to the world of Seattle a century later—to the global branding of Starbucks, the technological empires of Microsoft and Boeing, the in-migration of Filipina women and others to the rapidly expanding regional health care industry, the concern over dangers to the region's environment, and the city's continuing economic ties to the Pacific Rim.

Salmon Stakes taught me something else. As visitors moved from one corner of the story to another, they thrust themselves into the knife's-edge situation of people in the past—as we had in the LESTM. The drama of the tenement emerged by isolating the moment of crisis in each family. *Salmon Stakes* revealed a whole society skating on thin ice. Visitors could move from one situation to another, slowly grasping the systemic relationship of these efforts to transform the four corners of this industrial-natural complex. Fifteen years before, in our exhibitions on place such as *The Lay of the Land* in Providence, we enthroned visitors as omniscient observers of time's passing, watching places change before them. Now we used immersion to create another sort of "manysidedness," as Herman Melville calls it. We hoped our exhibition would help visitors reach for a deeper interpretation of the "Seattle way," that odd mix of entrepreneurial energy and ecological possessiveness, of hometown pride and an ever more diverse population.

When we came in the mid-1990s to plan the new museum for the central Arizona branch of the state historical society, we were dealing with a very different culture of "placefulness." The sprawling Valley of the Sun had encouraged a huge variety of communities to be planted without much connection to one another. While everyone in Seattle could orient himself or herself to Mount Rainier, Phoenix was tied together only by the interstate highways, I-10 and I-17. When we convened panels of local residents to unpack their notions of place, we discovered that most were better at recognizing landmark sites in New York or Paris than in metropolitan Phoenix. The folks working at Luke Air Force Base knew nothing of the university town of Tempe. The Yaqui-descended people in Guadalupe were unfamiliar with

SECOND FLOOR PERMANENT GALLERIES

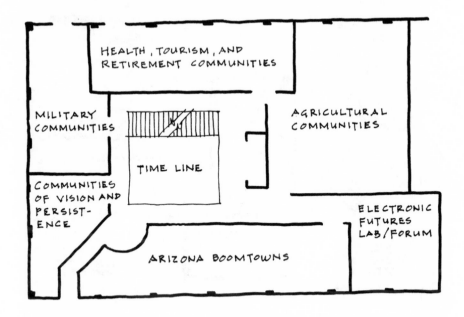

HEALTH, TOURISM, AND RETIREMENT COMMUNITIES

MILITARY COMMUNITIES

AGRICULTURAL COMMUNITIES

TIME LINE

COMMUNITIES OF VISION AND PERSIST-ENCE

ELECTRONIC FUTURES LAB/FORUM

ARIZONA BOOMTOWNS

the Iowa-descended people in Sun City, and vice versa. But even enumerating the separate places in a region of more than 3 million people, growing so rapidly, would be impossible.

In response, we resurrected our old "typology" strategy. We proposed an introductory gallery on nineteenth-century Arizona settlements and then suggested tracing the genealogy of five types of places: agricultural communities, military communities, recreation and retirement communities, utopian communities, and boomtowns. In each one, visitors would explore how a new form of Arizona's relationship to the rest of the United States led to implanting one type of landscape after another. Cotton and citrus farming, for example, found fertile ground for expansion from the American South once irrigation was in place. The reorientation of military tactics around air and armored vehicles at the beginning of World War II made central Arizona the logical location for new training bases. The clean and dry air in the desert attracted health-seekers and vacationers in the second quarter of the twentieth century, and subsequently wartime barracks-builders like Del Webb expanded that business into constructing and marketing huge colonies of retirement homes. Mining booms created a mindset for transients that later suited real-estate investors. And so on.

MILITARY COMMUNITIES

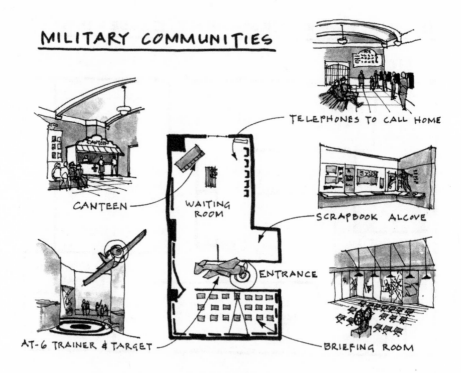

TELEPHONES TO CALL HOME

CANTEEN

WAITING ROOM

SCRAPBOOK ALCOVE

ENTRANCE

AT-6 TRAINER & TARGET

BRIEFING ROOM

MILITARY COMMUNITIES

Design: from an agenda of themes to real-life stories conveyed experientially.

As we aspired to strengthen the geographical literacy of our visitors, the central Arizona history museum also reminded me of *The Lay of the Land*. The Arizonans lacked the centuries of genealogical and historical research and of archival and museum collecting that we found in Providence, and the Rhode Island curators welcomed social history more warmly than the gun-toters on the Phoenix staff. But the bigger difference, I think, was in the experiential approach we brought to the project in the desert. Our plan was full of participatory opportunities and a focus on the life histories of individuals. Exhibits on vacation resorts would teach visitors to fox-trot to 1930s music; museumgoers, like raw World War II recruits, were directed to attend military briefings; engineering "workshops" engaged visitors in redirecting the flow of Salt River Valley water, posing challenges for local farmers, grain millers, and developers of residential communities. In sum, we tried to animate the geographical imagination through kinesthetic activity. Museum learning methods, we proved, could elicit a "sense of place" that was urgently desired in this era of globalization.

A big chunk of the Arizona Historical Society exhibition in Tempe was built, and more was planned until budget ceilings and board turnovers suspended the work. It had been our splendid laboratory to discover how visitors could transact relationships with unfamiliar histories by situating themselves in richly detailed narratives. Participatory exhibits no longer were simply tools for representing concepts but, rather, ways of engaging the "whole visitor" in an encounter with the past.

Gradually, over the years, I had learned to read clues to historical dramas everywhere. Once, in the Oregon Historical Society library, I discovered that Portland's Meyer and Frank department store had celebrated the long decades of service in bridal gowns by a salesperson—I think her name was Sonia. A little census research told me that she was a single woman, an immigrant from Russia, and the older sister to a prominent local doctor. A few minutes later, I was roaming the store itself, two blocks away, in search of the bridal salon. The current head was somewhat surprised at my questions: How many fittings did a customer have for a gown? How had the process changed over the years? My studies of Nathalie Gumpertz's tenement dressmaking led me to imagine a whole scenario, captured in two gestures: My Sonia's bending over to pin the waist of a young mademoiselle's gown, and then her returning home, later that night, to contribute her wages to the medical education of her kid brother. The ironies were obvious: fitting wedding dresses for dozens of women but never for herself. Then the whole life of my Sonia swirled around me: streetcars and delivery men in Meyer and Frank uniforms, fat volumes of *Gray's Anatomy* on the kitchen table at night, birthday parties for Aunt Sonia at a postwar suburban house. These imaginings were more entertaining than the movies.

THE STORYSCAPE EN PLEIN AIR

In 1993, American History Workshop (AHW) joined with two highly innovative design groups, Graham Landscape Architecture of Annapolis and Patricia O'Donnell of LANDSCAPES, to work with the staff of Historic St. Mary's City (HSMC) in fashioning a new program to interpret the history of Maryland's seventeenth-century capital. We called it the Outdoor Exploratorium of Colonial America. Decades of excellent historical and archaeological research at St. Mary's City had yielded valuable evidence of a startlingly distinctive colonial narrative. Because Maryland's proprietor, Cecil Calvert, the Baron of Baltimore, was a Catholic and most of his settlers were Protestant, the colony permitted a liberty of conscience unique in seventeenth-century English North America. St. Mary's City recognized the separation of church and state by siting the State House and the Chapel at opposite ends of the town. The community, situated on Maryland's western shore of Chesapeake Bay, near the convergence with the Potomac, thrived during the years of the tobacco boom in the middle of the seventeenth century, but religious dissension led to the end of the proprietorship in 1695 and the removal of the capital to Annapolis. The abandoned city slowly disintegrated, leaving almost nothing of its seventeenth-century architecture aboveground.

Though in many ways equal in importance to Jamestown and Williamsburg, the colonial capitals of Virginia, St. Mary's City never had the resources to develop its potential as a publicly accessible historic site in the first two-thirds of the twentieth century. The resulting interpretive landscape, begun in fits and starts, has always been a hodgepodge. An inaccurately reconstructed State House of 1935 is juxtaposed with meticulously documented exhibitions of archaeological materials in the visitors' center. Living history demonstrations and hands-on learning mingle with reconstructed ghost frames. It's hard for visitors to get a handle on the place or to follow a coherent pathway that does more than fill their heads with randomly encountered survivals of a remote civilization.

Our team proposed dividing the entire St. Mary's site into nine exhibition areas or "clusters," animating the existing structures and installing new indoor and outdoor learning stations. The key to our plan was to link the existing sites and the outdoor landscape with an interpretive boardwalk through "the world's first archaeology adventure park." The boardwalk would (practically and expressively) "protect and preserve as much as possible of the archaeological remains of the people who shared this site." It would lead visitors through "a vegetative environment that can suggest the varieties of ecological, economic, and cultural issues confronting seventeenth-century Indians and English in this place . . . [and] create opportunities for interactive learning about the social, cultural, technological, economic, and political (power relations) contexts of life in seventeenth-century St. Mary's City."

Those opportunities were expressed in a "lexicon" or family of learning tools. Among them were "Landscape Minus One" devices to "put visitors in the position of a historic character handling a tool or performing some period gesture." (It was modeled on the 1950s LP series Music Minus One, which encouraged young musicians, for example, to fill in the missing clarinet part of a Mozart concerto.) There were also cutout life-sized historical characters with quotations; archaeological "core samples," in which a Plexiglas tube showed the strata of a particular site; scale models; objects composed of interpretive elements ("mocuments"); a puzzle that revealed its secret on the opposite side when all its pieces were assembled; and many others.

The first cluster, Encountering, takes as its theme the ways in which the precontact Indians of the area lived in and understood the landscape. As visitors walk through this cluster, they move toward the "encounter" between the English colonists and the Chesapeake Indians and discover the effect on the latter's way of life. Visitors are introduced to the topography of this place, the physical challenges of moving through and living in this landscape (forest cover, ground surface, etc.), and the archaeological and historical methods used to uncover life here (reliance on English record-keeping and generalizations derived from studying nearby Indian groups).

Then visitors come to the Hunter's Blind station, which is surrounded by a lattice-like structure that serves as the intellectual launching pad for the experience therein. This element is composed of a band of text and illustrations that describe Powhatan religious beliefs. Visitors must walk completely around the station, stopping to recognize how the Indians had to appease severe deities with the power to manipulate natural forces (e.g., lightning) and punish wrongdoers. We went further. If this band (composed of aluminum, perhaps) were physically arranged so that the visitors would—as they read it—bend and stretch and lift and turn in particular ways, they could be reenacting the dance steps of local Indians documented by folklorists.[1]

1. The inspiration for this came from Kellom Tomlinson, *The Art of Dancing, Explained by Reading and Figures* (London, 1735), which represented the appropriate dance steps directly beneath the musical score, as reproduced and described

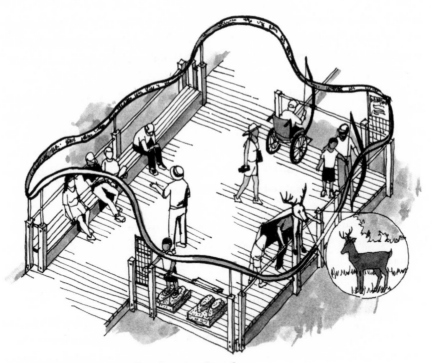

Enlist each of the visitor's skills in learning about the
encounter of Indian people and English settlers.

Within the Hunter's Blind station there were to be a series of interactive elements, pictured here. Several pairs of large stone "moccasins" invited young and old visitors to assume a stance before an altar (Pawocrance) of the type used by the Powhatans. On the altar, text explains how and why the gods needed to be appeased before the hunt. Adjoining this, visitors could poke their heads into a cast-resin mock deer headdress, modeled on those Indians used for stalking game. With the headdress on and looking out through the eyeholes (and through binoculars inserted within the mask), they could spot cutout life-sized figures of deer in the distant meadows. An accompanying text, perhaps delivered via audio in the headdress or on a nearby panel, would explain that though deer were not a critical component of the Indians' diet, hunting deer was an important step in proving one's manhood. The final element in this station was to be one or more large bows. Painted footprints on the ground instruct visitors to adopt the

in Edward Tufte, *Envisioning Information* (Cheshire, Conn.: Graphics Press, 1990), 114–15.

proper archer's stance, stretching their muscles, pulling the bowstring taut, and sensing the strength required. On the bows themselves visitors can read about the absence of bows in the archaeological record, the deduction of their use (from the number of arrowheads), and how the size of these hunting devices and the materials from which they were made have been calculated. A map on a facing panel lets visitors know that hostile and powerful Iroquois and Siouxan tribes surrounded the local Algonquin-speaking Indians. In sum, the Hunter's Blind station cognitively and kinetically transforms the visitors' sense of how hunting—far from only being a way of providing food—is also enmeshed in religious, political, and psychological life-patterns.

AHW produced similar plans and drawings for many other areas of the outdoor museum, dealing as much with issues of English colonist and Indian religious practice, family organization and roles, land use, and economic patterns as with the skills of ordinary life. But an upheaval in the administration of HSMC shut the project down before an experimental prototype could be tested in the summer of 1994. Still, the project yielded important value in shaping our approach to helping visitors acquire a sense of place.

Here is how we understood our process and its underlying learning theory:

The presentations American History Workshop are creating with the staff of HSMC take root in the splendid historical and archaeological research performed here over the past two decades, supplemented by the work of other scholars. Then we translate these understandings into concepts that have clear, almost physical, form, embodying basic human qualities and concerns—ideas about diet, seasonality, skill, family roles, power relationships, diplomacy, economic ambition, and most important, alienness. Finally, we imagine a process and a tool by which visitors—of all ages and backgrounds—can be helped to grasp that concept. And not just to grasp it but to fix it firmly in the mind through personal experience.

In our own voyage of discovery, we are learning that the past can be approached in many ways. Every human attribute, after all, can be a tool for investigation. Our legs can learn what it was to stretch oneself as well as the bowstring in hunting. Our backs can learn how important it is that we have planted our crops well. Our eyes can learn the difference

between an edible and a poisonous mushroom. Our ears can catch the difference between two bird songs, and we can hear the wind moving through the trees in which they sit. Our noses can smell the differences between medicinal herbs assigned to cure seventeenth-century diseases. Our parental fears can confront the commonness of infant mortality in that era. Our stubbornness can teach us something about the need to submit to familial or provincial authority.

THE ILLINOIS AND MICHIGAN CANAL CORRIDOR

In the late 1990s, the AHW team and Richard Hoyen applied a similar approach in developing a wayfinding system for the Illinois and Michigan Canal Corridor Association. Our *I&M Canal Passage* program proposed that towns along the ninety-six-mile-long canal towpath commission full-scale silhouette characters of figures in local history, to be constructed of Corten steel (this is a steelmaking valley!), with applied text. Modeled on the sculpture of George Segal and Georgia Gerber, and drawing special inspiration from Richard Beyer's *Waiting for the Interurban* public art in-

stallation in Seattle, the steel silhouettes aimed to animate and humanize
the history of this vital water connector between the Great Lakes and the
Mississippi River.

Our plan incorporated the silhouette figures in the landscape, often surrounded by mocked-up artifacts and settings. On the canal landing in Lock-
port, for example, visitors would come upon the figures of William Gooding
and Barbara Baird. Gooding was the chief engineer and oversaw the surveyors and contractors building the canal from 1836 to 1848. He is pictured
holding a rod for Baird, the first woman licensed as a surveyor by the state
in 1975. She is represented measuring the distance to Gooding through a
theodolite.

Farther down the towpath, the naturalist Robert Kennicott (1835–66)
is represented sketching birds such as the passenger pigeon, now extinct,
and the black-crowned night heron, now endangered, along the waterway.
Visitors pass by the figure of a young boy holding a jug in one hand and a
basket of food on his shoulders. They come across a man, half-buried in the

ground, shovel lifted high, apparently one of the thousands of workers who dug the canal from the prairie soil.

The long silhouette of a canal boat made of pressure-treated plywood stretches along the towpath, and to it are attached benches inscribed with the stories of canal boat passengers, as well as mocked-up objects of the trade that was making Chicago the commercial center of the nation's midsection.

In addition, AHW developed designs for directional signage, street furniture (bike racks, trash cans, benches, water fountains), and mile markers, all constructed of wood and steel to fit comfortably into this landscape. Each of the markers provided a glimpse into a richer back-story for the region:

In 1673, while traveling along the Illinois River, Marquette noted the presence of Carolina parakeets. The only parakeets native to North America, they were later hunted to extinction.

Keep a sharp watch for dead bodies. When passengers died on canal boats, often from infectious diseases, the captains would simply pull over to the bank and quickly bury them.

In 1830 the I and M Canal Commissioners laid out the town of Chicago for the sole purpose of being a canal port. They also platted Ottawa the same year.

The canal changed agriculture in Illinois. Prior to the canal, wheat was the chief cash crop grown in the state. The canal reduced the cost of shipping corn and made it more profitable than wheat, and production of corn increased tremendously.

The Western Clock Company, a/k/a Westclox, made Peru the alarm clock capital of the world in the early years of the 20th century.

Even slow marathoners run twice as fast as mules, but they don't have to pull 100 tons and a canal boat.

The *I&M Canal Passage* program aimed to infuse interpretation of the canal's history and geography into the ordinary life of the communities along the route. For our clients, the Canal Corridor Association, wayfinding and interpretation would draw positive attention and overcome decades of neglect as the canal towns turned their back on the canal. Rather than con-

*The Illinois and Michigan Canal Corridor is peopled
with dozens of full-sized Corten steel silhouettes.*

fine history in a downtown visitors' center, we aimed to bring it out into the streets. Aiming to increase recreational use and engender tourism along one of the most historically significant passageways in American history, the plan's design created coherence where there had been only scattered attention before.

ROSE KENNEDY GREENWAY, BOSTON

AHW served as interpretive consultants in many landscape design projects in the first years of the new century. Among the most interesting were two of the parks along the Rose Kennedy Greenway in Boston, open to the public in 2008. The chain of parks was designed to sit atop the tunnels that had replaced the elevated highway, the accursed Central Artery, that cut downtown Boston off from the North End neighborhood and the historic waterfront. We dug deeply into the topographical history of the site. The North End Parks would straddle what had long ago been a swampy lowland between Copps Hill, on which the North End sat, and Fort Hill, which became the site of Boston's downtown. Over the course of two centuries, the journey on Middle and Hanover Streets between one and the other was (in our interpretation) emblematic of the evolving split between home and community, on one side, and work and economy, on the other. The Wharf District Parks, by contrast, sat amid Boston's connection to the sea, evidenced in Long Wharf (1710), which extended King (now State) Street a third of a mile into the harbor.

In the nineteenth century, Boston leaped far beyond its regional seaport rivals by becoming a great railroad hub. But its geography required two termini: North Station received trains from northeastern Massachusetts, New Hampshire, and Maine; South Station drew in the traffic from Worcester, Providence, and points west and south. In the trench between the two, a succession of transit routes—wagon roads, street railways, automobile streets, and then the elevated expressway—were laid. Unhappily, the Big Dig engineers laid the chain of parks in this narrow slot where once the expressway hovered. The waterside buildings remain impediments to light and air, and the Greenway still feels more like a north-south median strip for cars than an east-west crossroads or connector to the sea.

In the furious debates that went on in public meetings and in the back offices of design firms for a quarter century, all sorts of suggestions were put forth to make these narrow strips into attractive public parks. The design of the Wharf District Parks by EDAW, a giant multinational firm, and Copley Wolff, a boutique Boston office, evolved from more urgent programmatic goals: to link the downtown to the waterfront; to create a "great room" that would accommodate festivals and performances; to define a plaza in front of the New England Aquarium with a spectacular, high-tech fountain; to house public art installations and programs; and so on. These aspirations for a glittering new urban park were laudable. Perhaps it could deliver the benefits promised and long deferred by the disruptions of Big Dig construction.

The landscape architects did try courageously to insert some historical character into the site, using granite blocks and planting native species. On the west or downtown side of the park blocks, a more formal allée of trees represents the orthogonal geometry of the cityscape; on the east or waterfront side, "an informal meander of groves . . . is a metaphor for the shoreline." Design ideas like these were conceptually rich but impossible for laypeople to experience. (They served the same purpose as writings by academics for fellow scholars.) But more fundamentally, these design objectives flatly contradicted the historical traditions of the site. The wharf district had historically been a place of bent shoulders and outstretched arms, of tight quarters and dark alleys. It was a man's world, inhospitable to proper ladies and well-born children. On this site, Bostonians got their first view of people and products from the Mediterranean and East Asia, got their first

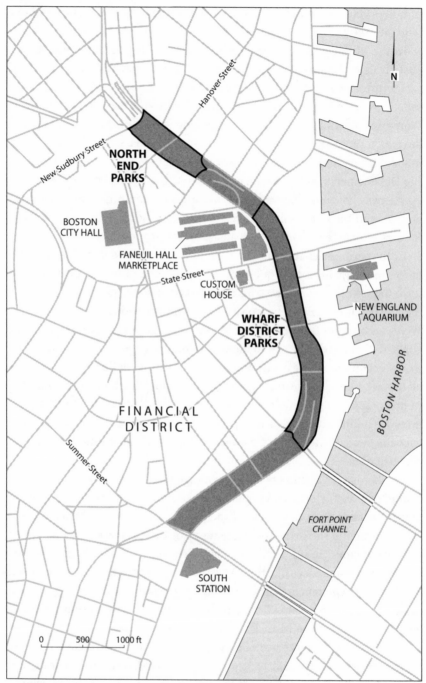

AHW worked on integrating interpretive elements in the design of two of the parks along the Rose Kennedy Greenway, Boston.

jobs on fishing schooners, strained to pass the scrutiny of immigration officials, gobbled down the newly invented meal called lunch because they lived too far to get home to dinner and back, and later decked themselves out in Sunday finery for boat trips to Provincetown and the Cape.

AHW and its scholarly consultants researched the site history, curated relevant maps and images, and wrote interpretive texts. In collaboration with the designers, we then created interpretive installations for the five segments of the Wharf District Parks, each with its own key theme: A Landscape Fit for Commerce (City Wharf); Boston and the Sea: Evolution of the Waterfront (Long Wharf); The Kingdom of Fish (Central Wharf); All the World's People: The Immigration Story (India Wharf); and Bostonians Discover a Playground in the Harbor (Rowes Wharf). We developed maps that traced the building (and building out of) the city and laid out the palimpsest of transportation systems in this area. We worked with artists to incise images showing the evolution of Boston's fisheries on granite blocks in another parcel. We excerpted the letters of six new Bostonians as they first stepped foot in their new home, and we placed them in the pavement of yet another segment. Some of these interactive and informative devices were playful. All tried to restore a sense of the historical importance of the waterfront to Boston's history, not by charts and statistics, or even by maps and personal narratives, but by reinserting clues to long-departed patterns of perception and action.

But in the end, the result was disappointing. Despite our best efforts, these interventions feel extraneous to the site. The marriage of muscular themes and refined garden designs was an unhappy one. The gardens, fountains, and park furniture of the Wharf District Parks, especially when it is animated by users, bespeak place, but not this place. They draw inspiration from Manhattan's Bryant Park, which was the beau ideal of this design moment; from Versailles; and from Ghirardelli Square in San Francisco. They address Boston's lack of access to open space, but they don't revive the spirit of this particular place. In a sense, they brought me back to the beginning of my journey as an interpretive historian. Once again, as I did in Providence and Boston in 1979, I was fostering the creation of clear and coherent materials *about* place, rather than experiences *of* place.

The North End Parks, by contrast, more successfully merged programmatic goals and a faithful derivation from topographical and historical characteristics of the site. Designed by the Seattle firm of Gustafson Guthrie Nichol and its Boston partners, Crosby Schlessinger Smallridge, these blocks evoked the scale and amenities of a neighborhood park, while preserving an openness to the soaring business district beyond. As with the Wharf District Parks, AHW did contribute "wonderfully obscure images and information bits that corrected and enriched our factual survey of the site's history," as project architect Shannon Nichol reports, but they

> more importantly led us into a less quantitative and more qualitative, interpretive, and intuitive understanding of the cultural history of this site. While we were still at a point of looking for hard evidence of the historic bridge locations that had crossed our site before it had been filled in, and while we were trying to accurately locate the merchant-occupied building footprints on the site over time, [AHW] helped us to step back from these details and confidently see them as evidence of something much simpler and more important. The place where many people met each other in crossing every day. The point of pause in a person's morning in 1780 and in 1980, during the walk to work. . . . The commonality of a human experience, over all the varying physical details across time, was the clear insight that sparked our design concept: "From Home to City."

"This understanding of the significance, heritage, and unique role of this very spot in the city," Nichol concludes, "was not just about the past but was about the timelessness of a living, breathing, place."[2]

For me, these parks, elegant and engaging at the same time, brought a powerful and fresh interpretation of the site, perfectly exemplifying my third definition of "interpretation," as the dictionary defines it, "the *recasting* of the thing in a new form." Both their hard surface and plant materials are tied to this place and feel expressive of its geology, topography, and local history. The park's fountain traces its source to the waters of the old Mill Pond, the Mill Creek, and the canal that was built along its route around the turn of the nineteenth century. The park's paths mimic the ancient street layouts. Specific historical and topographical information is inscribed along these pathways. True, a verbally comprehensive historical narrative is missing. But in providing a chain of benches on which older people and parents can watch the frolicking and waterplay of children, the design signifies "neighborliness" (captured in the idea that in urban settings, as Jane Jacobs put it, there are "eyes on the street"). And looking up, the benchwarmers can sense the "globalism" of the tall towers of the financial district ahead of them.

2. Email from Shannon Nichol to the author, February 20, 2014.

MARKERS AGAIN

Now I live in a designated historic district, the largest in New York City. At the corner of my block, a New York City Landmarks Preservation Commission sign—in a shade of terra cotta brown that was chosen to fit into the streetscape—tells me that I am standing within the Park Slope Historic District. The text says a lot about what the commission thinks is important, and who constitutes its primary constituency.

PROSPECT PARK, LARGELY COMPLETED BY 1873 AS THE MASTER-PIECE OF FREDERICK LAW OLMSTED AND CALVERT VAUX'S LAND-SCAPE DESIGNS, DEFINED PARK SLOPE AS A DESIRABLE RESIDENTIAL NEIGHBORHOOD. PRINCIPALLY BUILT BETWEEN THE MID-1880S AND WORLD WAR I, PARK SLOPE RETAINS ITS 19TH CENTURY PRO-FILE OF THREE- AND FOUR-STORY BUILDINGS, PUNCTUATED BY CHURCH STEEPLES, RECALLING BROOKLYN'S CHARACTER AS THE CITY OF HOMES AND CHURCHES. THE MONTAUK CLUB, A VENE-TIAN GOTHIC PALAZZO, BUILT IN 1891, AND MONTGOMERY PLACE, A BLOCK-LONG STREET, MUCH OF WHICH WAS DESIGNED BY ARCHI-TECT CASS GILBERT, ARE THE MOST DRAMATIC OF THE NEIGHBOR-HOOD'S ARCHITECTURAL CREATIONS. VICTORIAN GOTHIC, QUEEN ANNE, ROMANESQUE REVIVAL, AND OTHER STYLES ABOUND HERE.

I print it here in capital letters because that is how it appears, to the detriment of legibility, on the sign itself. In the world of this sign, only architecture matters: It has the power to "define" neighborhoods, "recall" urban character, and "dramatize" places ten or twelve blocks away. In this landscape, "styles abound," but there are no people. How Park Slopers made a living, chose their houses of worship, supplied themselves with food and clothing, responded to wars and depressions, welcomed or resisted waves of immigrant incomers, experienced anything of daily life, or even went about the highly relevant processes of gentrifying, rehabilitating, and celebrating their residences is not the concern of the Landmarks Preservation Commission. Nothing of note has happened here for over a century. The advent of automobiles, the Depression, two world wars, the invention of the name Park Slope, the closing of the big factories, gentrification, and the designation of the district all go unnoticed.

Like most markers of this type, it's great if you already know all this stuff—if you agree that Prospect Park is better than Central Park, if you recognize the architects' names, if you know how to find the nearly moribund Montauk Club. The markers hold up an admiring mirror to their writers. They stake a claim for the sponsors' knowledge and standing. But such neutron-bomb history is not a self-portrait of this community or an invitation to visitors to gauge the pulse of these streets in the twenty-first century. Beyond a vague notion of "Victorian" and a sure conviction of "expensive," most residents have no clue about the origins and evolutions of this neighborhood.

SENSING PLACE

Gaining a sense of a place is a process. History is essential to that process, but only if we understand history itself as a course of action instead of a repository of facts and concepts. A great British philosopher, R. G. Collingwood, defined history as the imaginative reenactment of past events. Another, Michael Oakeshott, viewed history as a mode of experience, basically a device for creating simpler order out of the potentially overwhelming "buzz and din" of lived experience.

I prefer to think of the process, at least in terms of making sense of the places we encounter, as dis-placement and re-placement. We come into a new setting (a scene, in Kenneth Burke's pentad of elements, composed by time as well as place). Kinesthetically we feel our disorientation. We don't fit; we have the wrong body and the wrong mind for this scene. We wobble. If all were instead consonant with us, we would be in the here and now, and we want to get to the there and then. If the historical marker or the text panel or the docent's chatter only confirms what I already know, it has no power to displace me. Only when I am displaced am I ready to be emplaced anew.

For that reason, we have stronger impressions of physically challenging spaces. I can "show" you more about a nineteenth-century room when it's dark than when it is illuminated. I can demonstrate the fear of a slave girl, newly arrived on a rice plantation, better if we go there by water, and I can feel the comforting connections between the slave quarters on adjoining plantations if we journey from one to the other through the woods. To gain a sense of the past we need to reawaken our native wit, our mental and physical skills. I learned that many years ago, in trying to read that 1820 newspaper in the Fenno House at Old Sturbridge Village, and I have to relearn it in every day of my professional life.

CONCLUSION

Almost a half-century of work had helped me visualize my dream of a lively, historically informed, and ceaselessly engaging landscape.

I want a landscape that can be read by anyone as everyone's. A hundred years ago, the City Beautiful belonged to the public but reflected the tastes and experiences only of the elite. Today it is the corporate, the propertied, that shapes access to the landscape. It invites us to purchase access to a world that actually has been expropriated from its roots in the commonality.

I want a landscape that registers the marks of passage and the implantations of settlement by one generation after another, so that every action we take feels as though we are connected to the generations that came before us.

I want a landscape that reveals more than names on the land but also evidences of habits of heart, hand, and mind; fields of struggle; faith and death; sites of invention and persistence.

I want a landscape that offers an adventure in discovery every day, rewarding curiosity, inclusion, and acute observation. We can well do without anything that obscures the past or "corrects" it so that it "conforms" to some historicized, invented consistency.

PART THREE

Beholding: Interpreting Stuff

12 ::: THE OBJECT OF THE OBJECT

I'm a material boy. As I've said, my immersion in the touchable past at Old Sturbridge Village (osv) transformed my vocation as a scholar and as a teacher of history. It revived my connection to the physical world of my upbringing, renewed my commitment to the "knowledge in the fingertips" of the men and women who reared me and those whom I studied in the field, and enriched my observations of the workaday world around me. I came to believe that even the most abstruse ideas in the human mind, such as the sense of spiritual infusion, were deeply rooted in the specific circumstances of material life. The old couplet says, "Man may work from sun to sun / But woman's work is never done." My dissertation tried to explain how this truism shaped personal religious experience in New England.

But I was not a museum rat as a kid. The objects in museum cases were not my kind of stuff. I've always found that there is something eerie about them. In the popular parlance, a museum object is a dead thing, but actually it is often all that remains of a life. Somehow a thing has survived after the men and women who made, owned, traded, treasured, and laid it aside are moldering in their graves. To wander through a gallery of historical relics sometimes feels like what I imagine it is like to tour a city deserted by plague victims or hit by nerve gas.

Nor was I born to a line of collectors, to say the least. Our foothold in America felt a little too tenuous for us to surround ourselves with a stockpile of objects superfluous for survival. I did create one collection as a child—stamps—and I lovingly searched out the Scott's catalogs to identify my acquisitions, one by one. But I chiefly treasured them for the stories they told, the ideas and places they introduced, and the feelings they engendered. I will never forget when Ohio gained admission to the Union because of the commemorative issued at its sesquicentennial in 1953. Stamp collecting was how I knew that Washington Irving, James Fenimore Cooper, and Ralph Waldo Emerson were "Famous Writers" before I had ever seen their names on the spines of books. Discovering a 1910 stamp from Montenegro sent me to atlases and timelines of the Balkan Wars. Collecting stamps even sparked political and ethical thinking. I recall puzzling over whether it was OK for me to collect and display the stamps of Hitler's Germany.

At my level, stamp collecting was an entertaining hunt. Sprawled on the living room floor on rainy afternoons, I aimed to replace the grayish squares in my album with the "real" vermillion and lilac examples. If there were world enough and time, one might assemble a "complete set." Though collecting, like any potentially obsessive human activity, may complicate individual lives, it ultimately simplifies the world for the collector. Filling up my stamp album became a surrogate for all the challenges of my ten-year-old world—a ready-made set of categories, a sure way of measuring progress, an adventurous way of linking my innermost thoughts to the most remote corners of the globe.

My stamp collecting, of course, dwelt on the outermost edges of the economically serious activity of philately. Each month I read *Stamps* magazine, the way other kids read movie star or motorcycle magazines, and I fantasized for a moment or two about acquiring the treasures *Stamps* described, the ones that were overstamped by military occupiers in 1919 or somehow mistakenly misprinted by the authorities. It never happened. I remained on the other side of the velvet rope from the collections that really counted—the stuff hunted, hoarded, cataloged, and presented by museums and connoisseurs.

My perspective changed on that day in 1967 when I came to Old Sturbridge Village. The simple contrast of the wing chair and the stick chair in the Fenno House parlor sparkled through the winter air and stirred my thoughts about new ways of defining hierarchy, family relationships, attitudes toward nature, and a dozen other phenomena of nineteenth-century rural life. But I wasn't particularly interested in the provenance of the chairs. I'm not sure I knew or cared if they were "original" or reproductions. Their shape and placement in the room and my engagement with them were far more instructive. (I took it for granted that OSV, as a reputable museum, had placed the correct chairs in the correct positions.)

As a costumed interpreter that spring and summer, I capitalized on my guests' familiarity with the basic lexicon of OSV's materiality. They knew many of these objects by their form and how to use them. They could unlatch a gate, slide into a school desk, or gather around a stove on a frosty day. That allowed me to jump right into the evocation of a nineteenth-century grammar lesson or legal case. That visitors already "know stuff" is the great advantage of museums as teachers, but some fritter away that advantage almost immediately, speaking of "Chippendale" or even "furniture" rather than tables and chairs, or speaking of "Romanesque Revival" before they invite visitors to pass through the arches into the next gallery. Too bad. The visitor's familiarity is a skeleton key that could open the doors to many museum mysteries, if fancy words did not block the passageway.

In the conventional view, of course, museums are all about stuff: collections and arrangements of things. Susan M. Pearce, among the most thoughtful contemporary scholars of museum practice, virtually identifies the modern museum with its collections of objects: "Our collections are what we are, and from this all our other functions flow."[1] For many museum people, the problem is that artifacts are mute. In our OSV journal, my friend and colleague Robert Post wrote, "Museum education struggles against the stubborn silence of things."[2]

But if objects are silent, museum people seldom are. Put a curator in front of an artwork, a specimen, or a relic, and the words gush. Whether in wall labels, catalog entries, or Acoustiguide recordings, and notwithstanding our desire to have visitors really *look*, we can talk, talk, talk about ob-

1. "Collecting Reconsidered," in *Museum Languages: Objects and Texts*, ed. Gaynor Kavanaugh (Leicester, U.K.: University of Leicester Press, 1991), 135.

2. *The Pedagogue's Panoplist* 2, no. 1 (November 10, 1972): 1. Post has subsequently gone on to become dean of the Yale Law School and an expert at decoding the loquacity of Supreme Court decisions. Even early in my tenure at OSV, I was caustically critical of too much lecturing at visitors. "Much of what passes for interpretation in the Village," I wrote to colleagues in 1973, "is the request to dismiss from thought what one is *seeing* in order to *hear* what is truly important."

jects until the visitor cries "Uncle." The key questions, then, are, What is best said? What's the best relationship between museum stuff and museum talk? How does language enhance the experience of museumgoing?

All would agree, I think, that the rhythms of James Joyce's parody of a museum tour in *Finnegan's Wake* do not fit the bill:

> This the way to the museyroom. Mind your hats goan in! Now yiz are in the Willingdone Museyroom. This is a Prooshious gunn. This is a ffrinch. Tip. This is the flag of the Prooshious, the Cap and Soracer. This is the bullet that byng the flag of the Prooshious. This is the ffrinch that fire on the Bull that bang the flag of the Prooshious. Saloos the Crossgunn! Up with your pike and fork! Tip. (Bullsfoot! Fine!) This is the triplewon hat of Lipoleum. Tip. Lipoleumhat. This is the Willingdone on his same white harse, the Cokenhape. ([New York: Viking, 1959], 8)

Many of the "other functions" that Susan Pearce refers to as flowing from our collections—acquisition, cataloging, conservation, and display, among others—require specialized languages that have little value for the encounter of museum visitors with the collection. Over time, as a young professional, I learned some of the codes and overcame the novice's feeling of intimidation in the company of professional chatter. Eavesdropping on my colleagues, I soon learned to pick out a few telltale signs of country vs. city furniture, Queen Anne vs. Sheraton legs, and federal vs. Greek Revival architectural details. After some reprimands, I learned how to lift chairs by their seats rather than their arms or rails.

But I had no particular method of talking about objects in the outdoor museum. As an interpreter working in the schoolhouse or the law office, I seldom had occasion to engage visitors about provenance or to testify to the authenticity of a particular piece. But then, in 1970, Barnes Riznik asked me to organize a course on the interpretation of artifacts for our graduate program in historical museum work. I was completely lost. I could not figure out how to help students distinguish between one approach and another. Instead we invited one curator after another to expound his or her methodology. One was all about distinguishing the correct names for things, another focused on the evolution of pieces, and a third addressed the challenge of bargain hunting and filling in a collection's gaps.

As I searched the literature, the prevailing wisdom in the museum field about artifact analysis came, as one might expect, from art historians and archaeologists, who had years of experience in studying the three-dimensional evidence that most general historians ignored. Most curators of decorative arts used the same kind of detailed description of the artifact's material, construction, and design that art historians applied to works of fine art. My osv colleagues convincingly used such scholarship to create timelines for the evolution of architecture, gardens, technologies and mechanical devices, textiles and clothing, household furnishings, and a hundred other material evidences of rural New England life.

But such genealogies still left most historians cold. What utility did evidence of this sort have for bigger questions in American history, such as the struggle for democracy, the conflict over slavery, or even the role of capitalism in forging a national economy built around industrialization and the expansion of commercial networks? History museum professionals insistently staked a claim to the value of their collections to this sort of scholarship. As my boss, Alexander J. Wall, president of osv, protested in his 1972 presidential address to the American Association for State and Local History, "The role of the historical artifact is more secure than ever before and is recognized as a necessary addition to the written record. It has become obvious that reliance on the written record alone can give just as incomplete a story as reliance solely upon an isolated artifact."

Wall cited the claim of E. McClung Fleming, education director at the Winterthur Museum in Delaware, "that early American decorative art objects serve as social documents by throwing light on the materials and the manufacturing techniques, trade, technology, the standard of living, social usage, and popular taste of a given period." Outdoor museums, Wall claimed, are particularly valuable for their "ability to give a sense of what it was like to live in a by-gone age."[3] In his proposed model, Fleming had posited that after analyzing the physical object, the student would move to cognitively "higher" operations—making aesthetic judgments, locating cultural contexts, and defining the historical significance of the piece. His own case study, for example, concluded that seventeenth-century court cupboards in Massachusetts looked a lot like those in the England of the time. This could mean, he explained, that their immigrant owners were conservative in their tastes, or else that they were innovative in their furniture design as they were not in town planning or family organization.[4] So?

This sort of painstaking research, yielding such paltry returns in historical understanding, was unappealing to the social historian in me and use-

3. Wall, "The Voice of the Artifact," *History News* 27, no. 10 (October 1972): 5, 8.

4. E. McClung Fleming, "Artifact Study: A Proposed Model," *Winterthur Portfolio* 9 (1974): 153–73; the conclusions of the study are at 171–73.

What can an object, such as this seventeenth-century court cupboard, say to us?

less for my work with the general museum visitor. I was not a Winterthur professor, charged with training a new generation of students of material culture or developing a theoretical approach to the field that would be most useful to academic researchers. My day job was equipping museum historians, educators, and interpreters in the challenge of engaging museum visitors. I needed, therefore, to discover and develop an approach to museum objects that would accomplish two things. First, it would document the location of artifacts within a variety of historical contexts, helping to explain the larger and more significant narratives of our national and regional history. And second, it would at the same time preserve the ability of these objects to spark the empathetic imagination of museum visitors, to allow them to use all their senses and skills to engage the stuff we showed. Or, to say this in reverse order, to encourage visitors first to pay close and rewarding attention to the materiality of the museum exhibition, and then to assist visitors in making personal meanings by integrating their experience of these objects into larger and larger stories of the American people.

Over the course of the twentieth century, several historians had written pioneering studies that valued material evidences evocatively and dramatically. In the 1910s and 1920s, Vassar professor Lucy Maynard Salmon unearthed the layers of historical influence in the contemporary social and physical world, asking, "Why search for hid treasure abroad when the history of the world was spread out in the back yard?" In her own backyard, she discovered an immigrant diversity worthy of any American place: "The crocus comes from the Levant, the hyacinth and the narcissus bear Greek names, the daffodil is a native of England, the tulip in its name is allied with Turkey and in its history with Holland, the fleur-de-lis is the insignia of France and also of Florence, our lilac is Persian, the wisteria is Japanese." And so on for another five or six blossoms.

Twenty-odd years later, John Kouwenhoven insistently broke down the boundaries between the fine and applied arts and exposed a vernacular streak in American design and production that underlay major social changes and distinguished the culture of the United States from its European antecedents. Carpets, automobiles, and skyscrapers, he contended, were as fundamental to the American narrative as westward expansion and constitutional thinking. Yet another quarter-century on, Thomas J. Schlereth, a professor of American studies at Notre Dame, produced a remarkable series of essays demonstrating the value of material evidence to American social history. Schlereth focused with particular adroitness on the amazing proliferation of mass-produced objects in the century after the Civil War, where plentiful evidence in visual and print culture, as well as three-dimensional material, could be marshaled to document the emergence of an integrated national industrial and consumer economy. Each chapter in his history of Victorian America—"Moving," "Working," "Housing," "Consuming," "Communicating," "Playing," "Striving," and "Living and Dying"—brought material artifacts into richly rendered stories of social transformation.[5]

Professors Salmon, Kouwenhoven, and Schlereth shared a populist antagonism to academic art history and its exclusion of almost everything one might encounter in the world outside the museum. Each was a disciple of

5. Salmon, "History in a Back Yard" (1915), reprinted in *Historical Material* (New York: Oxford University Press, 1933), 143–57, quotation at 144. See also Salmon, *History and the Textures of Modern Life*, ed. Nicholas Adams and Bonnie G. Smith (Philadelphia: University of Pennsylvania Press, 2001); Kouwenhoven, *Made in America: The Arts in Modern American Civilization* (New York: Doubleday, 1948) and *The Beer Can by the Highway: Essays on What's American about America* (New York: Doubleday, 1961); Schlereth, *Victorian America: Transformations in Everyday Life, 1876–1915* (New York: HarperCollins, 1991). Schlereth's *Cultural History and Material Culture: Everyday Life, Landscapes, Museums* (Ann Arbor, Mich.: UMI Research Press, 1990) is a valuable account of the evolution of history museums and scholarship in material culture.

John Dewey. The three of them found beauty, delight, and meaning in the stuff of everyday life, the tools of ordinary people, and even the detritus of a consumption-mad economy. They each wanted to expand the canon of vernacular objects deemed worthy of investigation to include the built environment, objects found in nature, things made after 1820, and even mass-produced goods. Buried inside all of their essays was a keen eye for the telling historical detail: how streamlining overcame traditions of luxury in the design of automobile bodies in the 1910s, how synchronized clocks reshaped industrial labor relations, and how clotheslines come and go with the changing demographics of a neighborhood.

This was fascinating stuff that I wanted to share with visitors immediately. But unless one happened to have one of these marvelous objects on hand, it was difficult to use this information in my museum teaching. And few of these discoveries, to tell the truth, involved looking first at an actual three-dimensional object. The stories these writers drew out came almost entirely from written or visual sources in the research library. The narrative flow of the historical essay rushes forward, collecting objects in the same way it snatches quotations from contemporaneous newspapers or images from advertising. Exhibitions work differently from essays. The epistemology of the museum encounter makes the methodology of these essays difficult to implement within the three dimensions of the museum gallery, the allotted time of a visit, and the physical capabilities of visitors' bodies. For the purposes of history museum interpretation and education, then, neither these wide-angle "vernacularists" nor the narrowly focused art historians had solved my problem.

What work, I came to ask myself, did objects do in the museum? What purpose were they serving? How did they engage visitors' attention? What did they cause visitors to do, to say, to think? As I began to be aware of the interpretive hexagon, I understood that objects were one part of a distinct configuration of the museum, and that as institutional purposes, themes, audiences, and pedagogical approaches evolved, so too did the meaning and value of the museum object.

OBJECTS IN MOTION
Most of the great European art museums—the Louvre, the Rijksmuseum, the Brera, and the Prado—descended from royal collections and from the plundering of the Bonaparte brothers. Lacking the blessing of a king or emperor, in the United States the task of choosing what their fellow citizens should behold, revere, and remember fell to local notables, the same gentle-

men who claimed the leadership of state. Imagine an upper chamber in the city hall or county courthouse in the first half of the nineteenth century, its walls lined with portraits of local and national luminaries, beneath which cases contained relics of Indian inhabitants and early European settlers, yellowing documents, buttons from the uniform of a Revolutionary War soldier, specimens of fossils, skeletal remains, and the trophies retrieved from exploratory expeditions and voyages to exotic lands. This is where the American history museum was born. *Oddity*, singularity, was the major message. Visitors were invited to gawk and exclaim their amazement. Superlatives adorned the India-ink labels: "the oldest," "the largest," "the first," or "the last." But welcoming outsiders was not the aim of the early historical societies. The collections were backdrop and illustration for regularly scheduled lectures, often by the members themselves. These enthusiastic amateurs took the rostrum to describe their researches, attribute names to their discoveries, and invite their peers to join in admiring the fecundity of God's creation, the wisdom of the founding fathers, and the value of discovery and enlightenment.

Even as early as the 1830s and 1840s, zealous promoters took over the display of weird stuff for paying spectators. P. T. Barnum is, of course, the most famous of this breed, whose attractions often juxtaposed strange (and sometimes wholly fraudulent) specimens, live performances of dramatic and musical works, and crowd-pleasing tableaux-vivants, panoramas, and giant cyclorama retellings of epic histories like the Mormon trek west or the Battle of Gettysburg. My friend Sherry Kafka Wagner recalls paying a dime to see the dead whale preserved on a railroad siding near Jonesboro, Arkansas, in the 1940s. Roadside attractions and "dime museums" still dot the older highways that parallel the interstates, and Ripley's Believe-It-or-Not remains open in Times Square, amazingly enough, for as long as sixteen hours a day.

But in the last third of the nineteenth century, the more serious and sustained investigation of the historical, aesthetic, and natural world diverged from this amateur and popular activity. Professional training in a hundred disciplines—learning to analyze the woods in furniture, the tooling on book spines, the morphology of fossils, the chemistry of paint and rocks, the baptismal records of rural parishes, or the sequential styles of decorative trim—became essential parts of the museum enterprise. The general museum (and the learned or "historical" society which was often its parent) was a legatee of the Enlightenment devotion to the unity of scholarship. In the middle of the nineteenth century, it was fragmenting into a variety

Museums used to be for gazing at weird oddities, like P. T. Barnum's Feejee Mermaid.

of institutions: the art museum, the science museum (eventually the science and technology center), the history museum, the research library, the botanical garden and arboretum, and the zoo. Each one developed its own sort of professional curatorship, where academic scholarship converged with techniques of studying, collecting, preserving, and interpreting the relevant "stuff," as well as an awareness of the politics and economics of public cultural institutions.

Exit those gentlemen sharing their amateur researches with their peers. Enter the professionals producing knowledge for "the public." Only rarely, and only in some corners of the United States (like the upper midwestern states), however, was there enough government support to pay for such erudition. In New York, Boston, Philadelphia, and a dozen other American cities, wealthy benefactors came forward to patronize these expensive endeavors. In the process, the architecture and interior design of the museum elegantly mixed the hush of the book-lined library, on one hand, and the plush of the gas-lit and carpeted drawing room, on the other. As a sanctuary for "high culture," the museum became an instrument for "uplift," raising the tone of social intercourse, associating with one's betters, and perhaps improving the quality of workmanship among local artisans.

Oddities, peculiarities, or eccentricities simply would no longer do. God's providential beneficence paled before the cash required to buy that lustrous gem that would reflect glory on the metropolis. The preferred object in this sort of museum was the *epitome*, the finest obtainable example of its type. The curator was an expert in identifying the criteria, the points by which a particular object excelled. The museum thus became a parallel universe— peopled by artifacts and specimens instead of plutocrats and laborers—that mirrored the social hierarchies of the Gilded Age. The best stuff strutted prominently; the lesser examples were stacked in back rooms and storage areas. Sometimes this mirroring was bizarrely racial as well as social, as when Charles Sprague Sargent arranged his plantings in Boston's Arnold Arboretum so that the American maples would stand in front of the European and Japanese ones.

Epitomes, in other words, are social creatures. They need companions to make sense. So museum objects now had to be grouped by type, by period, or by culture of origin. Empire-style gowns and early New England chests each had a separate space, each with its own hierarchy of quality. Visitors ranged from the cognoscenti, familiar with the fine points, for whom visiting confirmed their status as insiders, to the novices, who could often be intimidated by identification labels that presumed previous acquaintance with these objects. In this way, the museum of epitomes served as a social sorting instrument, like elite universities and other elements of the educational and cultural sector.

Epitomes, however, were built upon a paradox. Beginning around World War I, and for most of the next two generations, each of the humanities disciplines experienced a cleavage between the refined aesthetics of the social elite and the urge to explain and speak to the mass culture emerging in the advanced economies. Out in the field, archaeologists slowly turned away from hunting for treasures and toward objects that could evidence more fundamental social patterns. In the galleries, artists and art historians began to explore less exalted arenas of practice like photography, prints and drawings, design, murals, collage, and decorative arts. In the country-side, folklore, which had begun in late eighteenth-century collections of tales, songs, and other verbal evidence, now began to address the materiality of ordinary life. In the archive, the 1930s Depression brought on the first wave of "pots-and-pans" history, documenting the customs and objects of ordinary lives. As institutions grew and began to seek support from the wider public, as curatorial knowledge expanded, and as the needs of the middle-class and public-school audience demanded greater respect from the experts, it was no longer possible to claim that only the beautiful and the ornamental represented the true character of modern society.

Or rather, the standards of excellence changed. The Depression and World War II brought a greater sense of social cohesion, of living in a shared world of commodities and social practices. More Americans shared the distress of the 1930s and the material wealth of 1940s and 1950s consumer society. Automobiles, refrigerators, telephones, and televisions became nearly universal. While a Cadillac was still a Cadillac, it was a long way from the time when only a few urban families could afford a horse and carriage, and General Motors marketed even its low-end cars as vehicles for leisure ("See the U.S.A. in your Chevrolet"), not as functional replacements for buckboard wagons.

Typicalities became more important than epitomes: Because they were more present, they had greater influence on contemporary life. History museum curators removed objects from others of the same type and surrounded them with the stuff they once lived among in people's homes. Now an advertisement for breakfast cereals joined the bowls and spoons, the orange-juice glasses, the coffee cups, and the morning newspaper to form a suggestive mise-en-scène representing themes like Family Life, Changes in the American Diet, or The Rise of the Middle Class. Typicalities—like the historical phenomena described by Salmon, Kouwenhoven, and Schlereth—validated their place in the history museum by their frequent appearance in documentary sources. (Older patterns of display often continued, so even objects produced in huge multiples, like the Model T Ford, were displayed as a rare treasure.) Familiarity begat interpretive accuracy.

Each of these three phases of museum objects—oddities, epitomes, and typicalities—used a different sort of expertise, attracted different kinds of visitors for different purposes, and depended on a different sort of institutional authority and support system. Most important, each provided visitors with a distinctive way of engaging the otherness of "stuff," which is a good way of defining the basic purpose of the museum experience itself. At one time, visitors exclaimed, "Confounding!" Then Victorians and Edwardians intoned, "Very fine, indeed," before we all learned to say, after World War II, "That looks just like my grandmother's."

This is where I entered the story. osv was a hybrid. In one sense, its founders were high-minded collectors respectful of connoisseurship. They surrounded themselves, especially in the 1950s, with curators of impeccable credentials in the epitome world—the world of *Antiques* magazine and the dealers who advertised therein. I recall an anecdote about the visit to osv of the doyen of Fifty-Seventh Street dealers, Israel Sack, sometime in the early 1950s, which put the stamp of approval on this out-of-the-way museum. Each year, the museum's Antiques Collectors Weekend brought together professional and amateur students of the decorative arts to connect personal and museum collections.

Though the osv collection included some choice pieces, especially of clocks, glass, and country furniture, it was predominantly a museum of typicalities. My colleagues in the Curatorial Department, who were more and more often university- rather than dealer-trained connoisseurs, assiduously aimed to reunite all sorts of objects of everyday life with others of their kind and era. Of course, there were never enough original objects to furnish an entire village community, and its adoption of "living history" presentations meant that the museum had to use reproduction tools in demonstrations of craft, domestic, and farm work.

So the boundary between the original and the reproduction at osv was inevitably linked to the contest between the twin missions of the museum, as a repository for the best stuff and as a popular educational experience for the largest number. But this distinction, sharp but subtle, was seldom discussed. Nobody would dare harvest grain with the nineteenth-century sickles and scythes collected by the Wells brothers in the 1920s, but exact replicas were made to bring in the crops of the 1970s. On the other hand, reproducing an Eli Terry mantel clock was verboten. The Freeman Farmhouse at osv, in particular, was thus a strange mélange of "authentic" period artifacts and modern reproductions. This was emblematized for me when curator Jane Nylander, around 1973, covered an "original" (though quite ordinary) framed painting in the parlor with a piece of cheesecloth in the summer, describing this as a *typical* way of protecting the painting from flyspecks. Would any curator have deliberately obscured an artwork on display a decade earlier?

On another occasion, Nylander arrayed the Salem Towne House at osv in the funerary trappings of the time: crêpe hung over the doorways, clocks

Re-creating the inventory of the Asa Knight Store at OSV provided a history to global trade, shrewd merchandising, and attractive packaging.

stopped at the time of death, and mirrors covered. When osv acquired, moved, and re-erected Asa Knight's general store from Dummerston, Vermont, Nylander and historian Caroline Sloat oversaw the stocking of its shelves with reproduction objects that would have looked new, fresh, and attractive to shoppers in the 1830s: bars of imported Castile soap, bolts of printed cotton and woolen cloth, Irish linens, Chinese silks, locally woven straw hats, and panes of window glass.[6] There were no original objects at all, except a painstakingly restored architectural setting.

Nylander and Sloat drew upon the evidence of account books and probate inventories, as well as diaries, letters, and newspaper advertisements, to validate their notions of typicality. The most highly sought-after catch in New England manuscript repositories was what we liked to call "sudden death inventories," those lucky occasions when the researcher came upon the listing of household possessions for a forty-year-old man struck down

6. In this practice of mixing original artifacts and reproductions, as in many other ways, OSV followed the model of Colonial Williamsburg. A superb rendering of the material life of New England households is Jane C. Nylander, *Our Own Snug Fireside: Images of the New England Home, 1760–1860* (New York: Knopf, 1993).

by accident and before he had had time to give away his property to others.[7] But since the notations in historical sources were often vague and unfamiliar, the curatorial researcher also needed to know a great deal about the different words for fabrics or household utensils and how they would have been acquired, used, and maintained. Hence the knowledge gained in studying epitomes was invaluable throughout this search for typicalities.

THE TURN TOWARD MATERIAL CULTURE

Though Jane Nylander had been trained at Winterthur and had a splendid eye for the finest in the decorative arts, her practice marked her as an innovator in the curatorial shift toward "material culture" studies. This term, adopted from anthropology, became in the 1970s a useful umbrella for many different ways of exploring and representing the past. For devotees of decorative arts and the history of art and architecture, the term endowed their work with more intellectual heft and carved an escape route from an exclusive focus on the possessions of social elites. For social historians, material culture provided a concrete context for their images of groups usually excluded from the archival record—women, children, immigrants, the enslaved, and transients—and served to counterbalance the abstractedness of quantitative studies and words like "industrialization," "colonialism," or "modernization." Big-picture historians, like the French *Annalistes*, discovered patterns of over-the-counter trading beneath the history of kings and generals. Archaeologists, of course, had always claimed that material remains were truer evidences of past civilizations than the written record. Now that claim could be boldly extended to modern industrial and commercial societies, with their amazing proliferation of stuff and language about stuff (in advertising, regulation, and representation). Suddenly it appeared that consumer revolutions were everywhere in history. Perhaps this reflected deep cultural shifts in American society, where the role of con-

7. In those days, OSV aimed to represent rural New England from 1790 to 1840. So anything introduced after January 1, 1841, was off-limits. But so too were high-style objects, most objects of foreign manufacture, things characteristic of urban life, and "folk" artifacts. In representing a literate society deeply enmeshed in an interregional market economy, OSV steered away from the handmade, one-of-a-kind objects that were celebrated at sister institutions like the Farmers' Museum and Fenimore Art Museum in Cooperstown or the Shelburne Museum in Vermont. On what inventories reveal about the furnishing of rural dwellings, see Abbott Lowell Cummings, *Rural Household Inventories* (Boston: SPNEA, 1964), introduction.

sumer was fast outpacing other ways of describing oneself—citizen, congregant, or worker.

The advent of material culture studies exposed an important cleavage in my museum world. Grouping the entire universe of a particular society's stuff proved what was typical and what was not. If connoisseurship, detailing the "fine points," was the scholarship of the age of epitomes, material culture served the same function in the era of typicalities. As courses in material culture expanded, and as theoretical approaches to its study began to proliferate, the field became more deeply entrenched in the academy. At conferences of the American Studies Association or the Organization of American Historians, now, there were always comrades-in-arms: environmental psychologists, geographers, students of cultural landscapes, art historians, historians of technology, and folklorists, as well as the old decorative arts scholars and social historians wanting to adopt the theoretical and methodological innovations of these social scientists.

But once one left the convention center and walked out into the city, the utility of material culture faded. The new lingo only confused our audience. Why would audiences want to know what was most typical of New England farm households in the 1750s, of fine southern plantations a century later, or of suburban ranch houses in our own day? Indeed, individual objects might elicit a smile of recognition, but visitors seemed to disdain the whole question of the systematic relationship of one part of the material universe with another. I had friends and colleagues producing strokes of curatorial brilliance such as *The Clothes Off Our Backs* show at the Minnesota Historical Society in 1977 or *Getting Comfortable in New York: The American Jewish Home, 1880–1950*, at New York's Jewish Museum in 1990. But I observed that many of their visitors concentrated most on objects familiar from their personal experience. Many even refused to acknowledge the curators' (well-documented) insistence that other, unfamiliar pieces could also have belonged to their family's universe of things. "Never saw such a thing, we never had anything like that." Sometimes this attention to specific objects even conflicted with the overall thematic message of the show.

Material culture, appropriately for an academic discipline aspiring to some degree of scientific objectivity, still left the world of objects "out there." Visitors looked for a deeper, more immediate, and more visceral connection. We needed to draw them into the exhibition. We had to emphasize not the car, but its handling on the superhighway; not the mass of Chinese laborers at work on the Central Pacific, but one that came from a specific village in Fujian; not a recipe, but a chance to cook. Personal narrative, stagecraft, physical interaction, role-playing, and supplementary public programming started to dissolve the museum's "proscenium" separating the presentation from the visitor. Museum learning, it turned out, was all about what I came to call "stuffitude." Stuffitude built upon the materiality of the past, such as I had so dramatically experienced on my first visit to osv, but it was more. It incorporated as well the visitor's materiality in the present, the learner's sensory, physical, kinetic, and kinesthetic appropriation of the world. "Visible and mobile," the philosopher Maurice Merleau-Ponty says, "my body is a thing among things; it's caught in the fabric of the world, and its cohesion is that of a thing."[8] Stuffitude assumes that material objects are integral to all human actions, including the action of their historical moment and the action of our present-day engagement (and all those in between). Everything we do involves materiality and the perception of that material—from the chemicals within the brain to the tendons in our arms, the tools we employ, the anvils and computers we work on, and the ground on which we stand. And it acknowledges, conversely, that humanity is necessary to materiality, that stuff is constantly reconnected by and to human action.[9]

Along the pathway of interpretive design, historians, curators, and designers often fall prey to the tempting power of abstraction. Step away from the concrete realities of past lives, and historic objects easily become playthings for our own categorizing and system-building. Once, years ago, I worked on a major redesign of the Cheney Cowles Museum in Spokane, since renamed the Northwest Museum of Arts and Culture. Recognizing the importance of the museum's collection of fine Indian baskets, our architects proposed to ornament the new entry gallery with a high wall of glass boxes, a lattice of individual specimens. The sketches were intriguing to us, but not to the elders at the Spokane Indian reservation. When we went there to review the design ideas, the elders gently rebuffed our plans. Each basket, they told us, remained a part of the earth that had nurtured its cedar bark and swamp grass. Each was therefore still tied to the Great Spirit, cre-

8. Merleau-Ponty, "Eye and Mind," in *The Merleau-Ponty Reader*, ed. Ted Toadvine and Leonard Lawlor (Evanston, Ill.: Northwestern University Press, 2007), 351–78, quotation at 354.

9. "The perceiving mind is an incarnated mind," according to Merleau-Ponty, *The Primacy of Perception and Other Essays on Phenomenological Psychology, the Philosophy of Art, History and Politics*, ed. James M. Edie (Evanston, Ill.: Northwestern University Press, 1964), 3.

ator of all things. To isolate the basket in a glass cage high in the air, apart from its fellows, violated this lineage. The basket could serve a function and it would still always be both ornamental and spiritually rooted. But to make it a scientific specimen or an architectural feature was to violate its essential nature.

I recall asking my mother, whose memory of childhood in rural Poland and urban New York in the 1920s remained amazingly sharp all her life, how she and my grandmother prepared the Friday evening *Shabbos* dinner, the center of family life. "How did you make the chicken? What kinds of spices and herbs did you use?" I asked. Her reply was unforgettable and opened up a whole world for me. "What time of year are we talking about?" Chicken, in the days before anyone had ever heard of Tyson Foods or Frank Perdue, was not always the same critter. One had to feel its texture, judge its juiciness, give the bird "a good smell," before and during its preparation. One had to think about how to savor its liver, feet, and other parts. One had to consider how many it was meant to serve and what might be done with the leftovers. Making dinner on Friday night was also a way of learning and loving, of transforming the workweek into the Sabbath. The chicken was inseparable from the culture and from the surroundings. No chicken, no life story. If my mother ever had a religion, this was it. Her world was stuffitude, pure and simple.

This encounter reminded me of what material things meant in my growing up. In the era before day care and nursery school, I spent my first five years tied to my mother's apron strings. The advance of cognitive science in recent years suggests what a wonderful laboratory for concept development I must have had in Sarah Rabinowitz's kitchen. In infancy, it was doubtlessly there that I mastered basic-level categories, distinguishing chairs and tables, floors and walls, prams and cars—all things that are recognizable by their shape. Such categories are, according to George Lakoff and Mark Johnson's *Philosophy in the Flesh*, "the highest level at which a person uses similar motor actions for interacting with category members" ([New York: Basic Books, 1999], 27). It was there, probably as a toddler, that I learned to play with metaphors based on these sensorimotor experiences: "Bad is Stinky," so "this toy is stinky"; "Important is Big," so "tomorrow is a big day"; and "Time is Motion," so "time flies." Lakoff and Johnson contend that even the most complex and abstract reasoning emerges from this layering of metaphors atop fundamental relationships in the physical world. The brain, and hence the mind, is a biological phenomenon. "The very properties of concepts are created as a result of the way the brain and body are structured and the way they function in interpersonal relations and in the physical world. . . . From a biological perspective, it is eminently plausible that reason has grown out of the sensory and motor systems and still uses those systems or structures derived from them" (ibid., 37, 42).

Museum professionals, sometimes to the point of tedium, ardently insist that one can learn important things from objects. The new cognitive science teaches us that we cannot learn any other way. All our language, like all our skill of eye and hand, is rooted in our relationship to stuff, developed in conjunction with other people. Sitting in the crow's nest, far away from the messiness of life on deck, one can be easily convinced of our farsightedness. Beware! "Over Descartian vortices you hover. . . . Heed it well, ye Pantheists!"

WIDENING OUR GAZE

The evolution from oddities and epitomes to typicalities took in ever more of what surrounded the individual object. Then, in my generation, the typical began to collapse. We claimed descent from Ralph Waldo Emerson's notion of the "transparent eyeball," first broached in his essay "Nature" (1836), which encompasses the viewer as well as the viewed. In American intellectual life, the evidences of this have emerged everywhere—in the merger of biology and cognition by neuroscientists and linguists like George Lakoff, in Rachel Carson's notion of ecology, in Jane Jacobs's rendering of the organized complexity of urban life, and in many others. Museum learning was not so much an expedition into the unknown and exotic but the incorporation of the remote into the familiar. It no longer made most sense to probe deeper and deeper into the uniqueness of an object isolated from its contexts. Now its meanings were richer when it was allowed to inhale the worlds around it.

I had learned from Kenneth Burke that every object (or "agency") could provoke me to deduce its agent, its act, its scene, and its purpose. I ambled around OSV, bringing dead things to life with my imagination. But, of course, all of us know how to do this from childhood. When I was five, on a family trip through Ontario, my father had bought out the entire stock of a roadside vendor of little foot-high tepees. Installed behind the austere mohair-covered sofa of our living room, the Indian village and a dozen ten-cent plastic cowboys on horses became the terrain and performing cast of endless adaptations of the Wild West stories I devoured so voraciously on radio and television. Nothing was more exciting.

I found my museum career, similarly, in making motion out of stillness and story out of situation. Collecting, naming, categorizing, and displaying objects have been only small aspects of my relationship with stuff, and relatively thin ones at that. It is a fantasy that we can fix the meaning of an object for all time. Consider the infamous Confederate battle flag. Long after its use in war ended, it was revived as a symbol of southern heritage and especially the resistance of White supremacists to federal government intervention against Jim Crow. The battle flag was incorporated into state flags in South Carolina, Georgia, and Mississippi in the 1960s. After another half-century and the horror of a mass shooting in Charleston in 2015, the flag's basic offensiveness to Black Americans and others led, finally, to its removal from many places of public honor. The South Carolina governor and legislature resolved to lower the Stars and Bars from its place on the statehouse grounds. I was elated. But then my friend Christy Coleman, co-CEO of the American Civil War Center in Richmond, Virginia, told me that several of the dozens of Confederate battle flags in the collection of the Museum of the Confederacy were known to have been captured by members of the United States Colored Troops. That puts a different light on the story, doesn't it? Once a typical emblem of the war waged by Johnny Reb, now the flag becomes something more dramatic, a trophy captured on the battlefield in a war for freedom. Exhibiting those flags is a very different act.

Early in my museum career, I had thought that visitors move and the stuff in museums is perpetually still. I questioned that museums could even teach history, which is all about change. But now I know that the museum's objects are really not still. They are constantly in a motion of new meanings, staging and stage-managing new dramas.

13 ::: THE OBJECT AS EVIDENCE
AND EXPERIENCE

Collectors and collections come in all flavors. In the age of epitomes, local nabobs contributed Old Master paintings and other treasures of European art to museums that would adorn the industrial and commercial might of Cincinnati, Minneapolis, or Kansas City with a veneer of sophistication. Others assembled more eccentric arrays and endowed their own museums. A great example is Henry Mercer's collection of 30,000 artisanal tools, vehicles, and examples of folk and handcraft production. Mercer (1856–1930) devoted the profits of his tile-making enterprise to archaeological and historical study, made great advances in identifying and classifying these rather ordinary artifacts of everyday life, and constructed a six-story reinforced concrete castle to house the collection, now part of the Bucks County Historical Society in Doylestown, Pennsylvania. In many places across the North, town and county historical societies collected similar—though less encyclopedic—samples of local production.

By the 1980s, museums of such quaint objects were losing their audience. Collectors and local volunteers might feel nostalgic for those long rows of vitrines, filled with arrowheads or archaeological shards and littered with tiny identification labels handwritten with India ink. But few people wanted to visit. Visitors often complained that they didn't know how to make sense of so many similar objects. One might see the beauty in a handmade hammer, but fifty?

As with the Wells family collection that became the Old Sturbridge Village (osv) museum, the value of these assemblages gradually shifted. Where collectors and curators had cherished them as aesthetic epitomes, post–World War II educators viewed them as evidences of a *typical* pre-industrial or early industrial way of life. To show that shift, the old exhibition cases needed to be emptied and the objects redeployed to show their chronological evolution or their regional differences or, most ambitiously, their contribution to a larger historical narrative. My experience at osv provided me with the credentials for this kind of interpretive transformation and brought in much of the work in the early days of American History Workshop (ahw).

This reinterpretation depended on a crucial though unspoken working assumption. Connoisseurs had long emphasized the importance of the individual maker — Renaissance portraitist or country cabinetmaker. Devotees of the new "material culture" viewed the individual objects in their collections, instead, as having issued from a single, gigantic, interconnected, and internally consistent *system* of production and use, of rituals and performances, of values and ideas. Some unnamed but fundamental force operating beneath the turn-of-the-twentieth-century American society and economy, as an example, ensured that baby carriages and baseball bats, recipes and repair manuals, and almost everything else that was "modern" fit together. That consistency is what made this a material *culture*. So a huge Victorian ironstone soup tureen implied a mode of cooking and serving food, perhaps in a city boardinghouse, and that led, logically, to a kind of kitchen equipment and dining room furniture, and that in turn predicted likely forms of social interaction, even to the architecture of the building, its place in the landscape, and the kind of people who lived and worked there. Exhibitions interpreting this culture used contemporary illustrations and long interpretive texts to make these connections evident.

But a tureen filled with words and pictures rather than soup is more than a bit misleading. To see it as simply part of an internally harmonious cultural system substitutes the criterion of typicality for all the other possible meanings it can carry. Further, our curatorial cleverness — making these linkages — seldom impressed our audience as much as we hoped. Would visitors want to spend their Sundays in museums in analyzing and appreciating cultural systems? Was this insight into the fundamental unity of objects and social life appealing enough, important enough, to serve as a new raison d'être for the history museum? If one already could see the consistencies within a culture sufficiently through the illustrations in contemporary magazines, why did we need the museum objects at all?

Over time, my imagination wandered. I could not resist wondering, What happens if the soup spills? Or if the tureen is dropped on the way to the table? Or if the widowed boardinghouse keeper remarries and her tenants have to leave? Objects gain ever-new meanings as they move forward in time, become part of individual lives, and break out of their predicted typicality. Every object's life history is larger and more complex than the mold it came from. At the start of my career, I had been entranced by seeing the connections among a chair and a candlestand, a hearth, a newspaper, the ambient light in a winter room, and the instinct to read aloud to one's companions. Now I wanted to introduce contingency, mishap, second lives—something unexpected. These, I knew, would tell me new things.

Designing interpretive projects for collection-rich museums taught me a great deal about these questions and showed a pathway beyond the age of typicalities.

HIGGINS ARMORY MUSEUM

At the Higgins Armory Museum in Worcester, Massachusetts, a wonderfully eccentric collection of ancient, medieval, and Renaissance arms and armor had been assembled as a hobby by a local steel manufacturer. When the AHW team began our interpretive planning project in 1983, the museum had been open for about fifty years, but for most of that time it was an adjunct to a tour of the neighboring Worcester Pressed Steel Company. With over 2,000 pieces, the Higgins collection of arms and armor was second in the United States only to the Metropolitan Museum in New York.

John Woodman Higgins's museum building was a perfect starting point for imaginative voyages back in time. Designed in the late 1920s by Bostonian Joseph Leland, it was an Art Deco masterpiece of glass and steel (natch!) on the exterior and mock medieval halls inside, said to resemble those in Prince Eugene of Savoy's Hohenwerfen Castle in Austria. But after their initial stop at the admissions desk, visitors found little structure to their tour. They wandered from piece to piece. Too soon the wows gave way to yawns.

Some of its treasures were truly splendid: There were about two dozen full suits of armor. Others may have been not entirely trustworthy constructions of bits of old metal. The biggest crowd-pleaser was "Helmutt," the mannequin of a dog dressed in a reproduced suit of boarhound armor. Little identification tags defined and attributed each piece, but often with an unfamiliar terminology. Some of the most interesting facts were obscured—how this piece had been made, where Higgins had obtained it, or who'd owned it previously. The interpretive labels made comparisons among pieces that were out of sight of one another. In that era when *Dungeons and Dragons* was exploding in popularity, adolescent boys could quickly rival most curators in their ability to identify slight variations among such artifacts. To everyone else in the public, it was all a mystery.

But it was a compelling mystery. Burnished armor is a sensory self-contradiction. As we approach a suit of armor, we see ourselves reflected, distended and misshapen as in a funhouse mirror. And then we catch ourselves recognizing the cold, off-putting, hostile qualities of a warrior armed and shielded from the fellow feeling of human interaction. We have to pull away, stand back, aware that this prosthetic shell portends an ominous aspect of human culture. Every artifact in the museum of armor is thus an invitation to a dance.

Our first curatorial instinct, born of our inclination to typologies, was to group objects by culture of origin and historical era. We quickly realized this would stop the music and the dancing. Visitors would be lured into, even locked into, an interpretive pathway. Invited to read one label after another, they would probably look less and less intently at the armored figures before them. For the educated laypeople who constitute large proportions of the museumgoing audience, reading is so much easier than looking. Their walk through "Label-land" would become a confining tunnel of information, and references to Italy, to the Hundred Years War, or to "breastplates," "gorgets," and "gauntlets" would carry the visitors' attention far from the gallery.

In response, our goals were twofold. We wanted to encourage visitors to look more intently at the armor, to see its complexities, and to allow its physical strangeness to sweep over them. At the same time, we wanted to provoke the rich cultural associations already in the minds of visitors (like the medieval romances they'd read or seen in the movies, or the science fiction figures whose costumes are derived from historical armor) and to provide them with the tools that would allow them to categorize and interpret what they were seeing.

Our plan involved transforming the visitors' pathway into a series of short- and long-term encounters with object, story, and theme. First, an orientation film would introduce the basic contexts. Then a series of exhibitions varying in theme and experience would allow visitors to delve more deeply into the cultural and material contexts of the collection. Young visi-

tors could join a hands-on learning laboratory, where they could handle real pieces of armor, try to replicate their design and ornamentation out of cardboard, and participate in dress-up simulations of historical ceremonies.

If we had been professional students of the history of arms and armor or of warfare or of metalwork or of late medieval society or of anything else relevant, we might have conjured up a complex taxonomy to organize the collection. Instead, we were educators first. The most useful concept to give visitors is one that they will put to use immediately and that will lead them, confidently, to explore further. We found this tool in the simple division between the armor produced for use in actual warfare and that produced as ornamental display—War and Tournament.

We then allocated each wing of the museum's Great Hall into an evocation of the two, *The World of the Tournament* and *The World of Battle*. Incorporating the best pieces in the Higgins collection, the first of these interprets the tournament in 1600 as a sporting event that ritually transformed the objects, skills, and tactics of medieval warfare into a public "enactment," as our plan said, "on a mythic scale, of the codes of chivalric conduct and knight combat in a vanishing feudal society. Thus we find defenders in a tournament playing the allegorical roles of *Bon Espoir, Cure Loyal, Valiaunt Desire,* and *Joyeux Penser.* The strict rules and rituals of the tournament contrast strongly with the brutal violative (even if implicitly rule-dominated) conduct of contemporaneous and more modern wars."

The World of Battle, by contrast, aimed to bring visitors into the perspective of individual soldiers at the first Battle of Breitenfeld in 1631, a turning point in the horrific Thirty Years War. Here mayhem has replaced ritual, and slaughter and waste have taken the place of chivalry. Influenced by John Keegan's *The Face of Battle* (1975), this exhibition plan emphasizes the moment-to-moment, ground-level experience on the battlefield, when the strategy of commanders utterly failed to control events.

For fifty minutes of each hour, according to this plan, the exhibitions rely on elegant installations and beautifully designed settings and graphic information panels to convey the contrasting worlds of battle and tournament. But then, for ten minutes, five on each side of the Great Hall, a multimedia presentation adds sound and light, narration and projected images, to these stories. Visitors find themselves surrounded, alternately, by the ceremonials of knightly honor and the fearful dangers of hand-to-hand combat.

All this was to be supplemented, on the balcony overlooking the Great Hall, by an installation of a life-sized reproduction of the *Triumphal Procession of Maximilian I,* the Holy Roman Emperor. Originally produced by several artists and engravers in the 1510s and published by Albrecht Dürer and others after Maximilian's death in 1519, it is one of the largest prints ever made, 177 feet long. An extraordinary documentation of both ordinary life and fantasy in early Renaissance Europe, the imagined procession comprises dozens of carts, carriages, and marchers—far too expensive ever to have been realized. At the Higgins, visitors would be able to walk along the painted image, peer behind to see interpretive text, and take photos of their children dressed in the costumes of jousters and court musicians.

Over the years, AHW has tried to insert multimedia presentations like these right into the gallery space, rather than in set-aside theaters. Here it would have presented what every visitor craved, the chance to see all these glorious objects brought to life, moving, enhanced with voice and sound. But the director who had hired us was gone soon after, and his successors never returned our phone calls.

MÜTTER MUSEUM

Even more exotic was the Mütter Museum of the College of Physicians in Philadelphia, said to be the only significant cultural institution in the city not founded by Benjamin Franklin. The Mütter had everything you needed for a horror movie: skeletons of giants and of dwarfs, preserved specimens of every human abnormality and diseased organ, hundreds of criminals' skulls, and the remains of a dozen sideshow attractions. The Human Balloon, whose nine-foot-long colon contained forty pounds of feces at his death, was adjacent to the Soap Lady, whose corpse turned to gooey wax in the grave. I was stunned to discover a "horned lady" among the specimens—exactly like the one that White Jacket, Melville's title character, discovers in the captain's cabin in the novel that preceded *Moby-Dick*.

Gretchen Worden, the brilliant impresario of this swarm of ghouls, invited Nick Paffett and me to help re-order the museum's space in 1983. Her frequent appearances on the David Letterman late-night TV show, always accompanied by weird accessories and an infectious laugh, had begun to build the museum's annual attendance from the high three figures to over 60,000. Given Worden's success, nothing was going to undermine her attachment to the most peculiar parts of the collection. Visitors did not need a taxonomy to take pleasure in the Mütter's wacky stuff.

But, looking back, I'm intrigued to discover my proposed interpretive plan for the Mütter Museum. I began by asking, as I thought any visitor would, why there should be such a place inside the august halls of Philadelphia's oldest professional association. Was this some private cache of Dr. Thomas Dent Mütter, discovered and cracked open only after his death? Quite the contrary: Mütter had created something enormously useful in training nineteenth-century doctors. Here were specimens and models of the tumors presented by patients; here were instances of what ensued if treatment failed or if it was never offered. Here was the brotherhood and sisterhood of human variation for a society and a profession that scarcely knew how to cure any human ailment. When we say that a person had given his or her body to science, this is what we meant.

Of course, in the 1880s and 1890s, almost all of this became irrelevant. With the introduction of X-rays into clinical practice (1896), the body became much more permeable to medical investigation. The study of blood chemistry made similar advances at this time. The first pediatric textbook on hematology, for example, appeared in 1897, and the four blood groups— A, B, AB, and O—were identified four years later. After these two dramatic innovations, medical practice changed radically. The shift from relying on seeing, touching, and listening to the patient to examining evidence recorded on translucent plates or chemical charts profoundly altered the hierarchy of practice. And in Philadelphia, there were already two perfect images of the contrast, in two magnificent paintings produced by Thomas Eakins, *The Gross Clinic* (1875) and *The Agnew Clinic* (1889), representing the shift from doctors in business suits to skilled scientists wearing "whites."

By reintegrating the museum's collection into these two contrasting methods of medical diagnosis, before and after the introduction of these new technologies, we hoped to give visitors a more vivid way of engaging the Mütter's collection. These objects could now be experienced again as part of the thought process of doctors confronting the mysteries of bodily illness.

THE MUSEUM OF MISSING OBJECTS

AHW found its niche in creating public interpretive programs for institutions with few professional historians. Many museums did not need AHW to survey or study their collections. Their own staff members often came to their museum jobs as "collectors at heart," as Colonial Williamsburg's chief historian Cary Carson says. But they had less experience in developing exhibitions and programs about historical ideas, events, places, and patterns of life. As cultural institutions became more dependent upon audience members and government funding, they hoped to shape their long-standing collections into stories significant to a wider public, and to create dynamic learning encounters for visitors of all ages and backgrounds. Historic house museums wanted to transform themselves into mirrors of local history rather than displays of a leading family's Victorian furnishings. Industrial history centers wanted to show how critical their work had been to regional development. Even the most eccentric collectors wanted us to tell them what their assemblages might mean to a visiting public. To all these, we answered, in the eternal motto of the freelancer, "We can do that!"

We brought a venturesome pedagogical energy to this work. We heartily believed that great stories were out there, connecting local history to the richest narratives of the American people, and that these stories would be of great interest to contemporary audiences, even those descended from the most recent arrivals to these shores.

And then reality set in. The collections of most American museums and historic sites had been assembled in the age of the epitome. In the storage closets there were dozens of wedding gowns for every work apron, a hundred pieces of porcelain for each original wooden dish. My former OSV colleague Nicholas Westbrook, when creating exhibitions at the Minnesota Historical Society, fantasized that "an archaeologist unearthing the society's collection 500 years from now might well imagine ours to be a culture of a few men in military drab and a great many women who wore bridal white."[1] And that was at an institution which at the time had 10,000 items in its clothing collection. Whether by curatorial preference for finer objects, the larger role played by local elites, or the vicissitudes of wear and tear, history museum collections were almost always skewed toward a representation of upper-class life, leisure-time activity, patriotic symbols, and the tastes of private collectors and connoisseurs. Typicalities, as I have described them, were a more recent fashion, fed by academic interests in the experience of ordinary people and the desire of the historically excluded— women, second- and third-generation ethnics, and people of color—to have their stories represented in the gallery.

That wasn't all that was missing. Looking around any home taught you that people hoarded "string too short to save," last week's newspapers, the leftovers of a meal or the ingredients of a future one, socks that needed darning, letters that needed answering, and other "ephemera." No period room in a museum, built around invented or composite typicalities (e.g., a frontier family, a boardinghouse of Irish canal-diggers, or a split-level domicile for 1950s teenagers) could be curated with enough of these incidental objects.

There were other curatorial problems, particularly as museums began to interpret more contemporary eras. What could one do with the mass-produced objects of the industrial age, often lacking local provenance? As the American economy became nationalized, the objects in each place lost their distinctiveness. Why would a local history museum in Dallas, Texas, want to furnish a turn-of-the-twentieth-century room with material that was almost exactly the same as that in a historic house in Portsmouth, New Hampshire?

When one cast an eye at history beyond the front door and the garden gate, the problem got worse. Twentieth-century objects, especially in the public realm, were huge by comparison with those of previous generations. A single Bob's Big Boy outdoor fiberglass sculpture, originally installed in front of a fast-food restaurant in Glendale, Arizona, could by itself fill up one of the galleries in the Papago Park museum of the Arizona Historical Society. If you wanted to include one overhead directional sign for the Cross-Bronx Expressway in the exhibition on Robert Moses at the Museum of the City of New York, it would barely squeeze through the doorway. Of course, these objects were meant to be seen while moving quickly and through an

1. Nicholas Westbrook, "Collections: Decisions, Decisions: An Exhibit's Invisible Ingredient," *Minnesota History* 45 (Fall 1977): 292.

automobile window. When seen close up from a still position, and without the rest of the road landscape, they would dwarf the museumgoer.

The way we commonly represent such aspects of modern life, even the way we experience them, is through moving image media. In the 1980s museums began to face the challenge of collecting and preserving film and video, as well as recordings of oral history interviews. The conservation problems they posed were enormous. The selection criteria for what was recorded and what went unnoticed were impossible to determine. Simply owning and maintaining the appropriate playback equipment was often baffling. Since there's no simple way to scan a recording, cataloging was difficult and time-consuming.

As it turned out, therefore, the collections procedures, institutional history, architectural form, and financial basis of our history museums turned out to be inadequate for representing whole areas of the American experience. The scale and siting of gallery installations privilege certain aspects of our history, just as storage facilities have been designed around particular kinds of objects. The rest of what has happened to our people, and the way we recall and retrieve those stories, seems evidently to fall outside the capacity of our museums.

"Gotta have the real stuff! That's what museums are for!" We heard this over and over again. The conventional museum professionals' mantra was, in truth, a gigantic impediment in many early AHW interpretive projects. Curators and directors brought forth iconic artifacts they wanted on display. Important donors wanted their prize pieces to be featured. Fourth-grade teachers told their children to look out for that amazing furry creature they themselves had seen when visiting thirty years earlier. But twist and turn as we might, we had a difficult time incorporating many collection pieces into the arguments we were making or the stories we were telling. The transition to the "typical" had often proceeded without an alteration in collection policies. And the emergence of the "dramatic" would create even greater problems, since stories seldom come down to us with a full complement of accompanying artifacts.

Even if you could locate all the right objects, of course, you still might not be able to achieve the interpretive goals you had set. A prime example was AHW's work on the *16 Elm Street* project at the Smithsonian's National Museum of American History. Roger Kennedy, the museum's charismatic director, had decided to dedicate the largest artifact in his collection—a house built in Ipswich, Massachusetts, in 1696, removed and re-erected inside the museum in 1963—as the Time Machine, a multimedia orientation program for the whole museum. For almost twenty years, the reinstalled George Hart House had been used to demonstrate the late medieval post-and-beam construction technology of colonial America, with two mannequins positioned at either end of reproduction pit-saws and others locking mortise-and-tenon joints together. I actually liked that installation, and it reminded me of what I'd first seen on field trips with my colleagues at osv. But I also noticed that I was almost always alone in this gallery. Few visitors, it seemed, were interested.

The static, unsheathed Hart House could not contain Director Kennedy's ambition. So he did what energetic executives of that generation did: "Gather the best and the brightest" from outside, he decreed—never a good message to communicate to one's workers—and told us to hammer together a creative team for the Time Machine project. Rusty Russell had pioneered the development of hour-long multimedia, multiscreen presentations, including *The San Francisco Experience, The New York Experience,* and *Where's Boston?* Sherry Kafka Wagner had published a novel and short stories, collaborated on the design of the San Antonio Riverwalk, produced plays and films, and reinvigorated teaching in schools and museums throughout the country. Peter Wexler was a celebrated New York–based theater and opera designer, equally adept at photography, stage and costume design, lighting, and film production design. I don't know what I was doing in this mob.

Our idea, hammered out over a year of research and design meetings, was to transform the old house into a thirty-minute-long, walkthrough theatrical event. The storyline would trace the succession of families who had actually lived at 16 Elm Street in Ipswich, from cooper George Hart's patriarchal household in the eighteenth century (in which his son Nathaniel remained a dependent, voteless in town meetings, as long as the father survived) all the way through World War II, when it was rented by women who worked at the local Sylvania plant on proximity fuses for aerial bombing. Along the way, visitors would explore the lives of Abraham Dodge, a West India merchant (and his enslaved man, Chance) during the American Revolution; Josiah Caldwell, the town's leading abolitionist in the 1830s; and several households of Irish women who worked as laundresses for the Heard family next door in the 1860s and 1870s.

Since none of these people, so far as we knew, had left any of their possessions behind or had conveniently died in middle age and had their estates inventoried, reconstructing the family stories and the household's appearance was a challenge. I recruited Ellen Rothman, who had worked with me at osv before completing her Ph.D. in history, as the chief scholar on our team, and Ellen Rosenthal, trained at Winterthur and the Minnesota Historical Society, as our chief curator. Rothman dug at the archival records and did oral histories in Ipswich that brought to light the most recent denizens of 16 Elm. Finding very few relevant objects in the Smithsonian's own collections, Rosenthal surveyed twenty-five museum collections in New England, selecting over 1,500 objects that would have been appropriate in this house at various stages. The goal was to photograph these for inclusion in the Time Machine media program. This would, we hoped, provide a lexicon of material culture of American domestic life over the course of three centuries. And that would, we hoped, introduce a series of key social history themes for the museum: household composition, family roles, the expansion of material life in the century after 1750, slavery and abolition, education, reform movements, professionalization, immigration, working-class life and labor, war, and peace.

It didn't work, and its failure laid bare the weakness of material culture as a method for creating engaging museum exhibitions about the social history of the American people. The house's stories were exciting enough. Any one of the generational narratives we excavated could have provoked visitors to rethink their conventional understandings of domestic history and how families confront crisis and change: the fate of patriarchal authority in the middle of the eighteenth century, the commitment to radical social reform in the antebellum North, the emergence of ethnic and class diversity after the Civil War, or the struggle to survive economically through the Depression.

But the sources we used to represent these moments—each generation's array of domestic furnishings—had little to do with these stories. Chosen because of their typicality for each historical period in this region of the United States, they told a rather different tale, of shifts in technology, commerce, taste, and attitudes toward the home. "Typical" objects seldom helped us understand how these particular households coped with change—whether that came in publicly convulsive events like revolution, emancipation, or civil war or in more private crises like aging, orphaning, or immigration. Ordinary life is pretty extraordinary when looked at through the lens of individual households, as I would learn at the Lower East Side Tenement Museum a decade later. And often the objects we had located carried their own dramatic details, but these said nothing about the Ipswich folks we were tracing.

For me, the project brought into question the whole enterprise of material culture as it related to museum interpretation. We could do historical drama, as Director Kennedy wanted, or we could expound subtle anthropological distinctions, as our material suggested—but not both. We could provide a compendium of domestic furnishings over many decades, and we could define what Americans have meant by "home" in each generation (which would have probably been ideal!); but we could not introduce visitors to all the major stories of the National Museum's interpretation in this way.

Around the country, many other history curators were then creating exhibitions that traced the evolution of objects—communications devices, tableware, computers, clothing, the accouterments of smoking, or parlor furniture. In the *After the Revolution* exhibition at the Smithsonian's National Museum of American History, a splendid variety of object histories rendered the new material life of the young American republic. I found all of these quite interesting, and I was glad to sharpen my cocktail-party ability to note which sort of artifact preceded another in the inevitable sequence. But these projects, frankly, did little to expand my knowledge of American social history. As Cary Carson put it in 1997,

> Object-centered monographs and object-rich exhibits need not raise significant historical issues at all to attract publishers and sponsors or satisfy readers and visitors. Consequently, many do not bother. Those that make the effort almost always turn out to be derivative because they almost always borrow ready-made interpretations from some other branch of knowledge. "Culture and Comfort," for instance, however thoughtful, recycled historical ideas that had made their first appearance in feminist scholarship two decades earlier.[2]

By the late 1980s, object-oriented exhibitions had begun to disappear from many historical museums. In a volume reviewing a dozen interpretive exhibitions at institutions ranging in size from the Stearns County (Minnesota) Historical Society and the Indianapolis Children's Museum to the Henry Ford Museum, dealing with histories from prehistoric Florida to modern consumer cultures, only one exhibition—on Hispanic folk material

2. Carson, "Material Culture History: The Scholarship Nobody Knows," in *American Material Culture: The Shape of the Field*, ed. Ann Smart Martin and J. Ritchie Garrison (Winterthur, Del.: Henry Francis du Pont Winterthur Museum, 1997), 401–28, quotation at 408. *Culture and Comfort* was mounted at the Margaret Woodbury Strong Museum in Rochester, N.Y., in 1988–89.

in the Southwest—explicitly aimed to display key collection items. Virtually all the rest were "concept" shows, interpreting African American urban life in the 1950s ("the last decade in which American society was segregated"), the automobile in American life, and evolving ideas about fitness, folklore, and women's work in American history. Each plumbed collection resources from diverse collections but were chiefly organized around thematic narratives. And, finally, one was more explicitly narrative than conceptual, tracing how three Hidatsa Indians confronted the officially imposed reservation system at the turn of the twentieth century. Most of these shows relied heavily on objects in their designs, and several explicitly explored the problem of collecting and displaying. But the intellectual goals of the curators extended far beyond the challenge of informing the public about the collections themselves.[3]

Could the historical objects in museum exhibitions be more than illustrations? Could they be "sources" for new historical understandings? Were they actually evidence? It was fashionable, for a while, to advance theories about "visual literacy" and to analogize the linguistics of "three-dimensional documents" and try to encourage students to "*read* artifacts."[4] Archaeologists and folklorists like Henry Glassie and James Deetz tried to theorize explanatory schemes for American history, but in my mind they were only useful as new taxonomic categories for chairs or gravestones or whatnots. They did not explain anything beyond their own evidence or link these shifts in the design and production of artifacts to more significant social, economic, political, or cultural changes in American life. Visitors could actually experience for themselves Jane Nylander's interpretation of household life and labor by her curatorial work at osv, but *16 Elm Street*, I'm afraid, was more a sentimental soap opera than a challenging domestic history.

I learned more when Cary Carson and his colleagues at Williamsburg—careful students of stuff—began to speak about a "consumer revolution" in the eighteenth century, or when Richard Bushman began to define a process of refinement that extended from objects to manners to social roles.

3. Kenneth L. Ames, Barbara Franco, and L. Thomas Frye, eds., *Ideas and Images: Developing Interpretive History Exhibits* (1992; Walnut Creek, Calif.: Alta-Mira Press, 1997).

4. Tracey Rae Beck, Pauline K. Eversmann, Rosemary T. Krill, Edwina Michael, and Beth A. Twiss-Garrity, "Material Culture as Text: Review and Reform of the Literacy Model for Interpretation," in Smart Martin and Garrison, *American Material Culture*, 135–67.

This sounded like something that could be juxtaposed, comfortably or not, with the ideological shifts we used to explain the politics of the Revolutionary and Jacksonian eras. Here, finally, looking at stuff paid dividends in historical understanding. Rhys Isaac's *The Transformation of Virginia* extended this into a psychosocial inquiry into slaveholding society, in which investigations of language, landscape, and behavior, as well as material culture, underpinned a representation of a social crisis.[5]

The *16 Elm Street* project died along its journey through the Smithsonian's budget office, but it whetted my appetite for a more dramatic rendering of everyday lives in the American past.

5. Cary Carson, "The Consumer Revolution in Colonial British America: Why Demand?," in *Of Consuming Interests: The Style of Life in the Eighteenth Century*, ed. Cary Carson, Ronald Hoffman, and Peter J. Albert (Charlottesville: University Press of Virginia, 1994), 483–697, and other chapters in this volume; Richard L. Bushman, *The Refinement of America: Persons, Houses, Cities* (New York: Knopf, 1992); Rhys Isaac, *The Transformation of Virginia, 1740–1790* (Chapel Hill: University of North Carolina Press, 1982).

14 ::: THE INVENTION OF
THE CLUSTER

The scholarship of Cary Carson, Richard Bushman, and Rhys Isaac proved to me, even more than that of my early Old Sturbridge Village (osv) colleagues, that the materiality of place, stuff, and social situation was profoundly important to the history of American politics and culture. But they were still *writing* about objects. How could I incorporate these subtleties into my exhibition work? Giant introductory panels that spoke about the "transformation of material culture" would not do. I wanted to bring visitors into a more direct—physical, visual, and kinesthetic—relationship to the things we showed and, at the same time, help them generate fresh historical ideas that extended (rather than illustrated) what was already known through reading. And I aimed to embody that encounter in an experience that would provoke visitors to rethink their relationships to place, identity, and historical time.[1]

The answer, I discovered, was to expand the definition

1. See Scott G. Paris and Melissa J. Mercer, "Finding Self in Objects: Identity Exploration in Museums," in *Learning Conversations in Museums*, ed. Gaea Leinhardt, Kevin Crowley, and Karen Knutson (Mahwah, N.J.: Lawrence Erlbaum Associates, 2002), 401–23.

of the object. In the art museum (and especially in its permanent exhibition galleries), many visitors move deliberately, at a "cruising speed." They saunter, pausing to focus on this painting or that sculpture because it is familiar or newly intriguing. In the history museum exhibition, few relics or artifacts—whether oddities, epitomes, or typicalities—are magnets in their own right. They seldom stop visitors in their tracks. Instead, visitors are drawn closer by an ensemble of elements: an original or reproduced artifact, an idea, a person speaking about or reenacting a historical action, or an interpretive device (such as a model, a graphic panel, a multimedia presentation or a computer-interactive game).

In the visitor-centered museum, after all, the perceiving intelligence of the museumgoer, not the intervention of the curator, defines the museum object. We may as well say that everything that visitors encounter is an object in the museum setting. The distinctions museum people use to separate the "original" document, its interpretive context, and its physical surroundings are fundamentally useless. Visitors see them all and are influenced by all of them. It is foolish to hope that they will see only the ostensibly "authentic" document and ignore everything else. Accounts and reviews of exhibitions that take note only of the documents are half-blind. Curators and historians who ignore the communicative power of the stuff that is not an original document soon learn to their sorrow that much in their exhibitions is missed.

As I had learned long before in the outdoor museum, I observed a ritual, performative quality to gallery attentiveness. Visitors needed to be, first, invited into the encounter, then reinforced in that decision by its connection to previous experiences, stimulated to look at the whole and at details, provided with an intellectual scaffolding for examination and exploration, allowed to register a response and to witness that response, and then, finally, bade a farewell, perhaps by being given links to other encounters farther along the visitor pathway.

All this takes just a few minutes, and in a successful passage through an interpretive exhibition it happens dozens of times. Between these intermittent encounters, visitors regroup with their companions, smile or frown, change body position, and scan the pathway ahead for other invitations to attention. These ritualized encounters can hardly ever happen with individual objects. The only reliable way to initiate them is to break the typical pattern of library or art shows, in which similar objects are lined up in successive vitrines or wall mountings. Instead, we created what we called "the interpretive cluster."

As an example of this process, let me describe our installation of a few leaves from James Madison's notes on the 1787 Federal Constitution Convention in our exhibition *Miracle at Philadelphia*, mounted at the Second Bank of the United States building, just down the street from Independence Hall, in 1986–87. The best documentation we have for the proceedings of the convention, Madison's notes are enormously important treasures of American political and constitutional history. They came to light only a full half-century later, when his widow, Dolley, sold them to the Library of Congress a year after Madison's death in 1836. They were first published in 1840. As soon as I discovered in 1985 that the Library was not intending to mount a bicentennial exhibition on the convention, I leaped into action and persuaded James Hutson, the Library's manuscripts chief, to let us borrow them for the Philadelphia show.[2]

In our exhibition, we called these notes "the Rosetta Stone of American constitutionalism." That was truer than we realized. As important as the papers were, so too were they almost indecipherable to any but the most experienced archival scholar. (In fact, some of Madison's notes were written in code.) In an exhibition, it would be heavy weather for visitors to make any sense of these ink scratches, much less to approach them with the proper reverence. So, in addition to proclaiming the significance of the documents, the interpretive label transcribed the portions of Madison's notes actually shown on the table. Conservation requirements meant that the pages had to be changed frequently over the duration of the exhibition. How could our presentation clue visitors in to the importance of these papers and help them understand them?

Designer Nick Paffett and I donned the cloak of the set dresser. We decided to place the papers alongside the famous Syng inkstand that originally held the quill pens used by the convention secretary (close enough, but probably not the inkwell used by Madison himself), and we fit the two precious relics into a secure exhibition case sitting atop a replica of one of the tables at Independence Hall. Then we took a step further and commissioned Studio EIS in Brooklyn to supply a 5′3″-high white plaster figure of "Little Jemmy" Madison, which would stand next to the table.

The whole mise-en-scène functioned like one of those Venetian altarpieces I have long believed are the perfect models for exhibition elements. In the process, the (meaning of the) document was transformed. Seen by themselves within a vitrine, Madison's disembodied scrawls would at best come across as a major step in the evolution of the United States Constitution. Within our more elaborate dramatic setting, we wanted the document to live again as a work product. Visitors might peer over the (mock) Virginian's shoulder and try to see what he was writing on one particular day in the summer of 1787.

---

2. It was one of the most dramatic days of my career. I sped in a cab from my meeting with Hutson back to the offices of the National Endowment for the Humanities. As it turned out, gaining access to these papers was crucial to winning a major grant from the NEH for the Philadelphia exhibition.

Such immediacy required the engagement of the bodies of visitors as much as their eyesight. One was tempted to take the seat, pick up the pen, perk up one's ears to catch the drift of a delegate from Delaware, and scribble a note. Through visitors' physical connection to the convention and their theatrical proximity to one of the founders, we hoped to demonstrate that the Constitution was not an instantaneous revelation from on high, but something of a collaborative "construction project," where delegates advanced competing de-

signs and invented complicated institutional forms to reconcile political differences. Despite the exhibition's title, we deployed this design intervention
to emphasize the duration and unpredictability of the constitution-making
process in the barely united states of the 1780s.

In sum, it took a great deal of artifice to underscore the authenticity
of the original object. An inch of fakery was the only route to a mile of
"the real." Contextualizing and scene-setting would allow visitors to know

Madison's notes more intimately. Taken as a whole, this ensemble, or "interpretive cluster," became a model in our practice, an assemblage of heterogeneous elements that connect the cognitive, affective, and kinesthetic fragments of a human action. At osv, I had identified the museum experience as a sequence of "framing" encounters with an interpreter or a crafts demonstrator. In the gallery exhibition, similarly, we arranged for visitors to engage such clusters of elements. We wanted visitors to stay close to the cluster long enough to piece together an episode characteristic or constitutive of the story we wanted to tell. The key to museum learning is this relatively tight angle of vision, in which all of the visitor's body, and especially his or her eyes, encompasses the situation of a moment in a historical person's life. Exhibition design entails a careful placement of the visitor's body, his or her eyes and ears, as much as it does the historical document and the supplementary interpretive material we have created. Visitors look, they listen, they point, they jostle, and they connect to one another. The different elements of their perceptivity and rationality are set in motion. The exhibition cluster registers.

The cluster—and not the individual object, the historical idea, or the episode in the narrative—became the atomic particle, the irreducible constituent of our museum exhibitions. Our interpretive design work henceforth focused on the internal, experiential logic of the cluster itself and the arrangement of clusters along a temporal pathway. The oddity, the epitome, and the typicality all depended for their communicative power on a set of ideas and relationships to objects and forces outside themselves. The cluster, an artfully assembled array of objects and interpretive elements, was primarily experiential, not ideational, in character. Clusters could work in the history museum as art objects did in the art gallery: They would announce their significance and reward concentrated attention. Of course, we hoped that the whole series of clusters would convey historical themes and carry visitors through a historical narrative. But just as novelists have to write good paragraphs and dramatists stage good dialogues, the history curator has to arrest the wandering eyes and minds of visitors and fashion moments of illumination and excitement for them.

By the time American History Workshop (AHW) came to the 2006 exhibition at the New-York Historical Society, *New York Divided: Slavery and the Civil War*, we had learned to organize each gallery as a sequence of clusters. Right at the entrance to that show we wanted to show visitors that antebellum New York City was in economic thrall to King Cotton and its pro-slavery political and cultural attitudes. Our designer, Lynne Breslin, came up with the superb idea of suspending a (mock) 500-pound bale of cotton over the doorway to the first gallery. Everybody got the point. Cotton loomed over everything. The first gallery itself evoked the sights and sounds of the nineteenth-century seaport. Along one wall, visitors could trace a magnificent twenty-foot-long panoramic view of the New York streetscape and skyline, punctuated by church steeples and hundreds of ship masts. Produced in the 1840s by a Swiss amateur draftsman, Edward Burkhardt, the panorama is one of the great treasures of the historical society's superb collection of drawings. It served as a backdrop for four interpretive clusters.

The first, occupying the center of the room, featured a large exhibition case in the form of the slant-top desks of the seaport's many "counting-houses." Here visitors could explore the explosive growth of New York Port in the half-century after 1815. They could read the original letter (as well as a transcription) outlining a plan to establish packet-liner service between New York and Liverpool in 1818, survey a model of one of the Black Ball Line packet ships, read the lyrics and listen to the music of a song mourning the wreck of another of these ships, and admire a silver teapot gratefully donated by the passengers on a happier voyage. The next station on the "desk" displayed an early letterbook of the Brown Brothers firm (alongside an interpretive label), which would expand from cotton trading into global banking over the next century. Noting that the Browns had business dealings with 163 different merchant groups in dozens of cities, we designed and installed a mock Rolodex, organized by nation and region, that encouraged visitors to witness for themselves the wide range of trading partners spread all over the Atlantic world. (This was 2006, of course, before the Rolodex vanished into the Contacts file of everyone's smartphone.) Finally, a series of letters among correspondents explored the role of trust in a business world that lacked reliable information. This underscored how commerce engendered and depended on family, religious, political, and social bonds among merchants.

On the other side of the clerk's desk/exhibition case, we traced the progress of a single trade for fifty-seven bags of cotton. Starting with an 1821 invoice in the New-York Historical Society manuscript collection, supplemented by a map and accompanying narrative, we showed that the high-value Sea Island fiber was consigned by a planter in the islands off the Carolina coast to merchants in Savannah, Georgia, who then shipped it to England in a vessel that was owned, captained, and insured by New Yorkers, in a trade arranged by a New York merchant firm with its correspondents in Liverpool, and ultimately delivered to a textile manufacturer in Halifax, England. (The label copy for the invoice noted, "Everyone is mentioned here, except for the teamsters who brought the cotton to the wharf, the dockworkers who loaded the cargo in three ports, the sailors, and, of course, the slaves who had planted, cultivated, and harvested the cotton.") In adjoining panels, we traced other New York transactions in slave-grown produce, like the purchase and processing in Brooklyn of Cuban sugar. Another represented the purchase of Chickasaw Indian land in Mississippi in the 1830s, which would eventually be developed as cotton plantations.

This twin-sided and much enlarged slant-top standing desk was exhibition case, metaphor, and experience rolled into one. Experientially it invited people to bend forward to peer closely at the documents. In these bodily acts—leaning, focusing, reading, decoding, and moving on—visitors were reenacting the actions of the men who had once penned and read these letters. Bending at the waist and balancing with their hands were also tools in the learning process. The dimensions of the desk immersed visitors in a cloaked, semi-enclosed world of wood, paper, and ink. They could thereby connect to the historical "action" of the desk, which centered on the merchant's power to direct commodities, workers, and enormous vessels across vast expanses of ocean, in wildly uncertain conditions of weather and markets. Thus the museum could do its special magic by representing that this, rather than only statistical charts and maps, is what we mean by "trade."

We hoped that the bodily actions of the visitors and their intake and synthesis of information ultimately would bring them to a more emotional question: Whom can one trust? How can a social system operate if one's fate is repeatedly in the hands of total strangers? And then, after a few minutes of this immersion, some visitors might begin to ask even more profound questions: How does it feel to engage in this power, in this risk? What are the analogous experiences in our own day?

But our story is also a matter of historical perspective, and that can only be provided to museumgoers by charts, maps, and sweeping judgments about historical significance. So, on another side of the Burkhardt panorama, visitors came to Cluster 2, a graphically rich display wall. Here they might learn that raw southern cotton supplied seven-eighths of the world supply before 1860, constituted 60 percent of American exports, and delivered as much as thirty-eight cents of every American dollar earned in its trade to the merchants of New York. Next to that, visitors encountered a map of lower Manhattan, showing how South Street supplied the port, Pearl Street's wholesalers catered to visiting country merchants, and Wall Streeters pulled the financial strings. The map, which distilled many hours of research in city directories, represented the complex interrelationships of the city's import, export, and financial services businesses in a simple and familiar visual format, one that allowed New York visitors to compare the city's modern-day commercial geography. Here, too, they could see two lovely examples of imported printed English cottons, borrowed from the Cooper-Hewitt Smithsonian Design Museum, which showed what New Yorkers wanted to acquire in exchange for their handling of the raw southern cotton. Finally, this cluster concluded with a splendid lithograph, the

North River Drug and Patent Medicine Warehouse, dated 1848, borrowed from the Museum of the City of New York. It illustrated—as our interpretive label noted—"What the Country Storekeeper Found in the Big City."

The third cluster in this room focused on the dockside world itself. The entire back wall was covered with a much-enlarged *Harper's Weekly* print of the "street of ships" anchored along the East River in the middle of the nineteenth century. To further represent the importance of New York to southern planters and merchants, we located in the Bayou Bend Collection of the Houston Museum of Fine Arts a beautiful suite of Rococo Revival furniture from the celebrated Manhattan firm of John Henry Belter. Fortuitously the set of chairs, tables, sofa, and étagère were accompanied by a bill of sale to Colonel Benjamin S. Jordan of Milledgeville, Georgia. Jordan paid Belter $1,305.75 ($29,000 in 2006 dollars) for two similar suites of furniture, one for him and another for his widowed sister-in-law living on the adjoining plantation. Our interpretive focus was on intersectional trade (the tie of New York to a southern slaveholding clientele), not on design or construction, so we created an exhibition case that was two-thirds packing crate, with all the proper freight labels, and one-third Plexiglas. Then we attached the "crate" to a block and tackle, as if it were being hoisted onto a coastal packet bound for Savannah.

But, wishing to complicate the story a bit, we conjured up a second, almost tiny, accompanying crate. The brilliant New York doctor, political leader, and essayist James McCune Smith, a leader in the local African American community, had contributed a series of portraits of Black New Yorkers for *Frederick Douglass' Paper*. One of them evoked the ambition of a washerwoman to send a box of goodies to her sisters and their families, still enslaved in Carolina. Our interpretive text panel read,

> So into that southbound packet ship, along with the fancy New York furniture and clothing, the sacks of grain, barrels of whale oil, and boxes of "negro shoes," might also be loaded a small box of treats.
>
> What would be in it? Needles and thread, ribbons, toys, an outgrown boy's shirt, sugar candy, a Bible or religious tract, or maybe news of a New York nephew's success in school. Most important, the package proved that enslaved and free people were still connected, awaiting a reunion in freedom.

The little exhibition crate was stuffed full of original and reproduction objects—toys, ribbons, a book, cloth handkerchiefs—gathered less as evidence than as a visual contrast to the grand Belter armchair crate next to it. We aimed to demonstrate that American slavery, for all its horrors, was a strangely permeable system, an uneasy stewpot of coercion and autonomy.

This paradox was further amplified in the fourth and final cluster in this introductory gallery. Before leaving this space, visitors confronted a tuck-in space, labeled "Voices from the Edge," where they could begin an alternative journey through the exhibition themes. A sequence of six audio programs, accessed through individual sound sticks or wands, brought the voices of African American New Yorkers to life. Hidden away beneath the surface of public life in the booming metropolis, Blacks shared advice on finding work, evading slave-catchers, assisting fugitives, building communal bonds, and making ends meet. These brief audio dialogues reminded visitors that the surface history, the records of merchants and government agencies, missed the perspective of many actors in the story. Later in the exhibition, African American faces and bodies would come out of the shadows and be shown engaging in protest, performance art, and political activity.

THE "REAL STUFF" AND THE "OTHER STUFF"

As these examples show, the interpretive cluster is much more than an original object or document with annotative labels. Here is a description of the other sorts of "other stuff":

- *Mocuments* take the form of historical things but have information superimposed on or built into them. In AHW's 2011 exhibition, *Revolution! The Atlantic World Reborn*, reproductions of eighteenth-century newspapers from Boston, New York, Philadelphia, Williamsburg, Havana, and Cap Français were mounted on the wall of a re-created seaport tavern to show how imperial governments aimed to impose their will. On each, we scrawled graffiti to represent the resistance and resentment of colonial people. In the same gallery, drinking mugs were overprinted with scenes of the Royal Navy's impressment of civilian sailors, and a punchbowl contained the lyrics of Benjamin Franklin's 1737 ode to rum.
- *Artifictions* are "impossible" objects commissioned from artists and designers to communicate historical ideas. In the 1986 *Miracle at Philadelphia* exhibition at Independence National Historical Park, we adapted the orrery, a three-dimensional model of the solar system, to represent the elements of the new American

constitutional system—including "checks and balances," the separation of powers, the relationship of the federal and state governments, and the superiority of the Supreme Court. The device was derived from David Rittenhouse's orrery, produced in Philadelphia at roughly the same moment as the convention. In the *Revolution!* show, we commissioned a Mexican *alfeñique* artist to create a sculptural model of Versailles out of sugar paste. What better way to show that the vast wealth of Louis XVI's court relied heavily on the uncompensated labor of Africans in the sugar fields of France's American colonies!

- *Commissioned art objects* fill a void where historical materials don't exist. In the *Slavery in New York* exhibition, we know the names of the first dozen enslaved Africans brought to New Amsterdam by the Dutch in 1627, and we know something of the work they did to clear the land and construct the roads, docks, and mills of the new settlement. But we don't know what they looked like. So we commissioned Deryck Fraser, a Brooklyn artist of Surinamese extraction, to create a series of full-sized wire sculptures of these men and women at work, at rest, and in family relationships. Many visitors remarked on the haunting quality of these figures, prized only for their brawn and denied a historical face and voice.

- *Decoding and translating devices* help visitors engage with original materials that are visually complex, like historical cartoons with many obscure characters or written in a foreign language. In *Slavery in New York*, a computer-interactive program allowed visitors to transcribe and then translate and interpret the 1641 Dutch governor's decree that created a status of half-freedom for Africans in New Amsterdam. Another device in the same show allowed visitors to trace the slave-trading voyage of the sloop *Rhode Island* as it traveled along the African coast in 1748–49, exchanging American and British goods for human beings to be carried across the Middle Passage and sold in New York.

- *Visitor feedback devices* provide opportunities for visitors to evaluate and concretize their experiences. AHW created a simple visitor-activated video booth at its New-York Historical Society exhibitions, gently asking a sequence of questions that evoked more and more specificity about how visitors developed meanings from the exhibition elements. More than 10,000 visitors deposited their responses. Follow-up conversations with several visitors suggested

The imperial authorities boasted of controlling colonists, but every seaport tavern resounded with grievances (Revolution! The Atlantic World Reborn exhibition at the New-York Historical Society, 2011).

that what they recalled six months or a year later derived as much from these responses as from the materials we had presented. Such "externalization," as Jerome Bruner calls it, is a critical step in the informal educational process. As the French historian of psychology Ignace Meyerson says, "La personne n'est saisissable que par ce qu'elle produit: ses actes et ses oeuvres." Even we cannot know ourselves other than by our actions and the fruits of our labor.[3]

In addition to these, visitors to our exhibition confront a panoply of other interpretive devices: graphic panels (often including reproduced images and newly designed maps and charts); audio, video, and computer-interactive programs; simulation; and hands-on and other participatory programs. All of these, as well as the architecture of the space, work to situate the visitor both inside and outside the historical moment. On one hand,

3. Ignace Meyerson, *Problèmes de la personne: Exposés et discussions réunis et présentés par Ignace Meyerson* (Paris: Mouton, 1973), 9. See also Jerome S. Bruner, *The Culture of Education* (Cambridge: Harvard University Press, 1996), 22–25.

visitors are encouraged to connect themselves by immersion and reenactment to the actions of people in the past. On the other, they are reinforced in their historical distance, measuring the distance to our own day and their own stories. As at osv, we encourage visitors to move between first-person and third-person perspectives on the past.

The scholarly advisers to our projects, though scrupulous about historical accuracy, have never objected to the insertion of these curatorially created objects. Jean Hébrard, the noted historian of slavery in Brazil and the Caribbean, commented that the tavern setting in the *Revolution!* show, rich in mocuments and artifictions, was his favorite part of the exhibition: "It helped me feel the immediacy of the documents I'd been studying for years," he said. I had long been wary of crossing the line between artist and interpreter. All my efforts to write fiction or poetry had come to naught. I'd never felt free to call myself an artist, always internalizing the censure of my hardworking parents about such frivolous pursuits.

But, on the other side, I'd been haunted since my adolescence by a phrase in the "Whiteness of the Whale" chapter of *Moby-Dick*: "Without imagination no man can follow another into these halls." Melville is here speaking of the subtlety, complexity, and mystery of the mind. Focusing on the workings of the mind had been my chief interest, my most powerful entertainment, since late adolescence. Over the years I'd honed my passion for excavating the ways in which ideas, emotions, passions, and interests had played out across the screen of mental life. By the time of these ambitious New-York Historical Society exhibitions in 2005–11, I felt emboldened to engage the fellow humanity of all who came into my view: enslaved New Yorkers and slave-trading sea captains, impassioned abolitionists and embittered "draft rioters," matriarchs in the slave quarters and utopian dreamers, the Saint-Domingue women who refused, now that they were emancipated, to work in the sugar mill at night, as well as W. E. B. Du Bois striving again and again to define dignity across the oppressions of the color line.

As an accidental museologist, it falls upon me to view "stuff" as the vehicle for my exercises of historical imagination and pedagogical creativity. I use my imagination to honor the care with which my grandfather pulled down the heavy press in the coat factories of the 1920s, or the determination in my father's eyes when he made the last turn of the screw on a lighting fixture, or that perfect intoxication I could witness in my mother's face when she tasted and smelled the sauce she had cooked.

Is it old? Is it original? Is it real? Is it authentic?

Well, it all depends. Let me address the first two—old and original—first. These terms of art, applied to museum objects, rely on who's talking to whom and for what purpose, and on what objects by contrast do not qualify. One thing is sure: No old object comes down to us unchanged by time—alone, pure, untouched, free from meaning, unloosed from experience. During my visits to art museums with my friend Frieder Danielis, a painter, I'm always delighted when he bends toward the canvas, holds up his magnifying glass, and whispers something like, "There's not much of the sixteenth century left on this one." Even when condition is less important, as in letters, we know that most historical artifacts have been severed from their contexts. And the moment of an object's creation, like the writing of a letter, is only one moment in its long "career." We should always be aware that various people over many years made the decision to save it, to keep and conserve it, to categorize and interpret it in a way that makes it relevant to historical inquiries, and to make it available for study and exhibition.

By contrast, everything we say about an object (and perhaps much that we sense in it as well) belongs to our own time. We can only know it now. The meaning isn't in the object itself but in our use of it for our own purposes. Of all the many things that we can say about an object that was first created hundreds of years ago, we usually choose just one or two. In AHW's *Revolution!* exhibition at the New-York Historical Society, for example, we displayed a Roman marble bust of Attis wearing a Phrygian cap. Here's the label copy:

Ahead of the Revolution

A quarter-century before the French Revolution, this Roman sculpture was given to the royal library in Paris by the Comte de Caylus, a devoted scholar of antiquities. Though dating from the age of Rome's imperial glory, it could later have been a model for French artists and activists eager to represent the revolutionary spirit.

Revolutions shatter traditions. But their links with the past can strengthen them. In ancient Rome, slaves who had won their liberty wore a Phrygian cap, a soft conical cap with the top pulled forward.

Revolutionaries in America and France adopted this symbol of freedom from tyranny and mounted them on liberty poles. The cap found its place of honor on the national flags of Haiti and several Latin American countries, and the state flags of New York and New Jersey.

Attis enfant, marble de Paros sculpture, 2nd century C.E. Départe-

The Phrygian or freedom cap on a Roman marble bust, an inspiration to eighteenth-century revolutionaries in Paris (Revolution! The Atlantic World Reborn *exhibition at the New-York Historical Society, 2011).*

ment des monnaies, médailles et antiques, Bibliothèque nationale de France, Paris.

We said nothing about the artist or the moment of the bust's creation. We said nothing about the material (sourced from the same island as was the Venus de Milo!). We did not identify Attis. We said almost nothing about Roman slavery and nothing about the history of the library's stewardship of this artwork or why it should be in a national library at all. We ignored Caylus's vital role as an antiquarian and collector of ancient artwork. All very interesting subjects, but not here and not now. We left unstated the question of whether the then-recent discovery of this bust (in Italy) and its dis-

Girodet's painting of Jean-Baptiste Belley, 1797, borrowed from the Château de Versailles (Revolution! The Atlantic World Reborn *exhibition at the New-York Historical Society, 2011*).

play in Paris might have sparked or encouraged its adoption by artists and activists in 1789. Instead, we surrounded the bust with several eighteenth-century cartoons celebrating and caricaturing men and women wearing liberty caps. We mounted a touchable liberty cap alongside the bust to give sight-impaired visitors a chance to feel what we were talking about. (There was also a Braille version of the label.)

The cluster including the Roman bust, in other words, was an occasion to convey several ideas: the revolutionaries' claim to a long tradition of freedom-seeking, the way icons and symbols are created and how they evolve, how art forms intersect, and the presence of these symbols in our own iconography. But, most important, including the ancient sculpture also underscored the authority of the exhibition and, hence, of the curator's interpretive voice. A reproduction of the statue was impossible, and a photograph of it was much less powerful. The "original" object, authenticated by 250 years of scholarship, has an unmistakable presence.

Further on in the same exhibition, we included Anne-Louis Girodet's remarkable portrait of Jean-Baptiste Belley, borrowed from the Château de Versailles. Here's the text:

A Revolutionary Hero, in the French Mode

Girodet's stunning portrait of Belley is the iconic image of the Haitian Revolution. The artist, a student of the great Jacques-Louis David, provided several mixed messages in this portrait. Belley is dressed in the full regalia of the Convention, but his relaxed slouch seems undignified. He leans against a bust of the French *philosophe* Abbé Guillaume-Thomas Raynal, the author of *A Philosophical and Political History of the Settlements and Trade of the Europeans in the East and West Indies* (1770), who had called for the abolition of slavery, as if the very dark-skinned Belley needed the research of a marble-white Frenchman to argue against human trafficking. Though he stands in a three-quarters pose typical of royal and aristocratic portraits, Belley's forehead is shown as sloped (as Reynal's is not), indicative in this period of a low intelligence. And while he is comfortable in his clothes, his bulging breeches reveal an obvious sexuality. In sum, Girodet seems to see Belley as that well-known 18th-century figure, the "noble savage."

Anne-Louis Girodet de Roussy-Trioson, *Portrait of Citizen Jean-Baptiste Belley, Ex-Representative of the Colonies*, oil on canvas, 1797. Musée National des Châteaux de Versailles et de Trianon, Versailles.

Often reproduced, the painting is different "in person." Almost life-sized, the materiality of the original oil on canvas invites investigation, and hence our label aims to draw the visitors' eyes toward its details. Further, as we stand in front of it, we assume the position that the artist Girodet did, and somehow the artist's choices come back to life as if his palette was still wet. It is not a picture of someone else; it is an event in real time.[4]

In this case, there is real information to be gleaned from the original, as there was only narrative context and inference in the bust of Attis. That was overview and this is immersive. The Attis sculpture is, conjecturally, a missing piece in the history of revolutionary iconography, a building block for a historical argument. The Belley painting, contrarily, gives rise to many new inquiries—about race, revolution, and representation. But both contribute to the conversation we are conducting with our visitors, with their eyes and bodies, and their relationship to the concept and experience of revolution.

4. Laurent Dubois and Julius S. Scott, "An African Revolutionary in the Atlantic World," in *Revolution! The Atlantic World Reborn*, ed. Thomas Bender, Laurent Dubois, and Richard Rabinowitz (New York: New-York Historical Society, 2011), 139–58.

I find it difficult, therefore, to separate the "originality" of the object from all the meanings we attach to it now. Among those meanings is assuredly the hunger we have for the "real." In this may be the deepest power of objects and the deepest purpose of museums, to intermingle our changeableness with the seemingly immutable. The truth is that the object is real, but reality, necessarily, dances.[5]

Authenticity is something else altogether. A highly contested idea in contemporary philosophy, it has become the highest virtue for some. Authenticity is, in intellectual history, the successor to the faculty of Reason that the Romantics claimed was infused with the divine spirit. The inauthentic, for a generation and social class that has transcended material needs, is the realm of all that is hateful in contemporary life: the apparent falseness, artifice, meaninglessness, and shabbiness of modern life. In sum, the inauthentic is everything we see as shallow. As we become more knowledgeable about how meaning is constructed and presented in the media, we discover more and more inauthenticity.

Museums seem the perfect antidote. They have stuff whose edges we can't locate, whose emergence into the world we cannot completely fathom. The stuff in museums is prima facie the world's best raw material for achieving a sense of authenticity. When we define the museum visit as a process, as a transaction, we view its end product as a sense of authenticity, a validation of one's inner self in its connection to an object, an idea, or a place. This sense of fitness, fleeting as it must always be, is a great accomplishment. Thus, authenticity is not a quality of the stuff we encounter but, rather, what we call our satisfying experience with the unfamiliar.

---

5. This multifarious quest is the subject of Richard Todd's delicious *The Thing Itself: On the Search for Authenticity* (New York: Riverhead Books, 2008). One of the blessings of having parents who lived so long and observed so much was that they could describe what places and objects actually were before my generation discovered their "authenticity."

PART FOUR
Belonging: Interpreting Identity and Community

15 ::: THE BODY POLITIC
IN THE MUSEUM

Every museum visit tells me whether, where, and to whom
I belong. I go to the Baseball Hall of Fame and Museum in
Cooperstown, N.Y., and I'm reminded of my first extrafa-
milial identity, as a Brooklyn Dodgers fan. I drive farther,
stopping at the Corning Museum of Glass, and I discover
that I don't know the first thing about glass, but I want to
learn. Back in the car, arriving at the Albright-Knox Museum in Buffalo, I am reacquainted with the brilliant Abstract Expressionists I first met and loved in my twenties.
Crossing into Canada, I am repelled by the kitsch of "the
museums" in Niagara Falls.

In some museums, I feel emboldened to cross a track-
less wilderness in search of new knowledge. In others, I enjoy rediscovering my old attachments. And in still others, I
refuse to take a step. As Simon Schama says, "All history is
a negotiation between familiarity and strangeness."[1]

To explore this, I'll start with Nietzsche. "We need his-

---

1. Schama, "Clio at the Multiplex," *New Yorker*, January 19,
1998, 40.

tory," he says, "for the sake of life and action. . . . We want to serve history only to the extent that history serves life."[2]

But, of course, I didn't start my love affair with history by reading Nietzsche. That's an acquisition of my older years, along with anxieties about rising sea levels and dangerously low levels of money set aside for retirement. No, my romance with history started much earlier. Perhaps it was the mystery of my mother's going quiet when she was reminded of her maternal cousins lost in the Holocaust. "Hitler," she assumed without knowing for certain, "took care of them." But I also saw that she quickly let go of that moment and passed on to the business at hand. "Forgetting," says Nietzsche, "is essential to action of any kind."[3]

Or maybe it was my delight in historical stories. In third grade, when I told my favorite teacher, a guardian angel named Annette P. Goldman, that I'd read my sister's high school history text straight through, she presented me with a copy of Dorothy Canfield Fisher's *Paul Revere and the Minute Men*, number 4 in the Landmarks Books series. It was the first history book I owned. Each morning before school, Mrs. Goldman and I would sit and talk for ten or twenty minutes about my reading.[4] When we exchanged gifts the following Christmas, she gave me, presciently, it turns out (given my exhibition work sixty years later), the World Landmark story of *The Slave Who Freed Haiti: The Story of Toussaint Louverture*. And my dad and I scoured the shelves of every public library in eastern Brooklyn to find the Landmark and Signature books I hadn't yet read.

The history I imbibed from these books and from my school lessons was largely celebratory. History books created an America open to my belonging before the adult world did. I could identify with men and women I had never met and never would know but with whom I could feel a kinship. Reading American history, I felt much more connected to eighteenth-century revolutionaries and nineteenth-century pioneers than to their contemporaries, my genealogical forebears, in Poland and Russia.

It was easy in the 1950s to feel proudly American. My youthful patriotism was nourished by heavy doses of televised World War II documentaries like

2. Friedrich Nietzsche, "On the Uses and Disadvantages of History for Life," in *Untimely Meditations*, ed. Daniel Breazale (Cambridge: Cambridge University Press, 1997), 59

3. Ibid., 62.

4. Around 2006, a middle school in East New York, Brooklyn, was named for Annette P. Goldman.

Victory at Sea and *The Big Picture*, each with soaring musical scores and the rat-a-tat-tat of machine gun fire on the sound track. My country had defeated Nazism. My mother never doubted that the morning in August 1928 when her ship crossed in front of Lady Liberty was one of the greatest of her long life.

Yes, my youthful sleep was interrupted, I recall, by occasional nightmares of nuclear warfare and of hooded Klansmen carrying torches. And we were by no means complacent about American democracy. McCarthyism had cut close to the bone, my parents could smell anti-Semitism a mile away, we would never cross a picket line, and we embraced the fight for racial justice as our own. I was brought up less as a red diaper baby—my cousins were that!—but rather as a Popular Front kid, seeing the struggle for freedom and equality as indivisible. In addition to the "Star-Spangled Banner" and "My Country 'Tis of Thee," in school we sang "United Nations on the March," with a melody derived from Dmitri Shostakovich.

The events of the 1960s and 1970s, of course, and particularly the traumas of Vietnam, racial and political repression, urban violence, assassinations, and Watergate, complicated but did not substantially alter my politics. But while the basic framework of my political values remained consistent, my pedagogy evolved in a much more radical direction. Distrustful of formal educational institutions, I was dubious about the merits of what seemed a dull, one-size-fits-all system of classroom curricula and teaching methods. Invented in the era of industrialization, our educational system was so obviously ineffective in generating curiosity, imagination, social concern, useful skills, or intellectual mastery in the children of our own time. My pedagogy was, in a basic way, my politics.

Like many other young professionals in the 1960s and 1970s, these frustrations led me to press for alternatives. Day after day, I saw how the outdoor history museum offered students a rare chance to exercise all their senses and many of their skills in learning. To be sure, I knew that museum visits would have to prove valuable to teachers and administrators in achieving the school's goals for children, like preparing them for tests. Though innovative teachers and engaged students often expressed a desire to build their whole curriculum around the techniques of our museum education program, replacing sterile classrooms with museum learning was still a utopian ideal. (In the 1990s, this instinct led to the establishment of successful "museum schools" in New York, Boston, San Diego, and other cities.) Still, Old Sturbridge Village (osv) offered, as I have said earlier, a microcosmic test kitchen for cooking up good learning. Liberated from an overemphasis on deskwork, on rote assignments, and on working in isolation, our kids proved to be wonderful at making sense of this alien, long-departed rural world.

I embarked on a career-long search for more creative, joyful, and collaborative modes of teaching and learning. My experience at osv confirmed what I learned in my academic study of American thinkers from Jonathan Edwards to William James and John Dewey. The mind was always active, always inclined this way or that, and our reasoning usually followed, rather than preceded, our actions. We run from the danger, James taught me, and only then do we realize what has frightened us. Other philosophers and theologians prized the human capacity to judge disinterestedly after a period of investigation and thoughtful reflection. Both Edwards and James, though a century and a half apart, believed the mind is never neutral or indifferent before choices. It's always alert, moving, attracted or repelled by objects in the field of vision or morality. Pedagogically, it has always seemed much more effective first to encourage visitors to act and then to invite them to explore the grounds for their action, rather than to freeze them in place while they contemplate the competing claims for acting one way or another.

In 1973–74, a Kent Fellowship from the Danforth Foundation gave me a chance to take a leave from the museum and work on my Ph.D. dissertation more intently. Equally important during that year was my recruitment onto a team planning an exhibition on the American Revolution in Boston in connection with the national bicentennial celebration in 1975. I joined a team led by the designer Michael Sand and including the media guru Sam Miller and historian Bob McCaughey in planning a show that would inaugurate the restored Quincy Market in downtown Boston.

Already, in this, my first gallery exhibition, I was resisting a straightforward, illustrated textbook-on-the-wall chronology of the major events. In 1975, a dozen sites along the Freedom Trail piously intoned the heroic story of Boston's resistance to British tyranny. It had become the official memory of the city, enshrined in Boston's promotions for tourists as "The Cradle of Liberty," although scholars had been complicating the story for more than a generation. There were, I thought, three ways to subvert the dominant mythology. First, we could march visitors through a retelling of each milestone event: the celebration of George III's coronation in 1760, the Peace of Paris in 1763, the Sugar Act, the Stamp Act, the Townshend duties, the Boston Massacre, the Tea Act, the Tea Party, and the closing of the Boston port, culminating in Lexington and Concord. In each case, we would add juicy and unfamiliar factoids that suggested that EVERYTHING YOU THINK YOU

KNOW ABOUT THE AMERICAN REVOLUTION IN BOSTON IS WRONG. But despite all the clever surprises along the path, I feared that this approach would simply confirm for many visitors the inevitability of the Revolution, turning every crisis of the 1760s and 1770s into another predictable step to American independence. That hardly seemed worth the effort.

A second alternative was more thematic. A fellow team member advanced the idea of creating a series of "alcove" mini-exhibits detailing the role in the emerging conflict of women, African Americans, and children, as well as merchants, clergy, farmers, sailors, and local officials. This would accommodate the new interpretive tack of scholars like Jesse Lemisch and Staughton Lynd, who advocated "history from the bottom up," focusing on the role of the long-neglected and hard-to-document "rabble" and ordinary folk who actually did almost all of the fighting against British rule. A thematic approach might also allow for more subtle explanations. Perhaps we could stress the "ideological origins of the American Revolution," as Bernard Bailyn, one of my Harvard professors, had discovered in examining the pamphlet literature of the time. Or we could let visitors see the ways in which radical evangelicals pressed for revolution against the stodgy "liberals" who dominated Boston's pulpits, as Alan Heimert, another of my teachers, had suggested. But to adopt these complex formulations required removing and abstracting the exhibition entirely from the streets of Boston, from the rather remarkable fact that around us was the actual site of Revolutionary events. And in the end, visitors would be wearied, I thought, by repeatedly demonstrating that this group and that had "contributed" to the cause of liberty. Boring!

I returned to chronology, which is, after all, the easiest way to guide visitors through a historical narrative. Museum exhibitions by their nature convert historical time into visitor space, turning a timeline of events into a durational pathway. The downside: a conventional timeline often isolates visitors in their own zone, observing events from afar. I wanted the exhibition to bring visitors into the experience of revolution itself. My chosen alternative, in contrast to the other two, was to enlist the visitors in a different sort of chronology, rendering revolution as a personal and social experience. The events were now designed to evoke a sequence of *experiential* challenges: encountering mob violence, watching local authority crumble, feeling fear on the streets and shock at the Mother Country's fierce repressiveness, lending sympathy to neighbors, and so on. In this view, the struggle over independence would be seen as a collective psychological and social transformation.

During my stint with the project, we set out to achieve this through a rather media-rich approach that used role-playing and simulation as interpretive approaches. (I joked that we should call the show *Where Were You When the Rights Went Out?*) As we explained to Boston 200, the city's coordinating agency in 1974, "Utilizing role play as a major participatory strategy, we intend to allow exhibit goers to react to events, make decisions, declare their feelings, and find out how their own sympathies correspond to those of their forebears."

Characteristic of the design scheme is the treatment for a section called "How Willing are YOU to be Sur-taxed?" "The war with France cost more than the British thought it would," we wrote. "'Well, this exhibit cost more than we thought it would and we're sorry, we wish we didn't have to ask, but we must request that visitors ante up another nickel to continue through this exhibit.'—Another decision point. If visitors agree, they go through a turnstile. If they refuse, they must duck under it or go around it—the choices being recorded on the visitors' ballots [provided to them at the start of the show]."[5]

Some of the devices we imagined were just plain fun. Visitors might be offered a chance to chuck mock crates of the East India Company's tea overboard or sit down to a "British tea party" while listening to the music of George Frideric Handel. Or, while watching a mechanized puppet show, they could hear alternate accounts of the Boston massacre by an American narrator (that is, a mock John Wayne) and then by a Briton ("James Mason"). At the end, they could choose to sign the Declaration of Independence or get ushered into a small theater showing a travelogue of "beautiful Nova Scotia."

In a more serious vein, the exhibition plan relied on the visitors' bringing their own tacit and explicit understandings to bear on a succession of crisis moments in Boston's move to separation from the Crown. Many potential visitors, I knew, had themselves undergone the unsettling crises of the 1960s, as I had. They knew something about advocating and resisting change in both public and private life, and I wanted them to use that

5. Michael Sand & Associates, "The American Revolution Exhibit: A Progress Report, January 1974," Boston 200 Collection, box 11 NI, folder "Quincy Market," Boston Public Library. I want to thank Prof. Malgorzata Rymsza-Pawlowska for bringing this document to my attention. See her "Bicentennial Memory: Postmodernity, Media, and Historical Subjectivity, 1966–1976" (Ph.D. diss., Brown University, 2012).

as they proceeded through the exhibition landscape. I wanted to use their *memories* as a shaping device for reinterpreting the *history*. Here's how this might work. We imagined a role-playing situation in which the visitors would find themselves in a simulated crowded and noisy mob, standing outside Lieutenant Governor Hutchinson's Boston house during the anti–Stamp Act riot of 1765. As projectiles appeared to fly overhead and the sound of screams and breaking glass crested, some visitors might join in the chanting. Others, I predicted, would shudder and look for the exit. If we could, within the bounds of historical plausibility, make this feel a bit like Kent State or the streets of Newark, so much the better.

At the end of their journey, exhibition visitors would input the choices they had registered into a room-sized Honeywell computer and then receive a card that told them whose political evolution among Boston's political figures theirs most resembled: revolutionary, royalist, or fence-sitter. This wrap-up activity, along with some of our participatory elements, survived the project's succession of design firms and made its way into the actual exhibition. Even if all the patriotic Americans knew "the right answers" as to which side they should support, it turned out that the visiting public in 1975 came down much as John Adams (is supposed to have) said they did two centuries earlier: one-third for independence, one-third against, and one-third ambivalent.

Though I was long gone from the advisory team when the Boston 200 exhibition opened, I had learned a great deal. Turning the tour of an outdoor museum like osv into a storyscape had required tightly structuring the sequence of stops into a problem that would be introduced, explored, and resolved in a defined period of time—counteracting, in a sense, the appealing quality of wandering about in the rural landscape aimlessly. In the gallery exhibition, sequence was much easier to enforce, but the stops along the path were less involving. Creating a narrative was logical inside the walls of the museum, but we would need to challenge the conventional form of exhibit cases and graphic panels. The exhibition landscape had to be as lively as the events it described.

CONTRASTING POLITICAL AND SOCIAL HISTORY NARRATIVES
osv taught me the value of interactive and experiential learning, but I recognized that there were two very distinct pathways, depending on the historical issues we were presenting. Social history exhibitions called upon visitors to empathize with historical groups who were feeling the force of historical change. Whether we were focusing on the history of Fall River

or Altoona, Pittsburgh, or Phoenix, these were always stories about the global advent of modernity. We didn't foreground these massive forces—that would have been too abstract. But we cast our historical characters inside a vise of social and economic change. Every exhibition was grounded in this kind of historical pressure point. We wanted the gallery to feel like the hold of a slave ship, the crush of a union hall, the darkened hallway of a tenement. In exhibitions about enslavement, industrialization, immigration, and economic upheaval, our interpretive framework assumed that the world churned beneath the people we were exploring. To empathize with them is to perceive and shake with the tremors that were undermining their personal and social selves. Such social and economic transformations feel irresistible, irreversible, and even overwhelming. They grab the visitor.

Political exhibitions call for a different rhetoric. Reading Hannah Arendt's *The Human Condition* (1958) in the mid-1970s inspired me to define a chasm between freedom and coercion. In Arendt's rendering of the origins of politics in ancient Greece, she distinguishes between the realm of freedom and *public* life, belonging only to adult men of independent means, and the realm of coercion and *private* life, where work and family resided. The wives and concubines, children, slaves, and hirelings who lived in the darkness within the house were dependents, deprived (note the relationship of the word to private) of a voice in the public sphere, entirely subject to the violence of the master, beyond the scrutiny of law. In the nineteenth century, Arendt sees the gradual invention of a middle, a third sphere of life, the *social*, where the city or the nation is redefined as a household and where the well-being of such dependents becomes a central political concern. Working from these concepts, our political history exhibitions have, therefore, been about decision rather than coercion, action rather than deliberation. At a time when many in our audience feel powerless and alienated from politics, these exhibitions aim to encourage the visitors to assume the role of effective political actors.

Both social history and political history exhibitions offer visitors a chance to experiment with belonging, but in very different ways. Playing the role of a statesman or a citizen involves visitors in weighing alternatives and calculating their appeal to different interest groups, constructing coalitions of supporters, managing expectations, deflecting opposition, and so on. Most of the characters we meet in these stories are men, while our social history projects illuminate the lives of women, children, and others deprived of public voices. Through the visitors' participation, we hope, they would attach themselves to the body politic more vigorously, validating William

James's prediction that action generates emotional and cognitive learning. In Chapters 17 and 18, I will explore American History Workshop's approach to social history exhibitions, which generally aim to stimulate empathy with the (often constraining) circumstances of historical characters and identification with ethnic communities—other forms of "belonging." Chapter 19 concludes with an account of experiments, some of them successful and others not, with mixing social and political history in exhibitions.

Here our focus is on political history. In the forty-odd years since the Revolution bicentennial, American History Workshop has produced over two dozen exhibitions and public programs about the American Revolution, the Constitution, the early republic, and the Civil War. And our exhibitions about slavery and abolition, regional economic change, governance, the evolution of human rights, and symbols of national identity have invariably touched on political questions.

In all these projects I have wanted to make the story more accessible, more dramatic, and more relevant to contemporary affairs. While each of these projects says something significant about the United States, I want to oppose the idea that American politics is entirely exceptional. And, fundamentally, I want to subvert the notion that the American Constitution has been, as the poet James Russell Lowell once said (skeptically), "as if we had invented a machine that would go of itself," that is, a nearly perfect (and perhaps divinely inspired) instrument of government.

Over this half-century, the most common method of bringing the American master narrative down to earth has come through biographies of the republic's early leaders, in what some have called "founders chic." David McCullough, Joseph Ellis, Ron Chernow, and others have penned elegant portraits of the key figures in the struggle to establish independence from Britain and a federal constitution, especially Washington, Franklin, Adams, Jefferson, and Hamilton. Each biographer admits to complex contradictions in his hero's personality and social relationships, while generally admiring his political prescience. Their books, taken together, are an adroit intermingling of contemporary "peek-behind-the-curtain" celebrity journalism and uncritical "constitutional faith."[6]

Museum exhibitions work in other ways. I did not want to diminish the dignity of the public space by dwelling on individual personalities. My ap-

6. See the useful summary by H. W. Brands, "Founders Chic," *Atlantic*, September 2003. To my mind, the video versions of these, e.g., the HBO *John Adams* in 2008 and the Ken Burns *Jefferson* on PBS in 1997, were less successful.

proach has been to address the "making of the American republic" and its institutions as a step-by-step construction, replete with opportunities taken and missed and with choices made and evaded, rich with unintended consequences, and most important, produced by diverse hands and minds. Where other museum designers have taken the American federal Constitution as a completely integral invention, as the core exhibition at the National Constitution Center in Philadelphia does, showing how it ideally all fits together, I've constantly found that it's more instructive for visitors if I emphasize its jerrybuilt, lopsided, and historically evolving characteristics. Indeed, members of the founding generation were richly influenced by classical and Enlightenment theorists and historians, but their achievements came more often from constant compromise than from any rational blueprint. Some of their innovations, like the process of electing the president, the composition of the Senate, or the difficulty of constitutional amendment, effectively overcame eighteenth-century political roadblocks, but only at the expense of good governance in our own time.

Using the metaphor of a construction project to define the political process has its pedagogical advantages. This approach to constitution making offers visitors a chance to participate in balancing alternative governmental mechanisms, which raises questions about political ethics, equity, and efficiency. It slows down the rush of historical events and crystallizes the moments of decision. It constantly reinforces the notion that the political results are a product of human calculation and compromise.

PARADOXICALLY, CREATING "MIRACLES" STEP BY STEP

In our 1986 *Miracle at Philadelphia* exhibition for Independence National Historical Park in Philadelphia, for example, we underscored the factional nature of the Nationalists (men like Madison, Hamilton, Robert Morris, and ultimately Washington), who conspired to plan a convention that would replace the Articles of Confederation with a stronger national government. We "froze" the action during the Philadelphia convention at several points (for example, the debate over representation in the lower house of Congress) to demonstrate that there were some nearly intractable issues at stake. We unpacked some key historical documents on display, like James Wilson's manuscript draft of the plan of government, to show that institutions (like the presidency) that we now take for granted emerged only slowly, even accidentally, in the course of the 1787 deliberations. (Wilson's papers revealed that he stopped correcting "Governor" with the word "President" when he reached page 7 of his notebook, thereafter using only

"President": this is the moment that the office was actually named.)[7] We created a simulation exercise in the middle of the exhibition pathway, in which visitors could role-play various delegates in the thorny debate over the procedure for electing the president; the result was certainly no one's idea of a clear and simple method. Our designers adopted the metaphor of a slalom to organize our exposition of the state-by-state ratification process. All these interventions worked, I believe, to make room for the visitor's interaction with a more realistically rendered historical narrative of an event that is viewed by some Americans as the only possible product of such profound political wisdom.

After the successful launch of *Miracle*, I was introduced to John L. Bryant, president of the National Park Foundation. Bryant hoped to make Federal Hall National Monument on Wall Street, the site of the inauguration of George Washington as president in 1789, into the centerpiece of another bicentennial celebration. Weary of yet another Revolution-era exhibition project, I convinced Bryant to undertake a more radical experiment.

We would, indeed, install some modest exhibits on the main floor for general visitors, focusing on the work of the First Congress, which met at this site (and here passed the original constitutional amendments that became the Bill of Rights). But we would also create an educational program for middle-school students about American government. *Constitution Works*, as it was called, provides teachers and students with about a month's worth of classroom materials, preparing them for a highly dramatic role-playing experience at Federal Hall.

We created three different scenarios. The first, culminating in oral arguments before a simulated Supreme Court, involves the efforts of the U.S. Army to suppress publication in the *Denver Dispatch* about a biological-weapons plant in Boulder, Colorado. The class is divided into attorneys for the army, attorneys for the newspaper, Justices of the court, and journalists. (Students get elements of a costume—robes, vests, and press badges on porkpie hats—when they arrive at the mock courtroom for the Great Day. Usually dozens of parents come along with video cameras at the ready.) In the classroom, students prepare arguments and ready themselves for ques-

7. The important historical point is that the title "President" conveyed lesser authority than "Governor." In contemporaneous theological parlance, for example, God was often called "the Governor of the Universe." Presidents, like that of the Presbyterian Church or the men who occupied the shared presidency of the state of Pennsylvania, were less executives than presiding officers.

Vivifying the First U.S. Congress as inventors of government bureaucracy, including the "red tape" that held documents together (Launching the Republic *exhibition at Federal Hall National Memorial, 1989*).

tions with a "plain language" casebook that concisely briefs them on relevant cases dealing with the competing claims of national security and press freedom, starting with *Schenk v. U.S.* and including the Pentagon Papers case. The second scenario invites students to participate in a simulation of congressional hearings on Title IX equal protection for female student athletes. The third program asks students to work in the West Wing of the White House on a new law mandating two years of national service for all eighteen-year-olds. Again, thorny issues are presented: What should we do with expectant mothers or differently abled young people? Would job training be central to the program? How would business and labor unions be won over to the cause?

The *Constitution Works* program combines the excitement of a school play with a serious immersion in research, writing, and presentational skills. The program has proved a brilliant success, exfoliating into additional scenarios, expanding for a time to Philadelphia and Albany, fostering versions for students studying English as a second language, rewarding especially inventive teachers with grants and excellent students with internships in local law firms, and continuing to operate, twenty-six years later, along with other law-related educational initiatives, under the auspices of the Justice Resource Center in New York.

For a museum educator, *Constitution Works* provided a rare opportunity to get feedback on how the museum visit sparks learning. For decades I'd been frustrated by the brevity of my encounter with visitors. Here, finally, I had a way to hear from teachers, and see for myself when I went out to visit classrooms, how the ingredients of a participatory program steadily built the confidence, curiosity, and skill of our students. In addition, *Constitution Works* confirmed what I'd begun to learn at osv and in the Boston 200 project. The museum worked best as a stage, not as a library. I loved watching students climb the stairs at Federal Hall, readying themselves to take positions in the mock Supreme Court courtrooms and congressional hearing rooms we had outfitted, being respected by our educators as the stars of the show, and posing for snapshots by their parents. So much of a student's time is usually occupied by restraining his or her urge to act, to do something, while teachers (and museum docents) dish out oodles of information. Now I could apply the lessons of William James: In one's action, one could learn much about oneself and one's world.

Conventionally, many museums and historic sites have worked the other way around. They frequently narrated the careers of political leaders as if they were spring-loaded, shooting inexorably through our national history. More recently, and especially in the exhibitions at our presidential libraries, we encounter interactive programs. The Reagan Presidential Library invites visitors to "act in a movie with Ronald Reagan, deliver President Reagan's inaugural address on the steps of the U.S. Capitol, set the table for a state dinner, discover President Reagan's economic policies while playing six interactive games, read the president's handwritten diary by digitally turning the pages, and even ride a horse alongside President Reagan at Rancho del Cielo." Gerald Ford's presidential library, however, is more serious: "Visitors are invited to sit at the cabinet table while videos highlight three major events discussed by the President and his Cabinet: the pardon of Richard Nixon, the seizure of the uss Mayaguez, and the New York City financial crisis." The prime example of such a focus is, of course, the Cuban missile crisis, interpreted at the Kennedy library in Boston.

It's a mistake to ask visitors what they would do if they were in the hot seat. There's a falseness to this situation. Far better, I think, to construe the historical challenge as a shared dilemma, inviting visitors to become part of the team aiming to pull something off, rather than debating whether it was worth doing in the first place. *How* questions are much more engaging than *what* or *whether* questions. Visitors bring with them an array of surprisingly good instrumental skills—analytical, organizational, and political in the best sense—and engaging those skills will occupy their minds with the complexities of the challenge far more effectively than letting them stand outside the problem, looking in. Visitors should be brought to feel the urgency of the moment. That is not to say that deeper questions about the worthiness of political action should not be asked. But the time for that, from a pedagogically effective perspective, is in the aftermath, in the debriefing that follows the process. When visitors engage in an exciting process, even if they're not perfectly well informed, they create fragments of feelings and ideas in their minds. The teacher's role, then, is to help visitors understand what they have just done, what led to their actions, and how they might explain that as part of the historical narrative.

Embedded in this approach is a transformation of the curator's role. By sharing the challenge of the historical situation with visitors, we become their coaches rather than expert object-arrangers or information-givers. It's a style of pedagogy that is analogous to that of the teaching pro in skiing, tennis, golf, or other sports, and it rose to prominence in the years around World War II as Americans became more actively involved in such sports themselves. The teaching pro on the tennis court aims to reduce the difference between his or her backhand stroke and yours, rather than to magnify it as the professional athlete does in competition. Similarly, the teaching pro in the history museum tries to coach visitors in walking in the shoes of historical characters or researchers. The coach is a sympathetic figure, not a once-in-a-lifetime marvel, attentive to the client's immediate and long-term development rather than his or her own excellence—but no less a professional for all that.

In the early 1980s, when many of my projects brought me back to lower Manhattan, I spent my working days, as Ishmael observes in *Moby-Dick*, "pent up in lath and plaster—tied to counters, nailed to benches, clinched to desks." Often I would find my way down to Battery Park, becoming one of the "water-gazers," also to be occupied in "ocean reveries." And there I discovered a grove marked by eight nineteen-foot-high granite pylons, silent and un-attended. On the walls were inscribed the names of about 11,000 American servicemen and merchant mariners who lost their lives in the waters of the North Atlantic during World War II. A monstrous bronze eagle, almost as high as a pylon, stood as a sentinel over their symbolic watery grave. President John F. Kennedy dedicated the East Coast Memorial, as this site is known, on May 23, 1963. The president's "words were broadcast on the radio," the *New York Times* reported the next day, "but the audience actually on hand in the sunny green park was so modest that it barely exceeded the number of men being honored—the estimates ranging from 5,000 to 12,000."

Fast-forward almost twenty years to the dedication of the Vietnam Veterans Memorial on the Mall in Washington, D.C. Maya Lin's brilliantly designed twin walls, each about 250 feet long, slashed into the ground and tapering from about 10 feet high at their centers to 8 feet at their edges, list by date of death the 58,000-plus American service members who died in East Asia from 1957 until 1975, when the U.S. mission was abandoned. The stream of visitors, day and night, summer and winter, has never stopped: more than 4 million people a year for over thirty years. The "Wall" was controversial from the moment its design was chosen, and it was ultimately supplemented by two other figurative sculptural groups. But in "not telling us what to think," as the scholar Lora S. Carney has written, Lin's wall has singlehandedly re-invented the American way of commemoration. Most amazingly, the Wall began—almost from its Day 1—to attract offerings, deposited by visitors at its base. The first, legend has it, was a Purple Heart medal; the largest, a POW cage; the most extravagant, a Harley Davidson motorcycle.[1]

But first, let us ask why there is such a difference between the virtually neglected walls in Battery Park and those so often visited in Washington, D.C. The bereaved families presumably felt their loss equally. Neither is itself a burying ground, like the emotionally powerful cemetery at Omaha Beach in Normandy. The East Coast Memorial is not exactly in a remote area. Only a few steps away are the ramps that lead onto the ferries for the Statue of Liberty and Ellis Island, which attract nearly as many visitors in ordinary years as the Wall in Washington, D.C. But neither a flower nor a prayer intrudes on its stillness.

The simplest answer is the experience of Vietnam itself and its huge difference from that of World War II. The defeat of the United States compounded the divisiveness of the nation's politics during the long years of the war in Southeast Asia. Virtually all that Americans could agree upon was that the "grunts," the ordinary American soldiers in Vietnam, had unreasonably borne both the agony of the fighting and the shame of returning home empty-handed. As he watched *The Deer Hunter*, Michael Cimino's tough 1978 film dramatization of these scarred men, Jan Scruggs is said to have conceived the memorial project. Maya Lin's walls did the rest. Avoiding any effort to characterize the sacrifice of the lost or any interpretation of the war's history, the Wall's stark simplicity allowed both gung-ho hawks

1. Carney, "Not Telling Us What to Think: The Vietnam Veterans Memorial," *Metaphor and Symbolic Activity* 8 (1993): 211–19; the place of the memorial in the history of American commemoration is carefully dissected in Kristin Ann Hass, *Carried to the Wall: American Memory and the Vietnam Veterans Memorial* (Berkeley: University of California Press, 1998).

and peaceniks to grieve. The rivers and jungle killing-fields of Vietnam had almost magically been transmuted into the soft, restful turf of the National Mall.

Many observers noted that the reflective stone surface of the walls made visitors feel as though they were being absorbed into the monument as they approached. Perhaps this is what encouraged them to leave mementoes. What is certain is that the memorial kept the memories alive and kept the unresolved pain of Vietnam from "closure." Personal recollections here ceaselessly evolve into collective memory. More an altarpiece than an official monument, the Vietnam Veterans Memorial ushered in a new era of commemoration. The cool and cerebral summary judgments of historical meaning provided by the East Coast Memorial in New York, or the Lincoln, Jefferson, and Washington monuments on the Mall, seldom sites of repeated visitation, gave way to an ongoing and emotionally intense engagement with the past.

There is always a downside, a forgetting for every remembrance. The exquisite silence of the Wall stripped away the meaning of the war for the nation. Without eagles, flags, and patriotic language, this could conceivably resemble a memorial for victims of a storm or an epidemic disease. It was as if Vietnam was only a terrible zone of death in which not only 58,000 Americans but between 3 million and 4 million Vietnamese were killed, not a decades-long struggle between sectional, national, and global antagonists. In this way, the dead servicemen and servicewomen and their mourners— and not the nation itself—became the focal point of the commemoration. Theirs was an entirely personal, not a national, sacrifice. Nothing could be further from Lincoln at Gettysburg.

Almost every memorial built since the early 1980s partakes of this heightened emotionality and this personalization or has been criticized for failing to do so. It is as though America has replaced its older, more austere public culture of Protestant remembrance—engraved with moral authority—with rhythmically performative, physically present, acts of Catholic bereavement. Memorials for the Oklahoma City bombing, the 9/11 attack, hurricanes, and earthquakes, as well as a dozen Holocaust museums, each have areas for ritual acts of remembrance. Candles, prayer stools, flowing water, and eternal flames have often become more necessary to these memorials than words of wisdom.

As in memorials before the Vietnam Wall, the names of the lost are invariably listed. Indeed, the roll of names is more prominent than ever. But where they once were honored for their sacrifice to a great cause, now they are often mourned exactly because they died for no such clear purpose—because they were senselessly assaulted and/or inadvertently in harm's way. Why these, after all, and not others? Survivor guilt rules. Even when the lost are characterized as heroes, they are truly "victims." (The word stems from the Latin *victima*, or sacrificial animal.) These newly participatory memorials are no longer intended to impress by their grandeur, as if the sacrifice had yielded a bold new world.[2] They no longer intone the values of the nation or pronounce guideposts to civic virtues. Instead they operate as places accessible for personal, family, and group transactions—more like churches than monuments.

TOWARD A MORE CRITICAL HISTORY

How had this happened? I recall the shock of November 22, 1963, when the assassination of President Kennedy suddenly raised questions about "what sort of people we were," as if Lee Harvey Oswald's few bullets could shatter the veneer of our innocence. Fifty years later, none of us is immune from skepticism about the inherent goodness of the United States and its people, or at least about the "others" with whom we share this nation.

To be sure, I'd grown up witnessing episodes and patterns of oppression and injustice, including the persistent poverty Michael Harrington discovered in "the other America." But the word "anomaly" sprang easily to our lips, and we knew that we could mobilize opposition to the wrongs we noticed. We could use the power of American goodness to eradicate these ills. High schoolers like me, designated (without having accomplished anything) as "future leaders," sat at student forums sponsored by New York's newspapers and assertively scored debating points on how to advance a new and better world.

Then came Vietnam.

Several times a week, when I was a college freshman in 1962–63, I descended to the D level of Widener Library to dig out the pamphlets, magazines, and books—most of them in French—that traced the disastrous course of French and American policy in Indochina. I was contributing research for a newsletter, *The Correspondent*, which aimed to link the nuclear disarmament and antiwar movements on American campuses. While American newspapers and television newscasters dutifully parroted the line that Ngo Dinh Diem was "the Churchill of Asia," that South Vietnam

2. The World War II memorial on the National Mall is a remarkable exception to this evolution, and that has been a principal source of criticism.

was an internationally recognized sovereign state under attack from the foreign nation of North Vietnam, and that United States "advisors" could turn the tide of "subversion," I was learning a different story in the library's dimly lit subterranean study carrels.

The drumbeat of bad news in the 1960s radicalized us all, some to an even fiercer defense of American exceptionalism and the need for order, but most of my friends and classmates toward a questioning of established political and intellectual authority. As the memory of the nation's triumph in World War II—and its subsequent unity and prestige—faded, swords were drawn on every conceivable issue.

By the mid-1970s, both academic and public historians felt free—and for many, obligated—to explore the history of the American republic much more critically. Yes, the nation had expanded westward, but only in the process of "conquering" and displacing Indian peoples. Yes, the nation had experienced spectacular economic growth, but only at the cost of enslaving millions of Africans, exploiting immigrant workers, and subsidizing capitalist enterprise with government favors. True, the United States had had two centuries of constitutional stability, but only at the cost of excluding women, poor people, and people of color from political participation for most of our history and by privileging the role of slaveholders, urban bosses, southern racists, and corporate donors. Close friends and colleagues were busy tearing the veil from our eyes. Sanford Levinson showed me that America's reverence for the federal Constitution self-deceptively masked a fear of democracy and equal justice. Roberta Brandes Gratz explored the disastrous consequences of huge urban development projects. Martin Sherwin poked holes in the conventional explanations justifying the atomic bombing of Hiroshima and Nagasaki. Peter Wood firmly ensconced slavery at the heart of South Carolina's eighteenth-century economy and society.[3]

The same shift occurred in the world of American history museums. For two centuries, the essential purpose of American history museums had been the promotion of patriotism and civic identity. Most history museums had been uncritical celebrants of the "American way of life." As I've explained, the physical arrangement of most state history museums as a timeline of

3. Sanford Levinson, *Constitutional Faith* (Princeton: Princeton University Press, 1988); Roberta Brandes Gratz, *The Living City* (New York: Simon and Schuster, 1989); Martin Sherwin, *A World Destroyed: The Atomic Bomb and the Grand Alliance* (New York: Knopf, 1975); Peter Wood, *Black Majority: Negroes in Colonial South Carolina from 1670 through the Stono Rebellion* (New York: Knopf, 1974).

progress rendered the visitor into a spectator at a pageant or a pilgrim on the parade route. Triumph followed triumph in the triple advance of democracy, technological and scientific achievement, and the free-enterprise system. Even when I worked at and for institutions that were cheerleaders for these values, such as Old Sturbridge Village, I'd been pressing for a more critical perspective on history; for attention to a broader range of historical actors, issues, and voices; and for a more provocative pedagogy that would dislodge conventional wisdom and question American ethnocentrism and exceptionalism.

Within the museum world, a darker view of history first emerged, I think, in art galleries showing photographs or drawings. Edward Steichen's 1955 exhibition at the Museum of Modern Art, *The Family of Man*, juxtaposed more than 500 portraits of the agonized and the aspiring, produced by 273 photographers from sixty-eight countries. In the aftermath of the global wars of the 1940s and in the depth of the darkest Cold War years, the exhibition aimed to cultivate among viewers an empathetic identification with "All Men," "All Women," and "All Children," its accompanying book announced. Pain and suffering were bathed, in other words, in the exhibition's hopeful message and elegant presentation. Subsequent exhibitions of other great photographers, such as the Depression-era images produced by Dorothea Lange, Walker Evans, Russell Lee, Gordon Parks, and others, or earlier masterworks by Jacob Riis and Lewis Hine, represented the impoverished "other half" to American museumgoers, but they seldom escaped the ambiguities of self-congratulatory museum collecting, curating, and refined display techniques. More emotionally stirring, perhaps, were shows of drawings by Francisco De Goya or Käthe Kollwitz, but art museums provided only the slimmest historical contexts for these searing images.

The organizers of the Smithsonian's then-new Museum of History and Technology (NMHT) broached the idea of acquiring a "railroad-flat slum dwelling" for their portrayal of late nineteenth-century industrial society, and leaders in the secretary's office pressed for interpretations of "the seamier side of life," in part to balance "all those beautiful, gleaming machines" favored by the historians of technology among the museum's workers. But little came of that. Through the 1970s, the dominant national narrative held sway, but it was enlivened by the wizardry of staff and contracted outside designers. Graphic panels with simple pie charts became floor-to-ceiling assemblages of mock apple pies. Films of a speaker were projected onto a white sculptural head, which made it appear that a live person was talking directly to you. A dreary subject like American banking, sponsored by the financial industry's Washington lobbyists, displayed some treasures from the Smithsonian's numismatic collection, but more memorably the exhibit used mechanical devices and animated films to represent the flow of credit through the economic system. The low point in this progression, at least for me, was *A Nation of Nations* (*ANON*), the museum's major exhibition in the Revolutionary bicentennial years. It was hatched as the brainchild of NMHT director Daniel Boorstin, formerly a University of Chicago historian, controversial for his cooperation with the House Committee on Un-American Activities in the 1950s and who'd gained a reputation on campus as a fierce Cold Warrior. Boorstin had recently completed his lively three-volume romp through American history (*The Americans: The Colonial Experience, The Americans: The National Experience*, and *The Americans: The Democratic Experience*), celebrating the nation's exceptionalism by pointing out the repeated blunders, century after century, of utopians, theologians, scholars, legal theorists, doctors who preferred laboratories to bedside practice, and generals who debated strategy rather than corporals who stanched enemy attacks—in short, anyone with big ideas. He planned *ANON*, in particular, as a rebuttal to what he called the "mindless obsessive quest for power" of "the new barbarians," the 1960s radicals with their unwarranted criticism of American society. The exhibition "would emphasize the positive." It should be "a place of pride and patriotism."[4]

Boorstin brought in sociologist Nathan Glazer, a political soulmate, to collaborate on the exhibition plan with the New York design firm of Chermayeff and Geismar Associates. Glazer, an ardent opponent of affirmative action, cast the exhibition as a celebration of a distinctive American experience of cultural pluralism. Despite unfortunate episodes of discrimination, mostly in the past, the United States had in the bicentennial era successfully forged the political, economic, and cultural mechanisms that allowed children of immigrants to participate fully in American society. Carl Scheele and Ellen Roney Hughes, among other Smithsonian curators, pushed back. They pressed for greater attention to Indian peoples (immigrants who crossed the Bering Strait tens of thousands of years ago) and

---

4. William S. Walker, *A Living Exhibition: The Smithsonian and the Transformation of the Universal Museum* (Amherst: University of Massachusetts Press, 2013), 163–64. Marie Plassart, "Narrating 'America': The Birth of the Museum of History and Technology in Washington, D.C., 1945–1967," *European Journal of American Studies* 2, no. 1 (2007), is an excellent account of the museum's founding and early years (at http://ejas.revues.org/1184, accessed February 10, 2016).

enslaved people from Africa, and they diligently expanded the museum's collections so that *ANON* could richly display materials from diverse ethnic and religious traditions.

Inevitably, however, the plenitude of objects—and the color-coded labeling systems that allowed visitors to identify them with specific immigrant groups—vividly illustrated carryovers from the Old World, especially among the first generation. Such representations of diversity, the historian Matthew Frye Jacobsen argues, "made for a fairly sanitized and happy national narrative: diversity as feast, the nation as smorgasbord."[5] The design of the exhibition led visitors, implicitly, into the pathway of assimilation. The third and final section of the exhibition, *Shared Experiences*, explored the commonalities of postimmigration life in America—schoolrooms, voting booths, and consumer culture. Indeed, as we later learned at the Lower East Side Tenement Museum in a research project on the "material culture of the tenement," the utensils of day-to-day life do not differ substantially among different groups. Poor people, whether in 1815 or 1915 or 2015, buy secondhand goods or cheap, mass-produced knockoffs of the fancy designs of their richer fellow citizens. But real differences persist in the experience even of many third- and fourth-generation descendants of immigrants, as well as almost all American Indians, African Americans, and Latinos who have not, in the scholarly language of 2000, "become White," and the exhibition said little or nothing about that. The human suffering incurred in the foundation of the American republic and its economy left a debt that was still unpaid forty years after the bicentennial. The challenges of creating exhibitions of this history would largely remain unaddressed for decades to come.

A final wall of *ANON*, I remember, used the familiar BLACK POWER pin-back button as a model for dozens and dozens of others that the designers must have ordered from a lucky supplier: ITALIAN POWER, POLISH POWER, AFGHAN POWER, CANADIAN POWER, CHILEAN POWER, and so on. Everybody could be truly American, the exhibition winked, if they wore their ethnic identity more openly—so long as it had little or no bearing on their actual contemporary political positions or social lives. Just at the moment when identity politics was beginning to fracture the national consensus, the museum had turned multicultural diversity into an ornamental style.

In contrast, the Smithsonian's other bicentennial project, the *1876* ex-

5. Cited in Walker, *Living Exhibition*, 154.

hibition, installed at the Arts and Industries building across the mall, was a great success. The exhibition aimed to replicate both the event and the appearance of the national centennial exposition in Philadelphia, from which the Smithsonian had acquired many of its greatest mechanical treasures, and to interpret the exposition's huge significance in the evolution of American design, technology, and social customs. In a sense, the limitations of the Smithsonian project—it could represent only a tiny portion of the gigantic installation at Philadelphia's Fairmount Park a century earlier— became its virtues. It focused attention, in the way I think museums always do best, on a tight angle of vision, situating the visitor and the "object" in a provocative manner. The machines were enormous, but not so monstrous as their twentieth-century successors. The designs were elaborate, but still decipherable as an array of recognizable parts and materials. Even though the exhibition in 1976 hardly explored what had been omitted a century earlier, and though it reinforced the NMHT's faith in gadgets as the key to historical process, it showed that the exhibition form was more than the sum of its individual parts. For me, the obvious question was whether the elaborately labeled stuff in NMHT was as effective, pedagogically, as this effort to re-create the methods of the Philadelphia exposition.

These gigantic shows were a swan song for the Cold War master narratives in the museum world. As Daniel T. Rodgers demonstrates, the political rhetoric of both right and left fragmented the solidarity and consensus of the "word-pictures" Americans had of their own country. The more that Americans of all political stripes talked about "choice"—pro-choice, school choice, no-fault, opt-in, an all-volunteer military—the more they became aware of the obstacles they confronted in exercising their autonomy. To many, especially among the libertarian right wing, government ceased to be a legitimate vehicle for collective action. In the aftermath of Vietnam and revelations of CIA activities around the globe, left-leaning voices questioned the "imperial presidency" (Rodgers, *The Age of Fracture* [Cambridge: Harvard University Press, 2011], 89–91).

An eroded identification with the whole of American society and its government took its toll on political history exhibitions. It made less sense to ask visitors what they would do if they had responsibility for the nation. Cultural organizations responded to this weakening of collective identity. Grants from the National Endowment for the Arts and the National Endowment for the Humanities cultivated dissenting and minority voices and perspectives. When Roger Kennedy assumed directorship in 1979 of NMHT, soon to be renamed the National Museum of American History, he fostered the introduction of the new social history into the museum's exhibitions. *After the Revolution* (1985), an exhibition curated by Barbara Clark Smith, addressed the sharp differences among regional, racial, and economic groups in the first years of the new republic. Two years later, curator Spencer Crew and designer Jim Sims rendered the Great Migration of Black Americans from the Jim Crow South to northern cities in an exhibition called *Field to Factory: Afro-American Migration, 1915–1940.* Later that same year, the museum mounted *A More Perfect Union: Japanese Americans and the U.S. Constitution,* curated by Tom Crouch, which took the occasion of the bicentennial of the U.S. Constitution to explore its most egregious violation in the twentieth century, when 120,000 Japanese American residents were removed from their homes and sent to internment camps as potential enemy agents.

As at the Lower East Side Tenement Museum, these exhibitions and the many more that came in the flowering of ethnically specific history museums around the United States during the 1980s celebrated the agency of families and ethnic communities, rather than the "American way of life" or "the free-enterprise system." But the encouragement of these diverse voices drew fire from the right wing. Protests and threats of funding cuts roiled the climate in Washington, D.C., in the late 1980s and early 1990s, as Republicans lumped all these incidents together as an effort by "academic and cultural elites" to undermine and wage war on homegrown American values. "Revisionist history," right-wingers claimed, was an attack on patriotism and conventional morality.

For our purposes, the most important battle in this war—lost by the "revisionists"—was the controversy over the Enola Gay exhibition at the National Air and Space Museum (NASM). The plane, named for pilot Paul Tibbets's mother, had been acquired by the Smithsonian in 1949, four years after it had delivered the atomic bomb over Hiroshima. Long years of neglect, institutional planning, and then careful preservation had led to the idea that a major section (all that would fit) would be exhibited at the highly popular museum in 1995, on the occasion of the fiftieth anniversary of the mission. The curatorial staff and its historical consultants, reflecting the museum's gradual embrace of a more critical and contextual approach to the interpretation of its often-spectacular objects, decided to display the plane within a complex narrative about the decision to develop and use the bomb (and the B-29 bomber), the contribution of the Hiroshima and Nagasaki bombings to the Japanese surrender and the end of World War II, the local aftereffects of the bombing, and the postwar ethical debate about

Could political debates compete for visitors' attention with this shiny vehicle delivering nuclear death at the end of World War II? (Enola Gay B-29 bomber, National Air and Space Museum, 1995)

strategic bombing and nuclear warfare. If the Smithsonian history museum could observe the 200th anniversary of the federal Constitution by examining Japanese internment in World War II, the thinking went, the air and space museum could commemorate the end of the Pacific war by exploring the birth of the atomic age.

But of course there were important distinctions between the two. By 1987, the common wisdom was that Executive Order 9066, leading to the roundup of American citizens of Japanese origin, had been a tragic mistake. Not so the bombing of Hiroshima. Forty-plus years of Cold War had hardened the conviction among many Americans that the bomb's superior destructiveness had ended the war against Japan and led the superpowers to adopt nuclear deterrence in order to prevent the recurrence of world war.

No matter, then, how many museum professionals, scholars, and even veterans groups read, helped refine, and endorsed NASM's 350-page exhibition script; it was bound to spark opposition. The Air Force Association, a group of active and retired airmen and officers, backed by aerospace industry money, spearheaded the antagonists. It is possible, indeed probable, that no modifications to the exhibition plan would have satisfied the association. There was political hay to be made in tying the museum crowd in with a coterie of "political-correctness-spouting, America-hating, radical academics." But NASM tried hard to enlist supporters and significantly modified the script to mollify critics.

I was not involved in the Enola Gay controversy and have never read the draft exhibition script. More important, I have not read any exhibition treatments or seen any design sketches or object checklists that might indicate how visitors would engage with the subject. These are usually much more suggestive than the outline of the historical content. All I know comes from the splendid essays compiled in 1996 by Edward T. Linenthal and Tom Engelhardt in *History Wars: The Enola Gay and Other Battles for the American Past.*[6] I have read some of the scholarship on which the exhibition treatment was based, especially the monographs by Martin Sherwin and Gar Alperovitz. As a historian, I welcome the opportunity to explore anew the heavily freighted question of how World War II elided so quickly into the Cold War. My first high school politicking was on behalf of the Committee for a Sane Nuclear Policy, a leader among advocates of disarmament. In my teens and twenties, I read the *Bulletin of the Atomic Scientists* religiously. Every month its cover illustration—a clock showing only minutes to midnight—represented how close the world stood to a nuclear confrontation.

But as a curator of history, I find the reported complexity of the NASM draft worrisome. How would the museum actually represent the more abstract, verbal, and hard-to-decode debates that occurred behind the scenes, in the halls of power? How would such paper documentation fare, in the experience of visitors, against newsreel footage of aerial bombardment or, ultimately, against the big shiny B-29 bomber hovering overhead? How would thoughtful doubts about the Allied bombing of civilian populations and the use of nuclear weapons fit into such a populist exhibition?

For all their evocative power, exhibitions may deprive historians of some of their best tools. Moving from chapter to chapter, the author of a scholarly monograph can easily shift perspectives, timeframes, and central characters: "Having looked at the decision to deploy bombers" in chapter 2, say, we will now look in the next at the amazing technological prowess in the United States that brought along the B-29 so quickly. And then we will shift

6. Linenthal and Engelhardt, *History Wars: The Enola Gay and Other Battles for the American Past* (New York: Holt, 1996). A highly useful compilation of relevant documents by Edward J. Gallagher of Lehigh University is at http://digital.lib.lehigh.edu/trial/enola (accessed October 28, 2015).

in chapter 4 from the detailed narrative of the Enola Gay's mission, flying from the Tinian atoll to Hiroshima on the morning of August 6, 1945, to all the awful things that happened to buildings, objects, and people on the ground.

Convert those chapters into a series of exhibition galleries, and you're in some trouble. To the script's reviewers among the ranks of veterans and active military, its account of how the plane was designed, how the bomb was built, and how the bombing strategy evolved all seemed too cool and remote. It told a story of the triumph of science, engineering, and logistics rather than the struggles of patriotic men and women against a ruthless enemy. And then the following section, focusing on the sufferings of the victims in the bombed cities (illustrated by scorched and half-melted remains of everyday objects, to be borrowed from the Hiroshima Peace Museum), made it appear as if the Japanese were innocent victims of American technocratic violence. Or so the critics apparently believed.

Was there an alternative? The museum curators might have anticipated that veterans of war have almost always been sensitive to hints of postwar "betrayal" by their countrymen, their sacrifices taken for granted, their well-being neglected after they returned home.[7] Perhaps the museum might have instead focused throughout on how the Americans waged war: how they plotted a military strategy and came to adopt the bombing of civilians as a valid tactic; how they devoted enormous manpower, money, and intellectual resources to the development of the atomic bomb and the aircraft that might deliver it; how the troops in the Pacific theater conceived of their harrowing struggle; how political and military leaders debated the decision to deploy this superweapon over the course of its development; and how they assessed the damage it had done on the ground and the opportunities and challenges nuclear arms provided to policymakers in the immediate postwar years.

Such an exhibition, such a "Countdown to Cataclysm," would have represented conflicting positions within the American war machine. It could have foregrounded the creativity, but also the tragic limits, of American intelligence, geopolitical awareness, and economic resourcefulness. It might have built upon, rather than contradicted, the commonly held folk wisdom of the troops (especially U.S. soldiers) that their superiors are often

---

7. Jonathan Shay, *Achilles in Vietnam: Combat Trauma and the Undoing of Character* (New York: Scribner, 1994), uses the *Iliad* to tie the pain of combat to the soldiers' age-old sense of betrayal at the hands of their leaders.

clueless in the midst of battle. By carefully slowing down, reviewing, and measuring the U.S. actions against all the possible factors that had to be taken into account, this kind of Enola Gay exhibition would have more honestly represented the moment-to-moment confusions and potentially dangerous clarities of decision makers. (I see an obvious resemblance between this method and that of the exhibitions American History Workshop (AHW) has done on the process of creating the federal Constitution, dissecting and reassembling the decision-making stages so that visitors can see the human dramas firsthand.) It might have deflected the indictment of hindsight wisdom and superciliousness that doomed NASM's script. Of course, it would have said little or nothing about the Japanese version of events, except insofar as American authorities understood (or misunderstood) it. But a comparison of the American and Japanese narratives of the war would be better undertaken at another time, perhaps at another venue, and certainly not on the occasion of the fiftieth anniversary of the war's end. That is usually the "last hurrah" for a generation of historical actors before they pass from the scene. It's usually not the appropriate moment for sowing doubts.

After the abandonment of the original exhibition plan, the Enola Gay exhibition mounted at the museum focused almost entirely on the technical development of the B-29 and stripped away any concern with its historical context apart from the mission of the bombing run itself. It displayed major components of the plane: two engines, the vertical stabilizer, an aileron, propellers, and the forward fuselage that contains the bomb bay. A video presentation contained interviews with the crew. Much of the exhibition space explored the challenges facing the museum in conserving artifacts like this one. Nine years later, the fully assembled Enola Gay was installed in a permanent display at NASM's satellite facility in Virginia.

RETHINKING POLITICAL HISTORY IN THE WAKE OF AN EXHIBITION THAT BOMBED

Both sides in the Enola Gay controversy claimed to be staunch defenders of historical accuracy. During the "history wars" of the 1990s—concerning the degree to which classroom curricula should encourage either a critical perspective on or an abiding loyalty to the notion of America's exceptional role in world history—each side believed that "a knowledge of national history is essential to civic life." But in their important study of how Americans think about and use the past, based upon in-depth telephone surveys of over a thousand informants, historians Roy Rosenzweig and David Thelen "speculate that American nationalism (and a concomitant interest in the narrative of American national greatness) has significantly eroded since the mid-1960s for a variety of reasons—among them the globalization of the economy, the absence of unifying events like World War II or the Great Depression, and the socially divisive fallout of the 1960s" (*Presence of the Past: Popular Uses of History in American Culture* [New York: Columbia University Press, 1998], 123, 130).

During the bicentennial years, we had still assumed that the "national story" was everybody's story. We felt free to enliven its narrative by challenging conventional classroom understandings, by suggesting counterfactual alternatives, or, as in the case of the biographers, by delving almost novelistically into the inner lives and characters of the founders. As history became more entertaining, the past became less revered. Vietnam and Watergate sowed cynicism about political leaders that was read backward in time to taint the reputations of eighteenth- and nineteenth-century leaders. Feminist perspectives led to lumping "the whole lot of these dead white men" into one objectionable category, and the burgeoning interest in slavery dislodged the marble busts of Washington, Jefferson, and Robert E. Lee from their pedestals as paragons of virtue.

Rosenzweig and Thelen also discovered, in a more positive vein, that Americans attached themselves more strongly to family narratives and, especially among minority groups, to past stories of racial and ethnic groups. "When forced to say whether the past of their family or the past of the United States was more important to them," the historians reported, "Americans chose family history more than three times as often as their country's history." They were familiar with national history, often tied major shifts in personal life to the influence of national events like war and depression, and were thoroughly committed to history as a vital component of their children's schooling. But they most often detached personal history from the great tales of American greatness. A forty-year-old Georgia woman told the surveyors, "I feel that I have nothing to do with gaining our independence—that was done for me. I appreciate it, I celebrate it, but I did not have any relatives that fought for it or signed the Declaration of Independence" (ibid., 124, 129).

What did this mean for exhibitions and public history programs treating the political history of the nation? In the first decade of the new century, I had plenty of opportunities to find out. In 2004, the newly installed president of the New-York Historical Society (N-YHS), Dr. Louise Mirrer, described her intention to distinguish the Society from other local history groups by "seeing American history through the lens of New York." N-YHS has tremendously rich collections, especially in its library, that support scholarship far afield from the city's history—about colonial settlement and imperial commerce, westward expansion, and the Civil War. Mirrer's first foray into exhibitions enveloped Alexander Hamilton in an adulatory gaze (and wrapped the Society's building in a gigantic replica of a ten-dollar bill featuring the first treasury secretary). Curated by biographer Richard Brookhiser and designed by Ralph Appelbaum Associates, the glitzy exhibition felt to many historians, including me, more like a political campaign than a serious historical assessment.

So when Mirrer asked me to bring to fruition a long-gestating exhibition project on the history of slavery and emancipation in New York, I was a bit wary. But she proved the perfect client for AHW. Despite the presence on the N-YHS board of several important supporters of conservative causes, with our scholarly advisers we had a free hand to develop historical interpretations as we thought best. After the success of *Slavery in New York* and its follow-up, *New York Divided: Slavery and the Civil War,* AHW was contracted to do four more large history exhibitions in the next five years— *French Founding Father: Lafayette Returns to Washington's America*; *Grant and Lee*; *Lincoln and New York*; and *Revolution! The Atlantic World Reborn*—that focused on political issues. They culminate four decades of creating opportunities for visitors to understand their relationship to national and global communities of power and values.

We could no longer expect such programs simply to strengthen the visitor's identification with the nation. Even among the ranks of the cynical, New Yorkers excelled in sniffing out pious platitudes. Still, most of our visitors came thinking that the United States was formed full-blown in 1776–89—as a government, an economy, and a culture. The prestige of the Revolution and the Constitution has conventionally been used to fasten American attachments to institutions that did not exist in the eighteenth century: a nation-state of enormous reach and power, especially in military terms; a political party system sanctioning the pursuit of private interests; and a practice of judicial review by unelected judges with life tenure. Schoolbook chronologies suggest that the nation evolved in a fairly straight line to the American world we know today, through some sort of natural evolutionary process that would not have allowed real alternatives.

We decided, therefore, to embark on an effort—perfect for a series of museum exhibitions—to show how American national identity was constructed in the republic's first century. We knew that scholars like Benedict Anderson theorize the formation of a national identity as an act of collective imagination over the sweep of generations.[8] A museum exhibition, we thought, could represent that process as it happened, step by step, and in the material world.

The *Lafayette* exhibition (2007) was born as a loan exhibition of treasures from Mount Vernon, *A Son and His Adoptive Father: The Marquis de Lafayette and George Washington.* We convinced the N-YHS staff and board that a broader, historically focused exhibition would be more engaging and instructive for our New York audience. Although the materials from Mount Vernon were exhibited with great care, the New York installation concentrated on the astonishing tour Lafayette made to twenty-four states over a two-year period, 1824–25. It was a delightful curatorial enterprise. Almost every historical society in the eastern United States contains memorabilia of the Frenchman's journey. All these iconic Lafayette objects—commemorative plates, badges, clothing, and all sorts of tchotchkes—dovetailed with the creation of new methods of production and consumption. Robert E. Lee's tutor, Benjamin Hallowell, penned this ditty in honor of the occasion:

Each lover of Liberty surely must get
Something in honor of La Fayette
There's a La Fayette watch-chain, a La Fayette hat,
A La Fayette this, and a La Fayette that.
But I wanted something as lasting as life
As I took to myself a La Fayette wife.[9]

Further, by adorning themselves with this patriotic insignia, onlookers became both participants and spectators at a self-consciously historical occasion. The stuff and the memories of Lafayette's visit passed down in families and local repositories for generations. Dozens of towns, streets, and institutions bear the name of the hero or of his estate, La Grange.

On a more subtle level, the *Lafayette* exhibition demonstrated that contemporaneous newspaper reports treated the new nation to a very necessary two-year-long geography lesson and invented a set of icons that defined the United States as both exceptional and exemplary. At a moment of growing political polarization, Lafayette's tour provided a set of visual and tactile symbols, a litany of rhetorical expressions, and a geography of sacred

8. Anderson, *Imagined Communities: Reflections on the Origin and Spread of Nationalism*, rev. ed. (New York: Verso, 2006).

9. Cited in Elizabeth Brown Pryor, *Reading the Man: A Portrait of Robert E. Lee through His Private Letters* (New York: Viking, 2007), 42.

spaces that represented American nationality rather than the party or person in power at the moment. The tour, additionally, submerged regional loyalties in favor of national ones. The visiting hero did not dine on Louisiana gumbo or Yankee clam chowder, nor was he favored with the hat or title of a Kentucky colonel. Instead, frontier Little Rock mimicked cosmopolitan New York in its "Fayetting," as it was called, down to the menu and the toasts offered by the local notables. Thus did the Revolution evolve from a piece of personal memory to a socially binding array of associations. Every Fourth of July parade in twenty-first-century America—with its Stars-and-Stripes bunting, eagles, fireworks, and stem-winding speeches—is descended from these Welcome Lafayette festivities. (The hot dogs came later.) This theatricalizing of nationalism has long outlived the American public's awareness of the "French founding father."

In *Grant and Lee* (2008), co-curated by N-YHS public historian Kathleen Hulser, we revised a splendid Virginia Historical Society exhibition to explore the U.S. Army as an ambiguous expression of American nationality. The exhibition emphasized the pre- and post–Civil War experience of the leaders of the Union and Confederate armies, skirting the most familiar aspects of their biographies. Produced during the darkest months of the American incursion in Iraq, while my son was serving there as an army captain, *Grant and Lee* pondered two questions: What is the relationship of the military to civilian society in a nation founded on deep objections to a standing army? And how does military power shape the nation's political goals, domestically and internationally? On the exhibition's opening panel, Louise Mirrer invited visitors to "reflect on the application of military power to the achievement of our national goals. Visitors," she continued, "may find parallels and contrasts, to be sure, between the three Seminole Wars of 1817–1858 and our experience in Vietnam during the 1960s and 1970s, or between the army's paralysis during the crisis of Bleeding Kansas and our difficulties in Bosnia and Kosovo during the 1990s. Current-day immigration issues revive political disputes in the 1840s over the Mexican American War. The U.S. Army today faces challenges in Iraq that may recall its efforts of occupation and reconstruction in the post–Civil War South."

The *Lincoln and New York* exhibition (2009), scheduled to conclude the commemoration of the bicentennial of Lincoln's birth, enlisted Harold Holzer, the astonishingly productive scholar of Lincolniana, as our chief adviser. What particular contribution could our exhibition make? The Library of Congress had opened a magnificent display of letters, photographs, political cartoons, period engravings, speeches, and artifacts and arranged them artfully in a chronological sequence with excellent interpretive labels. That took care of the reverent antiquarians and Lincoln scholars. The National Museum of American History compiled a hodgepodge of terrific Lincoln artifacts: Abe's stovepipe hat and office suit, the gown made for Mary by Elizabeth Keckley, and plaster casts of Lincoln's hands and face. That took care of everything an eager parent needed in order to instill pride in a ten-year-old.

We decided to focus on the relationship of Lincoln's presidential career with the nation's greatest city and state—the largest supplier of Union troops and the funds for the war, home of the most important newspapers and magazines, and in its riots against the draft in 1863 the site of a little civil war on the streets. Our audience had grown so used to watching television coverage of Bill Clinton, George Bush, and Barack Obama that they could not think of Abraham Lincoln as anything other than a figure immersed in the minutiae of Washington, D.C., politics. In fact, the most thorough study of the Civil War in New York State was almost a century old.[10] (And this focus on Washington has been reinforced, of course, by blockbuster books like Doris Kearns Goodwin's gossipy chronicle of the Lincoln cabinet and by the murky machinations over the Thirteenth Amendment in Steven Spielberg's *Lincoln* film.) The political polarization of the Obama years spurred us to look hard at Lincoln's New York supporters, the Loyalists, and his antagonists, the Copperheads. Beyond their positions on the war itself, each side had advocated a shocking array of antidemocratic, racist, and authoritarian policies. To reconstruct the local context was thus to see another side of the Civil War, at once more ideological and more complicated by ethnic, religious, and racial antagonisms.

We wanted these exhibitions to demonstrate that museums could, in their attention to material sources, in their focus on the local aspects of our great national narratives, in their application of interpretive media, and in their engagement with a wider audience, actually provoke new scholarship about the past. In the process, they lost some of the sunnier qualities of our work in the 1970s and 1980s, when we could casually invite Americans to role-play, and thereby to rethink, the institutions and events of our nation's political evolution. A darker mood, a disenchantment, had set in. Perhaps the bloodshed at the Pettus bridge in Selma and at Hue in Vietnam were not historical anomalies. The nation's bold instruments of represen-

10. Sidney David Brummer, "Political History of New York State during the Period of the Civil War" (Ph.D. diss., Columbia University, 1911).

tative government, so promisingly launched 200 years ago, seemed paralyzed in the face of today's needs. West Point and the army it built, created with democratic promise and charged with providing the nation with the finest technical expertise, now seemed trapped in a series of imperialistic misadventures. The apparatus of nationalist celebration seemed an empty shell. From belonging we had descended to longing, merely hoping that attachment and participation might somehow be revived.

A more honest and critical appraisal of American history, beginning with the Vietnam Veterans Memorial wall, has fostered a change in exhibitions of our national political history. The long-standing master narrative of endless progress made increasingly less sense. Our audience seemed more willing to countenance stories without a happy ending, even, if I dare say so, with a sober awareness of human tragedy. While attendance at Independence Hall and Boston's Freedom Trail is declining, crowds flock to national parks commemorating Japanese internment, to the 9/11 Museum in Manhattan, to a dozen Holocaust memorials and museums, and to an ever-growing number of sites recalling the experience of enslavement. The Enola Gay controversy was a misstep, perhaps a necessary one, along this way toward a more mature assessment of our shared national triumphs and tragedies.

17 ::: TAKING THE NEW
SOCIAL HISTORY PUBLIC

Among history museum workers, the perspective of the
new social history swept away almost all competitors by
the 1980s. Focusing on the life histories of ordinary people;
exploring the ever-changing experiences of family, work,
and community; featuring in their storylines the darker
tendencies in American life; the new social historians portrayed the nation not as an express train to the future but
as a mule cart on a road heading off, bumpily, in many
directions at once.

Translating this perspective into museum exhibitions
and programs was an enormous challenge, not least because trustees, donors, and the general public generally
still viewed American history as a saga of presidents and
wars. As I've explained, it seemed obvious to us that "ordinary" people might more easily identify with the workaday
world we wanted to portray. Then, too, we had to worry
about whether our audience would be interested in "difficult" history. The history museum had almost two centuries of experience as a celebratory institution, and this
was a dramatic break. To undertake this new "interpretive
generation," we turned to unconventional sources, especially oral history interviews of people still living.

That, in turn, posed two further dilemmas. The communities who were the subjects of our interpretive programs, especially ethnic groups, began to insist on articulating their own histories rather than having them filtered through the conceptual frameworks of historians and anthropologists. Michael Frisch's papers, collected in *A Shared Authority: Essays on the Craft and Meaning of Oral and Public History* in 1990, introduced many historians, including me, to the subtleties of collaborating with the subjects of our investigations in developing interpretations of contemporary history. The museum historian was slowly evolving into a folklorist, a conduit for community voices, as responsibility for the interpretation was developed from the bottom up rather than from the top down.

Second, the introduction of new audiovisual media—valuable in communicating these "ordinary" faces, voices, and actions—turned up the temperature in the gallery. Stagecraft and audiovisual elements transformed the gallery's physical appearance. Importing this new expertise in design and media production, however, made greater community involvement difficult. Authorship of the interpretive program was becoming an ever more complicated affair. Exhibition deadlines were increasingly delayed by long meetings with community advisers and multiple planning team members. Even if one welcomed either or both of these two new trends, one had to wonder whether artistry and accuracy could survive.

The effects of these changes were felt as well in the substance of the historical interpretation. The old panel-and-vitrine exhibition, inviting visitors to see how historians, archivists, and curators could document historical change with period illustrations and relics, gave way to an experiential pathway—rich with media—that traced the dramatic saga of an individual family's or community's resilience and endurance in the face of dislocation and oppression. These were inspiring tales, but not in the way patriotic rituals had always been.

THE LEADERSHIP OF THE NATIONAL MUSEUM OF AMERICAN HISTORY

Perhaps the most surprising boost to the social history revolution in museums was the turnaround at the Smithsonian's National Museum of American History (NMAH). With Roger Kennedy's accession to the directorship in 1979, the museum recruited staff who had been schooled in the new social history and committed themselves to the museum's value in challenging the broader public with revisions of the conventional national narrative. Perhaps even more important, the staff now included several African American

The insults of segregation re-erected at the National Museum of American History's Field to Factory *exhibition (1987).*

professionals, including Fath Davis Ruffins, Spencer Crew, Bernice Johnson Reagon, and Lonnie Bunch. James Oliver Horton, who taught history at George Washington University, advised the director and tied the staff's work to that of historians around the country introducing new perspectives into that narrative. Two projects stand out from the 1980s.

In the 1987 exhibition, *Field to Factory*, visitors came across two doorways, one marked WHITE and one marked COLORED, into a replica of the Ashland, Virginia, railroad station. I have never seen an occasion in a museum, before or since, when everyone stopped dead in his or her tracks and suddenly confronted the shocking, embodied reality of an apartheid society.

Later that same year, *A More Perfect Union* explored the internment of 120,000 Japanese American residents (70,000 of whom were citizens) on the West Coast as potential enemy agents during World War II. This show featured a bold new use of media, including filmed interviews with former internees (some of them men and women of considerable achievement in postwar America). A meticulously re-created cabin represented the living spaces of the interned families, a conventional interpretive device in American history museums since the turn of the nineteenth century. But now, NMAH added a video, which re-created a visit by a middle-aged ex-internee to his childhood home. Visitors looked in at the room from one side, and the

A child's memory of life in a World War II internment camp translated into a father's explanation to his son many years later (A More Perfect Union, *NMAH, 1987*).

life-sized storyteller peered in from the other. One could not avoid his gaze or evade his shared memory of humiliation and resilience. The room was not "real."[1] The museum invented the characters and their dialogue, though they were based on oral histories.

The director and his staff had discovered that critical historical issues could be represented in momentary historical situations. Jim Crow found its emblematic experience in the split entrance to a railroad station. The national embarrassment over Japanese internment could be evoked, concretely and sensually, by the observable strain of a well-spoken, middle-class father in explaining his wartime confinement to his innocent son. The NMAH exhibitions showed that the big stories within the nation's history could be documented in the experience of ordinary people.

Though NMAH took some flak for washing the nation's dirty linen in public, Kennedy's forceful leadership was complemented by support from

1. None of the internment sites had been preserved by then. The act establishing Manzanar National Historic Site in the Owens Valley of California passed Congress in 1992, and the interpretive center opened in 2004.

the Black and Japanese communities. Also, the museum was not as completely dependent upon funding from outside (read corporate) sources as it would become in the 1990s and since. But for me, the most inspiring achievement of these shows, and of others in this era, was their ability to let visitors confront the history face on, without obscuring the pain of racism, wrapping it in adjectival excess, or using it to characterize the country as a whole. Exclusion and stigmatization are and have been public facts and private experiences throughout our history—pure, simple, and often repeated. But neither show assumed the burden of accounting for all of American history, and both discovered positive notes amid the pains they explored: the heroism of the almost all Japanese American 442nd Regimental Combat Team/100th Infantry Battalion in World War II, "the most decorated unit for its size and length of service in the history of American warfare," and the creativity of postmigration Black artists and musicians in northern cities, especially Chicago.

Of course, the most positive note was the national museum's taking notice of these troubling episodes in our national history at all. These stories did not necessarily have "happy endings" or lead to some beneficent state of affairs in the United States. As we saw in the months after 9/11, the nation is still inclined to the hasty detention and even deportation of allegedly "dangerous" elements in our citizenry. The trials encountered in the northbound migration of postemancipation Black people exemplified a fierce racism only slightly less violent than that of the Jim Crow South. It turns out that the purported value of telling these stories "so that we don't have to repeat them" is not quite foolproof. Still, the presence of these narratives does complicate and enrich our view of American history, and that is all to the good.

TURNING TOWARD INDIVIDUAL NARRATIVES

Both *Field to Factory* and *A More Perfect Union* explored the experience of groups of Americans, though their narratives were punctuated with portraits of and tales spoken by individuals. Social historians preferred it that way, attributing crises to whole groups rather than individuals. During my years at Old Sturbridge Village (osv), I have to confess, I did not warm up to the particular New Englanders whose way of life we tried to portray. I was in love with experiential learning and our narratives of economic transformation, but not with all the Priscillas and Jedidiahs we rescued from obscurity. In fact, we spent very little time delineating individual lives. I recall locating information about most of the families whose children went to a Killingly, Connecticut, school whose record book survived in the OSV library. I was astonished to discover that almost every one of the twelve children in one household had been born in a different town over the course of two decades — bitter evidence of a lifetime following jobs in one textile mill town after another. But I left their suffering to the past, bitter for them but data for me.

Even when we began to develop industrial heritage park projects, which entailed imagining ways to preserve and interpret working-class communities, the names slipped past us. I recall laughing out loud when told that a seven-foot-tall gas station attendant in Fall River was called "the Frenchman," rather than "Big Joe" or "the Giant," so fierce was the local emphasis on ethnic identity. When Philip Lax, head of the Ellis Island Restoration Committee, pounded the table at one meeting to accentuate the fact that his father and men like him "had built this country up with their bare hands," I shuddered. I shared his heritage and knew he was right, but as a historian I was dedicated to writing a collective narrative.

EMPATHIZING WITH HISTORICAL CHARACTERS
IN CHALLENGING SITUATIONS

Working on the Lower East Side Tenement Museum (LESTM), as I've explained, sounded the death knell for my use of composite historical characters and "typical" situations. Focusing on the dramatic moments of individual lives, especially given the museum's power to engage so many senses at once, proved tremendously effective in making history come alive. We had organized many role-playing experiences at OSV and in our early political history exhibitions, asking visitors to step into the shoes of historical characters and thereby altering their public memory of familiar historical events. A visitor to *Miracle at Philadelphia* could better understand James Madison by focusing on the interpretive cluster we created around his notes on the constitutional convention. At the end of that exhibition, when they were asked whether they would "sign" the draft Constitution or instead enter their objections in an adjoining notebook, perhaps they would feel a twinge of anxiety. That "three-fifths" clause, after all, that was pretty awful. But these ways of engaging the past were not deeply personal or emotional.

By contrast, at the LESTM or the Holocaust Museum or one of the many exhibitions we did on the history of slavery, the emotional stakes were much higher. Increasingly, through the 1990s and 2000s, more of my work focused on ordinary, unfamous people in tight spots. For my whole career, I'd been working hard to cultivate the learning skills of visitors to my public history programs, helping them to contextualize the fragments of stuff and story they encountered in my museums. But now I recognized that their empathy, their emotional connection, was essential in unlocking their best capacities for learning. I didn't want visitors to identify totally with people in the past but, rather, to "subjectivize" them, that is, to view them from the inside as fully human and complex historical agents. This required honing in on the circumstances in which the historical characters found themselves. Nathalie Gumpertz, the subject of our first tour at the LESTM, was many things—an immigrant, a deserted wife, a mother of three daughters (and of a son who had died as a toddler), a neighbor to other German immigrants, a Jewish woman, and a seamstress offering her skills to women better off than she. There were also things she could not be—a voter or a worshipper called to the Torah in the synagogue. To empathize with Nathalie in all of these circumstances, visitors would not lose themselves in her. They would, instead, "share" their own humanity—their hopes and fears, their skills in puzzling over choices and making decisions, and their imperfect memories of analogous situations—with a woman who died a century ago.

Empathy requires more than an outpouring of feeling toward another person. It is also a method of self-knowledge. In the process of connecting with the situation of a fellow human being, we can become aware of "the fears and needs established within one's own history," as museum scholars Jennifer Bonnell and Roger I. Simon note. Like Nathalie, we too have had instances of powerlessness, inequality, and abandonment. But ours are different from hers. Bonnell and Simon try to reconceptualize empathy

> as a capacity for reaching out to another's experience in which our distinctive psycho-social history is maintained. Rather than presume a similarity of feelings, empathy thus reconceived becomes a relation of acknowledgement, a responsiveness to the feelings of others that opens the question of what it might mean to live in proximity to these feelings, to live in ways in which one experiences the force of these feelings to alter one's experience of the world and actions in it. This acknowledgement of the other's situation neither presupposes nor implies that one actually feels what the other feels. It is a process of being responsive to and reaching out toward another in which the other remains other, a process within which our distinctiveness as individual persons is not obliterated.[2]

2. Bonnell and Simon, "'Difficult Exhibitions and Intimate Encounters,'" *Museum and Society* 5, no. 2 (July 2007): 65–85, quotation at 76.

To enter into this acknowledgment of others, including the long departed, takes time, patience, attention, and a mature understanding of one's own distance from the past. Museums often try to bridge this distance too casually. *Field to Factory* and the Ellis Island exhibitions quoted brief snippets of oral history, hoping that visitors would connect with such phrasemakers. But that's hard to do. As with anything else in the museum landscape, it takes real time, several minutes, to begin connecting with a story, an object, a performance, or most important, a historical personage. On the other hand, the Civil War reenactor who wanted to look exactly like the soldier in a daguerreotype portrayed by Tony Horwitz in his *Confederates in the Attic* (1998) is a mad caricature of true empathy. Past lives are both like and unlike ours. The most productive learning comes when we engage in a dialogue of resemblance and difference. Knowing and feeling the discomfort (the "wobble") of *not* fitting into the historical character is a critical element in good learning—about others and about ourselves. Empathy has to be mixed with critical judgment.

TO BIRMINGHAM

The LESTM, like NMAH, Ellis Island, and the Holocaust Museum, were top-down institutions. They incorporated the stories of ordinary people, but they did not emerge from within those communities. They expressed the openness of the American establishment to diversifying the national story. They allowed for the truly horrific episodes of American history to take place in the public historical record. Sometimes, as with the LESTM in New York, they were even situated in the midst of ethnically diverse communities, but they used an "uptown" voice in their public offerings.

The Birmingham Civil Rights Institute (BCRI) was different. Originally proposed in 1979 by Mayor David Vann, reputedly "the only White man in Birmingham willing to talk with the Reverend Dr. Martin Luther King, Jr.," the project had evolved in fits and starts under the succeeding administration of Richard Arrington, Birmingham's first Black mayor. The BCRI was shrewdly promoted more as a spur to the economic benefits of African American tourism than to community reconciliation, and the sponsors persuaded the city in 1985 to purchase a site on Sixth Avenue directly across from Kelly-Ingram Park, where the city's Black children marched for civil rights in the spring of 1963 and confronted Bull Connor's brutal water cannons and dogs. Catercornered to the institute site stands the Sixteenth Street Baptist Church, a center of the protest movement, where four young girls were killed in the bombing in September of that year. In 1986, Mayor Arrington created a task force to oversee the development of the project.[3]

That same year American History Workshop (AHW) was retained as a subcontractor to Bond Ryder James, the project architects from New York. They had sketched out an impressive classical-style building, with a large exhibition gallery ornamented with lovely clerestory windows. Immediately, my colleague Leonard Majzlin and I knew this was wrong. Telling the dramatic story of 1963 meant showing the television news footage that had broadcast the city's police brutality to a global audience two decades before. The interpretive gallery would have to be a darkened passageway, calling forth a different kind of architectural space. Beyond that, the key decisions over space allocation, thematics, and design would rest in the hands of the local BCRI task force members. Our job was to listen carefully to them and translate their thinking into an inspiring and challenging experience for the visiting public.

The task force was a wonderful client, with splendid individual talents. Horace Huntley, a labor historian at the University of Alabama-Birmingham, led us on tours of the steel mills and union halls that set Birmingham apart from other southern cities. Bob Corley, head of the local chapter of the National Conference of Christians and Jews, was a historian of racial politics in Birmingham. Dr. Abraham Lincoln Woods, who had helped organize the 1963 March on Washington, was a veteran of the local struggle. Marvin Whiting, archivist at the Birmingham Public Library, had amassed a superb collection of relevant documents over the last decade. Presiding over all was Odessa Woolfolk, a former teacher, urban affairs scholar, and university administrator, who envisaged an active, living institution enmeshed in community action. "Don't call it a museum," she frequently reminded us, and she kept the flame burning during all sorts of trials and tribulations in the years ahead.

Casting a glowing influence over our involvement was Dr. Fred Shuttles-

3. Glenn Eskew, "The Birmingham Civil Rights Institute and the New Ideology of Tolerance," in *The Civil Rights Movement in American Memory*, ed. Renee C. Romano and Leigh Raiford (Athens: University of Georgia Press, 2006), 28–66; Eskew, "Memorializing the Movement: The Struggle to Build Civil Rights Museums in the South," in *Warm Ashes: Issues in Southern History at the Dawn of the Twenty-First Century*, ed. Winfred B. Moore Jr., Kyle S. Sinisi, and David H. White Jr. (Columbia: University of South Carolina Press, 2003), 357–79.

worth, one of the heroes of my adolescence. Shuttlesworth had survived numerous bombings and death threats, and his Alabama Christian Movement for Human Rights had taken over leadership of the civil rights movement there when the state banned the NAACP in 1956. Historian David Blight reminds me of a phrase Shuttlesworth frequently inserted into discussions of past events: "If you don't tell it like it was, it can never be as it ought to be." Finally, the Reverend John Porter, the pastor of Sixth Avenue Baptist Church, provided our team with a spiritual and musical home every Sunday and a chance to sit down over Sunday dinner and talk with his parishioners.

Formidable as this group was, its members knew very little about making a history exhibition. One pressed for an IMAX presentation; another wanted "a Disneyland about the civil rights movement." For the sponsors, this did not mean employing high-tech presentations so much as creating a regional shrine operating at a high level of effectiveness and financial stability.

But they were clear on the really important questions. They were in full agreement about their target core audience: the young in Birmingham, especially African American children, who were growing up ignorant of the events of the 1960s and taking them for granted. The task force members knew their own story: the ability of ordinary people, even children, to transform a century-long practice of racial insult and injury. They knew their mission: "to promote human and civil rights worldwide through education." And through many conversations, I discovered the "key artifact" of the exhibition program. It was not the door of the Birmingham jail cell from which Dr. King had written his impassioned letter to those local clergy who urged him to be patient. It was not those "Whites Only" signs that were originally mounted in virtually every public place. These were important and impressive, but not so much as the sponsoring group itself. The men and women I was meeting, immaculately precise in dress, language, and manner, were the evidences of the transformation they themselves had wrought. Their individual narratives compelled attention and respect. They spoke of what segregation threatened, and they demonstrated what overcoming it could yield. I was convinced that visitors would be inspired simply by "meeting" them in the exhibition space.

Absent the task force, the project would likely have taken a very different direction. If we had constituted a panel of outside scholars to frame the story, as ordinarily happens (and is customarily mandated by funding from the National Endowment for the Humanities), it would likely have had a wider focus, like the civil rights museums in Atlanta and Memphis. Historian Glenn Eskew discerningly dissects the contribution of the task force members:

> The influence of the Task Force members can be seen in the thematic program designed by Rabinowitz. While internationally significant, the story told is a local one that features the indigenous movement rather than King and the SCLC [Southern Christian Leadership Conference]. Reference is made to Montgomery, but the chronology is rightly focused on the early 1960s as the pivotal period in civil rights history. The role of biracial communications in the postwar period, during the 1963 demonstrations, and since then is analyzed according to an interpretation proposed by Corley and [Arrington's chief of staff Edward] LaMonte. Black institutions appear as unequal byproducts of segregation as argued by Woolfolk. Rather than overemphasize the black bourgeoisie, the exhibit highlights the black working class, reflecting the interests of Huntley. Vann's opinion that the televised broadcasts of the fire hoses and police dogs marked the turning point in the movement is not only stressed in the exhibit but actually re-enacted through the [national news reports] shown on period television sets. Finally, the flow of events emphasizes Whiting's contention that Birmingham marked a watershed celebrated at the March on Washington.[4]

The overall narrative framework and many of its local connotations came from the task force, but the interpretive scheme was AHW's professional contribution. Majzlin and I designed the arc of the visitors' journey as an immersion in the civil rights struggle of the 1950s and 1960s. Approaching the building from Kelly-Ingram Park, visitors would look up at the glassed-in second-floor gallery and spot a series of life cast figures that would seem to march determinedly across the room—a physicalization, in fact, of the famous 1965 James H. Karales photograph of civil rights marchers across the horizon under a threatening sky. We anticipated that at a critical point in the course of the story, the pathway of visitors would bring them into that same "processional" space, joining those sculptural "marchers."

Between those two moments, the exhibition cast visitors as recruits in the movement. Entering the building, designed to resemble the church architecture of the region, visitors were invited to feel as though they were coming to a protest meeting in 1963. After a brief introductory audiovisual

---

4. Eskew, "Birmingham Civil Rights Institute," 52.

*The BCRI invites visitors to join the civil rights movement
as they reenact the events of the 1950s and 1960s.*

program emphasizing the migration of Black people to Birmingham's steel
mills in the early twentieth century and the creation of a vibrant local Black
community, visitors would be thrust into the "Barriers" gallery. Here they
sense again and again how Black Birminghamers were on the outside looking in, excluded and segregated by Jim Crow laws and social custom from
all manner of public spaces—schools, stores, theaters, buses, even the sidewalks (and, of course, the water fountains) of the city. As the story of the
protest movement begins, the exhibition moves between local events narrated personally, such as the repeated bombings of activists' homes in the
city known as "Bombingham," the legal struggles, and the violence of 1963,
and events occurring regionally (the Montgomery bus boycott; the attacks
on the Freedom Riders in Anniston, Birmingham, and Montgomery; and
the Selma march). Amid their journey, visitors could find a quieter space,
a chance to pause and contemplate, while looking out toward the park and
the site of the September 1963 church bombing.

By 1986, this storyline had been frozen into place as an unquestioned
mythos. There were no dissenters. The movement's opponents were silent
in public. The BCRI was a public-sector project. It had been promoted—and
funded with White support—for its value in attracting African American
tourists eager to connect with the heroism and heritage of the civil rights

movement of the 1960s. This rationale, Glenn Eskew points out, "insured that a constructive message had to accompany the negative racial history. . . . Thus the story line of the movement at the BCRI resolved into the Whiggish progressivism of the American master narrative, with a message that celebrates the moral righteousness of nonviolent protest, the potential of interracial unity, and the success of qualified integration."[5]

No one was naive or forgetful of the always lively contentiousness within Black politics. But all that was set aside in the unanimous support for "the cause." The task force members wanted to depict the 1960s civil rights movement as an example to today's youth of how civic action could empower individuals and the whole community. They wanted to narrate their own story in their own voice. They wanted to have the exhibition explain and illustrate what they could not convey in talks around the dining room table, at high school history classes, or even from the pulpit.

The clarity and harmony of the leadership was remarkable to me, but it was purchased at the cost of a critical perspective on their own movement histories. Given the state of scholarship in 1986 and the still-unclear effects of the Reagan administration's retreat from enforcement of civil rights legislation, I am not sure that an alternative explanatory framework was then available. The AHW plan pressed for educational programs that would help students explore and overcome the continuation of racial discrimination in Birmingham and its suburbs, arguing that the struggle was not over. But in large measure I felt no qualms about embracing the "Whiggish" narrative of the task force—in part because it dovetailed with my own commitment to the civil rights movement, but also because I knew that as a public historian and a "teaching pro" I was speaking on behalf of the sponsors, not for myself. If I were writing a scholarly article, aiming to win approval from journal editors and reviewers, hoping to gain tenure or promotion, I would have doubtlessly tried to tailor my approach to that of the scholarly community beyond Birmingham. All historians aim to tie their work to some community or another. Mine, at that moment, was the local task force.

The experience taught me that critical history and community participation are not necessarily happy bedfellows. Like all historians, I aspire to a quasi-academic freedom to create an open-ended and ceaselessly questioning historical narrative. While that's a lovely goal, it can be compromised by enthusiastic supporters as well as hidebound opponents. One has to ponder, Can a shrine also serve as a forum for debate?

5. Ibid., 29.

Despite these reservations, the BCRI sponsors achieved great things. The institute's public exhibitions continued the work of the local civil rights movement itself. In the 1950s and 1960s, Black Birmingham had fought for equal access to schools and public accommodations and for elemental decencies in social interaction. No longer would Black men, fearing for their lives, have to step off the sidewalk to let Whites walk by or avert their eyes from those of White women or answer to demeaning names rather than their own. Now their wives and sisters would be able to use the fitting rooms of the local stores or sit wherever they wanted in the movie theaters. A Black mayor and council members now oversaw the more equitable distribution of city jobs and benefits. The BCRI went a step further, aiming at an equally significant role in the public culture of the city. At the time of its planning, there was scarcely any African American presence in the city's fine arts museum, science center, or children's museum—among employees and volunteers, in program directions, and in community partnerships. After the BCRI opened in 1992, the history of Black Birmingham's struggle became fundamental to the history the region told about itself.

18 ::: THE COMMUNITY
AS CURATOR

Even in an innovative age, the most adventurous new museums in the 1980s emerged from within ethnic communities and spoke—as the Birmingham Civil Rights Institute (BCRI) did—with voices that had not previously been heard very much in the American civic space. African American museums, before 1950, had been almost always sited on historically Black college campuses. Under the leadership of local visionaries, a few dozen cities initiated local museums of African American history and culture in the next three decades, but the movement accelerated in the 1980s, most notably with the new building of the Charles H. Wright Museum in Detroit. Tribal groups founded dozens of American Indian cultural centers, especially in the West, many with active interpretive exhibitions welcoming tourists as well as local groups. The Japanese American National Museum in Los Angeles was established in 1982 and opened its impressive building a decade later. Even European American ethnic groups with longer museum histories rapidly expanded their geographical scope and educational ambitions during this period.

"Mainstream" museums like the National Museum of

American History, the United States Holocaust Memorial Museum, or the Lower East Side Tenement Museum had begun to incorporate the voices of long-silenced historical figures, survivors, and eyewitnesses in their presentations, but always with a strong curatorial hand at the helm. Like scholars, they might *quote* diverse American voices, but community-based museums actually try to *speak* with those voices. They would set aside the often-dominant voices of established scholars and substitute instead the perspectives of indigenous and local advocates, activists, artists, and intellectuals. Beyond interpreting the histories of their fellow ethnics in the United States, community museums adopt multiple missions: to enhance and express the community's voice in local affairs, to channel the creativity of community members toward an expression of group identity, to link intergenerational relationships to ethnic identity, and, in sum, to empower groups that felt they had been unfairly marginalized in the broader culture of the region and nation.

Before 1980, most museums sponsored by ethnic associations had combined displays of traditional Old World customs and costumes with a "hall of fame" celebration of the most successfully assimilated local members of the group. In the 1980s, ethnically specific museums, rooted in folklore and oral history research in minority communities, brought attention to everyday life practices that had usually been shunned by earlier community leaders. They visualized and concretized the often-attenuated memory of how immigrants and their descendants shared their work, family life, and community interaction. The Chinatown History Project in New York, a collaboration of historian Jack Tchen and community activist Charles Laiand, led off in 1980 with a brilliant exhibition called *Eight Pound Livelihood*, which excavated and represented the memories of laundrymen, the most common occupational group among early twentieth-century Chinese Americans. It brought this generation of immigrants into the historical light, explaining how laundry operators—often unmarried men living alone—converged on Saturday evenings in Chinatown after their long workweeks in far-flung American neighborhoods.

On the West Coast, the Wing Luke Museum of the Asian Pacific American Experience in Seattle pioneered a similar "from the bottom up" method of museum making. In 2001, I had the pleasure of spending several days observing the Wing Luke team put together an exhibition and public program series on Asian garment workers in Seattle. Rather than starting with a meeting of outside experts—one could have imagined a panel of labor economists, social historians, folklorists, and clothing historians—Director

Ron Chew and his staff instead began with community gatherings, where potential subjects for oral history interviews were identified. Then, beyond collecting stories, the oral history process became an opportunity to display garment-making skills; collect examples of the finest work, photographs, and other accouterments of the factory jobs; and develop hypotheses about the connections between shop employment and life in multigenerational households. At the center of the ensuing exhibition was an academic gown produced by an elderly seamstress for her grandson, who was graduating with a Ph.D. in economics from the University of Washington. Though it wasn't a "typical" artifact of the sweatshop system, as the exhibition promised, the gown dramatically embodied the contribution of women workers to the upward mobility of Seattle's Asian families. Would a conventional process of exhibition development have discovered and featured such an object?

The Wing Luke model collapsed the boundary between exhibition development and presentation, as it did the distinction between the development team and the audience. Exhibition-making itself became the educational method. Even after an exhibition was open, the museum staff continued to collect and incorporate stories and objects from visitors. In sum, the museum reinvented itself as a *method* of discovering, developing, and celebrating community identity—a verb, as we came to call it, not a noun.

Though deeply rooted in these urban communities, the New York Chinatown and Wing Luke projects were about more than ethnic identity. The people they portrayed were far more than exemplary Chinese or Filipinos. They were also workers and parents, worshippers and citizens. In constructing its interpretation around the actual families who lived at 97 Orchard Street, the Lower East Side Tenement Museum had liberated itself from its original simplistic assignment of its apartments to invented ethnic "composites." That allowed the museum to interpret other issues significant to immigrant, working-class life—family relationships, health, social mobility, entrepreneurship, and many other subjects that had little to do with German, Italian, or Jewish ethnicity. So, too, with the new ethnic history museums: They did not have to keep explaining "what it was like" to be Asian or Black.

These "outsider" groups brought lots of new stories to public light. These narratives fiercely undermined the stereotypes foisted on them for many years by the majority culture and its history textbooks. Even after ethnic slurs disappeared from polite public language, derogatory characterizations had endured. American historians, anthropologists, and sociologists had been deeply infected with assumptions about the supposed intellectual inferiority, susceptibility to intoxication and violence, cupidity, laziness, and childlike irresponsibility of the non-Anglo-Saxon groups they portrayed. The representation of aboriginal populations in natural history museums throughout the North American, European, and Australian world often emphasized the barbarism or savagery of their precontact histories. History museums enshrined only the most "successful" immigrants, often those who most comfortably assimilated into the mainstream, while ignoring traditionalists, stay-at-home mothers, and those who abandoned America to return to their countries of origin. Museum display methods implicitly communicated that Old World or precontact cultures were irreconcilable with modern American social, economic, and cultural norms.

Alternatives to this "professional" rhetoric have been difficult to develop. "Native" or "indigenous" perspectives often sound defensive, precious, and self-righteous. They convey stereotypes of their own.[1] At the Mashantucket Pequot Museum in eastern Connecticut, visitors can stroll through a recreated precontact village, with mock streams flowing alongside mock wigwams. Though the faces were life-cast from modern-day tribal members, the figures all look gorgeous—healthy, slim, and unscarred by childbearing, anemia, or arthritis. If only Europeans had not come to New England in the seventeenth century, one is led to suspect, the climate would have been milder and the landscape ready for development as a spectacular resort 400 years later. The people lived harmoniously in nature. They drew strength from ancient traditions and put mutual relationships ahead of business transactions. Peace reigned. The archaeological evidence, of course, contradicts many of these myths.

At least, in another exhibition area, the Pequot Museum acknowledges and traces the bloody history of conflict with the seventeenth-century English settlers and the ethnic cleansing of these ancestral homelands. Not so the Smithsonian's National Museum of the American Indian (NMAI). The museum scorned its origins in the natural history museum, where the skeletal remains of Indian peoples had been collected and studied for a cen-

1. Hilde S. Hein observes, "'Native interpreters' and 'resource people' are 'inexpert' when it comes to interpreting museum objects,' for their expertise, unlike that of the museum professionals, pertains to an earlier incarnation of the objects that have journeyed from a known world into a strange new environment" (Hein, *The Museum in Transition: A Philosophical Perspective* [Washington, D.C.: Smithsonian Institution Press, 2000], 43).

Connecticut has never looked so beautiful since the precontact Pequot people reimagined at the Mashantaucket Pequot Museum (1990s).

tury and a half in much the same way as dinosaur bones, butterflies, and tropical plant specimens. NMAI developed its independent existence in the 1980s, at the same time that the federal government mandated the restoration of these human remains, when possible, for ceremonial reburial by tribal members. In addition, the Smithsonian museum was greatly enriched by the 1989 acquisition of the George Gustave Heye collection of more than 700,000 objects in Heye's Museum of the American Indian in New York City. In 1994, a branch of the museum opened in the Custom House on Bowling Green in lower Manhattan. Five years later, the museum's Cultural Resources Center opened at Suitland, Maryland, housing the collections and making some of them available for reengagement by tribal members. The museum's exciting new building on the National Mall welcomed its first visitors in 2004.

NMAI's interpretive approach, focusing on the message that "We Are Still Here," gave participating Indian groups an opportunity to define and present themselves as radically distinctive systems of culture, ordinary life, spirituality, and material culture. Narratives of Indian-White relations in North America, especially since the seventeenth century, took a backseat to interpreting the contemporary life of Indian peoples, especially within their native soil. The museum abandoned conventional anthropological group-

The museum as an instrument of self-portraiture for Indian peoples
(National Museum of the American Indian, 2004).

ings such as "Algonquian language speakers" or "Plains people." The exhibitions themselves tried hard to respect and not elide the differences among all of the 500-plus tribal groups in North America.

Provocative as these decisions have been, they have often proved problematic for many in the museum audience. Curators can center their interpretations either on the perspectives of the sponsoring groups, as NMAI does, or on the learning process of visitors (like most children's museums), but it is hard to do both, and even harder when one sacrifices the contextual frameworks offered by scholarship. I can understand the motivations that underpinned NMAI's choices, but I remain more an advocate for the visitor rather than the sponsors. Consequently, as I walk though the beautiful building of the NMAI in Washington, D.C., I have been frequently confused and even embarrassed. I'm incapable of understanding the distinctions and the details presented. I'm put off by the ethnocentric, over-the-top pride in particularity. I don't see any place where a non-Indian visitor's experience of the world is connected to or validated by the exhibitions. I don't see enough complexity, and especially enough history and geography, to sharpen my sense of each group's particularity. For me, it's a mess. Except when I get to the museum restaurant, where the dishes on offer are grouped into reasonably recognizable cuisines: Northern Woodlands food (turkey, cranberry); Pacific Northwest food (salmon, wild rice); Mesoamerican food (which I'd always known as Mexican or Tex-Mex); South American (ceviche, calabasa squash); and Great Plains (buffalo, corn). What a treat, and what a lesson for the exhibition program upstairs!

HISTORY MUSEUMS AND IDENTITY MUSEUMS

Having felt excluded from the master narratives of American history for so long, or insulted by their racist condescension, the new ethnic museums have responded by becoming promoters of group identity and pride. History becomes a useful tool in changing the community's view of itself. We are not interlopers, not intruders on an Anglo world—no, we have been here for a long time. Though unnoticed, our forebears helped build this world, and their stories of resilience are sources of empowerment for their descendants today. Does a narrative of resilience and persistence actually yield power in the American context?

As they make this argument, however, many ethnically specific museum projects drift away from detailing the actual, often diverse, histories of their people in this particular place. Instead, they begin to interpret themselves through the lens of the standard American immigrant saga: We came, we were scorned, some of us began to succeed, we faced terrible setbacks but we have now overcome this challenge, and so on. Edward Rothstein, then a cultural critic for the *New York Times*, reviewing the much-expanded New York Museum of Chinese in the Americas, notes about these identity museums, "how similar the arcs of their stories are: they recount how after a long period of suffering, prejudice and hatred, a group has carved a distinctive place in the history of the United States, its once scorned identity now a source of strength. . . . The hardened formula of the identity narrative . . . overshadows the museum's ability to explore more fully the nature of Chinese culture and immigration."[2]

Further, these narratives often turn on a single villainous act in American history that exemplifies the host culture's racism, anti-Semitism, or nativism. For the Japanese American National Museum in Los Angeles, it is the experience of relocation to internment camps during World War II.

2. Rothstein, "Reopened Museum Tells Chinese-American Stories," *New York Times*, September 21, 2009.

For Chinese American museums, it is the Exclusion Act of 1882. For many Jewish museums, the Holocaust and America's failure to accept desperate refugees from Nazi Germany are an obligatory reference. The Irish experience in America is said to turn on the famine that drove emigration in the 1840s. German Americans had to hide from their proud heritage during the two world wars.

These are horrible, shameful stains on our national and global history. But they do not constitute the only or even the central factor in the evolution of these groups in the United States. Japanese citizens living east of the Mississippi were not interned. The vast majority of Chinese Americans have immigrated to the United States long after the offensive act was repealed. The dreadful life experiences of the "famine" Irish, historians tell us, made it very unlikely that they could form families and reproduce themselves, so there may in fact be very few Irish Americans descended from those arrivals. Most American Jews are descended from immigrants who came three decades or more before the Shoah. No single pathway characterizes more than a sliver of each group's population. We steal from one another's cultures shamelessly. Personality is larger than identity.

Early in my career, as I've explained, the storyline of social history exhibitions culminated in a vaguely described movement toward "modernization," and most shows ended with a limp conclusion like, "and that's why we live the way we do today." That narrative worked only so long as we thought of all Americans proceeding through the same historical evolution—sharing economic ups and downs, experiencing advances in technology, and occupying cities and homes that resembled one another from coast to coast. In the "age of fracture," this story had broken down. Now, the ethnic museums tell us, each of us seems to have marched in lockstep with our fellow ethnics.

Of course, this is nonsense. Immigration both broke apart and brought back together parts of each ethnic group. Subgroups, rooted in different experiences in the Old Country and different opportunities in this one, persist. One size does not fit all personal histories. In my own experience, I've always been bothered by museums purporting to tell me what was normal or correct in Jewish religion, culture, and ethnic experience. Almost every Jewish museum has a display of "the Jewish life cycle," with artifacts used in rituals from birth and circumcision to burial and mourning. Another exhibit typically proceeds through the Jewish ritual week, season, and year, bringing together Hanukkah menorahs and seder plates and Kiddush cups. But rather than demonstrate the amazing variety of Jewish experiences, making me both proud and fascinated by all these adaptions to host cultures around the globe, I come away feeling as though I've failed in my dutiful observance of most of the 613 prescribed commandments. Nobody I know practices this sort of "museum Judaism." I refuse to believe that some people and not others are "authentically Jewish" or "authentically Latino" or anything else.

BALANCING INSIDERS AND OUTSIDERS

Ethnically specific museums have to perform a balancing act. They can reinforce cultural identities by drawing attention to the historical experience of a particular community, but they are strongest when they allow visitors to develop their own definitions of what that identity is. The BCRI was not about what Black people were (or what they do if they are "authentically" Black) but, rather, what some Black people did at a particular time and place. Ethnic museums have an understandable impulse to emphasize the successes in a community's history—the businesses established, the advanced degrees won, the public positions achieved. But they also have an intellectual responsibility to explore the often-hidden, even shameful aspects of the group's experience in the United States: that first-generation immigrant men were often crude brawlers, for example, or that criminal gangs flourished on the Jewish Lower East Side or that French Canadian teenage girls who found themselves pregnant were consigned to lifelong semiservitude in convents.

It's not easy washing the dirty linen in public, risking embarrassing the group by showing its less attractive side, but it also can build a bridge to outsiders. Representing the day-to-day complexities of ethnic life in America without romanticizing the founding generations invites "others" to peer within the insider's curtain of privileged knowledge. Every group has experienced (and should interpret) the episodes of unemployment, intermarriage, isolation, bullying, and dependence upon charity and government assistance that are fundamental elements of becoming established in the United States—as fundamental as the examples of upward mobility and success. These experiences expose problems of political, economic, and cultural difficulty that we all share and that we all deserve to know about.

MUSEUMS AS SITES OF BOUNDARY CROSSING

My first visit to a museum on my own was, I think, for a seventh-grade school assignment, searching the Metropolitan Museum of Art to see if they had any work by the man who painted the picture of a young cadet my teacher had given me. It turned out to be Edouard Manet, and they did! It was scary, but I was brave. From that day forward, my museumgoing has always been a boundary-crossing business. Only gradually did I overcome my anxiety in these foreign terrains, and I accomplished that by displaying chutzpah as much as by learning the insider's code. My teachers told me in no uncertain terms that my adult social standing depended upon an acquaintance with, even an affection for, the great works of Western art, music, literature, theater, and dance. But for many years I always knew that I was an inch away from embarrassment.

I felt like an outsider as the child of an immigrant and as a novice among cognoscenti, and these two sources of anxiety—ethnic and professional—intermingled to make me aware that a museum would always be hard pressed to reduce such feelings among many visitors. In her thoughtful assessment of the contemporary museum, the philosopher Hilde Hein doubts that these institutions can welcome outsiders into "the embrace of . . . cognitive camaraderie" with insiders.

> The insider experience is doubly alien to former outsiders, in that the distinction marking this status exists only relative to the insider community, whose categories of meaning and rank do not apply elsewhere. So—if outsiders are to become insiders, they must adopt as their own the perception of themselves as reconstructed outsiders, a paradoxical option on both cognitive and ethical grounds. To remain an outsider is to be insensible of that condition, and to become an insider is to repudiate it—and so to disavow one's prior identity. Affirming "outsiderhood" positively is not an option.[3]

This seems to me basically wrong. While museums assuredly do legitimate the status of insiders, they also provide an exciting tremor of "crossing" for the less intimidated among our current "outsiders." As an American Jew and a native New Yorker, I'm very comfortable with the idea of "positive outsiderhood."

In fact, Hein later acknowledges that "most communities today are short-term, 'border' cultures with mixed and borrowed habits. Their members eat bagels with tuna and mayonnaise and put Chinese herbs on their pizza."[4] (That sounds dreadful.) Demographics is not destiny. We cannot assume, when we discover the composition of our audience, that we can predict its reaction to our program offerings. A wide variety of other factors

3. Hein, *Museum in Transition*, 39.
4. Ibid., 47.

may also shape the visitor's engagement: prior experience, cognitive styles, roles within the visiting group, and the like.[5] I've always been most interested in the eccentric mix of "cultures" that visitors bring, recognizing that my curatorial interventions will have to intersect with them. Ten-year-olds, for example, have a culture distinct from that of their parents or their siblings, characteristic of their developmental stage as well as their participation in their own distinctive idea-worlds of schooling, peer activities, media, and consumption. Good programs for them match what the museum offers with their mode of apprehension. Can we do this? Given how widely varied the visitors' cultures are in most circumstances—and given the brevity of the visit itself—this is a daunting but necessary challenge. But, on the positive side, it is also a chance to relearn the "content" of our programs as we reshape them to fit our different "responders."

The Wing Luke Museum had a built-in advantage over many other ethnic history centers. Aiming to connect all the diverse Asian immigrant populations of the Pacific Northwest—Chinese, Japanese, Vietnamese, Filipino, and South Asians, among others—the museum became adept at addressing noninsiders. Each specific story about one group—about Japanese market-gardeners, for example—was produced with the intention of making links to all the others, and even to Seattleites without Asian ancestry. If their struggles deserved representation in the museum, so too, logically, did the labor and home lives of other newcomers to the Pacific Northwest. The stories that the museum told were thus fragments of the collective memory of all the people of the Puget Sound region, of the Northwest coast, and indeed of the Pacific Rim.

WIDENING IDENTITIES TO ACCOMMODATE THE OTHER

Pierre Nora's *Realms of Memory: The Construction of the French Past* describes how an ongoing process of attachment to icons—architecture, symbols, cultural practices, and historical events—continues to reshape French identity. The basis for the attachment changes, too. The French, whether Catholic or not, love their cathedrals, but for reasons, as medievalist André Vauchez argues, that have changed radically over the years. These masterpieces of carved stone and stained glass began twelve or thirteen centuries ago as the seats of bishops. Then they became repositories for the relics of

5. John H. Falk and Lynn D. Dierking, *Learning from Museums: Visitor Experiences and the Making of Meaning* (Walnut Creek, Calif.: AltaMira Press, 2000). See "A Reader's Reflections" in this book for further references.

saints. By the fifteenth century, he notes, they had become both secular and religious emblems of the city around them. Even through the Enlightenment and the French Revolution, and notwithstanding the nation's growing commitment to secularism, the French cathedrals became symbols of national and civic pride. Every milestone in the nation's history—the liberation of Paris, the passing of Charles de Gaulle, or the mourning after a terrorist attack—invariably now incorporates a ceremony of dedication at Notre-Dame de Paris, in particular. The abbeys and monasteries that once dotted the French landscape, as they still do in Italy and Spain, have largely disappeared, but the cathedrals have become everyone's legacy.[6]

In a more modest way, of course, museums of American ethnicity need also to widen their communities of attachment. Both the BCRI and the Wing Luke Museum artfully deliver their key interpretive message to concentric circles of the public. First, they win the affection of a core group by describing a historical action that is familiar in time and place. (Often the exhibition "winks" knowingly at these visitors, using shorthand phrases to reinforce connectedness.) Second, they contextualize these actions in a way that is meaningful to a whole region or generation, such as those who crusaded for civil rights in the 1960s or who labored in Northwest factories alongside other immigrants. And, finally, they establish the importance of these stories for wider audiences and for succeeding generations. They have reinvigorated a key mission for history museums, providing opportunities for the public to transform personal into collective memory.

The rise of ethnically specific museums and historic sites can enrich how Americans think of themselves, or they can make us narrower. I want them to make every seventh-grader feel at home in the world. To find one's own way through their galleries is to discover new social and political identities.

6. André Vauchez, "The Cathedral," in *Realms of Memory: The Construction of the French Past*, 3 vols., ed. Pierre Nora, trans. Arthur Goldhammer (New York: Columbia University Press, 1996–98), 2:37–68.

19 ::: CAN THE HISTORY
MUSEUM FIX IT?

By the year 2000, the transformation was complete. New interpretive exhibitions had replaced the old-fashioned static display of dioramas, relics, and documents in state after state, on virtually every aspect of American history: industrialization, immigration, urban growth, war, race and slavery, reform movements, and so on. History museums and historic sites now typically enlisted the aid of outside scholars in framing their thematic presentations and hired skilled exhibition designers and media producers to enliven their galleries. "Promotion and marketing" became a line item on many museum balance sheets. Board meetings often began with anxious or reassuring announcements of attendance figures, and increasingly museums adopted measures to evaluate the quality of their offerings. School visits were keyed to local and state curricular objectives. A generation of young museum educators impatiently made a student-centered pedagogy the norm in their education programs.

Battles over school curricula, over historic preservation, over federal funding for arts and culture, and over the alleged "political correctness" of exhibitions brought

American history to page 1. Although Disney's Frontierland had lost some of its appeal, along with western movies, the Disney Company proposed a huge theme park about American history in northern Virginia. That failed, but Pleasant Rowland's American Girl venture, for which American History Workshop (AHW) did some early research, has actually included a well-researched historical vignette with each of its wildly popular dolls and themed merchandise.

If the fusty old history museum was now a thing of the past, the newer version rather suddenly became a project of broad interest in the community. Most new museum buildings were supported by public funds and often located on city or state property. Public and educational programs and exhibitions drew support from market-sensitive corporate donors. As museum stakeholders proliferated, news about the development process moved beyond the boardroom and into the press. And as funding appeals appeared in direct-mail envelopes and public service announcements, divergent goals for the museum and demands on its resources increased. This often left those of us in the vanguard of museum change mourning the passing of an era when museums were the quietest havens of the culture and everyone agreed that their fundamental purposes were purely aesthetic and educational. Now, many museums—particularly history museums—adopted a dizzying list of new social purposes. Far beyond engaging visitors in encounters with objects, museums felt obligated or seized the opportunity to improve the social climate in their cities by encouraging multicultural identities, revitalizing downtowns, exploiting heritage and ecotourism, reaching underserved populations, overcoming obstacles to participation by people with disabilities, promoting tolerance, assimilating new immigrants, creating "safe places" for community dialogue, and offering training and therapy programs for at-risk youth and others.

Among the most noteworthy of these efforts has been the Simon Wiesenthal Center/Museum of Tolerance in Los Angeles, whose exhibitions implicitly linked the often-casual racism of contemporary Angelenos with outbreaks of intergroup violence and even with the Nazi "Final Solution." The museum also developed a full-blown workshop program, training police and corrections officers and social service workers in recognizing and overcoming impulses toward acting out racist prejudices, in themselves and in those they confront every day at work.

My most extensive experience with this evolution in history museums came in Cincinnati. There the local chapter of the National Conference of Christians and Jews (later renamed the National Conference of Community and Justice) decided to mark its fiftieth anniversary by fostering the creation of a new museum interpreting the pre–Civil War Underground Railroad, the network that assisted people escaping southern slavery. From the outset, the sponsors aimed to celebrate the "greatest example of interracial cooperation" in American history. It was a noble idea, and necessary. Cincinnati has had a long history as well of racial violence and protests within the Black community about police brutality, housing and school segregation, and political exclusion. This project would be a contribution to intergroup harmony in Ohio's Queen City.

The National Underground Railroad Freedom Center (NURFC) project enlisted many progressive leaders in the local corporate world, in banking and the media, and in education and government, and it raised lots of money from similarly inclined figures on the national scene. The involvement of executives from Procter and Gamble was particularly important. Edward J. Rigaud, who'd risen from a 1965 job as a junior chemical engineer—one of the first Blacks in such a professional position—to a vice-presidency thirty years later, took over the reins of the Freedom Center.

NURFC did not quite fit comfortably inside my interpretive hexagon. Efforts to gain communitywide support and nationwide funding brought many diverse stakeholders to the table. A project of this scale (perhaps $100 million) generated lots of discussion about its proper mission. For civic leaders, a handsome new building, a piece of signature architecture, perhaps with a beacon that would signify "the pathway to freedom," might provide a new public identity for twenty-first-century Cincinnati. In the wake of Frank Gehry's Bilbao Guggenheim, this dream—dare I say fantasy?—was on everyone's wish list. Public officials also hoped that the center would be an engine of economic development. Recently, the Cincinnati History Museum (originally the Cincinnati Historical Society) and the Museum of Natural History and Science had merged to form the Cincinnati Museum Center at Union Terminal, the city's magnificent Art Deco railroad station. Soon the local children's museum would join them. NURFC, it was thought, would—if it were spectacular enough—make the city a tourist mecca. Across the river in Kentucky, the projected Newport Aquarium was making similarly promising noises. My team partners, the economic planners AMS Research and Planning, estimated that NURFC might attract about 200,000 visitors in a normal year (after the initial rush had stabilized its downward turn, say in five years).

It was a tall order, indeed: Could it be a history museum, tourist attraction, economic driver, civic symbol, agency of community reconciliation, urban revitalizer, community arts center, and/or educational resource? Nationally and even internationally significant, and/or locally focused? Planned from the top down or cultivated from the bottom up? What sort of new institution could successfully do all these things? AHW served as the programming partner on the three-legged consulting team, along with AMS and the architectural firms Blackburn Associates and BOORA. We tried to keep the steering committee together as we worked out the details, but the centrifugal pressures were formidable.

NURFC emerged at a critical moment in the historiography of the Underground Railroad. Local history and legend had long celebrated Cincinnati's role. As the city sits prominently on the Ohio River border with Kentucky, important events in the history of sectional conflict happened here. The Quaker Levi Coffin, who described himself as the "President" of the Underground Railroad, had harbored fugitives in his Cincinnati riverfront warehouse and raised funds for supporting freemen and freewomen. Ripley, Ohio, some fifty miles upriver from Cincinnati, contained the homes of Black businessman John Parker, who ventured into Kentucky himself to lead runaways across the Ohio River, and Judge John Rankin, whose family sheltered fugitives from slave catchers and government officials. The classic literary escape story, Eliza's carrying her children across the river ice in *Uncle Tom's Cabin*, was written by Harriet Beecher Stowe after she had lived in Cincinnati and visited those Kentucky plantations herself. The terrible story of Margaret Garner, later retold in Toni Morrison's *Beloved*, had transpired right here. Willard H. Siebert, the Ohio State University professor who wrote the classic 1898 history of the escape routes from southern slavery, had listed dozens of Ohio communities active in this surreptitious activity.[1] In dozens and dozens of towns, houses were identified as way stations for fugitives. Attic rooms, long-disused closets, fake panels, and cellar tunnels all were explained as hiding places for terrified travelers as they "followed the Drinking Gourd" north to Canada.

In the revived scholarly study of slavery and emancipation provoked by the civil rights movement of the 1950s, historians undermined the conventional Underground Railroad story. Larry Gara's *The Liberty Line: The Legend of the Underground Railroad* (1961) debunked many of the myths surrounding the escape routes and sanctuaries. Gara discovered that Siebert's research methodology was often a mélange of abolitionist propaganda, post–Civil War wishful thinking, and oral tradition. A good num-

1. See "A Reader's Reflections" in this book.

Four decades after the Civil War, White northerners reveled in their efforts to rescue fugitives from southern slavery, depicted in Charles Webber's 1893 painting of the Underground Railroad, now at the Cincinnati Art Museum.

ber of the sites claimed by local lore as stations along the Underground Railroad were in fact built decades after Appomattox. Loren Schweninger and John Hope Franklin's 1999 *Runaway Slaves: Rebels on the Plantation* determined that the number of slaves escaping to the North might not have exceeded 1,000 per year, most of them unassisted. It was particularly problematic to professional historians that the popular history of the antislavery struggle had for decades highlighted the role of White people. Charles T. Webber's painting *The Underground Railroad*, now in the Cincinnati Art Museum, had warmed the hearts of throngs and fixed the image of Black needfulness and White benevolence in American minds since its unveiling at the World Columbian Exposition in Chicago in 1893.

As AHW began planning the exhibitions for Cincinnati, we were tempted to scrap the whole business of attics, quilts, Quakers, dogs, and ice floes. In professional circles, the Underground Railroad seemed to be fading into myth. We assembled a star-studded cast of historians of slavery: David

Brion Davis of Yale, James Horton of George Washington University, Ira Berlin of Maryland, Eric Foner of Columbia, and David Blight of Amherst, among others. The project also enlisted others who also had experience in public interpretations of the subject: Fath Davis Ruffins from the Smithsonian; John Fleming from the Ohio Historical Society; Dan Hurley, formerly of the Cincinnati Historical Society; and Ted Rosengarten from Charleston, South Carolina. Their eminence underscored the opportunity to widen the interpretive framework of the new museum. It was too far a stretch to aim for a full-blown international slavery museum, as was then being planned for Liverpool in England. But perhaps we could create the nation's most comprehensive exhibition on the destruction of slavery in the United States.

In interviews with educators, tourism officials, and local residents, we confirmed our suspicion that NURFC's potential audience knew very little about the history and diversity of slavery itself—about its scale and duration in America; the enormous economic importance of plantation agriculture; slavery's significance in American law, political life, and culture; and its importance in shaping many aspects of the Cincinnati region in its period of formation. Focusing narrowly on the local story of rescuing fugitives would barely begin to transform the collective memory of many Cincinnatians. We would have to go back to the colonial period, address the apparent paradoxes of the Declaration of Independence, and carry the story forward through the antebellum sectional conflict to the Civil War itself. Cincinnati would be one focus, but we proposed also to explore the slave system as it operated and evolved in Charleston, South Carolina, and Natchez, Mississippi. The Underground Railroad would be viewed as one instance of the widespread opposition to slavery that included the day-to-day resistance of the enslaved on plantations and in urban households as well as the organized abolitionist movement. From a historiographical perspective, the expansion of NURFC's narrative ambit made sense. If it was anything, the Underground Railroad was a widespread activity, and places like Philadelphia could arguably stake stronger claims for a role in rescuing fugitives than Cincinnati.

If a political history exhibition might engage visitors by providing opportunities for choices and decisions, as we have seen, our social history projects instead sought to represent the weight of oppression. In Cincinnati, that meant putting the story of enslavement ahead of that of escape and rescue. But oppressed people, we contended, could not be viewed as passive in the face of their persecution. Since the 1960s, the idea of resistance had spread through the historical literature. Indigenous peoples had resisted colonizers and imperialists. Jewish partisan bands had resisted the Nazis. And the African men and women captured and enslaved had resisted the slave traders and slaveholders. The new magic word was "agency." Even in the most harrowing circumstances of plantation life, the historian Ira Berlin contended, Africans had found a space to carve out bits of autonomy—by sabotage, by short-term absences, by feigning illness or incapacity, and sometimes by shrewd negotiation with their owners. Historian Walter Johnson discovered that even on the auction block, slaves for sale could manipulate the market to have themselves sold to the least-objectionable purchasers. Even amid the fiercest fighting of the Civil War, Black people seized the chance to emancipate themselves by running to the U.S. Army lines and forcing often-reluctant Union officers to protect them from recapture. NURFC would be, in essence, a museum of resistance, and Black Americans would take center stage in the narrative of emancipation.

But the further the story drifted from its local roots and the more it focused on resistance, the more it also strayed from the celebration of intergroup harmony and from a "happy ending" to the struggle against slavery. No one needed reminding that 1865 was not the end of racial oppression in the United States. So community relations remained a sticking point. Simply raising the issue of interracial reconciliation, in conjunction with a new, expensive, cultural installation, sent up red flags. Some asked why the sponsors were spending money on this, when the need for health care, social services, and education in the Black community was so great. Others wanted to know, more cynically, "Why can't we put all this troubling history behind us and confront the future together?" The tag line among many Black Cincinnatians was "How can we have 'reconciliation' if we've never had 'conciliation'?"

Our advocacy of a museum exhibition program built around a critical historical perspective on slavery and race—while it gained enormous respect—did not truly satisfy any of the strong local interests. For White liberals, White businesspeople, the Black middle class, civic and religious leaders, and even the small contingent of Black nationalists in the area, NURFC's potential symbolic significance equaled or outweighed its value as an educational resource. Though coalition members each claimed different aspirations for the project, they courteously deferred to all the others, and remarkably the group held together through the years of fundraising and design development. Most of the professionals preached the need for coherence and consistency, hoping to clarify the integration of critical history,

*A slave jail, moved from Kentucky to NURFC, brings the
"second Middle Passage" to painful life.*

community involvement, and the multiple missions of a cultural institution. Most of the supporters felt little need to be so punctilious. I'm OK, you're OK, and our missions can overlap, right?

Then there was the question of what would actually be in the Freedom Center. NURFC had no collection of historical objects and wasn't equipped to acquire one. Authenticated material relating to the history of slavery and antislavery is rare and already exhaustively collected by well-established libraries and archives. Documents that reflect the actions and viewpoints of the enslaved themselves are even more difficult to find. Without a collection, how would NURFC establish its authority to tell this story? Would this be entirely a museum of reproductions or of temporary loans or of multimedia presentations?

At a critical moment, NURFC learned of the survival of Captain John Anderson's slave pen in Mason County, Kentucky, less than sixty miles from Cincinnati. Along its interior walls, a horror chamber of iron shackles, chains, and hooks left painful evidence of how Anderson held enslaved men and women before he shipped them "down the river." Few objects so poignantly represented the "second Middle Passage," the huge forced migration of a million enslaved African Americans, deported from the Upper South to the cotton, rice, and sugar fields of the lower Mississippi Valley. Reinstalled in NURFC, the slave pen became the dramatic centerpiece of the institution.

Still, even this would never accomplish the sponsors' dream of a direct intervention in the interracial dialogue in Cincinnati. That was in many ways more important to them than getting the story right. How could this be accomplished? I had incorporated a public forum into our planning from the very start, a kind of electronically equipped "town-meeting space," where visitors could participate in presentations and facilitated conversations that explored contemporary attitudes toward race and social justice. Aside from school groups, who might be offered a version of New York's *Constitution Works* program, would adult visitors want to join such dialogues? At the Lower East Side Tenement Museum, we had initiated a program of post-tour "kitchen conversations," in which visitors could talk among themselves and back to the museum on questions of immigration and ethnic identity.

Hot-button issues about freedom and equality are the agenda of the "public forum" AHW planned for NURFC (1995).

That had worked fairly well, though it needed constant tweaking and well-trained staff facilitators.

At one point in the planning process, I advanced a more radical solution: Let's cut back on the space devoted to a permanent historical exhibition, conceding that from October to April (with the exception of a week around Christmas) we could not attract a tourist audience. Let's instead create a program, in collaboration with local institutions such as the conservatory of music at the University of Cincinnati, the American Negro Spiritual Festival, various groups of enthusiasts for the music of German and Irish immigrants, and the Cincinnati Symphony and Pops, through which every student in the county's public schools would have free instrumental music lessons and be invited to join a choral group. At 5:00 or 5:30 every evening, the center might offer students and their families a chance to sit down to a healthy dinner, served family style. I hoped that NURFC would be sited not on the waterfront (where it would inevitably be a lonely cultural outpost, though it would represent the "border" between slavery and freedom more vividly), but in the middle of downtown, near the new Performing Arts Center, the Contemporary Arts Center, and the main branch of the Cincinnati Public Library (nationally renowned for its community outreach). Hughes High School, a districtwide magnet school, and the main University of Cincinnati campus were also close. I felt that this would more productively connect Black and White students than any historical exhibition or program. In tourist season, I hoped that performances by these students and their teachers and by local religious and musical groups would become a daily feature of NURFC's offerings.

It was not to be. NURFC opened with a glitzy, Hollywood-style orientation film, a drama of runaways and rescues produced by Oprah Winfrey, with the slave jail a bit too handsomely conserved and with a mélange of other exhibitions featuring borrowed objects and uncertain appeal. In the end, it has not transformed the racial climate of Cincinnati, nor has it kept up with the scholarship that has restored the political and cultural importance of the Underground Railroad in the coming of the American Civil War. But it is still the largest program dedicated to the history of race relations north of the Mason-Dixon line. Institutionally, it has soldiered on, its administration absorbed into the Cincinnati Museum Center, attendance always a problem, and funding a persistent crisis. NURFC has mounted an active schedule of loan exhibitions, many on issues of African American history and art, and it has more aggressively addressed the problem of *modern-day* slavery than any other cultural organization in the United States. And

Bringing community choirs in to demonstrate the majesty of art
and song in the freedom struggle (NURFC plan, 1995).

its surroundings have improved as "The Banks" waterfront development
has matured.[2]

NURFC was a lesson in leadership. Trying to serve so many masters, it
sometimes seemed to lack a simple, beating heart of its own as a museum.
It has never created the clear and coherent voice, message, medium, support network, and targeted audience of the Birmingham Civil Rights Institute, the Lower East Side Tenement Museum, or the Wing Luke Museum.
Its compromises, perhaps, reflect the many unresolved crises and controversies relating to race in the United States today. Its greatest achievement,
and its chief hope, is that it has—more than any other cultural organization I know in the nation—brought together Black and White people of
imagination, energy, commitment, and goodwill. Over time, its evolution

2. Mary E. Frederickson, "The Queen's Mirrors: Public Identity and the Process
of Transformation in Cincinnati, Ohio," in *Public Culture: Diversity, Democracy, and
Community in the United States*, ed. Marguerite S. Shaffer (Philadelphia: University
of Pennsylvania Press, 2008), 296–302.

is worth watching. Early in my career I scoffed at institutions. I cherished most the living relationship among a community of learners and a community of workers, not the shelter they found in organizations, where bureaucratic imperatives and overhead costs distracted people from creative work. I've since softened and come to value the capacity of institutions to foster growth, even when their initial state is disappointing. In a challenging climate, it makes sense to choreograph and perform the dance out of the inclement weather.

THE PRESIDENT'S HOUSE: THE AGE OF FRACTURE

Sam Bass Warner and I had founded AHW to press the case for the centrality of historical content in shaping the history museum's program, pedagogy, and approach to its local community. But a respect for accurate and powerfully relevant history could not subsume within itself all the demands put on NURFC. Instead the institution evolved as a compendium of ways to think about race and slavery—as dramatic story, as political challenge, as conduit of cultural expression, as social and economic problem, and as moral issue. All the stakeholders share the mast atop the building, but each flies a somewhat different flag of freedom. Can visitors from outside the circle of stakeholders fit this all together? What do they make of the place?

I'm still committed. Amid the fractionating impulses of American history and American culture in the past three decades, I have still tried in all our projects to locate a single history that can link locals and visitors, insiders and outsiders. Perhaps one of the most difficult examples in my career came in 2007, when AHW joined a team of architects, artists, designers, scholars, and media producers for the President's House project in Philadelphia. After years of protest, local historians and community activists had overcome the resistance of the administration of Independence National Historical Park (INHP), part of the National Park Service (NPS), to commemorate the site of the executive mansion occupied by Presidents Washington and Adams during the decade that Philadelphia was the national capital, from 1790 to 1800. While antiquarians decried the failure by INHP to interpret the executive branch—Congress and the Supreme Court had their own historic buildings adjacent to Independence Hall—the true passion for this project came from the local African American community. Organized into a group called Avenging the Ancestors Coalition, they seized on the significant fact that George Washington brought nine of the Mount Vernon slaves with him to serve in the president's residence. It is a great story. To evade the Pennsylvania law that would emancipate enslaved people after six months in the state, Washington regularly rotated this entourage in and out of Virginia. And then two of them escaped; at least one (Ona Judge) fled from the house on Market and Sixth Streets in 1796 and boarded a ship bound for Portsmouth, New Hampshire.

The park's long-range management plan had made no provision for recognizing the president's house, and the physical site (especially the location of the slave quarters) had been significantly compromised by the construction of a new pavilion for the Liberty Bell in 2003. After a public outcry, however, the NPS surrendered. Philadelphia's congressional delegation and the city council earmarked funds for an interpretive installation—but not a full-blown reconstruction of the house—to be built on the site. Little went smoothly thenceforward. The very public process of defining the project, establishing an oversight committee, and choosing the designers continually had contradictory effects, slowing the process and stirring up public fears that it would eventually be sabotaged.

Somehow, AHW found itself on the winning team, led by Emanuel Kelly, a gifted local architect and public citizen. As the interpretive planners, AHW and its scholarly advisers seized upon a single big theme: The house, like the nation it governed, was a dramatic, dynamic, and troubled convergence of freedom and slavery. We concurred with the architects in proposing a skeletal reconstruction of the house form, with interpretive texts and video pieces that would describe the interwoven narratives in this building. AHW's interpretive plan emphasized the "houseness" of the installation, reminding visitors that the eighteenth-century mansion admitted many to its back door but few to the front. And this insistence on social hierarchy permeated everything inside the house, including access to each of the rooms and their uses. We wanted the house to communicate to visitors that they were navigating delicate boundaries between high-born and ordinary folk, Black and White, slave and free, host and guest, government work and official entertainment. The ironies, after all, were profound and delicious. In the same rooms where Washington, Jefferson, and Hamilton debated and developed national policy about immigration and naturalization, fugitive slaves, and Indian treaties, enslaved Black men and women went about their duties, doubtlessly eavesdropping on the conversations, gossiping about them in the outdoor markets with other free and enslaved people of color, and groaning at the obvious inconsistency between the high-minded statesmanship of this newly independent nation and its protection for slaveholding. In the same streets where Ona and Hercules walked about with invisible shackles, Richard Allen and Absalom Jones were creating the

Recalling the intermixture of slavery and freedom at the President's House, Philadelphia, during the administrations of Washington and Adams.

first self-consciously public presence of free Black men and women just a few blocks south of the Executive Mansion at Sixth and Market.

Joseph Nicholson, our exhibition design partner, helped us shape the tour of the President's House into an experiential encounter with these twin sagas of domestic life and political innovation. Our plan featured a number of annotated architectural elements, graphic panels situating visitors as eavesdroppers on the house's "domestic politics" in every sense, maps that located Black freedom and revolutionary fervor in the streets of the capital city, and dramatic videos that would personalize the perspectives of the enslaved. We hoped to tie the visit to the house with new exhibitions at the city's African American museum, only a block away.

Getting it all designed, approved, and built was a titanic struggle. Though loyal to Kelly to the end of time, we still would periodically have to ask that legendary Hollywood question, "Who do we have to xxxx to get off this movie?" The process stretched on for years as a series of performance pieces. Most notably, there was the very public archaeological dig, staged by the NPS staff in the summer of 2007, complete with a viewing platform, graphic panels, a public television webcam trained on the site, and live interpreters who dramatically told the stories of each enslaved member of Washington's household. Radio and television reporters told how visiting the overlook was a life-changing experience. A correspondent for the *Philadelphia Inquirer* called to ask me if this was "the most important archaeological site in the history of African Americans, sort of like the Wailing Wall is for Jews?" That the dig actually produced very scant evidence of the life "below stairs" in the president's house was immaterial. (The major findings included the foundations for a basement below the kitchen, an underground passageway from the kitchen to the dining area, and the footings of a bow window added by Washington, perhaps to create an area for ceremonially greeting guests to the mansion—neither, in my mind, particularly consequential to the story of freedom and slavery.) The clamor it aroused mandated that the installation be redesigned to show the underpinnings of the house. This, however, delayed the project by a year and inflated the budget, and all this increased the anxiety.

Clearly, the President's House project had electrified the local Black community, and the project became a conduit for communicating its legacy of 325 years of anguish for having been tortured, reviled, or at best neglected by the city's purported paragons of brotherly love. In the monthly oversight committee meetings, nothing—and certainly not my ambitious interpretive plan—could compete with that emotional agenda. In a project with many stakeholders and no single responsible party, coherence like Birmingham's and comity like Cincinnati's were impossible. The community representatives on the oversight committee could focus only on George Washington's villainy. They had no patience for the other themes we advanced, although they had been prescribed in the original project brief. Facing such obduracy, the NPS representatives on the committee caved, the local historians caved, and ultimately we, too, gave up and resigned our commission.

What resulted is, to my mind, disappointing. It brought to mind the disconnected gleanings of a tour of the outdoor museum, as I remembered it from my early days at Old Sturbridge Village. Lengthy text panels exhaustively detail the chronologies of the era's political history, illustrated by the same images we've all seen in high school textbooks. The video reenactments of crises in the lives of nine slaves are dramatic, but they are quite long and hard to watch while standing up. In their effort to represent the sensibilities of the enslaved, they leave the minds of the slaveholder Washington a total mystery. A memorial to the enslaved sits off to the side, a ceremonial afterthought. Visitors can peer through a Plexiglas floor into the bowels of the site, straining to see the kitchen passageway to the main house. The NPS staff seems overburdened by the 24/7 maintenance of a complex site, complaining about the fragility of the electronics in a severe climate. The house is, for all practical purposes, simply a strange outdoor exhibition gallery. Nothing fits together to shape a coherent message. And in all of this, the needs of the visiting audience get meager concern. That families from Iowa can make any sense of this encounter with the nine enslaved people or George and Martha Washington and John and Abigail Adams, with all the important decisions made on this site, or with its ties to the emergence of Philadelphia's free Black community is doubtful. The long history of contention over the site could hardly overcome the centrifugal pulls of the project's diverse missions, target audiences, presentational media, and authorial voices.

MARRYING SOCIAL AND POLITICAL HISTORY

By the early 2000s, I had discovered my overall agenda for interpretive exhibitions: to marry the emotional intensity of social history with the public significance of political history, to situate historical figures as actors in a physical landscape, to balance the community's sense of involvement and stewardship with the historians' desire to construct an honest and open-ended narrative, and meanwhile, to stay sharply focused on visitors' use of all their sensorimotor and intellectual capabilities in the learning process. In 2004, Louise Mirrer asked AHW to undertake a major two-part exhibition at the New-York Historical Society (N-YHS) on slavery in New York. That gave us a wonderful opportunity to realize these long-maturing goals.

How could these slavery exhibitions marry our approaches to political and social history? Reflecting on our work on the American Revolution and the Constitution, I realized that we had depended on the visitors' attachment to the civic religion of American exceptionalism—which we could then aim to complicate or challenge. But as the public's faith in the master national narrative faded, the nation-state felt more remote and abstract to our public. Historyland, the terrain of schoolbook tales, seemed quite far away. On the other hand, the temperature of our social history projects had been dialed up. Where poor, female, immigrant, and Black Americans had once been excised from the history museum's attention, now their stories had almost become central to representations of the nation's past. Still, if these stories were disconnected from bigger narratives, they would come across as repetitive and formulaic. Did all these episodes of resilience and resistance add up to anything more than a catalog of courageous incidents? How had they actually changed the world? Or did each of these brave acts simply pass from the stage after a while, to be squashed by yet another instance of "man's inhumanity to man"? As I had learned again and again, political history leaned toward overview, and social history tended toward immersion. They needed to be balanced and arranged in a pedagogically powerful sequence.

Slavery in New York, the first of our N-YHS exhibitions, opened in 2005 and was designed so that visitors would slowly come closer and closer to an empathetic encounter with the city's African population. Then, having immersed themselves in the mostly hidden world of Blacks in mid-eighteenth-century New York, visitors would "walk alongside" them toward emancipation and public visibility in the early nineteenth century. In this way, the "outside," official, publicly documented, and political world, all in the voice of White New Yorkers, would frame an "inside" narrative that conveyed the perspective and voices of Blacks. We believed that the discontinuities (the "wobble") between the two worlds would provide a better picture of the situation of slavery in New York than a more straightforward overview from outside of the burdens that Blacks felt.

To externalize, objectify, and (excuse the expression) commodify the early Black people of New Amsterdam and New York, whose names but not their images or characters we knew, we commissioned wire sculptures of their emburdened bodies by Deryck Fraser, a Brooklyn artist of Surinamese extraction. We presented court and church records of their deeds, good and bad in the eyes of the Dutch. One document requested that the colonial governor's secretary shop for a slave, in addition to several cloves of garlic, at the market. A remarkable account book of a slave-trading voyage by New Yorkers to the coast of Africa revealed how human lives were exchanged for iron pots and barrels of rum and then enumerated the deaths of thirty-eight captives on the Middle Passage westward across the Atlantic. Almost every active merchant in New York participated in the slave trade, another document showed, and the whole front page of a newspaper could be covered with laws regulating and threatening punishment for the one-fifth of New Yorkers who descended from Africa.

Then, as if to turn the tables, we invited visitors to look again at a huge array of objects from the permanent collections of the N-YHS. Each item—a silver sugar pot, a cradle, a commode chair (for human waste)—could easily be interpreted, given what we knew of the owner or the maker, as a carrier of a slave's history. The enslaved had, after all, worked in this silver shop, cared for this infant, cleaned out the feces in this basin. Next, visitors came across a simulated three-dimensional water well, one of the few places that Black New Yorkers could ordinarily gather and converse in daylight without drawing suspicion. Looking down into the well, visitors could see (on a

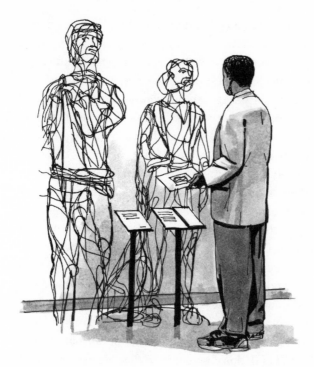

Feeling the strained muscles at work of the first dozen enslaved people in New Amsterdam (wire sculptures by Deryck Fraser and David Geiger, Slavery in New York *exhibition, N-YHS, 2005).*

video projected from below) four women of color discussing their lives in the city. These women often lived alone, in the attics and cellars of urban households, and were usually prevented from keeping their children with them at home; their conversation evoked sisterhood as well as desperation. After all our representation of the invisible, silenced, objectified slaves of New York City, it was especially powerful to see Black faces and hear Black voices telling Black stories.

An emotional identification with these women then became the armature of the visitors' journey through the subsequent stories of Revolution, emancipation, and the trials of second-class citizenship. For New Yorkers accustomed to celebrating independence from Britain, the creation of a federal constitution fostered by local heroes like Alexander Hamilton and John Jay, and the glorious expansion of their hometown to first place among American cities through the Erie Canal and regularly scheduled packet service to London and Liverpool, the stories of "somewhat more independent" Black New Yorkers describe an upside-down world. The American Revolution, we showed, gave Blacks an unprecedented opportunity to escape, and New York City during the war became the largest refugee camp in American history. The new federal constitution protected the property rights of slaveholders, but it also accompanied the movement toward the gradual abolition of slavery in the northern states. African Americans in New York, sometimes with the support of the White-dominated Manumission Society, created their own parallel universe of churches, schools, and mutual benefit and protection societies. In 1827, they established *Freedom's Journal*, the first Black newspaper in the United States, and witnessed the abolition of slavery in New York State.

But *New York Divided: Slavery and the Civil War*, our second slavery exhibition at N-YHS, showed that emancipation brought its own torments to New York's Black people. Once comprising as much as 20 percent of the population, African Americans were overwhelmed in the second quarter of the nineteenth century by new immigrants from Ireland, Germany, and the American hinterland. The city's link to the southern cotton trade was so valuable that the dominant Democratic political machine and its press were fiercely pro-slavery. The city's mayor even proposed in 1861 that New York declare its own independence from the United States so that it could continue trading with both North and South. From the popular culture of minstrelsy and the pseudoscience of "the separate creation of the races" to laws mandating segregation of schools and public transit and the constitu-

Hearing four Black women share their fears and dreams at "the Well" (Slavery in New York exhibition, N-YHS, 2005).

tional imposition of property requirements only for Black voters, antebellum New York City ceaselessly injured and insulted its Black residents. In this show, AHW employed a strategy similar to that of *Slavery in New York*, emphasizing the marginality of Black New Yorkers in the early galleries, securing visitors' empathy with their struggle for equality, and then allowing African American voices to take center stage in the march of events leading to the Civil War.

AHW's final exhibition for the N-YHS, *Revolution! The Atlantic World Reborn*, in 2011–12, also brought together the complementary approaches of political and social history. The exhibition narrated the multifaceted assault on monarchism, slavery, and inequality in the half-century after the Seven Years' War, roughly 1763 to 1815, contributing to the modern campaign for human rights. The trigger for this upheaval, we contended, was the disjunction between the ambitions of the imperial powers of Britain, France, and Spain and the zeal for autonomy among all the diverse people of their American colonies. The exhibition broke new ground among American history museums in taking a transnational approach to this history. In fact, the narratives of the American and French Revolutions, and of the beginnings of the abolitionist movement in Britain, were abbreviated in order to give greater emphasis to the revolution in French Saint-Domingue, which became the nation of Haiti after its people defeated Napoleon's invading armies in 1804. The Haitian Revolution embodied all three of these revolutionary assaults in destroying royal authority, the slave system, and the entrenched social hierarchies of the colonial world.

After an introduction to the proud and elegant perspective of royally endorsed cartography and military draftsmanship in the 1760s, visitors were immersed in a replica of a tavern like the one portrayed in the painting *Sea Captains Carousing in Surinam*, now in the Saint Louis Art Museum. The tavern was a mashed-up world of appetites and grievances, and visitors were introduced in turn to frustrated military officers, runaway slaves, mixed-race peddlers, piratical slave traders, corner-cutting Yankee merchants, stateless mercenaries, and other members of the eighteenth-century maritime underclass. The exhibition proceeded on two tracks, tracing the political events that led to the separation of North American states from the British Empire, on one hand, and the social dynamics that undermined and reestablished authority in America, Britain, France, and Haiti, on the other.

Revolution! was packed, perhaps overpacked, with treasures. Shoehorned into a narrow gallery, it was often too tightly compressed for easy viewing. Extraordinary curatorial borrowings filled the walls: the actual original parchment of the incendiary Stamp Act, in its first public viewing outside the Parliamentary Archives in London; the first display of the recently discovered first printing of the Haitian Declaration of Independence, from the National Archives in London; the first public proclamation ever issued in Haitian Krèyol, from the John Carter Brown Library in Providence; the chest of African objects carried around Britain by Thomas Clarkson to agitate for abolition of the slave trade; Thomas Jefferson's own copy of his *Notes on Virginia*, consigned to a French translator, from the New York Public Library; the N-YHS's own copy of the first printing of Thomas Paine's *Common Sense*; and on and on. They competed for attention with never-before-exhibited documents of ordinary life, including my favorite, a 1794 letter complaining that two unnamed African women mockingly refused after their emancipation to return to dangerous evening work in a Saint-Domingue sugar mill. Many visitors told us that they needed two or more encounters to engage with all the rich treasures of the exhibition.

N-YHS was not a community-based institution, and the funding for these exhibitions did not depend on public sources. Scholars, staff, and board members reviewed the exhibition script and design, but we were spared the oversight of community advisory committees—which undoubtedly allowed the exhibition team greater creative freedom. Still, the response from New York's African American and Haitian American communities was extremely positive. Strong promotional efforts drew in huge audiences, unprecedented in the society's two-century-long history. Collaboration between the N-YHS education department and New York City curriculum supervisors and teachers led to the official adoption and widespread use of exhibition-related materials long after the exhibitions closed.

After six exhibitions in seven years, we retired from the N-YHS collaboration. It had been an extraordinary run, which drew out of us decades of ideas we had long hoped to try. We learned a lot more about history and museums, which was worth digesting at leisure. Nothing was clearer than that the history exhibition is an extremely complex medium of scholarship and teaching, of artistry and public engagement.

POSTSCRIPT

So much of what I hoped and worked for has been accomplished. The history museum is a much more interesting and engaging place than it was a half-century ago. Visitors can use it to make connections and see their life histories in a new light. It's more likely than ever that my forebears, and yours, will have their stories told there—and more likely that their important places and their stuff will be preserved, studied, and interpreted. Professionalization has made museum architecture and operations much more expensive, and now—apart from the Smithsonian and a few other places—it often costs a hefty sum for a family to visit many of our sites and participate in our programs.

THREE ISSUES

But professional expertise has its limits. As forms of art and modes of humanistic study and expression, public history and museum work continue to evolve and to face new and exciting perplexities. In closing this volume, I want to address three of these: (1) the transformed status of "effortful attentiveness" in American culture and pedagogy and its relationship to the emergence of new media technologies, (2) the increased reliance on "insider" and eyewitness testimony in accounts of historical events, and (3) the problem of constructing storylines in the wake of the collapse of the master national narrative since the 1960s. I will conclude by talking about the role of the public historian in responding to these puzzles in the years ahead.

ATTENTIVENESS, COGNITION, AND TECHNOLOGY

I grew up worshipping at the altar of attentiveness. Nothing mattered so much as paying attention. It was the means and the end to every good thing. If you wanted to be successful in school, you had to pay attention. If you wanted to understand great music or great art, you had to concentrate. If you wanted to have a spiritual experience, you needed to focus on things beyond the ephemeral. I was a true believer. I came to understand that you could benefit enormously just by holding yourself still with a book in your hands—as if one could absorb wisdom from the hidden as well as the visible pages. I apportioned my time to ensure that I could work my way efficiently through my college assignments. I took to writing notes so that I was in a constant dialogue with my readings.

My studies in college and graduate school underscored the centrality of attention to religious life. Jonathan Edwards taught that the virtuous man is inclined by his "affections" or emotions to attend to spiritual truths, and that his attention thereby dictates his exercise of will toward good ends. William James concurred, "Attention with effort is all that any case of volition implies. . . . Effort of attention is thus the essential phenomenon of will."[1]

To my generation, the wandering mind was a dangerous outlaw. Threats abounded. While I loved watching *Sesame Street* with my young son (I was more attentive than he was) in its very early years, commentators blamed the program for abbreviating the attention spans of children. There then followed the epidemic of attention deficit hyperactivity disorder, in which a whole generation of (mostly) boys was judged incapable of focusing on their schoolwork. The Nobel-winning economist Herbert Simon worried publicly about the danger of short attentiveness to rational decision making.

But gradually those age-old antagonists of effortful thinking—instinct

1. Edwards, *Freedom of the Will*, ed. Paul Ramsey (New Haven: Yale University Press, 1966), pt. 2, sec. 9, pp. 217–24; James, *Principles of Psychology* (1890; rpt. New York: Dover, 1950), 2:561–62.

and intuition—have made a comeback. Psychologists, behavioral economists, sociobiologists, and spiritualists converged on the idea that yielding to "gut" feelings, jumping to snap judgments, and eliminating extraneous information could often yield truer results than laborious reasoning. Cathy Davidson, a guru of the digital humanities, calls upon us to cultivate distraction.[2] A greater emphasis on the unconscious mind, rooted in the evolutionarily early limbic system, has also undermined the dominance of logical reasoning. Researchers even located attentiveness, described as the organism's capacity to define and respond to particular stimuli, in the amygdala, part of the limbic system in the brain. Malcolm Gladwell's *Blink: The Power of Thinking without Thinking* (2005) popularized these ideas, linking them to a spreading dissatisfaction with the self-proclaimed expertise of elites in government, business, and the military. Daniel Kahneman's more balanced *Thinking, Fast and Slow* (2011) posited that the mind operates in two distinct and complementary modes: System 1, which is intuitive, fast, and emotionally rich, and System 2, or "effortful thinking," which is deliberate and logical.

As this intellectual shift was happening, the advent of smartphones, text messaging, and social media seemed either to stimulate or to accommodate shorter attention spans. Pro-techies declared this evolution inevitable; anti-techies thought it was awful. But both agreed that distraction was the new normal. Communications have indeed been speeding up rather continually since the 1980s, becoming visually, aurally, and verbally richer and more easily directed at larger and more carefully targeted audiences. All this has placed a premium on immediacy, on seeing, hearing, and sharing one's encounters in the world on demand and almost instantaneously. Such a vivid engagement appears to erase the sharp boundary between the original, in-person, on-site, physical encounter and its instant reproduction and dissemination. The real and the virtual have converged, even fused.

As has happened before, this convergence has spurred talk of a major cognitive transformation and moral crisis. Teenagers (it's always teenagers!) are said to have developed totally new and unprecedented ways of thinking—freed from adult supervision, more sensual, and therefore inherently perilous. The language of this critique echoes what has been said about the introduction of almost all other media over the past three centuries—newspapers, dime novels, photography, cinema, radio, television, comic

---

2. Davidson, *Now You See It: How the Brain Science of Attention Will Transform the Way We Live, Work, and Learn* (New York: Viking, 2011).

books, portable radios, the Walkman, and the Internet. Each of them has been greeted with predictions of intellectual decline and moral decay. New media always threaten the monopolies of established cultural elites, except for the entrepreneurs who sponsor and profit from these innovations.

In any case, it's not clear that the whole culture has been quickening. While Twitter limits its messages to 140 characters, feature films have been getting longer, and we're living through a new golden age of long-form television series. Even in the age of e-readers, I notice plenty of people carrying fat novels on the New York subways. (I was gladdened recently on the train when a young woman pulled a copy of *Moby-Dick* out of her beach bag and started to read. Everyone around her made encouraging noises.) In my own field, new cognitive styles and new social media have, in my mind, complicated and diversified the experience of museum visits but not fundamentally altered them.

Museum experience itself, as we have seen, is rooted in intermittent attentiveness. Unlike the cinema, the exhibition narrative is necessarily discontinuous as visitors move from one "museum frame" to another. Effortful thinking is always difficult in such circumstances, where one may be repeatedly distracted by others or fatigued by the frequent need to refocus. Much of my career has been occupied with finding ways to provide narrative continuity, reinforcement, and thematic development among these learning episodes.

I would describe two different ways in which media attach themselves to the exhibition experience: "the enriched environment" and "the virtual pathway."

Media technologies and design interventions enrich exhibitions by intensifying the sensory complexity of the environment. Audiovisual programs and interactive devices, incorporated into the flow of the narrative, punctuate the dramatic presentation and sustain attentiveness by encouraging visitors' use of multiple senses and skills. They close off the gallery from the outside world, allowing greater immersion in the story. Audio guides have the great advantage of allowing one to look and listen at the same time; but they can also lock one into a rigid sequence, moving from one featured work to another, often ignoring the in-between bits that don't have a recorded interpretation, and they isolate visitors from their companions. They work best at historic sites, like Alcatraz in San Francisco Bay or the Hyde Park Barracks in Sydney, where they can add ambient sound and character voices to animate the narrative of the space.

By contrast, the handheld device, either provided by the museum or available through visitors' own cellphones, creates a parallel and alternative virtual pathway. Visitors get access to a database of interpretive information by using a touchscreen keyed to a GPS locator, by punching in a number code, or by reading a barcode or QR square printed on a graphic panel. Images of the key objects are visible on the handheld screen. A menu lets visitors choose to see details of the object or access curatorial information, recorded interviews, or additional images. On some they may be able to "talk back" to the exhibition and to register their inputs and outputs for download later on a computer or mobile device. The more one's eyes focus on the screen, of course, the less one attends the objects in the exhibition themselves. So, experientially, this alternative pathway flattens the three-dimensionality and ambience of the physical site. Holding (one's own device) replaces beholding (what's unfamiliar in the actual object). Conversely, as the screen of the handheld replaces the museum frame, the visitor can move much more quickly through the content, maximizing the information most relevant to the visitor and escaping from everything else. And, as with websites, the user can exit easily, diverting his or her attention from the exhibition altogether, sending text messages, images, or tweets to absent friends.

Some museums have installed information kiosks or tablets, inviting visitors to delve more deeply or to comment on the exhibition at intervals along the pathway. Some devices allow visitors to register an interest in particular objects, so more information can be recovered and downloaded from a website after the visitor returns home. These programs allow a better balancing, I think, between the two modes. I've watched many visitors try out exploring the database at information stations or on their own handheld devices. But after three or four probes, they seem to give up. It's just too much trouble. And information-seeking of this sort seems generally incompatible with the social and aesthetic engagement that many visitors seek in their museum visits.

Of course, Marshall McLuhan was right in arguing that "the medium is the message." A more dismaying prospect is that the screen medium will become the environment. Installing a range of different media in an exhibition—clusters of objects and interpretive elements, audiovisual and computer-interactive programs, opportunities to contemplate and converse with companions—encourages visitors to immerse themselves episodically, diving in and out of the content. When, however, the information-giving device becomes the encompassing environment of the exhibition, then the engagement shrivels to the scale of a website; it's a handy medium for a quick visit, but you wouldn't want to live there.

THE TESTIMONY OF EYEWITNESSES

From the time of Herodotus in the fifth century BCE, historians—wisely skeptical of their own inadequacies—have seized upon the accounts of participants and eyewitnesses to provide ground-level evidence of momentous events and to measure the meaning of those events through the experience of contemporaries. Geographers, similarly, have always prized the descriptions of travelers who remarked on much that otherwise went unnoticed in local records—both of places and of the patterns of everyday life. Many memoirs, like this book, intermingle fragments of personal narrative with subsequent reflections. Though ancient examples exist, diary- and journal-keeping has especially flourished since the seventeenth century, and in the twentieth century, diaries obviously written for publication became an important literary genre. My research into the history of New England religious experience relied fundamentally upon such personal accounts.

But something significant changed with the advent of recordings of live interviews and commentaries captured in the midst of an occurrence—first on radio and then on television, on audio and video recorders, and now on smartphones. Even before we could receive transmissions of these recordings, we wanted them. Baseball games were re-created by radio announcers who translated telegraphic messages into simulated live broadcasts, feeding in the crack of the bat, the thud of the glove, and the cheers of the crowd. When I was young, I watched CBS's Sunday night *You Are There* to see Walter Cronkite and his colleagues narrate events such as the assassination of Julius Caesar and Wellington's victory at Waterloo through simulated interviews with costumed actors. Vietnam, famously, became the "living room war," in which news correspondents' interviews with American infantrymen and officers were quickly shipped across the Pacific to be shown on the following night's news. By the time of the first Gulf War in 1990, round-the-clock cable broadcasts followed events in Kuwait, Baghdad, and Washington, D.C., without interruption. And then came cell phones and social media. The distance between the event and the audience for these messages has totally disappeared. Americans can now easily follow protest marches in Egypt, cricket matches in South Africa, parliamentary debates in Britain, and missions to rescue survivors of tsunamis in South Asia, not to mention the activities of their own friends, all in "real time," as they happen.

Immediacy has thus become the key criterion of importance. Often, now, there seems to be no history except through its witnesses. John F. Kennedy's assassination becomes inextricable from the public's shock. Tornadoes, earthquakes, and hurricanes are "about" the experience of people near the epicenter of damage. Nowhere is this more evident than in the core exhibition at the National September 11 Memorial and Museum, which is organized as a carefully reconstructed timeline of the event's reportage, in which the witnessing of the horror is its most important quality. Interspersed throughout the museum are recordings captured at the scene, including deeply affecting phone calls from men and women facing death. These are dramatically surrounded by interviews with survivors, responders, and family members that add even more emotional intensity to a moment-to-moment recapitulation of that painful day. Our technological capacity to focus on recording and representing the experience at the site of the World Trade Center on that day has virtually extinguished any other possible narrative or any actors other than those who converged tragically, courageously, cruelly, and often painfully on that particular day. While the museum also traces the previous history of the site and follows the events of the postattack recovery in great detail, its focus remains throughout on this narrow frame. The hijackers are interpreted sensitively, with the same concentration on the immediacy of what they planned, prepared, and executed on that fateful day.

But aren't there other actors, other actions, other causes and consequences as well that are worth interpreting? Is what happened on 9/11 only what happened at the tip of Manhattan or at the Pentagon or at Shanksville, Pennsylvania, and only in those hours and days when the cameras were shooting and the microphones were catching voices? To be sure, the charge to memorialize the event was tightly focused; it's the 9/11 Memorial Museum, not the War on Terror Museum or the Western World Confronts Islamic Extremism Museum. What was available to the museum were the physical fragments of the ruins created by the attacks and, more important, the experiential fragments left in memories of victims, the survivors, and their families. Perhaps someday other kinds of documentation—detailing the wider contexts of that day's events—will be assembled for another sort of dramatic exhibition, but the quick decision to create the museum and the very active participation of the city, state, and federal governments all created fierce pressures toward a very sharp focus.

But all this is still more evidence that eye-level experience has become the preferred vantage point of this generation. I didn't recognize it at the time, but my embrace of personal experience in museum teaching and dissertation research in the 1970s and its elevation over grand themes in my interpretive design work in the 1980s were parts of a much larger cultural shift. The New Left's suspicion of "the system," converging with the New Right's antagonism to big government, amounted by 1980 to what historian Daniel T. Rodgers describes as "the narrowing down of institutional society into word-pictures of isolated individuals" (*Age of Fracture* [Cambridge: Harvard University Press, 2011], 73). Confronting the failure of macroeconomists to explain the topsy-turvy "stagflation" of the 1970s, the dominant analysis of the entire system of exchange was dethroned in favor of the microeconomist's focus on the decision making of individual actors. Among historians, an emerging school of microhistorians, led by the Italian scholar Carlo Ginsburg,

> placed their emphasis on small units and how people conducted their lives within them. By reducing the scale of observation [historian Sigurdur Gylfi Magnússon concludes], microhistorians argued that they are more likely to reveal the complicated function of individual relationships within each and every social setting and they stressed its difference from [the] larger norm. Microhistorians tend to focus on *outliers* rather than looking for the average individual as found by the application of quantitative research methods. Instead, they scrutinize those individuals who did not follow the paths of their average fellow countrymen, thus making them their focal point.[3]

The microhistorians focused on the concrete, the site-specific, and the peculiar, in a way that resembles the work of antiquarians and local historians. But the microhistorians were less interested, actually, in concreteness than in disputing the claims of conventional historians to have discovered universal norms of human action. Their tales of bizarre communities, with weird practices and oddball belief systems, only went to show that the "average individual" explored by mid-century historians was an arbitrary and culturally bounded construction.

Microhistory dealt a serious blow to the reign of the "typical." Its suspicion of generalizations was healthy, as it opened our eyes to human difference, to the complexities of all those who had been ignored, to women and

3. Magnússon, "'The Singularization of History': Social History and Microhistory within the Postmodern State of Knowledge," *Journal of Social History* 36, no. 3 (Spring 2003): 701–35, quotation at 709.

children, to LGBT people and the "differently abled," to the incarcerated, to the posttraumatic, and to people in all sorts of difficulties.

Across various academic disciplines and in public discourse, this focus on diverse individuals rather than the "normal person" has had profound consequences. Once the Lower East Side Tenement Museum abandoned the idea of assigning apartments to representatives of distinct immigrant and ethnic groups, it discovered that everyone's story is unique. Visitors no longer had to compare themselves with ideal types of the Jewish or Italian or Irish New Yorker, but only with Nathalie Gumpertz and Rosa Baldizzi, if at all. Once the stories in public presentations had to be somewhat capacious, capable of drawing visitors into emulation, mirroring, resemblance, and connection. In the ethnically specific museum, for example, the personal narratives derived from oral histories encourage us to identify ourselves with the informant and therefore with the ethnic culture. In projects like the 9/11 Memorial Museum, the diversity of responses is what matters, as it demonstrates the widely divergent effects of the event. Each of us is supposed and expected to have our own reaction, the more idiosyncratic the better.

The 2,500-plus "Portraits in Grief," capsule biographies of the 9/11 victims published in the *New York Times* over the year following the attack and now translated into an exhibition gallery at the memorial museum in lower Manhattan, almost always deny typicality. Each of the victims is special, remarkable for his or her interests, personal quirks, or biographical details. On the website still maintained after a dozen years, the peculiarities stand out: Persons lost in the tragedy include the firefighter with the largest-size boots, an enthusiast for biking on muddy trails, and the third-born of eight sisters.

What is the effect of encountering so many disparate stories? Only the most tenuous or tendentious links can tie the victims together. They don't *represent* anything (New Yorkers, functionaries of advanced capitalism, etc.). Simply and cruelly, they were in the wrong place at the wrong time. Others came forward with stories of "dumb luck" that were just as unlikely—they stopped off to have shoes repaired or to chat with a child's teacher and thus evaded the catastrophe. Of course, any of us could have been the victim or the randomly reprieved.

Now we are all anthologists, collecting bits and pieces of narratives. Can we pull them together, write ourselves an introduction or a postscript that summarizes what we make of all these stories?

To carry us across the frontier of fortuity and to share vicariously the unmerited pain of the lost and their loved ones, we intensify the immediacy of our encounter with the terrible event. Apps for our mobile phones can bypass the news media entirely, bringing us into the battle or the riot or the tornado even before professional reporters, photographers, and editors begin their work. Even if we don't have the app, the organized news media do, and soon their reports center on replays of the videos taken by bystanders, again and again. That the "amateur" eyewitnesses may be unreliable, biased, or unbalanced is beside the point. We look to them for rawer reactions—shock, disbelief, awe. We often hear them say, "It's unreal, it's like a movie!" Perhaps it's only real, in fact, if it corresponds to what we have learned to see by watching movies.

We slink out of this video "coverage" and turn to pundits and bloggers for commentary. But more often than not they only serve to inflame the wound—decrying injury, casting blame, or warning of the doom to come. By its nature, "news" wants always to proclaim that it is unprecedented and transformative. As historians, we instinctively reach for the pause button.

STORYLINES

What stories shall we tell of our national experience or of our home places? The old triumphalist American narrative masked a lot of troubling episodes in our past, and national flattery will get us nowhere. The old myth of inevitable upward economic progress has been shattered, and remedies rooted in the ideologies that survive from the twentieth century are scarcely credible. If our present is confusing and our future ominous, we surely need to rethink our past. How do we want to preserve and interpret our history?

Synthesizing the overall history of our nation has become as implausible as overcoming the fragmentation in our politics. Once, most regional history museums in the United States featured core exhibitions that presented a chronological survey of state or local history. Today most such installations are gone. In their place, there may be a brief, jazzy, multimedia orientation show that is designed more to jog positive associations through familiar images and sounds than to characterize the uniqueness of the place over time. The new core or "permanent" exhibition is generally a vast compilation of constantly changing odd bits of history. An Al Jolson movie poster, a scale from the California Gold Rush, a Cadillac hearse from a Black-owned mortuary, drill bits from the Iron Range, helmets from a Super Bowl–winning team—the exhibited collections can be as miscellaneous as the bricolage in a secondhand shop on a decaying Main Street.

In many ways, these hearken back to the original display cases, "cabinets of curiosities," of the earliest American historical societies. Those oddities exemplified the plenitude and variety of God's creation. Each piece of today's bric-a-brac, selected for its semifamiliarity rather than its exotic strangeness, is presented as part of a story. But it's meant to fit into the visitor's story, not that of the city or state. The history museum has become a communalized attic, especially for the surviving remains of the shared economy, commerce, and popular culture, but the message is fragmenting rather than unifying. Visitors are invited to engage and make connections to the items on the display walls, which are often accompanied by the stories of individuals or families. Much less effort is made to create object typologies or to shape larger communal narratives. Each of us can find a way to connect with the museum's collection but seldom with one another. Often using new interactive technologies, the exhibitions celebrate the ability of visitors to "make their own history." The Oakland Museum proudly announces that "there's nothing static about the new Gallery of California History, and for good reason: California—multilayered and ever evolving—has no single storyline, no fixed narrative." Absent the sweeping chronologies of the 1960s ("four-course dinners") or the overarching themes ("one-bowl meals") that formerly organized these galleries in the 1980s, they present history in short and snappy bite-sized "snacks."

Veterans of the 1960s struggles like me often complain that today's young'uns lack our fire for mobilizing protests that would change the world. I rather think that "millennials," as we call those born between 1980 and 1998, simply have less confidence that they can define the world so easily. So they gravitate to entertaining flashes of insight and individual attempts to effectuate social change. I'm not sure that they are wrong or less effective. But museums find it harder to engage such young visitors in connecting the little dots. From providing a vantage point for understanding the whole world, the museum's objectives have migrated downward, to assisting each visitor in replenishing a stock of facts and anecdotes worth sharing with friends.

If the core exhibitions of history museums retreat from telling "big picture" stories of place and time, their changing exhibition galleries do often feature narrative shows. These now often explore the living history, the recent past, of the city or state, such as the experience of "the Greatest Generation" of World War II veterans, the turmoil of the 1960s, or the settlement of new immigrant communities after the reforms of 1964 liberalized entries for Asians, Africans, and Latinos. These projects frequently depend on extensive, pathbreaking oral history and image-collecting research with surviving members of the population being interpreted. For those who join the research process—as informants as well as curators—the learning can be powerful, even transformative. Jan Ramirez, chief curator of the 9/11 Memorial Museum, comments on her colleagues' work in interviewing survivors of the 2001 attack:

> After listening to hundreds of survivor accounts, for instance, one becomes sensitized to not only the basic truths of that story construction but also language choices that become so meaningful to understanding the impact of 9/11 on the public psyche: time and again, survivors tell stories of near death and rebirth invoking all of their sensory intake— literally, the experience of being taken over by noise, smell, sound, physical pain and then total suffocating darkness. What often follows is the person's telling of the miraculous moment when he/she heard another human voice in that enveloping silence, began to distinguish a shaft of light in the blackness around them, had the freedom to wiggle a foot, throwing up ingested gunk, and then crawling toward the light/rescuer voices and emerging into a transformed world. (Email to the author, March 30, 2015)

For the 9/11 Memorial Museum, the Wisconsin Veterans Museum, and the multitude of Holocaust museums and interpretive centers around the country, the most precious artifacts in the collection are these recollections, increasingly focusing on life-and-death moments for individual mortals. These captured memories are as far as possible from the bric-a-brac one finds on eBay or in displays of "the 100 objects that made our world today." Building exhibitions from such complex personal narratives is the culmination of a huge transformation of history museum practice over two generations—in their inclusion of previously silenced voices, in their openness to "difficult history," in their embrace of unique stories rather than typicalities, and in their willingness to explore deep emotional states (even traumas) as well as physical actions.

These projects pose entirely new problems and paradoxes. For the museumgoing audience, the obstacle is analogous to that presented by the National Museum of the American Indian. The more deeply the curators and sponsors dig into the uniqueness (even alienness) of their narratives, the harder it will likely be for visitors to respond adequately. Given the discontinuities of attention in the gallery landscape, visitors at the 9/11 Memorial Museum inevitably absorb one sound bite, one brief disturbing revelation of distress, after another. For that museum to communicate the complexity of any one person's escape from death into life, it would need to block the distractions of competing stories, at least for longer stretches of time. But the museum's effort to represent the scale of the tragedy, the sheer multiplicity of these horrifying experiences, runs counter to the dramatic complexity of any one case. (Further, the capacity crowds make it difficult to establish an intimate connection to the stories told.) To be sure, visitors empathize with the victims, but I think it is hard for them to grasp the deeper textures of the stories that Jan Ramirez and her colleagues have collected. And they may feel disappointed by this failure. Museum educators now often extol the capacity of visitors to associate themselves with these evidences of the past, or even to "create" the exhibition out of their own memories, comments, and reactions. What would that actually require? As historians and curators produce more complex assemblages of historical materials—whether those are extracted from the archives, from the museum storage shelves, or through community oral history and folklore projects—they intensify the challenge of communicating this complexity to the general public. Or should we aim to make the exhibition-developing experience itself the goal of the project, as the Wing Luke Museum does in Seattle?

Second, what are we to do with the whole range of historical questions about which we no longer have (or can obtain) eyewitness testimony, or with which we cannot so deeply engage emotionally? How about the American experience in World War I, a largely untold and unknown narrative? It's not just that the last of the American doughboys have passed away. The quest for "user-generated content" has dangerously narrowed the range of subjects. Once, years ago, I asked a number of community members what they believed was most important to include in a new museum of African American history in Charleston, South Carolina. "Dr. Rabinowitz," one lady responded, "there are three kinds of people in the world. There are the dead, the living, and the living dead. You are interested in the dead, in the history of slavery. But we are interested in the living dead." When I asked her what she meant, she said it was "the past that lives on in our minds and hearts." As we talked further, I understood how passionately she cared about the lives of her grandparents, who had fished and farmed on the Sea Islands off the Carolina coast. They mattered to her more than the remote ancestors who arrived at Sullivan's Island in Charleston harbor in huge numbers throughout the eighteenth century and who earned for the city the title "The Ellis Island of Black America." Though I insisted that the history of slavery and the slave trade was therefore particularly vital for a Charleston museum, I also knew that I would need to connect that history to the ongoing memory project of these local people. I needed to attach that enormously important narrative to "her people," whose food, language, dress, work, and faith still infused their influence in every corner of her twenty-first-century life. It would be a different museum, therefore, from the one in Washington, D.C., or anywhere else.

We need to do much better. I've always been inclined to respond to one challenge with another, perhaps a more difficult one. Plenty of things in contemporary American life could use historical explanations, but museums often seem afraid to tackle them. Could we fold our possible World War I exhibition within a larger exploration of the history of American military engagements overseas, from the Barbary pirates to the confrontation with the so-called Islamic State and Al Qaeda? Rather than another bi- or tri- or sesqui-centennial exhibition about a political figure in our past, which inevitably slides toward hagiography, could we not locate this personage within a historical investigation of political polarization—from the contest of Jefferson and Adams in 1800 to the current stalemate? Couldn't an exhibition that traced the development of urban systems—a common project in city museums—tackle the resegregation of housing patterns over the past two decades?

These are all subjects capable of being represented dramatically and experientially in the gallery. There are powerful documents, images, and artifacts that can be assembled to engage visitors in exploring these histories. Curators and designers can develop opportunities for interactive devices that help visitors clarify their own perspectives on these matters. Educators can mount public programs that engage scholars and the wider community. They can serve as the spine of classroom curricula. There is no doubt that the public is interested.

Over the last two decades, the Gilder Lehrman Institute and the New-York Historical Society have promoted a full program of lectures, films, readings, dramatizations, and debates under the rubric of "Making History Matter." Sometimes these programs are keyed to current exhibitions, sometimes not. But they have become a vehicle for informal adult learning about an enormous range of historical subjects. When I attend, I am always astounded to find myself sitting next to an advertising copywriter or a schoolteacher or a subway motorman, people, "just curious," who return week after week to explore our shared past. They do not view history as a therapeutic enterprise or a contributor to social cohesion but, rather, as a journey into the unknown. Such people, I'm sure, dwell in every part of the nation.

These issues frame the responsibilities of the public historian today. In my mind, the historian, like T. S. Eliot's poet, "lives in what is not merely the present, but the present moment of the past."[4] What happens today is part of a chain of events, a confluence of life-patterns, and a connection to many narratives of our shared past.

As I write this in March 2015, the radio brings news of an explosion on Second Avenue in Manhattan's East Village that destroys four buildings, each with a business on the ground floor and tenement apartments above. Two dozen people are hurt; two others are missing and presumed dead. The cause, preliminarily, is said to be work on the gas connections to the Sushi Park restaurant, and the missing include a diner and a worker at that site. As a citizen of the city, I'm first concerned for the people immediately affected, and I'm upset to learn—three days later—that the bodies of the missing have been found in the ruins.

The journalists do their work, interviewing eyewitnesses, the family and friends of victims, and city officials. They remind us that a year earlier, a similar blast in East Harlem—also attributed to a faulty gas line—had killed eight people and injured more than seventy. They begin to probe the systemic problems of utility connections in buildings that were constructed even before indoor plumbing was available. They try to sort out responsibilities for the blast among the utility, the regulators, the landlords, and pure luck.

Meanwhile, I begin to think like a historian. I'm no longer the naïf who stumbled, half-frozen, into the Fenno House and discovered my ignorance about the touchability of the past I was dedicated to studying. Now I know the site of the sushi restaurant well. I went to high school nearby and have friends living just around the corner. Without returning to the scene, I can conjure up its layers of personal memory, of food and clothing and conversation and theater: I saw my first *Hamlet* at the Phoenix Theatre just up the street. I had plenty of meals at the famous Second Avenue Deli, now on Thirty-Third Street. My memory merges into the larger, public history of this part of my hometown. The land was once a part of Peter Stuyvesant's "bouwerie" (farm) in mid-seventeenth-century New Amsterdam, on which African slaves worked. In the nineteenth century, it was near the

4. Eliot, "Tradition and the Individual Talent," in *Selected Essays*, new ed. (New York: Harcourt, Brace, 1950), 11.

heart of Kleindeutschland, the third-largest German-speaking community in the world. (Only Vienna and Berlin were larger.) Later still, Second Avenue was the Broadway of the Yiddish theater. In the 1960s and '70s, the neighborhood evolved into the East Village, a center of the counterculture. Ultimately, the pressures of gentrification and the proximity of the ever-expanding campuses of New York University and Cooper Union have made this one of the most heterogeneous meeting grounds in the city. The explosion has also destroyed Pommes Frites, a place for Belgian-style fries, and Sam's Deli, a sandwich shop.

I begin to think about the history that lies behind this event, about the patterns of life that ignited, so to speak, these explosions? My trained intuition conjures up stories of colonization, immigration, ethnicity, and entrepreneurship; of urban planning and social geography; of cultural history and disaster relief; of the history of food and music and architecture. Each has a cast of interesting characters, eccentrics, heroes, and villains.

I also think like a curator. I begin to assemble, at least in my mind, an archive of relevant images and film clips and oral histories of several dozen people I could interview. Are there people in the story who can serve to carry the drama? Does the Municipal Archives or the Museum of the City of New York or the New-York Historical Society have images of the street over time? Of the earliest sushi restaurants in the city? (What does that say about the post–World War II reconciliation of the United States and Japan?) I conjure up a scale model of the street or cutaway sketches of the buildings, visualizing how pipes, wires, and cables transformed the streetscape, the work lives, and the dwellings of this street. Is this a good subject for a computer interactive? How can we display examples of the equipment used by first responders or the paraphernalia of building inspectors to describe the uneasy relationship of modern technologies to older urban forms?

Not least, I think like an educator. Who will see my exhibition? What experience of the cityscape do they bring? What kind of narrative will engage their interest most? How will the show strengthen their awareness of urban problems and their capacity as citizens to respond? Can the exhibition work for fifth-graders? For professional students in architecture or construction management?

And then I end the exercise. I have to get back to writing this book. I file the Second Avenue explosion away in the unused story portion of my brain. Maybe someday . . . .

That's what I do as a public historian. I perform balancing acts. I balance the past and the present, the immediately personal and the documented collective, the weight of our history and its power to interrupt (to explode) and shape the course of our present. I have to balance the moments of drama with the narrative of longer historical transformations, the thread with the yarn, the anecdote with the saga. Focusing on the critical moment, I can discover what will draw the interest of visitors, energize their senses and skills, and help them engage and identify with the characters in my story. Attentive to longer time frames, I can help visitors situate themselves and their families in the movement of history and its great events.

As always, I have to balance the epistemology of my research with the epistemology of my teaching. As I work with dusty old documents or through interviews with my contemporaries, I listen to the inner logic of their communication. As I work alongside talented artists and scholars, I try to trace their way of turning words into shapes and stories. I hum along with gospel preachers in Clarksdale, hold my breath at cattle auctions in Ogallala, or brace myself on the gunnels of a fishing boat out of Manemsha, all the time trying to figure out how these people construct a world for themselves and their neighbors. But I'm also aware that fidelity to these voices may mean frustration for my responders. I need to map out workable pathways for their explorations, inserting as many cues, clues, and rewards along the way as I can, without obscuring the content that comes from historical sources.

Finally, I balance the schedules so that all three story trains—the stories my exhibition plan tells, the stories my conjured-up characters from the past tell, and the stories my visitors are telling—are running on distinct tracks and often crossing one another. A metaphor comes up in a design meeting that puts a new spin on the story we want to tell. Reconstructing in our minds the often-interrupted conversation of enslaved women in colonial New York suggests that our gallery design needs to communicate discontinuity. A visitor turns to her companions and notes a connection between the riots of 1863 and the violence of protest on last night's network news. Each of these, overheard and intermingled, pushes and pulls the others ahead. The historical inquiry remains open-ended as it traverses ever-new landscapes of meaning.

A few curators, it must be said, regard the "opening" of their exhibitions as the absolutely last time they cross the threshold into the spaces they have remade. As an old theater fellow, I like to take the word literally. I prowl the galleries for weeks and months thereafter, talking to visitors—sometimes announcing my role, most often incognito—and observing how the show has been received, translated, interpreted, and transformed into new meanings. I marvel at my fellow citizens and delight that we have these moments of shared understanding and conversation.

A READER'S REFLECTIONS

Once, a dozen or more years ago, I received an inquiry from an old friend in the museum world, asking me to list the books or articles that had been most instrumental in shaping my approach to this work. She hoped to produce a bibliography for emerging curators and educators. I ruminated long and hard, made my list, and then realized that my professional colleagues would think I was nuts to say out loud that the works of Jonathan Edwards, William Wordsworth, Herman Melville, William James, John Dewey, and Ralph Ellison were my strongest inspirations. At that moment, I also understood that my devotion to these writers was not academic. I no longer viewed them as "interesting." I stopped wanting to probe their strengths and weaknesses as philosophers, psychologists, and poets, or to put them into historical context. I wanted instead to let their evocations of human passion and action serve as my ideal models for learning and doing. I've wanted the young Kimberlys, Kevins, and Dareshas who have come to my exhibitions to experience the world as these writers predicted.

Here, in a nutshell, is the problem of footnoting a book like this, and my editor and I have gone round and round trying to define what sort of documentation would be most honest, most appropriate, and most useful to my readers. To footnote only specific citations to others' writings seems to inflate the significance of relatively few words and works. But in such a book, I cannot aim to trace the genealogy of my working assumptions to particular texts or guide readers to all of the literature relevant to my wide range of subjects.

Instead, this set of reflections. It records fragments of an interior conversation that I've been having for decades with practitioners and students of my various fields of interest. A character in a recent novel "never expected," she says, "to find so many things she already knew about written down in a book." That's how I feel. While I didn't learn most of my craft by reading, I have been fascinated to discover how some others have witnessed and described work like mine.

1. AMERICAN HISTORY WORKSHOP MATERIALS
AND OTHER PROFESSIONAL WRITINGS

I have relied here most heavily on the materials collected as the American History Workshop (AHW) Records, which are deposited at Special Collections and University Archives, University of Massachusetts, Amherst, Libraries, housed in the W. E. B. Du Bois Library on the Amherst campus. Unless otherwise noted, excerpts from AHW project proposals and reports are taken from these records. Here are a few of my published pieces: "Museum Education at Old Sturbridge Village," *Pedagogue's Panoplist* 2, no. 3 (November 10, 1972): 1–26, http://files.eric.ed.gov/fulltext/ED083088.pdf (accessed October 14, 2015); *Learning in Public Places: The Museum*, delivered at the meeting of the American Educational Research Association, New Orleans, February 23, 1973 (available via Educational Resources Information Center); *The Spiritual Self in Everyday Life: The Transformation of Personal Religious Experience in Nineteenth-Century New England* (Boston: Northeastern University Press, 1989); "Story Time and Exhibit Time: Designing an Interpretive Exhibit at the Monmouth Battlefield State Park," *Culturefront*, Summer 1997, 57–65, 72, 95 (available on the AHW website: www.americanhistoryworkshop.com); "Forum: Religion and American Autobiographical Writing," *Religion and American Culture: A Journal of Interpretation* 9, no. 1 (1999): 20–29; "Eavesdropping at the Well: Interpretive Media in the *Slavery in New York* Exhibition," *Public Historian* 35, no. 3 (August 2013): 8–45.

2. RESEARCHING THE PAST

Every American History Workshop project entails a good deal of historical research, of course, and it is impossible now to reconstruct the documentation and scholarship for hundreds of efforts in dozens of cities and states. Still, in producing this account, I did go back to key sources on a small number of subjects.

Old Sturbridge Village

The first involves interpreting the past at Old Sturbridge Village (osv). The most thorough study of the museum's history is Laura E. Abing, "Old Sturbridge Village: An Institutional History of a Cultural Artifact" (Ph.D. diss., Marquette University, 1997); it is stronger on organizational evolution than on museum practice or cultural context. In the AHW Records, there are these additional sources: Barnes Riznik, "Education Resources in Museums: A Personal Perspective," *Roundtable Reports* 9, no. 2–3 (Spring–Summer 1984): 10–14; Riznik, "Reflections on Old Sturbridge Village 25 Years Ago," typescript of a lecture delivered at osv, June 6, 1996; my interview with Barnes Riznik, recorded July 8–9, 2013; and the notes of my phone interview with architect Allen Moore, August 13, 2013. A very useful compendium of family reminiscences was assembled by Ruth D. Wells and published privately as *The Wells Family: Founders of the American Optical Company and Old Sturbridge Village* (Southbridge, Mass., 1979).

For examples of the scholarship undertaken at osv in the 1950s and 1960s, one can scan the Village Booklet Series, 30 vols., written by various hands and edited by Catherine Fennelly (Sturbridge, Mass., 1955–70); also see Kenneth Wilson, *Glass in New England* (Sturbridge: Old Sturbridge Village, 1959), and Wilson, *Glass and Glass-Making* (New York: Crowell, 1972). The sophistication of the museum's restoration process is documented in John O. Curtis, "The Move and Restoration of the Hapgood Wool Carding Mill: A Case History from the 1960's," *Bulletin of the Association for Preservation Technology* 12, no. 1 (1980): 30–51.

Among published reports of the new generation of scholarly research at osv in the 1960s, see Barnes Riznik, *Medicine in New England, 1790–1840* (Sturbridge: Old Sturbridge Village Booklet Series, 1965), and Roger N. Parks, *Roads and Travel in New England, 1790–1840* (Sturbridge: Old Sturbridge Village Booklet Series, 1967). The Village's exploration of early industrialization is discussed in the introduction to Gary Kulik, Roger Parks, and Theodore Z. Penn, eds., *The New England Mill Village, 1790–1860* (Cambridge: MIT Press, 1982). For the expansion plan, see Roger N. Parks,

"Manufacturing Villages in New England before 1840: A Preliminary Report" (1967) at http://resources.osv.org/explore_learn/document_viewer .php?Action=View&DocID=744 (accessed October 13, 2015). On the living historical farm idea, see Darwin Kelsey, "Outdoor Museums and Historical Agriculture," *Agricultural History* 46 (January 1972): 105–28, and John Mott, "The Making of a Farm at Old Sturbridge Village," at http://resources .osv.org/explore_learn/document_viewer.php?Action=View&DocID=989 (accessed October 13, 2015). There are many other valuable documents in the osv "Explore and Learn" digital database.

Among the scholarly works that later systematized the museum's understanding of this historical change, see Steven Hahn and Jonathan Prude, eds., *The Countryside in the Age of Capitalist Transformation: Essays in the Social History of Rural America* (Chapel Hill: University of North Carolina Press, 1985), and Christopher Clark, *The Roots of Rural Capitalism: Western Massachusetts, 1780–1860* (Ithaca: Cornell University Press, 1990). Also see Prude, *The Coming of Industrial Order: Town and Factory Life in Rural Massachusetts, 1810–1860* (New York: Cambridge University Press, 1983), and Prude, "Protoindustrialization in the American Context: Response to Jean H. Quataert," *International Labor and Working-Class History*, no. 33 (Spring 1988): 23–29.

The standard source for tracing the transformation of rural life in New England is likely to be Robert A. Gross's long-awaited study, *The Transcendentalists and Their World* (New York: Farrar, Straus and Giroux, forthcoming), which brilliantly synthesizes the conceptual sophistication of the new social history and an astonishingly fine-grained attention to the life-courses of three generations of people in Concord, Massachusetts—the famous ones and those hitherto obscure.

On living history, see Jay Anderson, *Time Machines: The World of Living History* (Nashville: American Association for State and Local History, 1984), and Scott Magelssen, *Living History Museums: Undoing History through Performance* (Lanham, Md.: Scarecrow Press, 2007).

osv, of course, remains as much a reflection of popular mythmaking as it is an ongoing research project into the actualities of rural life on the edge of industrialization. A paper by one of my interns in 1971, Herbert Levine's "In Pursuit of the Nucleated Village," was among the first to challenge the ancient tale that all New England towns began with their earliest settlers clustering together around a town common. In the town of Sturbridge itself, the "center village" was invented by merchants and professionals created at the confluence of trade networks during the second quarter of the *nineteenth* century. This work has been expanded by M. J. Bowden, "Invented Tradition and Academic Convention in Geographical Thought about New England," *GeoJournal* 26 (February 1992): 187–94, and Joseph S. Wood, *The New England Village* (Baltimore: Johns Hopkins University Press, 1997).

The history of OSV as a preservation project is contextualized authoritatively by Charles B. Hosmer Jr., *Preservation Comes of Age: From Williamsburg to the National Trust, 1926–1949*, 2 vols. (Charlottesville: University Press of Virginia, 1981), esp. 1:109–21. The background of tourism and regionalism in New England is provided by James M. Lindgren, *Preserving Historic New England: Preservation, Progressivism, and the Remaking of Memory* (New York: Oxford University Press, 1995); Lindgren, "A New Departure in Historic, Patriotic Work: Personalism, Professionalism, and Conflicting Concepts of Material Culture in the Late Nineteenth and Early Twentieth Centuries," *Public Historian* 18, no. 2 (Spring 1996): 41–60; and Dona Brown, *Inventing New England: Regional Tourism in the Nineteenth Century* (Washington, D.C.: Smithsonian Institution Press, 1995). Also see the very valuable essays and studies in John K. Wright, ed., *New England's Prospect: 1933* (New York: American Geographical Society, 1933). The cultural meanings of the post–World War II shift in interpretations of New England history away from filiopietism and toward social history, including the reuse of the region's industrial patrimony, still remain to be explored in depth.

Brooklyn

In looking back at Brooklyn, my personal memories of East New York have benefited from a conversation with several works of historical scholarship. Alter F. Landesman, *Brownsville: The Birth, Development and Passing of a Jewish Community in New York*, 2nd ed. (New York: Bloch Publishing, 1971), is a rich compendium of institutional histories, interspersed with shrewd observations on the evolution of Brooklyn's Jews. Wendell E. Pritchett, *Brownsville, Brooklyn: Blacks, Jews, and the Changing Face of the Ghetto* (Chicago: University of Chicago Press, 2003), helpfully puts the explosive events of the 1960s and 1970s into a longer historical perspective. Walter Thabit, *How East New York Became a Ghetto* (New York: New York University Press, 2003), and Jonathan Rieder, *Canarsie: The Jews and Italians of Brooklyn against Liberalism* (Cambridge: Harvard University Press, 1985), add useful detail. Hillel Levine and Larry Harmon, *The Death of an American Jewish Community: A Tragedy of Good Intentions* (New York: Free Press, 1992), shows us that this phenomenon of displacement and replacement had a much larger national scope. For a wider perspective on the pre- and post-war era, I have turned to, among others, Joshua B. Freeman, *Working-Class New York: Life and Labor since World War II* (New York: New Press, 2000); Marc Linder and Lawrence S. Zacharias, *Of Cabbages and Kings County: Agriculture and the Formation of Modern Brooklyn* (Iowa City: University of Iowa Press, 1999); and Suleiman Osman, *The Invention of Brownstone Brooklyn: Gentrification and the Search for Authenticity in Postwar New York* (New York: Oxford University Press, 2011). The many popular histories of the great era of the Brooklyn Dodgers from 1947 to 1957, especially those focused on the experience of Jackie Robinson's emergence, yield important insights into the public culture of lower-middle-class Brooklyn life. Fiction is an important source, and I've learned a lot from Paul Auster, Michael Chabon, Daniel Fuchs, Bernard Malamud, Gerald Green, Jonathan Lethem, Paule Marshall, Chaim Potok, Philip Roth, Lynne Sharon Schwartz, and Irving Shulman—though no one has, to my regret, captured the exact cultural moment of my own cohort of "war babies."

More generally, in thinking about the evolution of historiography in the past half-century, I recognize my debt to the "new social historians," a few years older than I, including the following: John Demos, *A Little Commonwealth: Family Life in Plymouth Colony* (New York: Oxford University Press, 1970); Philip J. Greven, *Four Generations: Population, Land, and Family in Colonial Andover, Massachusetts* (Ithaca: Cornell University Press, 1970); Kenneth Lockridge, *A New England Town, the First Hundred Years: Dedham, Massachusetts, 1636–1736* (New York: Norton, 1970); and Michael Zuckerman, *Peaceable Kingdoms: New England Towns in the Eighteenth Century* (New York: Knopf, 1970). An even stronger influence on my own work was Richard L. Bushman, *From Puritan to Yankee: Character and the Social Order in Connecticut, 1690–1765* (Cambridge: Harvard University Press, 1967).

Beyond the context of American historical scholarship, I've enjoyed reading William J. Bouwsma, "From History of Ideas to History of Meaning," *Journal of Interdisciplinary History* 12, no. 2 (Autumn 1981), The New History: The 1980s and Beyond (II): 279–91; John E. Toews, "Intellectual History after the Linguistic Turn: The Autonomy of Meaning and the Irreducibility of Experience," *American Historical Review* 92, no. 4 (October 1987), 879–907; Anthony Grafton, "History's Post-Modern Fates," *Daedalus* 135, no. 2 (Spring 2006): 54–69; Peter Burke, "History and Folklore: A Historiographical Survey," *Folklore* 115, no. 2 (August 2004): 133–39; Joan W. Scott, "The Evidence of Experience," *Critical Inquiry* 17, no. 4 (Summer 1991): 773–97; Scott, "After History?," in *Schools of Thought: Twenty-Five Years of Interpretive Social Science*, ed. Joan W. Scott and Debra Keates (Princeton: Princeton University Press, 2001); and Paul Steege, Andrew Stuart Bergerson, Maureen Healy, and Pamela E. Swett, "The History of Everyday Life: A Second Chapter," *Journal of Modern History* 80, no. 2 (June 2008): 358–78.

3. INTERPRETING PLACE

Nothing in my academic training as a historian had prepared me to consider the significance of geography, archaeology, or the history of architecture and landscape. I spent many hours in the osv research library poring over the fat Victorian-era histories of New England towns. Over the next four decades of my professional practice, I tried hard to express this more deeply textured interpretation of American locality over historical time. In place of gauzy talk about the "authentic" this or that or the cherished "sense of place" there, I wanted to find a critical language about placefulness.

Travel taught me a great deal. Between my twenty-fifth and thirty-fifth years, I made my first trips back and forth across the United States by car, went to Europe for the first time, and spent most spring and fall weekends exploring obscure corners of New England. I began carrying around the *AIA Guide to New York City* when I visited my hometown. I found no perfect models, either in print or in exhibitions, for what I wanted to do. I pieced together an approach from different sources. Traditional architectural histories, concentrating on great buildings by famous architects, were mostly useless. As much fun as it was to bring Nicholas Pevsner's *Buildings of England* volumes along into the churches of East Anglia, say, straining to recognize the "Early English Perpendicular" style and to notice the "hammerbeams" and other obscure architectural elements, this hardly helped me understand the historical contours of the place. W. G. Hoskins's *The Making of the English Landscape* (London: Hodder and Stoughton, 1955) was a better exemplar. His 1973 bbc television production took that septuagenarian geographer and historian aloft by helicopter, from which he could point out thirty generations of change in the countryside below. On this side of the Atlantic, J. B. Jackson's essays in the journal called *Landscape* created a pattern language for American places — strip malls along the highway, the stranger's path from the bus station to City Hall, the famously contrasting right and wrong sides of the tracks in a rural market town. Grady

Clay's *Close-Up: How to Read the American City* (New York: Praeger, 1973) was, as he calls it, "a kind of Baedeker to the commonplace."

Given my fascination with interior and subjective experience, I sought out books that expounded on how ordinary people perceived and used place. In *The Image of the City* (Cambridge: MIT Press, 1960), Cambridge urban planner Kevin Lynch pioneered the use of "cognitive maps," in which residents visualized on paper their everyday passages through their hometowns. In the process, Lynch shifted his focus from a top-down, aerial view of place, as seen by architects, planners, and public officials, to the eye-level perspective employed by users. I snapped up everything I could find on architectural and environmental psychology, on the relationship between architecture and education. Among the key works for me are Harold M. Proshansky, William H. Ittelson, and Leanne G. Rivlin, eds., *Environmental Psychology: Man and His Physical Setting* (New York: Holt, Rinehart and Winston, 1970), and Robert Sommer, *Personal Space: The Behavioral Basis of Design* (Englewood Cliffs, N.J.: Prentice-Hall, 1974). Jay Appleton, *The Experience of Landscape*, rev. ed. (Chichester, U.K.: Wiley, 1996), has been my essential tool for linking environmental perception to the cognitive process. Appleton's memoir, *How I Made the World: Shaping a View of Landscape* (Hull, U.K.: University of Hull Press, 1994), is an inspiring model for this book.

Jane Jacobs's *The Death and Life of Great American Cities* (New York: Random House, 1961), built upon street-level observation rather than aerial surveillance and statistical abstraction, was a sacred text, not least because the last chapter in that book, "The Kind of Problem a City Is," provided me with exactly the sort of epistemological grounding I wanted in my own work. Viewing the city as an organism, as a problem of "organized complexity" resistant to the reductionist efforts of urban planners, Jacobs framed her own work in the context of the history of scientific problem-solving. Jacobs's rich descriptions of urban life were complemented by William H. Whyte's cinematographic capture of the dense human interactions in the streetscape (*The Last Landscape* [Garden City, N.Y.: Doubleday, 1968] and *City: Rediscovering the Center* [New York: Doubleday, 1988]). Together Jacobs and Whyte exploded the modernist myth, identified with Le Corbusier, that urban crowding was dangerous and dirty and that planners and architects might impose their visions onto the landscape just as they could on the white spaces of their design drawings. That there was in fact no empty or white space in the real world, and that we must begin by looking at and celebrating the hectic, mysterious, undisciplined, overlapping activities of ordinary life—these became crucial to my thinking about place and about education. Before reading Jacobs I was a seeker after rarity. After that I relished plenitude.

Beneath the level of behavior and beyond the realm of the material, philosophers and psychologists offered explanations for how people transformed *space* (raw, physical, and measurable) into *place* (human, historically evolved, and full of meaning). At Sturbridge, I trained myself to focus on the dramas that occurred in my immediate field of vision, in the eight to ten feet between where I stood and the weaver at the loom or the potter at the wheel. Yi-Fu Tuan's *Space and Place: The Perspective of Experience* (Minneapolis: University of Minnesota Press, 1977) provided elegant ways to surround that immediacy with architecture, nature, weather, and the rhythms of days and seasons. Henri Lefebvre's *Everyday Life in the Modern World*, trans. Sacha Rabinovitch (New York: Harper & Row, 1971), had the marvelous power to turn the space around us into an artifact, a thing produced by the culture and the economy. Gaston Bachelard's explorations reminded me that lived experience always left its residue in consciousness (*The Poetics of Space*, trans. Maria Jolas [Boston: Beacon Press, 1969]; *The Poetics of Reverie*, trans. Daniel Russell [New York: Orion Press, 1969]; and *The Psychoanalysis of Fire*, trans. Alan C. M. Ross [Boston: Beacon Press, 1969]). A potter's wheel spins concentric circles around our prior encounters with rotating things. The fabric slowly emerging from a loom becomes a perfect metaphor, as the ancients knew, for the fatefulness of a human life. More recently, I have enjoyed reading works that have taken a "spatial turn" (e.g., Edward W. Soja, "Taking Space Personally," in *The Spatial Turn: Interdisciplinary Perspectives*, ed. Barney Warf and Santa Arias [London: Routledge, 2009], 11–35), though I am concerned less with spatiality in itself, or even with the history of spatial consciousness, than with its explanatory power for social lives in the past. A former project partner, Dennis Frenchman, cogently expresses the importance of more complex understandings of place for the architect and urban designer in "Narrative Places and the New Practice of Urban Design," in *Imaging the City: Continuing Struggles and New Directions*, ed. Lawrence Vale and Sam Bass Warner Jr. (New Brunswick, N.J.: Center for Urban Policy Research, 2001), 257–82.

Finally, I gravitate to those historical works that really understand the situation and movement of human actors in actual landscapes. One example is James S. Young, *The Washington Community, 1800–1828* (New

York: Columbia University Press, 1966), where difficult traveling through the mud and marsh seems to shape political alignments as significantly as party alignment.

4. CREATING THE STORIES

My immersion in Kenneth Burke's dramatistic approach came with reading *A Grammar of Motives* (Berkeley: University of California Press, 1945); *A Rhetoric of Motives* (Berkeley: University of California Press, 1950); *Language as Symbolic Action: Essays on Life, Literature, and Method* ((Berkeley: University of California Press, 1966); and *The Rhetoric of Religion: Studies in Logology* (Berkeley: University of California Press, 1970). The following books by Mary Douglas were fundamental: *Purity and Danger: An Analysis of the Concepts of Pollution and Taboo* (New York: Praeger, 1966); *Natural Symbols: Explorations in Cosmology* (New York: Pantheon, 1970); *Implicit Meanings: Essays in Anthropology* (London: Routledge & Paul, 1975); and *Essays in the Sociology of Perception* (London: Routledge & Kegan Paul, 1982). Douglas also edited *Rules and Meanings: The Anthropology of Everyday Life* (Harmondsworth, U.K.: Penguin, 1975) and, with Baron Isherwood, *The World of Goods* (New York: Basic Books, 1979).

The metaphor of theatricality was an important stepping-stone in my effort to see how museum design could represent historical actualities. Erving Goffman was an important influence—*The Presentation of Self in Everyday Life* (Garden City, N.Y.: Doubleday, 1959) and *Frame Analysis: An Essay on the Organization of Experience* (New York: Harper & Row, 1974)—as was Elizabeth Burns, *Theatricality: A Study of Convention in the Theater and in Social Life* (London: Longman, 1972), and Tom Burns and Elizabeth Burns, eds., *Sociology of Literature and Drama* (Harmondsworth, U.K.: Penguin, 1973).

Only much later did I discover Pierre Bourdieu, *Outline of a Theory of Practice*, trans. Richard Nice (Cambridge: Cambridge University Press, 1977), and Michel de Certeau, *The Practice of Everyday Life*, trans. Steven F. Rendall (Berkeley: University of California Press, 1984). For many social scientists and some historians, these works are foundational in interpreting the structures of ordinary life. The terms "praxis" and "habitus" are everywhere in academic circles. But I still prefer to use the term "pattern," or "pattern of action," out of respect for the work of Christopher Alexander and his colleagues in *A Pattern Language: Towns, Buildings, Construction* (New York: Oxford University Press, 1977). "Each pattern," Alexander writes, "describes a problem which occurs over and over again in our environment" (x); this approach weaves together action and its physical aspects and allows us to see how each individual element emerges from and fits into a "pattern-language."

My understanding of narrative was significantly advanced by reading Paul John Eakin, including *Fiction in Autobiography: Studies in the Art of Self-Invention* (Princeton: Princeton University Press, 1985); *How Our Lives Become Stories: Making Selves* (Ithaca: Cornell University Press, 1999); and *Living Autobiographically: How We Create Identity in Narrative* (Ithaca: Cornell University Press, 2008). Jerome S. Bruner's turn toward an interest in stories (see below) sparked my interest in the role of narrative in learning. More recently, I've been intrigued by Gregory Currie, *Narrators and Narratives: A Philosophy of Stories* (Oxford: Oxford University Press, 2010).

5. THE LEARNING PROCESS

I came to museum work deeply interested in epistemology and the philosophy of mind. As an undergraduate I'd spent a summer reading widely in nineteenth-century treatises and texts on the workings of the human mind, in psychology before psychology. I have always been fascinated by the substratum of human consciousness, "above" sensorimotor perceptivity and "below" articulated belief systems, in which ordinary workaday thought is shaped by diurnal work rhythms, social roles and relationships, gender identity, personality types, and the like. And I believe that this sort of thinking is particularly responsive to changes in work, family, and community life and hence of particular value to historians. In searching for ways to analyze this form of mental life, I've learned much from philosopher Alfred Schütz's *The Phenomenology of the Social World* (Evanston, Ill.: Northwestern University Press, 1967) and *The Structures of the Life-World* (Evanston, Ill.: Northwestern University Press, 1973). Going further back, I'm inspired by the wit and wisdom in George Herbert Mead, *Mind, Self and Society*, ed. Charles W. Morris, annotated by Daniel R. Huebner and Hans Joas (Chicago: University of Chicago Press, 2015).

As this book shows, Jerome S. Bruner has been a key figure in my thinking as an educator—in three distinct generations. Bruner's early books on learning—*The Process of Education* (Cambridge: Harvard University Press, 1960) and *On Knowing: Essays for the Left Hand* (Cambridge: Harvard University Press, 1962)—allowed me to connect my interest in epistemology (how a mind works) to pedagogy (how a person learns). The first Bruner emphasized the discovery of a discipline's conceptual underpinnings. The somewhat later Bruner focused on how narratives are constructed and communicated from one person to another, in legal cases as in oral histories and works of fiction: *Actual Minds, Possible Worlds* (Cambridge: Harvard University Press, 1986); *Acts of Meaning* (Cambridge: Harvard University Press, 1990); and *Making Stories: Law, Literature, Life* (New York: Farrar, Straus and Giroux, 2002). And subsequently, Bruner's lens—and therefore mine—widened to emphasize the cultural and interpersonal contexts of learning, as in his *The Culture of Education* (Cambridge: Harvard University Press, 1996). Bruner's *In Search of Mind: Essays in Autobiography* (New York: Harper & Row, 1983), however, is an inadequate guide to this evolution in this great man's thinking, and an intellectual biography would be deeply welcomed.

Only after leaving OSV did I learn the term "embodied cognition," based on the central role played by the body's sensorimotor inferences in creating and shaping even our most complex ideas. See George Lakoff and Mark Johnson, *Philosophy in the Flesh: The Embodied Mind and its Challenge to Western Thought* (New York: Basic Books, 1999), 77–78 et passim, and Lakoff and Johnson, *Metaphors We Live By* (Chicago: University of Chicago Press, 1980).

A compendium of recent research in cognitive development is John D. Bransford, Ann L. Brown, and Rodney R. Cocking, eds., *How People Learn: Brain, Mind, Experience, and School* (Washington, D.C.: National Academies Press, 2000).

And I continue to be interested in the history of the philosophy of mind. See Udo Thiel, "'Epistemologism' and Early Modern Debates about Individuation and Identity," *British Journal for the History of Philosophy* 5, no. 2 (1997): 353–72, and Thomas Dixon, *From Passions to Emotions: The Creation of a Secular Psychological Category* (Cambridge: Cambridge University Press, 2003). There is still much more to learn in reading David Hume and Samuel Taylor Coleridge. But of course every work of history, as of science and literature, also contains a philosophy of the mind at its core— a theory of knowledge, of motives, and of human interaction.

6. INFORMAL LEARNING: WHAT HAPPENS IN MUSEUMS
Museum learning and teaching are different from the world of the classroom, a hybrid of organized schoolwork and the enormously important interactions within families and communities. On the latter, see Hope Jensen Leichter, *Families and Communities as Educators* (New York: Teachers College Press, 1979). The notion of "situated learning," stressing

the social and institutional interactions involved in mastering new skills, seems increasingly important to me. See Jean Lave and Étienne Wagner, *Situated Learning: Legitimate Peripheral Participation* (Cambridge: Cambridge University Press, 1991). I wish we had more work in the museum field akin to that of Bruce McConachie, *Theatre and Mind* (New York: Palgrave Macmillan, 2013) and *Engaging Audiences: A Cognitive Approach to Spectating in the Theatre* (New York: Palgrave Macmillan, 2008). The closest we have come is the provocative work of Ken Yellis, especially "Cueing the Visitor: The Museum Theater and the Visitor Performance," *Curator* 53, no. 1 (2010): 87–103.

George Hein, *Learning in the Museum* (London and New York: Routledge, 1998), is the bible of the professional museum educator today. I do wish Hein gave more room to the fun of museum learning. Understanding my own approach has also been helped by the research of the Museum Learning Collaborative, based at the University of Pittsburgh in 1998–2003. The research was reported in Gaea Leinhardt, Kevin Crowley, and Karen Knutson, eds., *Learning Conversations in Museums* (Mahwah, N.J.: Lawrence Erlbaum Associates, 2002). The collaborative's approach was rooted in "sociocultural theory," which posits that "meaning emerges in the interplay between individuals acting in social contexts and the mediators—tools, talk, activity structures, signs, and symbol systems—that exist in that context." On "sociocultural theory," see Barbara Rogoff, "Cognition as a Collaborative Process," in *Handbook of Child Psychology*, ed. William Damon, 5th ed., vol. 2, *Cognition, Perception, and Language* (New York: John Wiley & Sons, 1998), 679–744.

For a quarter-century, John H. Falk and Lynn D. Dierking have been extraordinarily insightful analysts of what happens in the course of the museum visit. See their *Learning from Museums: Visitor Experiences and the Making of Meaning* (Walnut Creek, Calif.: AltaMira Press, 2000); *Museum Experience Revisited* (Walnut Creek, Calif.: Left Coast Press, 2012); and, as coeditors with Susan Fouts, *In Principle, In Practice: Museums as Learning Institutions* (Lanham, Md.: AltaMira Press, 2007). Lisa C. Roberts, *From Knowledge to Narrative: Education and the Changing Museum* (Washington, D.C.: Smithsonian Institution Press, 1997), is the clearest exposition of the transformation of museum learning in this generation. For the designers' perspective on the experience of the gallery, see Herman Kossmann, Suzanne Mulder, and Frank den Oudsten, *Narrative Spaces* (Rotterdam, The Netherlands: 010 Publishers, 2012).

Invaluable reports from the field are collected in *Patterns in Practice:*

Selections from the Journal of Museum Education (Washington, D.C.: Museum Education Roundtable, 1992) and Joanne S. Hirsch and Lois H. Silverman, eds., *Transforming Practice: Selections from the Journal of Museum Education, 1992–1999* (Washington, D.C.: Museum Education Roundtable, 2000).

Of course, most of the serious thinking about teaching focuses on the schools. Here are a few works that have bridged the chasm between schools and museums for me: Eleanor Duckworth, "The Having of Wonderful Ideas," *Harvard Educational Review* 42, no. 2 (May 1972): 217–31; Bruce Van Sledright, "Confronting History's Interpretive Paradox while Teaching Fifth Graders to Investigate the Past," *American Educational Research Journal* 39, no. 4 (Winter 2002): 1089–1115; Thomas Fallace, "John Dewey's Influence on the Origins of the Social Studies: An Analysis of the Historiography and New Interpretation," *Review of Educational Research* 79, no. 2 (June 2009): 601–24; Sam Wineburg, *Historical Thinking and Other Unnatural Acts: Charting the Future of Teaching the Past* (Philadelphia: Temple University Press, 2001); Jacques Rancière, *The Ignorant Schoolmaster: Five Lessons in Intellectual Emancipation*, trans. Kristin Ross (Stanford: Stanford University Press, 1991); and Meira Levinson, *No Citizen Left Behind* (Cambridge: Harvard University Press, 2012).

7. STUFF

In the era when it was felt necessary to underscore the importance of learning from objects, Jules David Prown's article, "Mind in Matter: An Introduction to Material Culture Theory and Method," *Winterthur Portfolio* 17, no. 1 (Spring 1982): 1–19, was very influential. A useful examination of the transformation of decorative arts into material culture is Catherine L. Whalen, "American Decorative Arts Studies at Yale and Winterthur: The Politics of Gender, Gentility, and Academia," *Studies in the Decorative Arts* 9, no. 1 (Fall–Winter 2001–2): 108–44.

A compendium of scholarship in this area, vital for its self-regard, is Robert Blair St. George, ed., *Material Life in America, 1600–1860* (Boston: Northeastern University Press, 1988). A useful meditation on the relationship of material culture and social history is John Demos, "Words and Things: A Review and Discussion of 'New England Begins,'" *William and Mary Quarterly*, 3rd ser., 40, no. 4 (October 1983): 584–97. A widening analytic framework for material culture study is suggested in Edward S. Cooke Jr., "The Study of American Furniture from the Perspective of the Maker," in *Perspectives on American Furniture*, ed. Gerald W. R. Ward (New York:

W. W. Norton for the Henry Francis du Pont Winterthur Museum, 1988), 113–26. But it is crucial, too, to discover what the maker thinks about, and I've been long devoted to David Pye, *The Nature and Art of Workmanship* (Cambridge: Cambridge University Press, 1968). More recently, it has been a pleasure to read David Esterly, *The Lost Carving: A Journey to the Heart of Making* (New York: Viking, 2012), and the pleasure is enhanced by knowing that the author was once my college roommate.

In the 1980s, anthropologists and geographers began to develop a more theoretical and cross-cultural approach to stuff and its roles in diverse cultural settings. Among the highly provocative works I've enjoyed are Ian Hodder, ed., *The Meanings of Things: Material Culture and Symbolic Expression* (London: Unwin Hyman, 1989); Mihaly Csikszentmihalyi and Eugene Rochberg-Halton, *The Meaning of Things: Domestic Symbols and the Self* (New York: Cambridge University Press, 1981); John Brewer and Roy Porter, eds., *Consumption and the World of Goods* (London: Routledge, 1993); and Mary C. Beaudry, Lauren J. Cook, and Stephen A. Mrozowski, "Artifacts and Active Voices: Material Culture as Social Discourse," in *The Archaeology of Inequality*, ed. Randall H. McGuire and Robert Paynter (Oxford: Blackwell, 1991), 150–91. More recently, Daniel Miller has undertaken fascinating studies of materiality itself, beneath and beyond its particular cultural and physical form. See his edited volume, *Materiality* (Durham: Duke University Press, 2005), as well as *Material Culture and Mass Consumption* (Oxford: Blackwell, 1987). A useful connection to thematic complexity appears in Robin Bernstein, "Dances with Things: Material Culture and the Performance of Race," *Social Text* 27, no. 4 (Winter 2009): 67–94.

8. HISTORY MUSEUMS: A HISTORY

When I began working at Old Sturbridge Village, I quickly learned that our closest sister institutions were other outdoor history museums, especially Colonial Williamsburg. Plimoth Plantation, under the charismatic leadership of Jim Deetz, was doing the most innovative things—abandoning the display of original materials, re-creating the minutiae of an early modern British outpost on an alien continent, and training interpreters to talk like the groundlings at the Globe Theatre. Mystic Seaport addressed problems most similar to Sturbridge's—a romantic (or rather romanticized) setting, an imprecise historical context, and a confusing mix of original "antiques" and modern reproductions.

As a fledgling participant at meetings of the American Association for

State and Local History, I began to learn something of the history museum movement, forged by (mostly) men who directed state historical societies and (mostly) women who operated historic house museums. At an association seminar in Albany in October 1969, when I could be diverted from sneaking off to watch my Mets win their first World Series, I met several of these leaders: Bill Alderson, Jerry Swinney, Louis Jones, and Fred Rath. They had fought hard to turn old-line historical agencies, dominated by genealogies of pioneers and first settlers, toward stronger public and educational purposes and more relevant historical contexts. I can recapture the sense of their time by consulting my copy of Frederick L. Rath and Merrilyn Rogers O'Connell, *A Bibliography of Historical Organization Practices* (Nashville, Tenn.: American Association for State and Local History, 1975).

Most of the early histories of history museums told a story of happy professionalization emerging out of a raucous, undisciplined, and Barnumesque past, including G. Brown Goode, *Museum History and Museums of History* (Washington, D.C.: Government Printing Office, 1901); Arthur C. Parker, *A Manual for History Museums* (New York: Columbia University Press, 1935); Walter Muir Whitehill, *Independent Historical Societies: An Enquiry into their Research and Publication Functions* (Boston: Boston Athenaeum, 1962); Clifford L. Lord, *Keepers of the Past* (Chapel Hill: University of North Carolina Press, 1965); and Whitfield J. Bell Jr., *A Cabinet of Curiosities: Five Episodes in the Evolution of American Museums* (Charlottesville: University of Virginia Press, 1967).

Already by the mid-1960s there were warnings of too much popularization, of vulgarization, of a loss of authentic historical fiber in order to appeal to wider audiences. In Chapter 2 above, I have cited David Lowenthal's 1966 article, "The American Way of History" in the *Columbia University Forum* as an example. Architectural critic Ada Louise Huxtable took up the cudgels against the scrape-and-clean restoration policy in her "Dissent at Colonial Williamsburg," *New York Times*, September 22, 1963; also see the letters her column provoked, *New York Times*, October 13, 1963.

9. POPULAR HISTORY AND ITS CRITICS

By the 1970s, as I have shown, museum exhibitions began to be more lively in their use of media, more visitor-centered in their pedagogy, more inclusive in their subject matter, and more diverse in their authorial voices. The American Revolution bicentennial in the United States encouraged local celebrations, public programs, and publications for the general reader. In Britain, the History Workshop movement—the inspiration for the name of my own consortium of public historians—carried history out into many communities facing deindustrialization. It organized oral history workshops, performances, exhibitions, and publications aimed at many who had no connection with the academic history world. Raphael Samuel, an early leader of the movement, portrayed a dizzying array of creative projects all over Britain in his two-volume compilation, *Theatres of Memory* (London: Verso, 1994) and *Island Stories: Unravelling Britain* (London: Verso, 1999). The *History Workshop Journal*, founded in 1976, brought the history of women and other unvoiced communities to light and significantly reshaped academic scholarship in Britain and other countries.

Not surprisingly, popular history could also be profitable history. Artists' happenings evolved into urban festivals, and festivals into festival marketplaces. As museums came to view artifacts as evidence of themes, so too did marketers increasingly realize that merchandise could also be endowed with thematic overtones. First the diner was drenched in symbols (e.g., Golden Arches), and then the symbol was turned into a full-blown narrative (Planet Hollywood). The outdoor museum was particularly susceptible to overlap with the ever-expanding array of theme parks. By September 1975, the Sunday *New York Times* travel section comfortably compared Walt Disney World and Colonial Williamsburg as equally splendid places for family vacations. It became a commonplace in the museum world that "we were competing for the visitors' leisure time and their travel budgets." By the 1990s, everything—from lectures in philosophy and religion (TED talks) to college courses (One-Day University) to going to the dentist and rafting along the Colorado River—had dissolved into the soup of "consumer experiences." In B. Joseph Pine II and James Gilmore, *The Experience Economy: Work Is Theater and Every Business a Stage* (Boston: Harvard Business School Press, 1999), the confluence of culture and commerce is complete and unembarrassed. It is more than a little shocking to discover that the literature of "theming" and "branding" is vastly greater than that of museum development, and it is rooted much more carefully in consumer research than anything nonprofit arts groups have attempted in audience evaluation. Among the works I've explored are Mark Gottdiener, *The Theming of America: Dreams, Media Fantasies, and Themed Environments*, 2nd ed. (Boulder, Colo.: Westview Press, 2001); Scott A. Lucas, *The Themed Space: Locating Culture, Nation, and Self* (Lanham, Md.: Lexington Books, 2007); Kevin Meethan, Alison Anderson, and Steve Miles, eds., *Tourism Consumption and Representation* (Wallingford, U.K.: CAB International, 2006). Scary stuff, indeed.

The encroachment of marketplace values in the cultural realm, of course, did not pass unnoticed in the halls of academe, and a critical counterattack had been launched. Accepting that the world of the "thematizers" is as they describe it, the critics locate its motivations in the enlarged ambitions of "late twentieth-century capitalism" to dominate and profit from every aspect of human life. Influenced by a renewed interest in Marxism, as well as the work of Michel Foucault and Antonio Gramsci, and energized by opposition to Margaret Thatcher and Ronald Reagan, several British, Australian, and American scholars worked to expose the complicity of museums in supporting elitist political interests. Seeing everything as based in what British geographer David Harvey calls "the condition of postmodernity" (in a book of that title [Oxford: Blackwell, 1989]), museums and cultural activity in general came to exemplify the devastating substitution of surface glitz for deep and authentic substance. Under the guise of a phony positivism, so went the argument (as in Tony Bennett, *The Birth of the Museum: History, Theory, Politics* [London and New York: Routledge, 1995], natural history museums cruelly invented a hierarchy of racial groups, art museums spiritualized art-making as a device to anesthetize opposition to ruling-class politics, and history museums enlisted visitors in a passionate subservience to master national narratives of progress. Other works in this vein, particularly relevant to historical museums, include Robert Hewison, *The Heritage Industry: Britain in a Climate of Decline* (London: Methuen, 1987); Donald Horne, *The Great Museum: The Re-Presentation of History* (London: Pluto Press, 1984); Peter Vergo, ed. *The New Museology* (London: Reaktion Books, 1989); and Robert Lumley, ed., *The Museum Time Machine: Putting Cultures on Display* (London: Routledge, 1988).

The most substantive critique of this populist history was David Lowenthal's brilliant *The Past Is a Foreign Country* (Cambridge: Cambridge University Press, 1985). A decade later, Lowenthal had just become downright cranky, and his *Possessed by the Past: The Heritage Crusade and the Spoils of History* (New York: Free Press, 1996) flailed mercilessly against anything other than scholarly research. In the American context, Michael Sorkin's edited volume, *Variations on a Theme Park: The New American City and the End of Public Space* (New York: Hill and Wang, 1992), compiled a dozen of these gloomy critiques. The statements in Mike Wallace, *Mickey Mouse History and other Essays on American Memory* (Philadelphia: Temple University Press, 1996), are, as Huck Finn says of *Pilgrim's Progress*, "interesting, but tough." A wider range of responses to the new museology was collected in Ivan Karp and Steven D. Lavine, eds., *Exhibiting Cultures: the Politics and Poetics of Display* (Washington, D.C.: Smithsonian Institution Press, 1991), and Ivan Karp, Christine Mullen Kreamer, and Steven D. Lavine, eds., *Museums and Communities: The Politics of Public Culture* (Washington, D.C.: Smithsonian Institution Press, 1992).

10. MUSEUM THEORY

By the mid-1990s, museums had become a favorite arena for discovering the vacuousness of contemporary culture. While much that occurred within the gallery was closely linked to new work in theater, film, and performance art, the relative placidity of the museum made it an easier target. Performances come and go, but the grand museum space emerged as a perfect simulacrum for the corrupt socioeconomic world outside its doors. For me, "theorizing" the museum has often meant reducing its complexity to its political role, concentrating on "how museums were embedded within a network of power relations that supported dominant interests" (Kylie Message and Andrea Witcomb, introduction to *Museum Theory: An Expanded Field* [Online: Wiley, 2015], xxxvii). Serving as both premise and conclusion, this can get rather tired.

Many works in museum theory start with fascinating anecdotes, offering empirically verifiable data-points, noting something the author had actually experienced in a recent museum visit. But after they link this one particular action to a praxis dissected in other theoretical works, however, they begin to lose me. Each of the following compiles a wide variety of pieces: Bettina Messias Carbonell, ed., *Museum Studies: An Anthology of Contexts* (Malden, Mass.: Blackwell, 2004); Susan A. Crane, ed., *Museums and Memory* (Stanford: Stanford University Press, 2000); Sandra H. Dudley, ed. *Museum Materialities: Objects, Engagements, Interpretations* (New York: Routledge, 2010); Simon J. Knell, Suzanne MacLeod, and Sheila Watson, eds., *Museum Revolutions: How Museums Change and Are Changed* (Abingdon, Oxon, U.K., and New York: Routledge, 2007); Sharon Macdonald and Gordon Fyfe, eds., *Theorizing Museums: Representing Identity and Diversity in a Changing World* (Oxford: Blackwell: Sociological Review, 1996). I've learned much from Didier Maleuve, *Museum Memories: History, Technology, Art* (Stanford: Stanford University Press, 1999).

Much of this work has been produced by academics with slender work experience in museums. It is very rare to discover anyone working in museums who thinks or talks this way. Perhaps museum workers are all self-deceiving creatures, unaware of how their work advances the interests of the top One Percent. Or, more likely, the very complexity of museum work—taking account of each slice of the Interpretive Hexagon—makes such reductiveness impossible. That multifariousness is very challenging. Often, nearing the end of their careers, museum directors and association leaders pen books that outline a new and distinctive vision for institutions like theirs: S. Dillon Ripley, *Sacred Grove: Essays on Museums* (New York: Simon and Schuster, 1969); Gerald George, *Visiting History: Arguments over Museums and Historic Sites* (Washington, D.C.: American Association of Museums, 1990); Stephen Weil, *Rethinking the Museum and Other Meditations* (Washington, D.C.: Smithsonian Institution Press, 1990); Weil, *A Cabinet of Curiosities: Inquiries into Museums and Their Prospects* (Washington, D.C.: Smithsonian Institution Press, 1995); Edward P. Alexander, *The Museum in America* (Walnut Creek, Calif.: AltaMira Press, 1997); Julian Spalding, *The Poetic Museum: Reviving Historic Collections* (London: Prestel, 2002); and Robert Archibald, *The New Town Square: Museums and Communities in Transition* (Walnut Creek, Calif. AltaMira Press, 2004). These works, invariably, sound an optimistic note, trying hard to encourage the young to keep pressing forward.

Some observers have captured more of the complex challenges of museums in the future. I would highly recommend Gaynor Kavanaugh, ed., *Making History in Museums* (London: Leicester University Press, 1996); Andrea Witcomb, *Re-Imagining the Museum: Beyond the Mausoleum* (London and New York: Routledge, 2003); Hilde S. Hein, *The Museum in Transition: A Philosophical Perspective* (Washington, D.C.: Smithsonian Institution Press, 2000); Hein, *Public Art: Thinking Museums Differently* (Lanham, Md.: AltaMira Press, 2006); and Steven Conn, *Do Museums Still Need Objects?* (Philadelphia: University of Pennsylvania Press, 2010).

11. TRACING THE EVOLUTION OF THE MODERN HISTORY MUSEUM

My taste as a historian is for studies that situate museums in time and place rather than prescribing for or theorizing about them. Critical studies of the evolution of modern history museums and historic sites did not come until the 1980s. Ian M. G. Quimby's edition of the papers given at a 1975 Winterthur Museum conference, *Material Culture and the Study of American Life* (New York: Norton, 1978), represents for me the status quo antebellum, the moment before the terrain of public history interpretation shook itself into a new life. Evidence of the change was an important national conference in 1984, sponsored by the New York Council for the Humanities, which brought together around 150 historians, preservationists, artists, curators, and educators to discuss the interpretation of historic sites and narratives for the wider public. Jo Blatti helped organize the conference and edited a volume of wide-ranging essays that it inspired, including a wonderful introductory piece of her own: *Past Meets Present: Essays about Historic Interpretation and Public Audiences* (Washington, D.C.: Smithsonian Institution Press, 1987). Warren Leon and Roy Rosenzweig, eds., *History Museums in the United States: A Critical Assessment* (Urbana: University of Illinois Press, 1989), surveys the variety of interpretive institutions, and David Glassberg, *Sense of History: The Place of the Past in American Life* (Amherst: University of Massachusetts Press, 2004), widens the context of commemoration in American history. Looking back, David Lowenthal, "The Bicentennial Landscape: A Mirror Held Up to the Past," *Geographical Review* 67, no. 3 (July 1977): 253–67, is valuable. The keenest assessment of the new generation of interpretive exhibitions is Kenneth L. Ames, Barbara Franco, and L. Thomas Frye, eds., *Ideas and Images: Developing Interpretive History Exhibits* (Walnut Creek, Calif.: AltaMira Press, 1997). I found Claire Bishop, *Installation Art: A Critical History* (New York: Routledge, 2005), very helpful. Much more work in this vein needs to be done.

Within the history museum profession, these are some landmark documents: Lonn Taylor, ed., *A Common Agenda for History Museums: Conference Proceedings, February 19-20, 1987* (Nashville, Tenn.: American Association for State and Local History; Washington, D.C.: Smithsonian Institution, 1987); Thomas A. Woods, "Getting Beyond the Criticism of History Museums: A Model for Interpretation," *Public Historian* 12, no. 3 (Summer 1990): 77–90; and "Curating History in Museums: Some Thoughts Provoked by *The West as America*," a valuable roundtable discussion with contributions by several noted museum professionals, which appeared in *Public Historian* 14, no. 3 (Summer 1992).

Colonial Williamsburg itself has been the focal point of important comment and criticism: Richard Handler and Eric Gable, *The New History in an Old Museum: Creating the Past at Colonial Williamsburg* (Durham: Duke University Press, 1997); comments by Rhys Isaac in *Public Historian* 20, no. 3 (Summer 1998): 100–105; comments by Cary Carson in "Lost in the Fun House: A Commentary on Anthropologists' First Contact with History Museums," *Journal of American History* 81, no. 1 (June 1994): 137–50; Anders Greenspan, *Creating Colonial Williamsburg: The Restoration of Virginia's Eighteenth-Century Capital*, 2nd ed. (Chapel Hill: University of North Carolina Press, 2009); Cary Carson, "Colonial Williamsburg and the Practice of Interpretive Planning in American History Museums," *Pub-

lic Historian 20, no. 3 (Summer 1998): 11–51; and Marie Tyler-McGraw, "Becoming Americans Again: Re-Envisioning and Revising Thematic Interpretation at Colonial Williamsburg," *Public Historian* 20, no. 3 (Summer 1998): 53–76. More generally, see John D. Krugler, "Behind the Public Presentations: Research and Scholarship at Living History Museums of Early America," *William and Mary Quarterly*, 3rd ser., 48, no. 3 (July 1991): 347–86.

Other institutions and types of institutions are portrayed in Jennifer L. Eichstadt and Stephen Small, *Representations of Slavery: Race and Ideology in Southern Plantation Museums* (Washington, D.C.: Smithsonian Institution Press, 2002); Catherine M. Lewis, *The Changing Face of Public History: The Chicago Historical Society and the Transformation of an American Museum* (DeKalb: Northern Illinois University Press, 2005); Paul Harvey Williams, *Memorial Museums: The Global Rush to Commemorate Atrocities* (New York: Berg, 2007); and Denise D. Meringolo, *Museums, Monuments, and National Parks* (Amherst: University of Massachusetts Press, 2012).

Among studies of interpretation at preserved industrial sites and heritage parks, see Martha Norkunas, *Monuments and Memory: History and Representation in Lowell, Massachusetts* (Washington, D.C.: Smithsonian Institution Press, 2002); Cathy Stanton, *The Lowell Experiment: Public History in a Postindustrial City* (Amherst: University of Massachusetts Press, 2006), an incisive ethnographic analysis of the "makers" of the Lowell national park; and Carolyn L. Kitch, *Pennsylvania in Public Memory: Reclaiming the Industrial Past* (University Park: Penn State University Press, 2012).

I've been stimulated by several more theoretical studies of history museum interpretation: Jeff Malpas, "New Media, Cultural Heritage and the Sense of Place: Mapping the Conceptual Ground," *International Journal of Heritage Studies* 14, no. 3 (April 2008): 197–209; John McCarthy and Luigina Ciolfi, "Place as Dialogue: Understanding and Supporting the Museum Experience," *International Journal of Heritage Studies* 14, no. 3 (April 2008): 247–67; Tammy S. Gordon, "Heritage, Commerce, and Museal Display: Toward a New Typology of Historical Exhibition in the United States," *Public Historian* 30, no. 3 (Summer 2008): 27–50; Penny Edgell and Eric Tranby, "Shared Visions? Diversity and Cultural Membership in American Life," *Social Problems* 57, no. 2 (May 2010): 175–204; and Benjamin Filene, "Passionate Histories: 'Outsider' History-Makers and What They Teach Us," *Public Historian* 34, no. 1 (Winter 2012): 11–33.

12. CONTEMPORARY MUSEUM PRACTICE

The most active site for thinking and teaching about museums in many dimensions is the University of Leicester in England. Out of that program have come several very useful works in museum craft, though they are more focused on art and archaeological than on historical collections (and, quite naturally, on Britain rather than the United States). The most important are by Susan M. Pearce, including *Museums, Objects and Collections: A Cultural Study* (Leicester, U.K.: Leicester University Press, 1992); Pearce, *On Collecting: An Investigation into Collecting in the European Tradition* (London: Routledge, 1995); Pearce, ed., *Interpreting Objects and Collections* (New York: Routledge, 1994); Pearce, ed., *Museum Studies in Material Culture* (Leicester, U.K.: Leicester University Press, 1989; and Pearce, ed., *Objects of Knowledge* (London: Athlone Press, 1990). A colleague of Pearce's, Eilean Hooper-Greenhill, is the author of *Museums and the Shaping of Knowledge* (London: Routledge, 1992) and *Museums and the Interpretation of Visual Culture* (London: Routledge, 2000). In the American context, see Gail Anderson, *Reinventing the Museum: Historical and Contemporary Perspectives on the Paradigm Shift* (Walnut Creek, Calif.: AltaMira Press, 2004), and Michael Belcher, *Exhibitions in Museums* (Washington, D.C.: Smithsonian Institution Press, 1991).

13. AN EXCURSUS ON AUSTRALIA

The Australian context of this transformation in history museum practice focuses on the brilliant innovations of Peter Emmett and his colleagues at Sydney and subsequently in the political travails of the National Museum of Australia in Canberra. A good introduction is Andrea Witcomb, "How Style Came To Matter: Do We Need to Move beyond the Politics of Representation?," in *South Pacific Museums*, ed. Chris Healy and Witcomb (Melbourne: Monash University Press, 2006), 21.1-1–21.16; also see Kate Gregory, "Art and Artifice: Peter Emmett's Curatorial Practice in the Hyde Park Barracks and Museum of Sydney," *Fabrications: The Journal of the Society of Architectural Historians, Australia and New Zealand* 16, no. 1 (June 2006): 1–22; Armanda Scorrano, "Visions of a Colony: History on (Dis)play at the Museum of Sydney," *Public History Review* 19 (2012): 1–20; and Scorrano, "Constructing National Identity: National Representations at the Museum of Sydney," *Journal of Australian Studies* 36, no. 3 (2012): 345–62.

For the wider story of the politics of culture in Australia, see Stuart Macintyre and Anna Clark, *The History Wars* (Carlton, Vic.: Melbourne University Press, 2004). The Australian conflict was of course paralleled by the right-wing attack on "revisionism" in U.S. school curricula and history museum interpretation, as summarized in Gary B. Nash, Charlotte Crabtree, and Ross E. Dunn, *History on Trial: Culture Wars and the Teaching of the Past* (New York: Random House, 1997). The Enola Gay controversy was a major chapter in the American story, but the damage in Australia was probably greater, as Liberal (i.e., conservative) politicians forced museum officials to redo almost the entire initial installation of the new National Museum of Australia in Canberra. See Guy Hansen, "History Curatorship: Case Studies from the National Museum of Australia, 1991–2008" (Ph.D. diss., University of Technology, Sydney, 2009).

THE TABLE IN ONE'S MIND

All these readings coalesce with all those design meetings and conferences and all those after-work dinners to form one rich ongoing rap session, my very own Platonic symposium, in my own head. Once, a half-century ago, I was taught to read carefully and slowly, to savor Hawthorne's elusiveness and Melville's fearlessness as I did my mother's noodle pudding. I can still do that when the occasion arises, parsing every noun as if it were a galaxy unto itself, every verb as if it were a piece of stage direction, and every sentence as if it were a cloud chamber revealing the traces of a subatomic collision. As a scholar, I'm embarrassed if I approach a text in any other way. But the sort of reading I've described in these pages is quite different. Around my own interior symposium table, my companions (the authors I have read, the friends I have listened to, the self I left behind decades ago) and I (my self of this moment) talk on and on. My interlocutors do not wince at my misreadings. Creative misreading is fundamental to my creativity, and perhaps to yours, gentle reader. I urge you not to follow the instruction manuals too faithfully.

ACKNOWLEDGMENTS

For the historian, writing a book rooted in one's own history is a huge personal and professional challenge. I started believing that I knew the plot of the past forty-plus years. Then I reread the archives of the work I've done since 1967. Oh, that was painful. I was occasionally pleased to discover bits of precocity in the early work and just as often disappointed by later evidences of inexplicable stupidity. And, of course, in the process I learned that the documents often contradicted my memory and the stories I'd been telling myself and others for decades. Probing further, I realized that many of the documents, too, had their problems. My plans for all these museum projects were hardly the trustworthy stuff of objective journalistic observation. They were often written with an eye to persuading my clients to alter their ways of thinking and operating. To deduce the actual situation, I had to re-create the circumstances of each plan's birth and read the documents ironically, as if the opposite of what I proposed was often the status quo. At some point I also discovered the interpretation of chroniclers, others who had reviewed the work I had done and tried putting it in context. These were fascinating but invariably frustrating. The commentators didn't know the story from the inside; they judged from inadequate evidence; they misconstrued final results as evidence of intention. Now I had come to the critical moment: how to evaluate and weave together these strands of memory and archive and commentary. I learned once again Melville's wisdom, that the truth is everlastingly elusive, and, most disconcertingly, it is glimpsed only momentarily.

Eventually I realized that such evidence testing is a key step in every project of historical investigation. But I wasn't done, yet. My fifty cartons of archival material, even excavated as carefully as an archaeological exploration in ancient Mesopotamia, could not tell their own story. The reader, ah, yes, the reader—how could my reader make sense of 500 projects? Would I not have to construct a narrative that put all this into an orderly progression, as if my life and work manifested some manageable coherence? Here was another weaving challenge, to tie together the evidence and a through-line of account and argument. In sum, dear reader, what you hold in your hands is a book of unexpected discoveries about what I once thought I knew thoroughly. The comedian Gracie Allen used to say that "sometimes I need to say something three or four times before I know what I'm talking about." I had to practice history for almost a half-century before I seemed to know what I was doing.

There were other lessons. The American History Workshop archives also relate the tale of an independent curator/educator/museum planner, working at the edges of revolutions in both museum practice and historical scholarship. In picking up my free lance forty years ago, I set aside some of the undeniable benefits of steady employment in solvent institutions: the opportunity to nurture an organization by building collections, staffs, or programs over many years; the chance to work alongside fellow specialists to create a historical program (for example, a college course or graduate seminar, or an interpretation of the same era) through successive experiments; and a reliable patron to cover my overhead expenses and cast a safety net below my tightrope. On the other hand, I have had the inexhaustible freedom to explore new questions in American history and new techniques of teaching, a lifelong get-out-of-committee-meeting card, and a chance to create many ad hoc working communities to do good work and to get paid for it. And, most of all, to keep the question pot boiling, one domain of knowledge after another.

Finally, the archives told me that much of the past is truly gone. The museums we planned have gone on to other challenges and the exhibitions we did have had their moment in the limelight. But the fellowship of my companions in this work has always been its chief joy. Many have long ago transmogrified from colleagues to very close friends, our original collaborations over drawing boards and library tables having given way to long evenings of cooking dinners and sharing memories. Even the following long list of my comrades is insufficient and incomplete. Some of these names are gone from my life or from this earth, but they deserve recognition here as coauthors of the work described in this book.

So my deepest affection goes out to Kevin Allen, Anna Arabindan-Kesson, Regan Backer, Minju Bae, Robert Bailey, Edward Ball, Jake Barton, Anna Bean, Rick Beard, Sven Beckert, Jacob Bender, Thomas Bender, Michael Berkowitz, Ira Berlin, David Blight, Flora Boros, Bill Braverman, Jason Bregman, Lynne Breslin, Stan Brimberg, Fred Brink, Steve Brosnahan, Carlyle Brown, Clare Brown, Vincent Brown, Bryan Burke, Margaret Burke, Irene Burnham, Claudia Bushman, Richard Candee, Jean Casimir, Gillian Chaplin, Barbara Cherington, Aileen Chumard, Cynthia Copeland, Nancy Dallett, David Brion Davis, Avi Decter, Thomas DeFrantz, Ellen

Denker, Laurent Dubois, Dianne Durante, Moira Egan, Jeffrey Eger, Anne Emerson, John Englund, John Findlay, Ellen Fineberg, Paul Finkelman, Ellen Fletcher, Jonathan Fogelson, Eric Foner, Michael Frisch, Charles Froom, Lisa Garrison, Christine Gebhard, Susan Geib, Gary Gerstle, Les Gilbert, Thavolia Glymph, Fred Golinko, Roberta Brandes Gratz, Elly Greene, Robert Guest, Gail Guillet, Philip Gura, Karl Haglund, Pauline Chase Harrell, Leslie Harris, Jean Hébrard, Emily Hiestand, Peter Hinks, Graham Russell Hodges, Marjorie Hoffman, Harold Holzer, James O. Horton, Lois Horton, Jeanne Houck, Richard Hoyen, Kathleen Hulser, Daniel Hurley, Henry Huston, Peter Iverson, John Jacobsen, Annie Johnson, Martha Jones, Lynda B. Kaplan, Martha Katz-Hyman, Melissa Keane, Darwin Kelsey, Albert Klyberg, Peter Knupfer, Lloyd Kramer, Ed Krent, Bob Krim, Daresha Kyi, Ted Landsmark, Mindy Lang, Jack Larkin, Chris Lawrence, David Layman, Mindy Lehrman, Mark Lender, Molly Lenore, Ann LeVeque, Hillel Levine, Cynthia Levinson, Leslie Lindenauer, Albert Lorenz, Allen Lubow, Anne Maher, Meg Maher, Leonard Majzlin, Paula Maliandi, Lisbeth Mark, Cathy Matson, Lorraine McConaghy, George McDaniel, Sheila McDowell, Jane McNamara, Jawad Metni, Laurie Mittenthal, Allen Moore, Christopher Paul Moore, Nina Morais, Andrea Most, Sarah Muir, Cory Munson, Minda Novek, Jane Nylander, Peter O'Connell, Bud Oringdulph, Nancy Grey Osterud, Meg Ostrum, Nick Paffett, Max Page, Ann Parsons, Liz Patterson, Jennifer Patton, Theodore Penn, Carla Peterson, Millery Polyné, Jeremy Popkin, Bernard Powers, David Quigley, Steve Rabin, Keith Ragone, Arie Rahamimoff, Jan Ramirez, Marci Reaven, Carole Rifkind, Richard Rifkind, Barnes Riznik, Brett Robbs, Ann Rochell, John Rogers, Melanie Roher, Dolores Root, Michael Roper, Elizabeth Rose, David Rosen, Dale Rosengarten, Theodore Rosengarten, Ellen Rosenthal, Ellen Rothman, Terrie Rouse, Gary Rowe, Fath Davis Ruffins, Rusty Russell, Michael Sand, Michael Sant'Ambrogio, Linda Sargent Wood, Dana Schaffer, David Schmitz, Eric Schneider, Emily Schottland, Susan Schreiber, Martin Schweizer, John Sears, Liz Ševčenko, Holly Sidford, Michael Singer, Caroline Sloat, Peggy Smith, David Spatz, Jeanie Stahl, John Stauffer, Joseph Stein, Jason Steinhauer, A. T. Stephens, Elizabeth Stines, Lou Storey, Cara Sutherland, Robert Sutton, Dianne Swann-Wright, Ken Takeuchi, Bill Tally, Joan Tally, Nick Tanis, Hal Tiné, Phillip Tiongson, Zev Trachtenberg, Miriam Trementozzi, Lilly Tuttle, Jessica Unger, Jasmine Utley, Lara Vapnek, Peter Vermilyea, Steve Victor, Sherry Kafka Wagner, Mike Wallace, James Walvin, Sam Bass Warner, Amy Waterman, Marjorie Waters, Michael Weber, Nicholas Westbrook, Virginia Westbrook, Peter

Wexler, Craig Wilder, Talvin Wilks, Julie Winch, Lynn Wolff, Kara Yeargens, Ruthie Yow, Christina Ziegler-McPherson, Jonathan Zimmerman, and Shomer Zwelling. I love seeing all these names in one paragraph.

Over all these years I've been blessed by sharing what Rabbi Abraham Joshua Heschel calls "radical amazement" in the work and the fellowship of my dear friend Holly Sidford. And my chaverim, the Second Shabbat group in Park Slope, have been my steadiest source of intellectual and spiritual companionship over these decades.

I have a special debt to people who have remembered things that I could not and helped contribute to the accuracy of this narrative: David Blight, Richard Candee, John Demos, Susan Geib, Emily Hiestand, Ana Koval, Shannon Nichol, Max Page, Barnes Riznik, Ellen Rosenthal, and Caroline Sloat. And then there are the brave souls who read early and late versions of this text and vigorously marked it with lots of "?" and a few "!@#$#$!." The book found a voice in being written for these ears. Thanks to Rick Beard, Anne D. Emerson, Randy Fertel, David Fleischmann, Roberta Brandes Gratz, Robert Gross, Philip Gura, Leonard Majzlin, Anne C. Rose, Andrea Witcomb, the anonymous readers for the University of North Carolina Press, and most especially Lynda B. Kaplan. As the images in this book attest, Richard Hoyen has for decades been a treasured alter ego with astonishing power to comprehend and represent my best ideas visually. Mark Simpson-Vos, my editor at UNC Press, has been a wonderful literary and intellectual companion along the way, mixing encouragement with mildly expressed dismay in just the right proportions. I'm also grateful for the splendid professional work of his colleagues at the Press.

These readers saved me from many errors. But the infelicities, inconsistencies, and absurdities that remain in this book are all my own, proofs of what my ancient friends, the Puritans, would have called my inborn obduracy.

One of my anonymous readers asked me to judge whether, in career terms, I blazed a trail for others to follow or pulled up the bridge behind me. Even among my generation of historians who entered the museum field because they loved the opportunities it provided for teaching and learning history (rather than because the job market was weak), I have been unusual in remaining independent for so long. Many others have worked as freelance consultants or guest curators for a few years. So, then as well as now, most nonacademic public historians have sought regular employment—in cultural organizations, government agencies (National Park Service, Bureau of Land Management), preservation groups, and design firms. The public history field has matured and professionalized. We have a national organization, the National Council on Public History; a juried journal, the *Public Historian*; and dozens of graduate and undergraduate programs.

Self-employed entrepreneurship is not for the faint of heart. The required accounting, legal, and insurance regulations can almost make one a Republican. Most important, one has to find and dwell on the consistent principles in one's own work—reading and reflecting on one's past work, serving as one's own toughest critic, knowing that one cannot afford an "off day" when the work of others hangs in the balance. This is why I've always had this book in mind all through these many years. It was a promise to myself to keep track of my own issues as I met the concerns of so many clients.

Perhaps running my own business was in my blood. I loved being the fellow at the American Association of Museums meetings who was known as "a real historian" and the fellow at the Organization of American Historians who is "the museum guy." But such positive marginality does have its costs. I was not asked to speak to a university class, much less to teach, for over thirty years. Academic fellowships, research grants, and summer seminars have been almost totally unavailable to independent and public historians like me. In the past decade, finally, I've been invited to lead workshops at CUNY, Duke, Michigan, Princeton, UMass Amherst, Vanderbilt, Yale, and three universities in Australia—Sydney, Deakin, and Monash. In 2014, I was even invited to make my first return to a Harvard classroom, after forty-five years. These workshops have been very helpful in framing the ideas in this book, as have a number of weeklong institutes we have organized with the support of the New York Council on the Humanities, the National Park Service, and the Gilder Lehrman Center for Slavery, Resistance and Abolition at Yale University.

Happily, the last few years have provided me with some wonderful opportunities to lift my head from the deadline pressures of producing exhibitions and to take time for reflection and research. Through Professor David Blight, director of Yale's Gilder Lehrman Center and a great mensch, I've been privileged to have a fellowship, a desk, and the companionship of a terrific succession of historians of slavery in New Haven. Through the good offices of Professor Shane White, I was fortunate to have a fellowship in March–May 2014 at the United States Studies Centre at the University of Sydney—where I wrote much of this book. And now I complete the writing with a Guggenheim Fellowship for 2015–16. I am enormously grateful to all of these benefactors. I also want to thank Franklin Roosevelt, Lyndon Johnson, and the Social Security Administration.

Readers will know how much I have learned from Sarah Rabinowitz, my mother, who died halfway through her one-hundredth year, on the day I completed this manuscript. Her memory has been a blessing.

My greatest debt is inscribed on the dedication page.

INDEX

Page numbers in italic indicate illustrations.

9/11 Memorial Museum. *See* National September 11 Memorial and Museum
16 Elm Street (project proposal), 208–13
1876 (exhibition), 258–59

Abram, Ruth, 75, 148–49
Accessibility, of public history, 85
Acoustiguide, 82
Actions: comprising objects, human senses, etc., 6; "daily rhythms," 32–33; dramatism and, 34–38; exhibitions representing, 114; facts as deeds, 33; historian of, 33–38; symbolic, 34; tactility and understanding of, 31–33; as threshold to dialogue, 45
Adams, Abigail, 312
Adams, John, 245, 308, 312
African Americans: Birmingham Civil Rights Institute, 6, 278–84, *282*, 285, 293, 296; in Boston's history, 99n, 133; Charleston, S.C., museum, 331–32; critical history and, 257–60; *Field to Factory*, 260, *273*, 273–74, 278; historical markers and, 92–95, *95*; museum professionals at NMAH, 272–73; National Underground Railroad Freedom Center, 298–308; N-YHS slavery exhibitions, 6, 220–25, *226*, 266, 312–17; President's House, 308–12, *310*; public art and, 135; public history and, 6–7, 22, 41; social distinctions and, 37
After the Revolution (exhibition), 211, 260
"Agency," 303
Age of fracture, 292, 308–12, 328–32
The Agnew Clinic (painting), 206
"Aha!" moment, 46–47
AHW. *See* American History Workshop
Air Force Association, 261–62
Alaska-Yukon-Pacific Exposition (1909), 154–55
Albany Urban Cultural Park, 71
Aldrich House, 107–12
Allen, Ethan, 123–24
Allen, Richard, 309–10

Alperovitz, Gar, 262
Altoona, Pa., industrial heritage park in, 137
American Association for State and Local History, 183, 351–52
American exceptionalism, 255–57, 312
American Girl, 298
American History Workshop (AHW): creation of, 6, 67, 112; defining the products of, 69; early years of, 105, 120; Heritage Trails New York approach of, 96n; inclusion and diversity in, 6–7; place focus of, 89; process and theory of, 164–65; project focus of, 8, 68–69; reader's reflection (resources) on, 338; role in industrial heritage parks, 137–38; selling of interpretation, 69–70; situated learning approach of, 153–59; social history approach of, 245; typologies of, 112. *See also specific exhibitions, programs, and sites*
American Studies Association, 194
American Textile History Museum, 141
America's Historylands (National Geographic Society), 90
AMS Research and Planning, 299
Anderson, Benedict, 266–67
André, Jean Jacques, 82
Annalistes, 193
Annapolis, Md., as museum without walls, 133
ANON. See A Nation of Nations
Archaeological core samples, 162
Architecture: OSV, 18; OSV education center, 63, *64. See also specific facilities and projects*
Arizona Historical Society, *156, 157*, 207
Arnold Arboretum, 189
Arrington, Richard, 278–79
Art: commissioned objects, 226; critical history and, 256; redefining public space, 135; silhouettes for *I&M Canal Passage*, 165–68, *168*; *Waiting for the Interurban*, 165–66; wire sculptures for *Slavery in New York*, 313, *314*
Artifictions, 225–26, 228

The Art of Dancing, Explained by Reading and Figures (Tomlinson), 162n

Asa Knight Store, OSV, *192*, 192–93

Asian Americans: Chinatown History Project, 286, 287; Chinese Exclusion Act of 1882, 154, 292; *Eight Pound Livelihood*, 286; Japanese American National Museum, 285, 291–92; Japanese internment, 7, 83, 260–61, 270, 273–74, 291–92; *A More Perfect Union*, 83, 260, 273–74, *274*; Museum of Chinese in America, 291; Wing Luke Museum, 286–87, 295, 296, 331

Attendance: as goal of interpretive program, 76–78; OSV, 17, 76–77

Attentiveness, 320–24

Attis, marble bust of, 229–32, *230*

Audiences, for interpretation, 76–78, 118–19

Audiovisual media, 82–85, 120–24, 272

Aural evocation of place, 120–24

Australia: *Eat Your History: A Shared Table* (exhibition), 121n; political partisanship in, 74; reader's reflection (resources) on, 359–60; representation of aboriginal people, 288

Authenticity of objects, 75–76, 233

Avenging the Ancestors Coalition, 308

Bailyn, Bernard, 241

Baird, Barbara, 166

Baldizzi, Josephine, 149–51

Baldizzi, Rosa, 327

Baltimore, *Rowhouse: A Baltimore Style of Living*, 147

Barnum, P. T., 187

Base camp, metaphor of visitors' center as, 135

Basic data-point, 31

BCRI. *See* Birmingham Civil Rights Institute

Belley, Jean-Baptiste, portrait of, *231*, 231–32

Beloved (Morrison), 300

Belter, John Henry, 224

Berger, Peter, 65

Berlin, Ira, 302, 303

"Best practices," 8, 63

Beyer, Richard, 165–66

Bilbao Guggenheim, 299

Birmingham Civil Rights Institute (BCRI), 6, 278–84, *282*, 285, 293, 296

Blacks. *See* African Americans

Blatt, Marty, 138

Blight, David, 280, 302

Blink: The Power of Thinking without Thinking (Gladwell), 321

Body politic, 237–50

Bond Ryder James (architects), 279

Bonnell, Jennifer, 277

Boorstin, Daniel, 257–58

Borges, Jorge Luis, 97

Born to Trouble (Meade), 61

Boston: Arnold Arboretum, 189; author's experiences in, 130; bicentennial exhibit, 240–43; diversity lacking in public history, 99n; Freedom Trail, 90, 125–26, 240, 270; Museum of Afro-American History, 133; Old South Meetinghouse, 125–27; *Place over Time*, 108, *110*, 111; Rose Kennedy Greenway, 168–72, *170*; *Where's Boston?* (multimedia presentation), 82–83

Boston 200, 240–43

Boston Landmarks Commission, 108

"Bottom up" approach, 272, 286–87

Boundary crossing, in museums, 293–95

Branding of experiences, 353

Breslin, Lynne, 220–21

Brink, Fred, 108n2

Brookhiser, Richard, 266

Brooklyn, N.Y.: author's origins in, 99–104; author's return to, 130–31; reader's reflection (resources) on, 341–43

Bruner, Jerome, 55–56, 80, 227, 347–48

Bryant, John L., 247

Bucks County (Pa.) Historical Society, 199

Bulletin of the Atomic Scientists, 262

Bunch, Lonnie, 6, 273

Bunker Hill Monument, 90

Burke, Kenneth, 34–38, 118, 197, 346

Burkhardt, Edward, 221–22

Bushman, Richard, 212, 214

Buten, David, 76n

Buten Museum of Wedgwood, 76n

Calvert, Cecil, 161

Caramoor estate, 121–22

Carney, Lora S., 252

Carson, Cary, 206, 211, 212–13, 214

Carson, Rachel, 197

Carter, Jimmy, 67

Cathedrals, French identity and, 295–96

Cavell, Stanley, 30

Charles H. Wright Museum, 285

Charleston, S.C.: museum of African American history, 331–32; visitors' center, 135

Cheney Cowles Museum, 195–96

Chermayeff and Geismar Associates (design firm), 82, 257

Chernow, Ron, 245

Chew, Ron, 286–87

Chicago: Creating New Traditions (exhibition), 147

Chicago Historical Society, 147

Chinatown History Project, 286, 287

Chinese Exclusion Act of 1882, 154, 292

Chronology, exhibitions based on, 98–99, 241, 255–56, 328

Cincinnati: National Underground Railroad Freedom Center, 298–308; public art installation in, 135

Cincinnati History Museum, 299

Cincinnati Museum Center, 299, 306

Cities: districts of, 132; as museums without walls, 132–34

City Beautiful movement, 90–91, 93, 175

Civil War battlefields, politics and, 74

Clark, Horace, 35–37, 40

Classroom space, in museums, 79

The Clothes Off Our Backs (exhibition), 194

Clusters. *See* Interpretive clusters

Coach, curator as, 250

Coffin, Levi, 300

Cognition, attentiveness and, 320–24

Cognitive development theory, 55–56

Cold War narrative, 255–57

Coleman, Christy, 198

Colfax, La., massacre, 93n

Collaboration, 29, 60–67; with artistic partners, 84–85; with classroom teachers, 62; with costumed interpreters, 60–62; in OSV education program, 60–65

Collections: authenticity of, 75–76, 233; author's relationship with, 179–81; as element of interpretation, 74–76, 179–98; museum function flowing from, 181–82. *See also* Objects

Collingwood, R. G., 174

Colonial Williamsburg: African American interpretation at, 7; historical features of, 90; mix of originals and reproductions in, 192n; pedagogy of, 23; *The Story of a Patriot* (film), 82

Commissioned art objects, 226

Common Sense (Paine), 317

Community, as museum education theme, 58–59

Community museums: Birmingham Civil Rights Institute, 6, 278–84, *282*, 285, 293, 296; "bottom up" approach, 272, 286–87; ethnically specific, 285–96; new social history and, 271–84; sponsor versus historian interests in, 283; sponsor versus visitor interests in, 290–91

"Comparables," 76

Concept shows, 212

Confederate flag, 197

Confederates in the Attic (Horwitz), 278

Constitutional Convention: Madison's notes from, 216–20, 276

Constitution Works (exhibition), 77, 78, 79, 247–50

Cooper-Hewitt Smithsonian Design Museum, 223

Cooper at OSV, understanding experience of, 38–39, *39*

Copley Wolff (design firm), 169

Corley, Bob, 279, 281

The Correspondent (newsletter), 254

Cosmology, 38–39

Costumed interpreters, OSV: author's collaboration with, 60–62; author's work as, 6, 10, 15, 181; inspiration from, 1–6; learning in interactions with, 27–29, 44–49; sequence of encounters with, 44–45

Craftsperson's work, 29

The Cranberry and Its People (exhibition), 66–67

Crew, Spencer, 260, 273

Critical history: community sponsorship versus, 283; Enola Gay exhibition and, 260–64, *261*, 270; "history wars," 262, 264–65; master national narrative versus, 257–60; National Museum of History and Technology and, 256–60; National Underground Railroad Freedom Center, 303–4; New-York Historical Society and, 265–70; origins of, 254–55; Vietnam Veterans Memorial and, 251–53, 270

Crockett, Karilyn, 99n

Cronkite, Walter, 324

Crosby Schlesinger Smallridge (design firm), 171–72

Crouch, Tom, 260

"Culture wars," 74

Curator: as coach, 250; community as, 285–96; thinking like, 334

Curatorially created objects, 225–28

Curriculum, and museum education, 56–57, 79, 239, 297, 317

"Daily rhythms," 32–33

Dance, depiction of, 162

Danforth Foundation, 240

Danielis, Frieder, 229

Davidson, Cathy, 321

Davis, David Brion, 301–2

de Bretteville, Sheila Levrant, 135

Decoding and translating devices, 226

The Deer Hunter (film), 252

Deetz, James, 212, 351

Demography, 76

Demos, John, 32

Dennis, Marsha Saron, 149

Depression-era photography, 256

Deschooling Society (Illich), 54

Design: as element of interpretation, 80–85; Parker's methodology for, 81. *See also specific facilities and projects*

Dewey, John, 54–55, 78, 79, 185–86, 240, 337

Dialogue, museum as a site for, 305–6

Dinkins, David, 95

Dis-placement, and sense of place, 174

Diversity: Boston, lacking in public history, 99n; critical history and, 257–59; ethnically specific museums and, 285–96; historical markers and, 92–98; industrial heritage parks and, 144–45; *A Nation of Nations*, 82, 257–58; public history and, 6–7, 22, 41

Dodge, Lucie Bigelow, 121–22

Dodge, Walter, 121–22

"Does the Museum of History Teach History?" (Heslin), 23

Dolkart, Andrew, 75

Doorways to Statehood (exhibition), 112

Douglas, Mary, 36–40, 346

Downtown revitalization, 134–35

Drama: interpretive clusters, 215–33; museum visit as, 11, 123–24; new social history and, 272; reader's reflection (resources) on, 346–47, 349; Tenement Museum storyscape, 149–53; three-act plays at industrial heritage parks, 138–39; visitors as cast members in, 128–30

Dramatism, 34–38, 118, 197

Drucker, Peter, 65

Du Bois, W. E. B., 228

Duffey, Joseph, 65–67

Dutch Reformed Church (Brooklyn, N.Y.), 100, 104

Eakins, Thomas, 206

Eames, Charles, 82

Eames, Ray, 82

East Coast Memorial, New York, 251–52

East New York neighborhood. *See* Brooklyn, N.Y.

Eat Your History: A Shared Table (exhibition), 121n

Eavesdropping on history, 120–24

EDAW (design firm), 169

Education: cognitive development and, 55–56; curriculum and museums, 56–57, 79, 239, 297, 317; Dewey on, 54–55, 78, 79; exhibition-making and, 287; in interpretation, 78–80; museum, synthesis of, 58–59; Museum Education program at OSV, 49–65; new social history and, 55–56, 129. *See also* Learning

Edwards, Jonathan, 30, 240, 320, 337

Effortful thinking, 320–24

Eight Pound Livelihood (exhibition), 286

Eldridge, Elnathan, 66

Eldridge Street Synagogue, 84, 146

Eliot, T. S., 333

Ella Sharp Museum, 134

Ellis, Joseph, 245

Ellis Island, 7, 148, 252, 278

Ellis Island Restoration Committee, 276

Ellison, Ralph, 337

Embodied cognition, 164–65, 196–97, 348

Emerson, Ralph Waldo, 197

Emlen, Robert, 108n1

Empathy, 276–78

Engelhardt, Tom, 262

Enola Gay exhibition, 260–64, *261*, 270

"Enriched environment," 322

Ephemera, 207

Epistemology, 29; author's interest in, 44, 60; balancing act in, 335; cosmology in, 38–39; Douglas's mental constructions and practices in, 36–38; dramatism in, 34–38; human actions in, 33–38; reader's reflection (resources) on, 347–48; structuralist methodology in, 37; understanding experience in, 38–42; visitor's way of learning, 44–53

Epitomes, 189–91, 193, 206, 220

Equal Justice Initiative, 93n

Eskew, Glenn, 280–81, 283

Ethan Allen: Man and Myth (exhibition), 123

Ethan Allen Homestead, 123–24, *124*

Ethnically specific museums, 285–96; "bottom up" approach, 286–87; concentric circles of public for, 296; identity and pride in, 291–92, 295–96; insiders versus outsiders, 293–96; mainstream museums versus, 285–86; narratives in, 287–91; sponsor versus visitor interests in, 290–91; stereotypes conveyed in, 288; stereotypes undermined in, 287–88

Ethnic communities: author's "unnotable" place, 99–104; *Chicago: Creating New Traditions*, 147; historical markers and, 92–93; industrial heritage parks, 144–45; Lower East Side Tenement Museum, 146–53

Evans, Walker, 256

Everyday life, history of, 90–91, 96, 99, 105

Evidence, objects as, 184–86, 199–213

Exhibition-making: as educational method, 287. *See also* Interpretation; Objects; *and specific exhibitions*

"Exhibit of, not [simply] in," 126

Experience: exhibition, 38–42; eye-level, 325–26; new social history and, 272; objects as, 184–86, 199–213; themes versus, 115–17, 125–27, 138–39, 146; understanding, in learning, 38–42

Experiential learning, 53–59

Explanation, interpretation as, 69

Externalization, 227

Eye-level experience, 325–26

Eyewitness testimony, 324–28

The Face of Battle (Keegan), 204

Factorial ecology, 114

Facts, as deeds, 33

Fall River Heritage State Park, 71–72, 73, 138

Family, as museum education theme, 58–59

The Family of Man (exhibition), 256

The Farmer's Year (exhibition), 81

Federal Hall National Monument, 247, *248*

Feedback devices, 226–27

Fences, knowledge from, 30–31, 41

Fenno House, OSV: actions in, 33, *34*, 36; author's inspiration in, 2–3, *4*, 5, 43–44, 180–81, 333; costumed interpreter of, 60–61; dramatism and, 36; objects of, 180–81

Fenton, Edwin, 55

Field studies, by schoolchildren, 51, 62, 64

Field to Factory: Afro American Migration, 1915–1940 (exhibition), 260, *273*, 273–74, 278

Filene, Benjamin, 121n

Filmmaking, 82–85

Film preservation, 208

Fisher, Dorothy Canfield, 238

Fitzgerald, Geraldine, 84

Fleming, E. McClung, 183

Fleming, John, 302

Folklorist, museum historian as, 272

Foner, Eric, 302

Foster, Abby Kelley, 35

"Founders chic," 245

France: Annalistes, 193; identity and attachment in, 295–96

Franklin, Benjamin, 225, 245

Franklin, John Hope, 301

Fraser, Deryck, 226, 313, *314*

Frederick Douglass Papers, 224

Freedom's Journal, 315

Freedom Trail (Boston), 90, 125–26, 240, 270

Freelance work, 68

Freeman Farm, OSV, 3, 49–50, 191

French Founding Father: Lafayette Returns to Washington's America (exhibition), 266–68

Frisch, Michael, 272

Gallery installations in history museums, 98–99

Gara, Larry, 300–301

Garner, Margaret, 300

Garrison, William Lloyd, 34–35

Gay rights movement, 92, 94

Gehry, Frank, 299

Geib, Susan, 108n2

Geiger, David, *314*

Generalizations, 114–15, 118. *See also* Themes; Typologies

George Hart House, 208–13

Gerald R. Ford Presidential Library, 249

Gerber, Ga., 165

Germantown Preserved, 134–35

Getting Comfortable in New York: The American Jewish Home, 1880–1950 (exhibition), 194

Gilbert, Stuart, 132–33

Gilder Lehrman Institute, 332

Ginsburg, Carlo, 326

Girodet, Anne-Louis, *231*, 231–32

Gladwell, Malcolm, 321

Glassie, Henry, 212

Glazer, Nathan, 257

Glockner, Lucas, 149

Goldman, Annette P., 238

Golinko, Fred, 108n2

Gooding, William, 166

Goodwin, Doris Kearns, 269

Goya, Francisco de, 256

Graham Landscape Architecture, 161

A Grammar of Motives (Burke), 34

Grant and Lee (exhibition), 266, 268

Graphic design, 82

Gratz, Roberta Brandes, 255

Greven, Philip, 32

The Gross Clinic (painting), 206

Growth of the United States (exhibition), 141–42

Guiliani, Rudolph, 95

Guldbeck, Per, 81

Gumpertz, Nathalie, 149–51, 160, 277, 327
Gura, Philip F., 171n1
Gustafson Guthrie Nichol (design firm), 171–72

Haitian Revolution, 34, 231–32, 238, 317–18
Hallowell, Benjamin, 267
Hamilton, Alexander, 245, 246, 266, 314
Handheld devices in museum galleries, 323–24
Harper's Weekly, 224
Harrell, Pauline Chase, 108n2
Harrisville, N.H., woolen mill, 142
Hart-Celler Act of 1965, 152
Harvard University: author's studies at, 6, 15–17,
    22–23; turmoil in 1960s, 15–16, 22–23
Heald, Candace, 108n1
Hébrard, Jean, 228
Heimert, Alan, 241
Hein, Hilde S., 288n, 294
Heinrich's Day (interpretive proposal), 144–45,
    145
Hemings, Sally, 7
Henry Ford Museum, 211
Heritage mythos, of OSV, 19–21
Heritage Trails New York, 95–96
Hermann-Grima House, 117–18
Herodotus, 324
Heslin, James, 23
Heye, George Gustave, 289
Heye's Museum of the American Indian, 289
Hiestand, Emily, 108n2
Higgins, John Woodman, 201
Higgins Armory Museum, 201–4, *203*
Hill, James J., 117–18, 120–21
Hine, Lewis, 256
L'histoire èvénementielle, 98
Historical content, in interpretation, 70–73
"Historical features," 89–90
Historical markers, 90–98; conventional, prob-
    lems with, 97–98; *I&M Canal Passage*, 167;
    neglect of "all of us," 91–93, 97; New York
    City, 93–96, *95*, 173–74; Pennsylvania, 91–93;
    REPOhistory, 93–95, *95*; southern states, 93n
Historic American Buildings Survey, 136
Historic American Engineering Record, 136
Historic American Landscape Survey, 136
Historic houses: aural experiences in, 120–24;
    Germantown Preserved, 134–35; thematizing
    of, 117–19. *See also specific houses*
Historic St. Mary's City (Md.), 161–65
Historiography, author's, 64–65

History museums. *See* Museum(s); *and specific
    facilities and topics*
"History wars," 262, 264–65
*History Wars: The Enola Gay and Other Battles
    for the American Past* (Linenthal and Engel-
    hardt), 262
History Workshop (Britain), 352–53
Hodgkinson, Ralph, 61
Holocaust museums, 253, 270, 276, 278, 286,
    292, 330
Holzer, Harold, 268
"Hook," 45
Horsmanden, Daniel, 94
Horton, James Oliver, 273, 302
Horwitz, Tony, 278
Houston Museum of Fine Arts, 224
HSMC. *See* Historic St. Mary's City
Hughes, Ellen Roney, 257
Human remains, Native American, 288–89
Huntley, Horace, 279, 281
Hurley, Dan, 302
Hutson, James, 217
Huxtable, Ada Louise, 148

I&M Canal Passage (wayfinding program),
    165–68, *168*
Identity: basis of attachment, 295–96; ethnically
    specific museums and, 291–92, 295–96; mas-
    ter national narrative and, 257–60
Illich, Ivan, 54
Illinois and Michigan Canal Corridor Associa-
    tion, 165–68
IMAX shows, 83
Immediacy, 324–25
Immersion, 48; contrast with overview, 53; en-
    hanced by audiovisual technology, 322; in
    industrial heritage parks, 138–39; at Lower
    East Side Tenement Museum, 149–53; at
    Seattle Museum of History and Industry, 157–
    58; within re-created environments, 81–82
Immigrants: backyard history of, 184–85; *Chi-
    cago: Creating New Traditions*, 147; Chinese
    Exclusion Act of 1882, 154, 292; ethnically
    specific museums, 285–96; historical markers
    and, 92–93; industrial heritage parks and,
    144–45; *A Nation of Nations*, 82, 257–58; stan-
    dard saga of, 291–93. *See also* Lower East Side
    Tenement Museum
Independence Hall, 90, 270
Independence National Historical Park: *Miracle*

at *Philadelphia*, 216–20, 225–26, 246–47, 276; President's House, 308–12
Indianapolis Children's Museum, 211
"Indigenous" perspectives, 288
Individual narratives, 275–78, 324–28
Industrial heritage parks, 136–45, 276; AHW involvement in, 137–38; background for, 134–37; Fall River, 71–72, 73, 138; inclusion of work and workers in, 142–44; industrial community (landscape) in, 139–40, *140*; machines in, 141–44; politics and, 137; three-act play at, 139–45
Inhelder, Bärbel, 55
Insiders versus outsiders, 293–96, 308
Internships, Old Sturbridge Village, 17
Interpretation: author's overall agenda for, 312; collections (objects) in, 74–76, 179–98; contemporary representation in, 72; definition of, 69; elements of, 70, *70*; ethnically specific, 285–96; historical content in, 70–73; new social history and, 271–84; pedagogy in, 78–80; politics and, 74; process, at outdoor museums, 43–44; resistance to, 72; selling by AHW, 69–70; stakeholder interests in, 73–74; thematic, limitations of, 118–19. *See also specific topics and exhibitions*
Interpretive clusters, 215–33; Madison's notes installation, 216–20, 276; *New York Divided: Slavery and the Civil War*, 6, 220–25; origins and context for objects in, 229–33; "real stuff" and "other stuff" in, 225–28
"Interpretive generation," 271
"Interpretive Hexagon," *70*
Interpretive media, 80–85, 120–24, 272; diversity of, among historians, 10
Intuition, effortful thinking versus, 320–21
Invention, as concept of historical change, 111–15
Irish Americans, standard narrative for, 292
"The Iron Chink," 154–59, *155*
Isaac, Rhys, 213, 214
Italian Americans, in Lower East Side Tenement Museum, 149–51, 327

Jacobs, Jane, 93, 172, 197, 344–45
Jacobsen, Matthew Frye, 258
Jacobson, Anita, 75
James, Henry, 147–48
James, William, 240, 249, 320, 337
James J. Hill House, 117–18, 120–21
Japanese American National Museum, 285, 291

Japanese internment, 7, 83, 260–61, 270, 273–74, 291–92
Jay, John, 314
Jefferson, Thomas, 245, 265, 317
Jewish history: author's personal, 41–42, 99–104, 196; Eldridge Street Synagogue, 84, 146; *Getting Comfortable in New York: The American Jewish Home, 1880–1950*, 194; Holocaust museums, 253, 270, 276, 278, 286, 292, 330; "museum Judaism," 293; Simon Wiesenthal Center/Museum of Tolerance, 298; standard narrative for, 292–93. *See also* Lower East Side Tenement Museum
The Jewish Museum (New York City), 194
John F. Kennedy Presidential Library and Museum, 249
Johnson, James H., 114
Johnson, Mark, 196–97
Johnstown, Pa., industrial heritage park in, 137
Jones, Absalom, 309–10
Jordan, Benjamin S., 224
Joy, Henry, 61
Judge, Ona, 309

Kahneman, Daniel, 321
Kantor, Rosabeth Moss, 65
Karales, James H., 281
Kazin, Alfred, 102
Keech, Pamela, 75
Keegan, John, 204
Kelly, Emanuel, 309–10
Kelsey, Darwin, 21
Kennedy, John F., 15, 249, 251, 254, 325
Kennedy, Roger, 208–13, 259–60, 272–74
Kennicott, Robert, 166
Kent Fellowship, 240
Kinesthetic engagement, 48, 74, 139, 174, 195
King, Martin Luther, Jr., 15, 278, 280, 281
Klyberg, Albert T., 108n1
Kollwitz, Käthe, 256
Kouwenhoven, John, 185–86, 190
Kramer, Pam, 62
Kulik, Gary, 81
Kyongju, Korea, museum without walls, 133

Lafayette, Marquis de (Gilbert du Motier), 266–68
LaGuardia, Fiorello, 148
Laiand, Charles, 286
Lakoff, George, 196–97

LaMonte, Edward, 281
Landscape. *See* Place
Landscape Minus One, 162
LANDSCAPES (design firm), 161
Lange, Dorothea, 256
Larkin, Jack, 37n, 62
Laslett, Peter, 130
Launching the Republic (exhibition), *248*
Lax, Philip, 276
The Lay of the Land (exhibition), 107–12, *109*, 158, 159
Learning: "aha!" moment in, 46–47; cognitive development theory and, 55–56; collaboration in, 29, 60–67; Dewey on, 54–55, 78, 79; epistemology in, 29, 44; experiential, for children, 53–59; flow of human actions in, 33–38; history of place, 106–7; immersion and overview in, 48; interactions with costume interpreters in, 27–29, 44–49; kinesthetic engagement in, 48; museum episode in, 47–48; museum frame and, 46–48, *47*; new social history and, 55–56, 129; objects and, 29–33, 41–42, 194–98; open-ended love of, 57; in OSV education program, 49–65; reader's reflection (resources) on, 347–50; scaffolding in, 28, 71, 215; situated, 153–59; tactility in, 29–33; understanding experiences in, 38–42; visitor's way of, 44–53. *See also* Embodied cognition
Lee, Robert E., 265, 266, 267, 268
Lee, Russell, 256
Leicester, Andrew, 135
Leland, Joseph, 201
Lemisch, Jesse, 241
LESTM. *See* Lower East Side Tenement Museum
LeVeque, Ann, 108n1
Levinson, Sanford, 255
Lexicon, 162
The Liberator, 34–35
The Liberty Line: The Legend of the Underground Railroad (Gara), 300–301
Library of Congress, 217, 268–69
Lin, Maya, 251–52
Lincoln (film), 269
Lincoln and New York (exhibition), 266, 268–69
Linenthal, Edward T., 262
Lippard, Lucy, 94–95
Living history museum, 17n2
Living memory, 331–32
Local history research, 15
Location theory, 114
Lockridge, Kenneth, 32

Lohman, Ann, 94
Los Angeles: Japanese American National Museum, 285, 291; public art and inclusion in, 135; Simon Wiesenthal Center/Museum of Tolerance, 298
Louisiana, historical markers in, 93n
Lowell, James Russell, 245
Lowell, Mass., industrial heritage park in, 137, 138, 141, 143–44
"Lowell girls," 144
Lowenthal, David, 20, 354
Lower East Side, Manhattan, author's personal connection with, 146
Lower East Side Tenement Museum (LESTM), 6, 7, 75, 146–53, 258, 286, 287; authenticating versus authenticizing, 75–76; author's turning point with, 151, 153; discovery of site for, 148; goals of, 148–49; individual narratives of, 276–77, 327; milestone of, 146–47; planned expansion of, 152; post-tour "kitchen conversations," 305–6; storyscape of, 149–53
Lower Manhattan Sign Project, 94
Lynd, Staughton, 241

Machines: industrial heritage parks, 141–44; *Salmon Stakes*, 154–59, *155*
Madame Restell, 94
Madison, Dolley, 217
Madison, James, notes from Constitutional Convention, 216–20, 276
Magnússon, Sigurdur Gylfi, 326
Maguire, Matthew, 131
Maine, *Doorways to Statehood*, 112
Majzlin, Leonard, 84, 279, 281
"Making History Matter," 332
Malraux, André, 132–33
Manet, Edouard, 293–94
Manual for History Museums (Parker), 81
Manzanar internment camp, 7, 274n
Markers. *See* Historical markers
Mashantucket Pequot Museum, 288, *289*
Mason, Biddy, 135
Massachusetts, industrial heritage parks in, 137
Massachusetts Spy, 3, 36
Material culture, 193–97, 210–13, 214
McCaughey, Bob, 240
McClellan Law Office, OSV, 2, *3*, 28, 61
McConachie, Bruce, 48
McCullough, David, 245
McDaniel, George, 76
McLuhan, Marshall, 323

Meachum, Mary, 135

Meade, Patrick (McClellan Law Office lawyer), 2, *3*, 28, 61

Media: attention/cognitive effects of, 320–24; audiovisual, 82–85, 120–24, 272; graphic design in, 82; interpretive, 80–85, 120–24, 272; preservation of, 208; public history, 9–10

Meetinghouses, OSV, 2, *2*, 4–5, *5*, 18; Old South (Boston), 125–27

Melville, Herman, 228, 337

Memorials: critical history and, 251–54; emotionality and personalization of, 253

The Memory Theater of Giulio Camillo (play), 131

Mercer, Henry, 199

Merleau-Ponty, Maurice, 195

Merrimack Valley Textile Museum, 141

Metropolitan Museum of Art, 293–94

Meyerson, Ignace, 227

Mickey Mouse History and Other Essays on American Memory (Wallace), 114n

Microhistorians, 326–27

Miller, Perry, 16, 41

Miller, Sam, 240

Mills, Robert, 90

Minnesota Historical Society, 194, 206–7

Minnesota History Center, 121n

Minnesota Labor Interpretive Center, 144

Miracle at Philadelphia (exhibition), 216–20, 225–26, 246–47, 276

Mirrer, Louise, 265–66, 268, 312

Mise-en-scène, of interpretive clusters, 215–33

Mission 66 (National Park Service), 81

Moby-Dick (Melville), 228, 251, 322

Mocuments, 162, 225, 228

Monterey, Calif., visitors' center, 123

Monticello, African American history at, 7

Monuments, 90

Moore, Allen, 63, 66

Moore, J. Fred, 108n1

A More Perfect Union: Japanese Americans and the U.S. Constitution (exhibition), 83, 260, 273–74, *274*

Morgan, Philip, 20

Morris, Robert, 246

Morrison, Toni, 300

Moses, Robert, 207–8

Mott, John, 21

Mount Vernon, 267, 308

Le Musée Imaginare (Malraux), 133

Museum(s): author's frustration with "sacred spaces," 105–6; as base camp for exploration, 135; body politic in, 237–50; "bottom up" approach, 272, 286–87; boundary crossing in, 293–95; costs of professionalization, 319; current issues/challenges facing, 319–32; differences from schools, 116; envisioning place in, 98–99, 105–19; ethnically specific, 285–96; experience of exhibitions, 115–17; function flowing from collections, 181–82; insiders versus outsiders, 293–96, 308; museum without walls versus, 134; objects' evolving role in, 186–93; reader's reflection (resources) on, 351–52, 356–59; role in teaching history, 23; sponsor versus visitor interests in, 290–91, 330–31; theory of, 8–9, 355–56; visit as performance, 11, 123–24; visitors as cast members in ongoing drama, 128–30; visitors' time as organizing frame for, 124. *See also specific museums, topics, and exhibitions*

Museum Education program, OSV, 49–65, 78; architectural design for, 63, *64*; Bruner's visit to, 56; cognitive development theory and, 55–56; collaborative efforts in, 60–65; curriculum reform and, 56–57; different minds and experimentation in, 63; diversity of activities in, 53–54, 59; experiential learning in, 53–59; field studies in, 51, 62, 64; in-house journal of, 62; innovation versus OSV institution, 63–64; name change to, 49; "rice cakes" model in, 49–53; synthesis of education in, 58–59; thematic approach in, 51–53, 58–59; wobble between past and present in, 55

Museum episode, 47–48

Museum frame, 46–48, *47*, 322–23

Museum moment, 59

Museum of Afro-American History (Boston), 133

Museum of Chinese in America, 291

Museum of Modern Art, 256

Museum of Sydney, 121n

Museum of the City of New York, 207–8, 224, 226

Museum of the Confederacy, 198

Museums without walls, 132–45; implications for museum professionals, 134; use of term, 132–33

Museum theory, 8–9, 355–56

Mütter, Thomas Dent, 205

Mütter Museum, 204–6

Mystic Seaport, 351

Napoleon, 34

Narrative: attentiveness and, 322–24; in ethnically specific museums, 287–91; individual, 275–78, 324–28; in interpretation, 70–73; reader's reflection (resources) on, 346–47; standard immigrant, 291–93. *See also* National narrative, master; Storyscape; *and specific exhibitions*

National Air and Space Museum: Enola Gay exhibition, 260–64, *261*, 270; *To Fly* (film), 83

National Conference of Christians and Jews, 298–99

National Conference of Community and Justice, 298–99

National Endowment for the Arts (NEA), 259

National Endowment for the Humanities (NEH), 65–67, 129, 259, 280

National Geographic Society, 90

National Museum of African American History, 6, *290*

National Museum of American History (NMAH): *After the Revolution*, 211, 260; *Field to Factory*, 260, *273*, 273–74, 278; inclusion and diversity in, 285–86; leadership of and new social history, 259–60, 272–75; Lincoln artifacts, 269; *A More Perfect Union*, 83, 260, 273–74, *274*; name change to, 259; *16 Elm Street*, 208–13. *See also* National Museum of History and Technology

National Museum of History and Technology (NMHT), 82; Boorstin and, 257–58; critical history and, 256–60; *1876*, 258–59; initial exhibition, 141–42; master national narrative and, 257–60; name change, 259; *A Nation of Nations*, 82, 257–58

National Museum of the American Indian (NMAI), 288–91, 330

National narrative, master, 256–60, 269, 272–73, 354; American exceptionalism, 255–57, 312; collapse of, 328–32; standard immigrant, 291–93

National Park Foundation, 247

National Park Service: audiovisual media of, 82; historical documentation by, 136; industrial heritage parks of, 137; Mission 66, 81; Old South Meetinghouse, 125–27; politics and, 74. *See also specific sites*

National Register of Historic Places, 136

National September 11 Memorial and Museum (9/11 Memorial Museum), 253, 270, 325–27, 330, 331

National Trust, 133

National Underground Railroad Freedom Center (NURFC), 6, 298–308; acquisition of collection, 304–5; ambitious goals for, 299–300; critical history and, 303–4; developing narrative for, 301; lesson in leadership, 307–8; music program proposed for, 306, *307*; promoting dialogue in, *305*, 305–6; resistance and agency in, 302–3; slave pen, *304*, 304–5

A Nation of Nations (*ANON*), 82, 257–58

Native Americans: critical history and, 257–58; encounter in Historic St. Mary's City, 161–64; ethnically specific museums, 285; historical makers and, 92, 97; inclusion in public history, 7; Mashantucket Pequot Museum, 288, *289*; National Museum of the American Indian, 288–91, *290*, 330; objects versus abstraction, 195–96; skeletal remains of, 288–89; social distinctions and, 37; traditional museum presentation of, 98–99; "We Are Still Here," 289

"Native" perspectives, 288

Natural Symbols: Explorations in Cosmology (Douglas), 38–39

The Nature and Art of Workmanship (Pye), 57

NEA. *See* National Endowment for the Arts

NEH. *See* National Endowment for the Humanities

New England village, 18

New Orleans, Hermann-Grima House, 117–18

Newport Aquarium, 299

New social history: building blocks for, 32; education and learning in, 55–56, 129; goal of inclusiveness, 41, 134; National Museum of American History, 259–60, 272–75; perspective of, 271; translation into exhibitions, 271–84; visitors and, 119. *See also* Social history

New York (state), industrial heritage parks in, 137

New York City: author's origins in "unnotable" place, 99–104; author's return to, 130–31; Chinatown History Project, 286, 287; *Constitution Works*, 77, 78, 79, 247–50; East Coast Memorial, 251–52; Ellis Island, 7, 148, 252, 278; historical makers of, 93–96, *95*, 173–74; *Lincoln and New York*, 266, 268–69; Museum of Chinese in America, 291; National September 11 Memorial and Museum, 253, 270, 325–27, 330, 331; Park Slope Historic District, 173–74; Peddler's Park tours, 147–48; reader's reflection (resources) on, 341–43; responsibilities of historian in, 333–36; *The South*

Street Experience, 124; Statue of Liberty, 252. *See also* Lower East Side Tenement Museum; New-York Historical Society

New York City Landmarks Preservation Commission, 173

New York Divided: Slavery and the Civil War (exhibition), 6, 220–25, 266, 315–16

New-York Historical Society (N-YHS), 220–25, 265–70, 312–17; *French Founding Father: Lafayette Returns to Washington's America*, 266–68; *Grant and Lee*, 266, 268; *Lincoln and New York*, 266, 268–69; "Making History Matter," 332; *New York Divided: Slavery and the Civil War*, 6, 220–25, 266, 315–16; *Revolution! The Atlantic World Reborn*, 6, 225, 227, 228, 229–32, *230*, 266, 316–17; *Slavery in New York*, 6, 226, 266, 313–15, *314*

New York State Museum, 81

New York Times, "Portraits in Grief," 327

Nichol, Shannon, 172

Nicholson, Joseph, 310

Nietzsche, Friedrich, 237–38

NMAH. *See* National Museum of American History

NMAI. *See* National Museum of the American Indian

NMHT. *See* National Museum of History and Technology

Nora, Pierre, 295

North End Parks (Boston), 168–69, *170*, 171–72

North River Drug and Patent Medicine Warehouse (lithograph), 223–24

Northwest Museum of Arts and Culture, 195–96

Notes on Virginia (Jefferson), 317

NURFC. *See* National Underground Railroad Freedom Center

N-YHS. *See* New-York Historical Society

Nylander, Jane, 191–93, 212

Oakeshott, Michael, 174

Oakland Museum, 329

Objects: abstraction versus, 195–96; authenticity of, 75–76, 233; author's approach to, 184, 195, 197–98; author's relationship with, 179–81; concept shows versus, 212; diversification of, 79–80; dramatism and, 197; as element of interpretation, 74–76, 179–98; epitomes, 189–91, 193, 206, 220; as evidence and experience, 184–86, 199–213; evolving role in museums, 186–93; expanded definition of, 214–15; interpretive clusters of, 5–6, 215–33; learning from, 29–33, 41–42, 194–98; machines and technology, 141, 154–59; material culture and, 193–97, 210–13, 214; missing, curatorial problem of, 206–8; museum function flowing from, 181–82; oddities, 187–91, *188*, 220, 328–29; old and original, 229–33; Old Sturbridge Village, 180–81, 191–93; originals versus reproductions, 191–93; outdoor museum, 183–84; "pots-and-pans" history, 190; reader's reflection (resources) on, 350–51; "real stuff" and "other stuff," 225–28; size and scale problems of, 207–9; "stuffitude," 195; typicalities, 190–93, 207, 220; visitors' knowledge about, 181

Ocean Spray visitors' center, 66–67

Oddities, 187–91, *188*, 220, 328–29

O'Donnell, Patricia, 161

Ohio, industrial heritage parks in, 137

Oklahoma City bombing memorial, 253

"Old" objects, 229–33

Old South Meetinghouse (Boston), 125–27

Old Sturbridge Village (OSV): attendance at, 17, 76–77; author as assistant director of interpretation and education at, 6, 16–17; author as costumed interpreter at, 6, 10, 15, 181; author as director of education at, 6, 49–65, 78, 239–40; author's departure from, 64–65; and author's discovery of calling, 1–6, 29, 43; collections (objects) of, 180–81, 191–93; cooper of, 38–39, *39*; establishment and growth of, 18–19; heritage mythos of, 19–21; interactions between visitors and costume interpreters, 27–29; internships, 17; mission statement of, 20, 24, 48–49; as outdoor history museum, 17; pedagogy of, 19–26; reader's reflection (resources) on, 339–41; "time of change" approach at, 21–26, 27; touchable past in, 29–33

On Knowing: Essays for the Left Hand (Bruner), 56

Oral history: in cranberry growers exhibition, 66–67; in ethnically specific museums, 286–87; in new social history, 271; reliance on, 329–30; testimony of eyewitnesses, 324–28

Oregon Historical Society, 160

"Organic historians," 72

Organization of American Historians, 194

Original objects, 191–93, 229–33

Orlando, Fla., downtown redevelopment, 134

Osterud, Nancy Grey, 62, 108n1

OSV. *See* Old Sturbridge Village

Oswald, Lee Harvey, 254
"Other stuff," 225–28
Outdoor Exploratorium of Colonial America, 161–65
Outdoor history museum: objects in, 183–84; OSV as, 17; touchable past of, 29–33
Overview: in learning, 48; in political history exhibitions, 312; themes in OSV Museum Education program, 58–59

Paffett, Nick, 205, 217
Paine, Thomas, 317
Parker, Arthur C., 81
Parker, John, 300
Parks, Gordon, 256
Park Slope Historic District (New York City), 173–74
Past, image of, 4
Patriotism: challenged in museum exhibitions after 1960s, 259–60, 266, 269–70; inculcated in youth, 238–39
Paul Revere and the Minute Men (Fisher), 238
Pausanius, 129
Peale Museum, 147
Pearce, Susan, 181, 359
Pedagogue's Panoplist, 62
Pedagogy: as element of interpretation, 78–80; for OSV, 19–26; student-centered, 297; transformation in, 22–23. *See also* Learning; Museum Education program, OSV
Peddler's Pack tours, 147–48
Pennsylvania: historical markers in, 91–93; industrial heritage parks in, 137
Pennsylvania Historical Commission, 91–93
Performance: museum visit as, 11, 123–24; visitors as cast members in ongoing drama, 128–30
Perry, Shaw and Hepburn (architects), 18
The Phenomenology of Landscape: Places, Paths, and Monuments (Tilley), 103
Philadelphia: Germantown Preserved, 134–35; Independence Hall, 90, 270; indoor "museum without walls," 133; installation of Madison's notes, 216–20, 276; *Miracle at Philadelphia*, 216–20, 225–26, 246–47, 276; Mütter Museum, 204–6; President's House, 308–12; *The Private City* (Warner), 112, 113; Robeson residence, 92–93
Philadelphia Inquirer, 310–11
A Philosophical and Political History of the Settlements and Trade of the Europeans in the East and West Indies (Raynal), 232

Philosophy in the Flesh (Lakoff and Johnson), 196–97
Phrygian cap, 229–32, *230*
Piaget, Jean, 55, 58
Picasso's Mask (Malraux), 133n
Piven, Frances Fox, 102–3
Place: AHW focus on, 89; aural evocation of, 120–24; author's approach to, 105–7; author's hopes and goals for, 174–75; City Beautiful movement and, 90–91, 93, 175; distinctiveness of, 8; "exhibit of, not [simply] in," 126; *l'histoire èvénementielle*, 98; "historical features" of, 89–90; historical markers of, 90–98; industrial heritage parks, 136–45; *The Lay of the Land*, 107–12, *109*, 158, *159*; monuments of, 90; museum educator's approach to, 106–7; museum envisioning of, 98–99, 105–19; museums without walls, 132–45; neglect of workaday world of, 90–91; past and present merging in, 128–31; *Place over Time*, 108, *110*, 111; reader's reflection (resources) on, 343–46; REPOhistory and, 93–95, *95*; sense of, 115, 159, 174; thematizing historic houses, 117–18; themes for, 107–19; typologies for, 111–15, 158; "unnotable," author's origins in, 99–104; "unnotable," historical richness of, 100, 104
Place over Time (exhibition), 108, *110*, 111
Place-units, 108, 111
Plimoth Plantation, 23, 351
Political correctness, 262, 297–98
Political history: author's personal, 237–40, 254–55, 262; family history versus, 265; "founders chic," 245; marrying with social history, 312–17; social history versus, 243–44. *See also* Political history exhibitions and programs
Political history exhibitions and programs: *After the Revolution*, 211, 260; author's approach to, 244–46, 249–50; author's first (Boston 200), 240–43; *Constitution Works*, 77, 78, 79, 247–50; critical history and, 251–70; curator as coach in, 250; emotionality and personalization of, 253, 260; Enola Gay, 260–64, *261*, 270; *Field to Factory*, 260, *273*, 273–74, 278; *French Founding Father: Lafayette Returns to Washington's America*, 266–68; *Grant and Lee*, 266, 268; *Launching the Republic, 248*; *Lincoln and New York*, 266, 268–69; *Miracle at Philadelphia*, 216–20, 225–26, 246–47, 276; *A More Perfect Union: Japanese Americans and the U.S. Constitution*, 83, 260, 273–74, *274*; New-York Historical Society and, 265–

70; presidential libraries, 249; provoking new scholarship, 269–70; *Revolution! The Atlantic World Reborn*, 6, 225, *227*, 228, 229–32, *230*, 266, 316–17; shared challenges for visitors in, 249–50

Politics: and industrial heritage parks, 137; and interpretation, 74; and NEH, 67; and public history, 9

Popular history, reader's reflection (resources) on, 352–55

Porter, John, 280

"Portraits in Grief" (9/11 biographies), 327

Post, Robert, 181

"Pots-and-pans" history, 190

Powhatan people, 161–64

Preservation, historic, 7, 173

Presidential libraries, 249

President's House (Philadelphia), 308–12, *310*

Prince Hall Grand Lodge of Masons, 92

The Private City (Warner), 112, 113

Privatism, 113

Procter and Gamble, 299

Professionalization, costs of, 319

Projects: as AHW focus, 8, 68–69; author's preference for, 68; use of word, 68n1

Promotion and marketing, 297

Psychologie de l'Art (Malraux), 133

Public art. *See* Art

Public history: age of fracture, 292, 328–32; complication and accessibility in, 85; current issues/challenges in, 319–32; ephemeral and local nature of, 7–8; heritage mythos in, 19–21; historian's responsibilities in, 333–36; inclusion and diversity in, 6–7, 22, 41, 285–96; intellectual discovery in, 9; interpretation in, 69–70; media and modes employed in, 9–10; pedagogy of, 19–26; politics of, 9; as public dialogue, 73; transformation of, 7–10

Purity and Danger: An Analysis of Concepts of Pollution and Taboo (Douglas), 36, 38

Pye, David, 57

Quaint, as code word, 20

Queer Spaces, 94

Quincy Market (Boston), 240–43

Rabinowitz, Richard: as AHW cofounder, 6, 67; credo of, 105; departure from OSV, 64–65; discovery of calling, 1–6, 29, 43–44; Harvard studies of, 6, 15–17, 22–23; historiography of, 64–65; love affair with history, 237–38;

museumgoing experiences of, 237, 293–94; museum theory of, 8–9; origins in "unnotable" place, 99–104; as OSV assistant director, 6, 16–17; as OSV costumed interpreter, 6, 10, 15, 181; as OSV director of education, 6, 49–65, 78, 239–40; Ph.D. dissertation, 40–41, 240; politics of, 238–40, 254–55, 262; reader's reflections, 337–60; responsibilities as historian, 333–36. *See also specific topics*

Rabinowitz, Sarah, 22, 41–42, 100–103, 146, 196, 238–39

Race, as a theme in history exhibitions, 303, 307–12

Ralph Appelbaum Associates (design firm), 266

Ramirez, Jan, 330–31

Rankin, John, 300

Rath, Fred, 352

Raynal, Abbé Guillaume-Thomas, 232

Reader's reflections (resources), 337–60

Reading artifacts, 212

Reagan Presidential Library, 249

Reagon, Bernice Johnson, 273

Realms of Memory: The Construction of the French Past (Nora), 295

"Real stuff," 225–28

Recasting, interpretation as, 69

Religion, author's Ph.D. dissertation on, 40–41

Re-placement, and sense of place, 174

REPOhistory, 93–95, *95*

Reproductions, 191–93

Resistance, as theme, 302–3, 312

Resources (reader's reflections), 337–60

Responders, visitors as, 77–78

"Revisionist history," 260

Revolution! The Atlantic World Reborn (exhibition), 6, 225, *227*, 228–32, *230*, 266, 316–17

Rhode Island Historical Society, *The Lay of the Land*, 107–12, *109*, 158, 159

Rigaud, Edward J., 299

Riis, Jacob, 256

Ripley's Believe-It-or-Not, 187

Rittenhouse, David, 226

Riznik, Barnes, 6, 16–17, 24, 49, 182

Roberts, Laura, 108n1

Robeson, Paul, 92–93

Rochester (N.Y.) Museum of Arts and Sciences, 81

Rodgers, Daniel T., 259

Rogers, John, 63

Roosevelt, Eleanor, 82

Rose Kennedy Greenway, 168–72, *170*

Rosenblatt, Yossele, 84n
Rosengarten, Ted, 302
Rosenthal, Ellen, 210
Rosenzweig, Roy, 264–65
Rothman, Ellen, 209–10
Rothstein, Edward, 291
Rowhouse: A Baltimore Style of Living (exhibition), 147
Rowland, Pleasant, 298
Ruffins, Fath Davis, 72, 273, 302
Runaway Slaves: Rebels on the Plantation (Franklin), 301
Russell, Rusty, 209
Rust Belt: industrial heritage parks in, 136–45; openness to landscape interpretation in, 136; politics and, 137

Saar, Betye, 135
Sack, Israel, 191
St. Louis, African American history in, 135
St. Mary's City, Md., 161–65
St. Michael's Church (Shenandoah, Pa.), 92
St. Paul, Minn., James J. Hill House, 117–18, 120–21
Salmon, Lucy Maynard, 184–86, 190
Salmon Stakes (exhibition), 154–59, *155*
Sand, Michael, 240
Sargent, Charles Sprague, 189
Scaffolding, in learning, 28, 71, 215
Schama, Simon, 237
Scheele, Carl, 257
Schlereth, Thomas J., 185–86, 190
School and Society (Dewey), 54–55
Schoolchildren: cognitive development of, 55–56; experiential learning by, 53–59; field studies by, 51, 62, 64; OSV education program for, 49–65; "rice cakes" model for, 49–53
Schweninger, Loren, 301
Scruggs, Jan, 252
Sea Captains Carousing in Surinam (painting), 317
Seattle: *Salmon Stakes*, 154–59, *155*; *Waiting for the Interurban*, 165–66; Wing Luke Museum, 286–87, 295, 296, 331
Segal, George, 165
Self-guided tours, 82
Sense of place, 115, 159, 174
The Senses of Walden (Cavell), 30
"Sensible" knowledge, 30
Sensuality of past, 29–30

September 11. *See* National September 11 Memorial and Museum
A Shared Authority: Essays on the Craft and Meaning of Oral and Public History (Frisch), 272
Shaw, Henry, 135
Sherwin, Martin, 255, 262
Shurcleff, Arthur, 18
Shuttlesworth, Fred, 279–80
SIA. *See* Society for Industrial Archeology
Siebert, Willard H., 300
Silhouettes, for *I&M Canal Passage*, 165–68, *168*
Simon, Herbert, 320
Simon, Roger I., 277
Simon Wiesenthal Center/Museum of Tolerance, 298
Sims, Jim, 260
Situated learning, 153–59, 348–49
Skill, homemaking, 41
Slavery: inclusion in public history, 6–7, 41; modern-day, 306; National Underground Railroad Freedom Center, 298–308; N-YHS exhibitions, 6, 220–25, 226, 266, 312–17; President's House, 308–12, *310*
Slavery in New York (exhibition), 6, 226, 266, 313–15, *314*
The Slave Who Freed Haiti: The Story of Toussaint Louverture (Scherman), 238
Sloat, Caroline, 192–93
Smith, Barbara Clark, 260
Smith, Edward A., 154
Smith, James McCune, 224
Smith, Margaret, 108n2
Smithsonian Institution: critical history and, 256–64; politics and, 74; technology and machines, 141–42. *See also specific museums*
Social history: age of fracture, 292, 308–12, 328–32; AHW approach to exhibitions, 245; Birmingham Civil Rights Institute, 6, 278–84, 282, 285, 293, 296; building blocks for, 32; education and learning in, 55–56, 129; empathy in, 276–78; ethnically specific museums and, 285–96; individual narratives in, 275–78; marrying with political history, 312–17; museum historian as folklorist in, 272; National Museum of American History, 259–60, 272–75; National Underground Railroad Freedom Center, 298–308; new, translating into exhibitions, 271–84; new, visitors and, 119; objects as evidence of, 184–86; political history ver-

sus, 243–44; President's House, 308–12, *310*; transformation of, 297–98; widening focus in, 41, 134

Society for Industrial Archeology (SIA), 136

Society for the Preservation of New England Antiquities, 116

A Son and His Adoptive Father: The Marquis de Lafayette and George Washington (exhibition), 267

"Soul, Character, and Personality" (Rabinowitz), 40–41

Sound, in historic spaces, 4–5

Sound presentations, 120–24

South, historical markers in, 93n

The South Street Experience (exhibition), 124

South Street Seaport Museum, 124

Spielberg, Steven, 269

Stakeholder interests, 73–74, 299, 311

Stamp Act, original parchment, 316–17

Stamp collecting, 180

Staples and Charles (design firm), 82

Statue of Liberty, 252

Stearns County (Minn.) Historical Society, 211

Steichen, Edward, 256

Stevenson, Bryan, 93n

The Story of a Patriot (film), 82

The Story of Old Sturbridge Village (van Ravenswaay), 19–20

Storyscape, 11–12, 124; author's affinity for, 160; in ethnically specific museums, 287–91; in industrial heritage parks, 139–45; interpretive clusters, 215–33; in Lower East Side Tenement Museum, 149–53; in museum without walls, 134; en plein air (Historic St. Mary's City), 161–65. *See also specific exhibitions*

Stowe, Harriet Beecher, 300

Structuralist methodology, 37

Stuart, Evelyn Marie, 90

Studio EIS, 217

"Stuffitude," 195

Swinney, Jerry, 352

Tactility, 29–33, 41–42; diversification of objects, 79–80; and human actions, 31–33; and importance of ideas, 31–32. *See also* Objects

Taylor, Alice Thompson, 60

Taylor, Iral D., 60–61

Teaching pro, as model for museum curator, 250

Technology: attention/cognitive effects of, 320–24; industrial heritage park, 141–44

Tenement Museum. *See* Lower East Side Tenement Museum

Theater. *See* Drama

Thelen, David, 149, 264–65

Themes: author's disenchantment with, 25, 125–27, 138–39; in exhibitions of typicalities, 190; experience versus, 115–17, 125–27, 138–39, 146; in historic houses, 117–18; in history of place, 107–19; in interpretive clusters, 220; limitations of, 118–19; master, for OSV, 24–26; master, in typology, 111–15, 130; in OSV education program, 51–53, 58–59

"Theming." *See* Branding of experiences

The Thing Itself: On the Search for Authenticity (Todd), 233n

Thinking, Fast and Slow (Kahneman), 321

Thomas, Selma, 83

Thoreau, Henry David, 30

Three-dimensional documents, 212

Tilley, Christopher, 103–4

"Time of change" approach, at OSV, 21–26, 27

Time-plan analysis, 114

Time-units, 111

Todd, Richard, 233n

To Fly (film), 83

Tomlinson, Kellom, 162n

Top-down approach, 278

Totalizing frameworks, 114–15

Touchable past. *See* Tactility

Tourism and pilgrimage, 129, 354

Toussaint L'Ouverture, François-Dominique, 34, 238

The Transformation of Virginia (Isaac), 213

Translation, interpretation as, 69

"Transparent eyeball," 197

Triumphal Procession of Maximilian I (print), 204

Typicalities, 190–93, 207, 220

Typologies, 111–15, 130, 158; ad hoc, 114; historians' imposition of, 113–14; visitors' recall of, 113

Uncle Tom's Cabin (Stowe), 300

Underground Railroad: history versus myths, 300–301; information on historical markers, 92–93; National Underground Railroad Freedom Center, 298–308

The Underground Railroad (painting), 301, *301*

United States Holocaust Memorial Museum, 276, 278, 286

"Unnotable" place: author's origins in, 99–104; historical richness of, 100, 104
Urban Geography (Johnson), 114

Vann, David, 278
van Ravenswaay, Charles, 19–20, 21, 24
Vauchez, André, 295–96
Ventura, Jesse, 144
Victoria, British Columbia, life-sized model of, 82
Vietnam Veterans Memorial, 251–53, 270
Vietnam War, 15, 239, 251–55, 265
Villainous act, in ethnic narrative, 291–92
"Virtual pathway," 322
Visitor feedback devices, 226–27
Visitors: as audience for interpretation, 76–78; as cast members in ongoing drama, 128–30; fragmentary experience of, 23–24; as heart of museum experience, 10–11, 115; "hook" for, 45; interactions with costumed interpreters, 27–29; interests of, sponsor interests versus, 290–91, 330–31; new social history and, 119; objects and, 181, 194–98, 214–15; as responders, 77–78; sequence in encounters with, 44–45; time of, as organizing frame, 124; way of learning, 44–53
Visual literacy, 212

Wagner, Sherry Kafka, 187, 209
Waiting for the Interurban, 165–66
A Walker in the City (Kazin), 102
Wall, Alexander J., 183
Wallace, Mike, 114n
Walt Disney World, 77, 83
Warner, Sam Bass, Jr., 6, 67, 112
Washington, D.C.: Vietnam Veterans Memorial, 251–53. *See also* Smithsonian Institution; *and specific national museums*
Washington, George, 90, 245, 246, 265, 266–68, 308–12
Washington, Martha, 312
Washington Monument, 90
Watergate, 239, 265
Wayfinding, *I&M Canal Passage*, 165–68
Webber, Charles T., 301

Wells, Albert B., 18, 191
Wells, Joel Cheney, 18, 191
Westbrook, Nicholas, 57, 206–7
Westbrook, Virginia, 62
Wexler, Peter, *203*, 209
Wharf District Parks (Boston), 168–71, *170*
"What is the Effect of Urban Renewal on Crime?" (sign), 94
"Wheeler-Dealers" (AHW program), 96n
Wheeling, W.Va.: *Heinrich's Day*, 144–45, *145*; model of, 140, *140*
Where's Boston? (film), 82–83
Whiting, Marvin, 279, 281
"Who Owns Your Life?" (sign), 94, *95*
Willard, Solomon, 90
Williams, William Carlos, 42
Williamsburg. *See* Colonial Williamsburg
Wilson, James, 246–47
Winfrey, Oprah, 306
Wing Luke Museum of the Asian Pacific American Experience, 286–87, 295, 296, 331
Winterthur Museum, 183–84
Wisconsin Veterans Museum, 330
Wobble, between past and present, 55, 174, 278, 313
Women: inclusion in historical narratives, 22; social distinctions and, 37
Wood, Peter, 255
Woods, Abraham Lincoln, 279
Woolfolk, Odessa, 279, 281
Wool Technology and the Industrial Revolution (exhibition), 141
Worden, Gretchen, 205
Wordsworth, William, 26, 44, 337
Work: inclusion of labor in industrial heritage parks, 142–44; as museum education theme, 58–59
"Workmanship of certainty," 57
"Workmanship of risk," 57
The World We Have Lost (Laslett), 130

You Are There (TV program), 324

Zuckerman, Michael, 32